Cases on Muslim Law of India,
Pakistan, and Bangladesh

Cases on Muslim Law of India, Pakistan, and Bangladesh

ALAMGIR MUHAMMAD SERAJUDDIN

OXFORD
UNIVERSITY PRESS

OXFORD
UNIVERSITY PRESS

Oxford University Press is a department of the University of Oxford.
It furthers the University's objective of excellence in research, scholarship,
and education by publishing worldwide. Oxford is a registered trademark of
Oxford University Press in the UK and in certain other countries

Published in India by
Oxford University Press
YMCA Library Building, 1 Jai Singh Road, New Delhi 110 001, India

ISBN-13: 978-0-19-945761-8
ISBN-10: 0-19-945761-1

Typeset in Dante MT Std 10.5/13
by Tranistics Data Technologies, New Delhi 110 044
Printed in India at Rakmo Press, New Delhi 110 020

To Azmeh, Ehsan, and Ayan
With love
Dadu

Contents

Section II: India

Part II: Text of Cases

Section I: Colonial India

Section II: India

Section III: Pakistan

Section IV: Bangladesh

Abbreviations

AD	Appellate Division
ADC	Appellate Division Cases
AIHC	All India High Court Cases
AIR	All India Reporter
All.	Allahabad
All ER	All England Reports
All.W.C.	Allahabad Weekly Cases
A.P.	Andhra Pradesh
Ass.	Assam
BLC	Bangladesh Law Chronicle
BLD	Bangladesh Legal Decisions
Bom.	Bombay
Bom.L.R.	*Bombay Law Reporter*
Cal.	Calcutta
Civil P.C.	Civil Procedure Code, 1908
C.J.	Chief Justice
Cri.L.J.	Criminal Law Journal
CrPC/Cr.P.C.	Code of Criminal Procedure
CWN	Calcutta Weekly Notes
Dac.	Dacca
Del.	Delhi
DLR	Dhaka Law Reports
DMMA	Dissolution of Muslim Marriages Act, 1939
F.B.	Full Bench
FLC	Family Law Cases
FSC	Federal Shariat Court
Gau.	Gauhati

GLR	Gauhati Law Reports
Guj.	Gujarat
HLC	House of Lords Cases
Hyd.	Hyderabad
I.A.	Indian Appeals
IC	Indian Cases
ILR	*Indian Law Reports*
J.	Justice
Jhar.	Jharkhand
JJ.	Justices
J&K	Jammu and Kashmir
Kant.	Karnataka
Kar.	Karachi
Ker.	Kerala
KLT	*Kerala Law Times*
Lah.	Lahore
Luck.	Lucknow
Mad.	Madras
M.B.	Madhya Bharat
MFLO	Muslim Family Laws Ordinance, 1961
Mh.L.J.	*Maharashtra Law Journal*
M.I.A.	Moore's Indian Appeals
MLD	Monthly Law Digest
MLR	Mainstream Law Reports
M.P.	Madhya Pradesh
MWA	Muslim Women (Protection of Rights on Divorce) Act, 1986
Mys.	Mysore
Nag.	Nagpur
O.C.	Oudh Cases
Pat.	Patna
PC	Privy Council
Pesh.	Peshawar
PLD	*Pakistan Legal Decisions*
PPC/P. P. C.	Pakistan Penal Code
Que.	Quetta
Raj.	Rajasthan
Rang.	Rangoon

SC	Supreme Court
SCC	Supreme Court Cases
SCJ	Supreme Court Journal
SCMR	*Supreme Court Monthly Review*
SCR	Supreme Court Reports
W.P.	West Pakistan

Table of Cases

Colonial India

India

Pakistan

Bangladesh

Table of Statutes

Indian High Courts Act, 1861
Indian Law Reports Act, 1875
Indian Penal Code, 1860
Indian Succession Act, 1925
Land Reforms Regulations, 1959
Kazis Act, 1880
Limitation Act, 1877
Limitation Act, 1908
Majority Act, 1875
Muslim Family Laws Ordinance, 1961 (Pakistan and Bangladesh)
Muslim Family Laws Rules, 1961 (Pakistan and Bangladesh)
Muslim Marriages and Divorces (Registration) Act, 1974 (Bangladesh)
Muslim Personal Law (Shariat) Application Act, 1937
Muslim Women (Protection of Rights on Divorce) Act, 1986 (India)
Mussalman Wakf Validating Act, 1913
Oaths Act, 1873
Offences of Zina (Enforcement of Hudood) Ordinance, 1979 (Pakistan)
Punjab Muslim Personal Law (Shariat) Application Act, 1948
Registration Act, 1908
Special Marriage Act, 1872
Special Marriage Act, 1954 (India)
Transfer of Property Act, 1882
United Nations Declaration of Rights of the Child, 1959
Wakf Act, 1954
West Pakistan Family Courts Act, 1964
West Pakistan Muslim Personal Law (Shariat) Application Act, 1962

Preface

The introduction of the principles of English law, especially the doctrine of precedent, has made a lasting impact on the administration of justice in South Asia. Under the doctrine of precedent a decision of a higher court on any point of law is an authority to be followed by the lower courts under its jurisdiction. Whatever the opinion of a lower court on the issue, it is bound to follow the decision of the higher court, recognized as competent to bind it, and administer the law as declared by such a court. As Professor Tahir Mahmood (1997: 4) succinctly puts it, 'Under this system the law on a given point is what the highest court dealing with it says it is'. Thus, the binding force of precedent is firmly rooted in South Asian jurisprudence. The judgments pronounced by superior courts are as much the laws of the South Asian countries as their legislative enactments. The Privy Council served as the highest court of appeal from the decisions of the High Courts and its decisions were binding on all the courts in India. After independence in 1947 it was replaced, in India and Pakistan by their Supreme Courts, and in Bangladesh the Pakistan Supreme Court was replaced by the Appellate Division of the Supreme Court of Bangladesh. The decisions of the High Courts are binding on all the subordinate courts within their jurisdiction.

Case law is the core and kernel of a precedent-bound legal system. The necessary concomitant of this doctrine is an organized system of law reporting. Professor M.P. Jain (1972: 654) explains its importance thus: 'Publication of decisions is a condition precedent for the theory to operate; there must exist reliable reports of cases; or, if the cases are to be binding there must be precise records of what they do lay down and it is only then that the doctrine of *stare decisis* can function meaningfully.' Law reporting began in India within a decade of assumption of *diwani* of Bengal by the East India Company in 1765. Reporting in the early period was a private enterprise of practising lawyers and judges. Following the enactment of the Indian Law Reports Act, 1875 the first official series of law reports, known as the *Indian Law Reports* was started in 1876, containing decisions of the High Courts of Bombay, Calcutta, Madras, and Allahabad. The more popular and widely used law reports are *Indian Appeals* (I.A.) on colonial India, *Indian Law Reports* (ILR), and *All India Reporter* (AIR) on colonial India and India after 1947, *All Pakistan Legal Decisions* (PLD) on Pakistan, and *Dhaka Law Reports* (DLR) on Pakistan and Bangladesh.

Law reports are a sampling of judicial philosophy and thought, offering the readers an excellent opportunity of observing and learning how the judicial mind and judicial process operate in a given situation and time. In the resolution of family law litigation, the courts cannot ignore the cultural and social norms of a society, nor can they stand as barriers in the way of social change and transformation. Case law is not only a means of winning cases in courts, but also a useful social barometer and tool of social change. It is, therefore, of considerable interest to sociologists, social reformers, and social historians. By studying many different problems as they arose for courts' decisions, law students and young practitioners can learn how to apply the principles of law to various fact situations they may encounter in their everyday lives and professions. Hence, case studies are indispensable for them.

Muslim law, which governs the personal lives and family relations of about 500 million Muslims of South Asia, is an integral part of the South Asian legal system and case law has come to play a major role in its interpretation, application, and development. In its classical formulation this law was more jurist's law than judge's law. 'It was expressed in textbooks as the doctrine of the jurists, not in the law reports containing the decision of the judiciary' (Coulson 1969: 9). Often, the founders of various schools of Muslim law and their disciples differ among themselves on different points of law. Muslim law of South Asia also remains largely uncodified. The few legislative enactments that are there, like any other laws, are themselves subject to interpretation and exposition by the courts. These factors largely explain why judicial decisions constitute the single most important source of Muslim law as applied in South Asia and why this law is regarded as Muslim law as interpreted by the courts. They also explain why judicial exposition of the principles and rules of this law has occupied thousands of pages of law reports. The objective of this book is to enable the students, scholars, and practitioners of Muslim law to form an idea of the volume, variety, and richness of law reports and have easy access to primary source material. The collection of cases in this volume is also intended to show how religion-based rules of personal law have been interpreted by secular courts at certain epochs in history and how the trend of interpretation has changed over the last 150 years.

Asaf A.A. Fyzee's *Cases in the Muhammadan Law of India and Pakistan* (1965) is the only case law book on this important field of law. What is the necessity for another volume on the same subject now? The answer is simple: Fyzee's *Cases* has become almost obsolete. Of its forty-three cases, thirty-eight come from the colonial period, only four from independent India, and one from Pakistan—that too overruled in a later decision. The second edition adds Bangladesh to the title but does not include any Bangladeshi case. A good number of decisions of the colonial period, handed down in the nineteenth and early-twentieth centuries, have either been overruled in the post-1947 period and are no longer law, or dissented from. So most of Fyzee's cases are of academic rather than practical legal interest. Noting that momentous developments have taken place in the area of Muslim law in the last three decades of the twentieth century and early years of the new millennium, Professor Tahir Mahmood, editor of the second edition, says: 'It is just not possible to update an old text so as to accommodate all these new trends and changes. Yet, I have done my best to edit and revise Fyzee's forty-year old *Cases* to give the readers a fair idea of where its original contents now stand' (Fyzee 2005: viii). In this edition he has neither discarded any old cases nor included new ones; instead, he has added at the end of each of the nineteen chapters of the book 'brief updates indicating the later developments'.

These developments, some of them almost revolutionary, have had far-reaching consequences on the evolution of Muslim law and Muslim societies of South Asia. After independence, the South Asian courts were required, in the changed circumstances, to take cognizance of the social needs and requirements of the new states, recognize the social changes and transformations taking place at a rapid pace, develop, adapt, and reconcile law to changing needs and trends, and meet the challenges of social justice. This they did by giving an activist, creative, and liberal interpretation to laws. The phenomenon, known as judicial activism, was perhaps nowhere felt more than in the sphere of Muslim family law. The new judicial thinking greatly impacted laws relating to the interpretation of sources of Muslim law, the institution of marriage including polygamy, marriage guardianship, 'option of puberty' and restitution of conjugal rights, nature of dower, Muslim husband's unilateral power of *talaq, talaq-i-tafwid*, judicial divorce under statuary provisions including cruelty and non-maintenance as grounds of divorce, *khula* divorce without husband's consent, maintenance of wives, divorced wives, and children under traditional sharia law and statutory law, guardianship and custody of children, and the interpretation of social legislations like the Dissolution of Muslim Marriages Act, 1939 (DMMA), Muslim Family Laws Ordinance, 1961 (MFLO), Code of Criminal Procedure (CrPC), 1973 (Sections 125–7), and Muslim Women (Protection of Rights on Divorce) Act, 1986 (MWA). These are the areas that affect family life and relations most and where Muslim women suffer grave injustice; these are also the areas where judicial activism has made the deepest inroad.

To demonstrate the major changes in the Muslim family laws of India, Pakistan, and Bangladesh, one case from each jurisdiction is cited here. Contrary to traditional talaq law that a husband can divorce his wife at will, in a number of cases, the Indian High Courts decided that talaq given without assigning a reasonable cause and reconciliation efforts by two arbiters was invalid. In *Shamim Ara* v. *State of U.P.*, the Supreme Court agreed with this statement of law. Dispensing with the requirement of traditional law that the husband's consent is necessary for a khula divorce, in *Khurshid Bibi* v. *Muhammad Amin* (Case 37), the Pakistan Supreme Court held that a wife is entitled to a khula divorce, as of right, if she satisfies the conscience of the court that it will otherwise mean forcing her into a hateful union. In *Md Abu Baker Siddique* v. *S.M.A. Bakar* (Case 58), the Appellate Division of the Bangladesh Supreme Court decided that as custody rules are only juristic views and not based on the Qur'an or Sunnah, the courts may diverge from them, the paramount consideration being the children's welfare. These and all other cases, which have either modified traditional law or will assist the reader in comprehending the salient features of Muslim family law and its current trends, have been included in this book. Fyzee's *Cases* includes only five post-1947 cases, while this compilation contains forty-eight, most of which are leading ones. As the laws of *waqf*, gift, will, and inheritance remain more or less static and important cases on them are available in Fyzee's book, they have been excluded here.

This volume has been prepared primarily as a textbook for use in law schools. Members of the legal profession may also find it useful as a handy reference book. The cases—not all of them leading, although no leading cases have been omitted—illustrate not only the basic principles of law but also different fact situations. The book is divided into two parts and each part is subdivided into four sections: colonial India, India, Pakistan, and Bangladesh. Part I summarizes each of the sixty-one cases under three heads: issues of law, case summary, and court decision, and comments. Part II reproduces the full text of thirty-five cases. Part I, a novelty in case law books, is designed to explain case laws to students in a simple and intelligible manner, encourage them to read the original reports, which they do not generally do, and make the study of Muslim law interesting and meaningful. The comments are intended to enable them to compare with other relevant decisions and materials. At the end of Part II, a chapter titled 'A Comparative Survey of Muslim Personal Law in South Asian Countries' assesses the judicial trends of pre- and post-independence cases of India, Pakistan, and Bangladesh, and the extent of their convergence with or divergence from each other.

A few remarks may be added here regarding the quality of judgments. The language of the higher courts of the subcontinent has been English since the establishment of the High Courts of Calcutta, Bombay, and Madras in 1862, and so it has continued since independence. Fyzee, the celebrated jurist, contends that simplicity of language, lucidity of style, and cogency of arguments should be the hallmark of higher court judgments. He observes: 'A loose expression or confused thinking would lead to serious consequences to litigants. It is an unfortunate fact that in certain Courts of Records, greater attention is not paid to the use of simple words, the avoidance of clichés and to accuracy in grammar, spelling and idioms' (1965: ix). The vast majority of judges of superior courts have displayed a high standard of legal scholarship and acumen and a number of them have earned proverbial reputation amongst the legal fraternity for their wisdom and sagacity. But the quality of some recent judgments would appear to suffer from the weaknesses mentioned by Fyzee. As the quality of judgments reflects the quality of the judiciary of a country, deviant courts would do well to heed Fyzee's advice.

This book is intended to be a companion volume to recognized textbooks on Muslim law in India, Pakistan, and Bangladesh and should be read in conjunction with one or more of them. The more widely read textbooks are:

1. Syed Ameer Ali, *Mahommedan Law*, vols. 1 and 2
2. Paras Diwan and Peeyushi Diwan, *Muslim Law in Modern India*
3. Asaf A.A. Fyzee, *Outlines of Muhammadan Law*, which, in the words of Professor Joseph Schacht (1964: 249), an eminent authority on Islamic law, is 'the most elementary but the most scholarly of these handbooks'.
4. Tahir Mahmood, *The Muslim Law of India*
5. D.F. Mulla, *Principles of Mahomedan Law*
6. David Pearl and Werner Menski, *Muslim Family Law*
7. Tanzil-ur-Rahman, *A Code of Muslim Personal Law*, vols. 1 and 2
8. K.P. Saksena, *Muslim Law as Administered in India and Pakistan*
9. Faiz Badruddin Tyabji, *Muslim Law*

The bibliography contains the names of other textbooks on the subject. Keith Hodkinson's *Muslim Family Law: A Sourcebook* and Tahir Mahmood's *Islamic Law in Indian Courts since Independence: Fifty Years of Judicial Interpretation* are useful contributions to the study of Muslim family law. Students, researchers, and lawyers may also find it worthwhile to consult my two studies, *Shari'a Law and Society: Tradition and Change in South Asia* and *Muslim Family Law, Secular Courts and Muslim Women of South Asia: A Study in Judicial Activism*. In passing, it may be noted that sources of Muslim law as administered in India and found in textbooks consist mainly of the following classical texts:

1. The *Hedaya* of Burhanuddin Marghinani, translated by Charles Hamilton
2. The *Fatawa Alamgiri*, compiled by Shaikh Nizam Burhanpuri and others, translated by N.B.E. Baillie
3. The *Shara'i' al-Islam* of Nizamuddin Hali, also translated by Baillie
4. *Al-Sirajiyah*, translated by Sir William Jones

To provide readers information about the legal rules and an adequate number of fact situations and yet keep the manuscript manageable is itself a difficult task. It is still more difficult since due weight should be given to each of the four divergent South Asian jurisdictions. Considering that the judicial philosophy on which colonial decisions were based has lost its relevance and thirty-eight of Fyzee's forty-three cases are devoted to the colonial period, the colonial cases could have been omitted altogether from this compilation. But that would have meant that the South Asian countries began their judicial journey in a vacuum. Moreover, the foundation of the case law system on which administration of justice in South Asia is based was laid on a firm footing during colonial times. However, only three of the thirteen cases extracted here are in common with Fyzee's cases. In selecting the text of cases for the book, a choice had also to be made between a larger number of cases with reproduction of key extracts from judgments, as some textbooks on case law do, and a complete presentation of a lesser number of judgments more or less in full. I have chosen to follow the latter course with some inconsequential pruning here and there. For example, extracts from Arabic texts quoted in the judgments have been excised, but their English translation retained. In a few cases, a number of lengthy extracts, consisting mainly of narration of complicated facts, which are not essential for understanding the law, have been eliminated. In *Khurshid Bibi*, to save space only the leading judgment has been reproduced and the concurrent judgment dropped. Similarly, in *Khurshid Jan* v. *Fazal Dad* (Case 31), the dissenting and concurrent judgments have also been scissored off.

Some other features of the book may be noticed. Copious endnotes in Part I have been avoided and where found unavoidable, short references have been inserted in the text. Similarly, an elaborate bibliography has been avoided. The brief bibliography contains only a select list of books and articles which are directly relevant to the theme of the book. The statutes are listed separately; so also the relevant cases. For users of the book not familiar with Arabic and Persian terms and usages, a glossary has been added. Abbreviations are also given. Students, researchers, and practitioners interested in further study may consult the comprehensive bibliography in my treatise *Muslim Family Law*. I hope that the present book will stimulate interest in the study of Muslim law, provoke discussion and debate, and lead to a better understanding of this much misunderstood and misinterpreted subject.

I would like to put on record my deep gratitude to the American Institute of Bangladesh Studies and Indian Council for Cultural Relations for their grants to enable me to work on this book at Georgetown University, Washington, DC, and Indian Law Institute, New Delhi. I am very grateful to Mr Justice Mohammad Fazlul Karim, former chief justice of the Bangladesh Supreme Court, Professor Tahir Mahmood, a leading scholar of Muslim law in South Asia, late Mr M.J. Asa'd, my brother-in-law in Karachi, Professor Abdullah Al Faruque, Dean of the Faculty of Law, Chittagong University, and Professor Ridwanul Hoque, Faculty of Law, Dhaka University for their help and advice, and Mr Rana Dasgupta and Mr Ziauddin Ahmed, senior advocates of the Chittagong Bar, Mr Md Nasirul Islam, Assistant Librarian, Appellate Division, Bangladesh Supreme Court, and Mr Mohammad Ali of Anupam Gyan Bhander for making available to me a number of important Indian, Pakistani, and Bangladeshi decisions. I have also greatly benefited from exchange of ideas with my friends Professor John L. Esposito, Founding Director of Prince Alwaleed Bin Talal Center for Muslim-Christian Understanding, Georgetown University and Werner Menski, Professor of South Asian Law, SOAS, London University. I remain deeply indebted to Professor Nazrul Islam, former chairman of the Bangladesh University Grants Commission (BUGC), and the then members of BUGC, especially Professor Abdul Hakim, for appointing me BUGC professor and to Professor M. Anowarul Azim Arif, Vice Chancellor of Chittagong University and members of the University syndicate for electing me Professor Emeritus, which positions have helped me to continue my research. My thanks are also due to Mr S.M. Abu Taher, Librarian, Mr Iskander M. Reshadul Karim, Deputy Registrar, Mr Harun-ur Rashid, and Mr Tarequl Islam, administrative officer and administrative assistant respectively, History Department, Chittagong University for their efficient and valuable services. The text of cases reproduced in Part II have been selected from the following reputed law reports of India, Pakistan, and Bangladesh: *All India Reporter, Indian Law Reports, Indian Appeals, All India High Court Cases, Family Law Cases, Kerala Law Times, Supreme Court Cases, Pakistan Legal Decisions, Dhaka Law Reports,* and *Bangladesh Choronicles.* I gratefully acknowledge my debt to the publishers of these reports. I am much indebted to the Oxford University Press, Delhi, for undertaking publication of this volume and their editorial staff for skilful coordination of the long and tedious process of publication.

I am very happy to acknowledge my deep sense of gratitude to my wife Professor Asma Serajuddin who, as in the case of my previous books, went through the manuscript several times and came up with useful comments and suggestions, and to my daughter-in-law, Rosana, and my son, Umar, for looking after my well-being in Washington, DC. The main inspiration behind this book has been my three grandchildren, Azmeh, Ehsan, and Ayan in whose cheerful company it was completed and to them, in love and affection, I dedicate this book.

Alamgir Muhammad Serajuddin

University of Chittagong
Chittagong, Bangladesh
April 2015

PART I

CASE SUMMARY AND COMMENTARY

SECTION I

COLONIAL INDIA

Aga Mahomed Jaffer Bindaneem v. Koolsom Bee Bee

Interpretation of Qur'an

Aga Mahomed Jaffer Bindaneem—Appellant

v.

Koolsom Bee Bee and Others—Respondents

(1897) 24 I.A. 196

(Lord Watson, Lord Davey, and Sir Richard Couch)

Decided on 16 March and 7 April 1897

Issues of law

Interpretation of Qur'an; rights of widow regarding maintenance

Case summary and decision

Haji Hussain Bindaneem, a Shia Muslim, died in February 1890, leaving behind a widow, Kulsoom Bibi, and no children. Among other things, the widow claimed maintenance from the estate of her husband for one year from the date of his death. The Recorder of Rangoon awarded the childless widow maintenance at the rate of 150 per month for a year. For his decision he relied on the Qur'anic verse 2:240 which says, 'Those of you who die and leave widows should bequeath for their widows a year's maintenance and residence.' He also cited the observations of Syed Ameer Ali in his celebrated work on the personal law of Muslims that several jurists have held that a wife has a right to be maintained out of the husband's estate for a year, independently of any share she may get in the property left by him. On appeal, pronouncing the decision of the Judicial Committee of the Privy Council, Lord Davey said that the Recorder's decision conflicted with the long-established rule stated in the *Hedaya* and *Imamia*, the two paramount authorities on Hanafi and Ithna Ashari Shia law respectively in South Asia. According to the *Hedaya* (Hamilton, 1870: 145), 'maintenance is not due to a woman after her husband's decease', and according to the *Imamia* (Baillie, 1869: 171), 'a widow has no right to maintenance even though she be pregnant'. The Judicial Committee, he said, must follow these two authorities and hold that a Muslim widow 'is not entitled to maintenance out of her husband's estate in addition to what she is entitled to by inheritance or under his will'. It was not their domain to speculate on how to reconcile the Qur'anic verse with the law laid down in the *Hedaya* and *Imamia*. In what has ever since come to be regarded by courts as a classic statement of the rules of interpretation of Qur'anic text, the Judicial Committee held that 'it would be wrong for the Court on a point of this kind to attempt to put their own construction on the Koran in opposition to the express ruling of commentators of such great antiquity and high authority'. In other words, where a Qur'anic verse is interpreted in a particular way by the classical jurists of recognized merit and authority, it is not open to a judge to construe it in a different way; he must follow their authoritative exposition of the law.

Comments

The rules of interpretation of the Qur'an and Sunnah laid down by the Privy Council in this case and in *Baker Ali Khan* v. *Anjuman Ara Begum* (Case 2) were criticized by Chagla J. in *Ashrafalli Cassamalli* v. *Mahomedalli Rajaballi*. He was of the opinion that the ancient texts must be considered with utmost respect, but they should be so applied as to suit modern circumstances and conditions. Since 1947 the Indian courts have generally followed these rules as binding precedents, for example, in *Imdad Ali* v. *Ahmad Ali*, *Amad Giri* v. *Begha*, *K. Veerankutty* v. *Pathummakutty Umma*, *Usman Khan Bahmani* v. *Fathimunnisa Begum*. But deviations are also noticeable in a few cases, for example, in *Jiauddin Ahmed* v. *Anwara Begum*, *Mohd Ahmed Khan* v. *Shah Bano Begum* (Case 27), *Zeenat Fatema Rashid* v. *Md Iqbal Anwar* (Case 19), *Dagdu Chotu Pathan* v. *Rahimbi Dagdu Pathan* (Case 20),

Shamim Ara v. *State of U.P* (Case 21), *Masroor Ahmed* v. *State* (unreported case; see Mahmood [2007: 7]). The Pakistani courts refused to abide by the decisions of the Privy Council and asserted their right to independent interpretation of the rules of sharia law, for example, in *Balqis Fatima* v. *Najm-ul-Ikram Qureshi* (Case 36), *Rashida Begum* v. *Shahab Din, Khurshid Jan* v. *Fazal Dad* (Case 31), *Zohra Begum* v. *Latif Ahmad Manawwar* (Case 42), *Sardar Muhammad* v. *Nasima Bibi* (Case 45), *Khurshid Bibi* v. *Muhammad Amin* (Case 37). In *Md Hefzur Rahman* v. *Shamsun Nahar Begum*, the High Court Division of Bangladesh claimed the right to interpret the Qur'anic verse but in an elaborate judgment in *Md Hefzur Rahman* v. *Shamsun Nahar Begum* (Case 61), a Full Bench of the Appellate Division of the Supreme Court overruled the High Court's decision.

2

Baker Ali Khan v. Anjuman Ara Begum

Interpretation of traditions

Baker Ali Khan—Defendant

v.

Anjuman Ara Begum and Another —Plaintiffs

(1903) 30 I.A. 94

(Lord Macnaghten, Lord Lindley, Sir Andrew Scoble, Sir Arther Wilson, and Sir John Bonser)

Decided on 4 March 1903

Issues of law

Interpretation of the traditions of the Prophet; creation of testamentary waqf under Shia law

Case summary and decision

Haji Begum, daughter of the king of Oudh, executed a will on 10 July 1890, bequeathing to the defendants Sadiq Ali and Baker Ali Khan, mainly for religious and charitable purposes, a portion of her estate not exceeding one-third. The plaintiffs Anjuman Ara Begum and Wasi Ali Khan challenged the validity of the will on the ground that it was not a will but a *waqf-bil-wasiat* or endowment by will, and hence invalid under Shia law by which the parties to the suit were governed. Thus the question before the court was whether a Shia Muslim can create a waqf by will. Following the decision of a Full Bench of the High Court of the North-Western Provinces in *Aga Ali Khan* v. *Altaf Hasan Khan*, in which the judgment was delivered by Mahmood, J., both the Additional Civil Judge of Lucknow and the Judicial Commissioner of Oudh held that under Shia law a waqf cannot be created by will. The Privy Council however held that under Shia as well as Sunni law waqf can be created by will, and overruled the law laid down by Mahmood, J. The Privy Council observed that the more important of the ancient Shia texts have long been accessible to lawyers. In none of them has the author himself drawn the conclusion that creation of a waqf by will is not permissible, nor have the modern writers who have collected and translated these texts held that view. The Privy Council cited a number of cases where testamentary waqfs were created and given effect to, and observed that the decision of Mahmood, J. was not based on 'any positive statement by any of the recognized authorities on Shia law'(Fyzee 1965:16) but on his inferences, drawn from 'a number of more or less ambiguous texts'. For the guidance of the courts, the Judicial Committee laid down the following principles of interpretation of Hadith and ancient texts:

> In *Abul Fata* v. *Russomoy Dhur Chowdhry* [1894], in the judgment of this Committee delivered by Lord Hobhouse, the danger was pointed out of relying upon ancient texts of the Mahomedan law, and even precepts of the Prophet himself, of taking them literally, and deducing from them new rules of law, especially when such proposed rules do not conduce to substantial justice. That danger is equally great whether reliance be placed upon fresh texts newly brought to light, or upon fresh logical inferences newly drawn from old and undisputed texts. Their Lordships think it would be extremely dangerous to accept as a general principle that new rules of law are to be introduced because they seem to lawyers

of the present-day to follow logically from ancient texts however authoritative, when the ancient doctors of the law have not themselves drawn those conclusions. (Fyzee 1965:16)

Comment

See comments in Case 1.

3

Aziz Banu v. *Mohammad Ibrahim Husain*

Divergent juristic opinions, 'option of puberty'

Aziz Banu—Defendant, Appellant

v.

Mohammad Ibrahim Husain—Plaintiff, Respondent

AIR 1925 All. 720

(Sulaiman and Mukerji, JJ.)

Decided on 23 April 1925

Issues of law

Application of the law of the defendant; differences of opinion among jurists; authoritative text of Shia law; marriage of a Shia woman and Sunni man; 'option of puberty'

Case summary and decision

The plaintiff's case was that the defendant was married to him by her father acting as her guardian but she refused to move to the matrimonial home. He prayed for restitution of conjugal rights. The defence of the defendant was that she was not aware of the alleged marriage; her father had never consented to it; she being a Shia and the plaintiff a Sunni, no valid marriage could have been contracted; and, lastly, on attaining puberty she had repudiated the marriage. The trial court found that the defendant was duly married to the plaintiff and her own father had acted as her guardian. The marriage of a Shia and a Sunni was not illegal, and since the marriage was contracted by her own father, she could not repudiate it. The court decreed the plaintiff's claim, which was confirmed by the lower appellate court. In the second appeal, the defendant raised two points: (i) under Shia law the marriage of a Shia woman and a Sunni husband was illegal and a nullity and (ii) In any case such a marriage was voidable.

The Allahabad High Court held that it is a well-settled rule that the law to be observed in the trial of suits shall, in the absence of any enactment or usage having the force of law, be the law of the defendant, and in the absence of any specific law and usage, be justice, equity, and good conscience. Therefore, the law that would apply in this case was Shia law. But there were differences of opinion among Shia jurists as to whether the marriage of a Shia woman and a Sunni man was legal. The court held that in case of divergent opinions where it seems impossible to ascertain the comparative merits of the authorities, it is the duty of the court to accept the view which is more in consonance with equity, justice, and good conscience. According to *Sharaya-ul-Islam*, which is regarded as the most authoritative text of Shia law in South Asia, such a marriage is not illegal. The court considered this view to be 'most conformable to equity and requirements of the times' (p. 278) and accordingly, held that the marriage of a Shia woman and a Sunni man is not absolutely illegal so as to make it void. Was such a marriage voidable even though contracted by the father? The court held that if a Shia girl was given away in marriage by her father while she was a minor, when it was impossible for her to have any voice in the matter, and on attaining puberty, she considered the marriage repugnant to her religious sentiments and grossly disadvantageous to herself, it would be contrary to all rules of equity or justice to force such a marriage on her and thereby compel her to live with a person who is abhorrent to her. She must be allowed the option to repudiate it. If she allows the marriage to be consummated, or in some other way ratifies the marriage, then her 'option of puberty' would be lost and the marriage would be a perfectly valid marriage and her issues legitimate. In the present case it was found that the marriage was not consummated; no fraud was practised by the minor's father in negotiating the marriage; the marriage was to the minor's manifest disadvantage; and she repudiated the marriage on attaining puberty. Thus, though the marriage was not illegal, the defendant had an option of repudiation, which was duly exercised. In consequence, the marriage tie no longer subsisted.

Comments

Under the law prevailing until 1939, a minor girl given in marriage by her father could not exercise her 'option of puberty' and repudiate the marriage. But Section 2(vii) of the DMMA gives her this right, even though the marriage was contracted by her father. This case also reiterates the rules of interpretation of Muslim law as laid down in Case Nos. 1 and 2.

4

Ghulam Kubra Bibi v. Mohammad Shafi

Essentials and formalities of marriage

Ghulam Kubra Bibi—Defendant, Appellant

v.

Mohammad Shafi—Plaintiff, Defendant

AIR 1940 Pesh. 2

(Mir Ahmad, J.)

Decided on 8 December 1939

Issues of law

Essentials and formalities of valid marriage; marriage of a girl contracted by her legal guardian

Case summary and decision

Mohammad Shafi sued Ghulam Kubra for restitution of conjugal rights. Her defence was that she was never married to him. The trial judge found that the girl was of age when she was married and the solemnization of the marriage had been proved. He ordered restoration of conjugal rights, which was upheld by the Additional District Judge. In the second appeal the Peshawar High Court held that, for a marriage to be valid, it is absolutely necessary that the man or someone on his behalf and the woman or someone on her behalf should agree to the marriage at one meeting and the agreement should be witnessed by two adults. In the case the woman was in *parda*, one of her relations must obtain her consent to the marriage within the hearing of two witnesses, and for a specified dower. In the case under review, the grandfather of the adult woman gave her away in marriage without taking her consent under the impression that she was a minor, though, in fact, she was not. Therefore, no valid marriage took place, and Mohammad Shafi had no right to file a suit for restitution of conjugal rights.

Comments

This case is of special importance for delineating the customary formalities and procedures followed with respect to the marriage ceremony in traditional Muslim societies in South Asia. For essential conditions of a valid marriage, see also *Abdul Kadir v. Salima* (Case 5).

5

Abdul Kadir v. *Salima*

Nature of marriage and dower

Abdul Kadir—Plaintiff

v.

Salima and Another—Defendants

ILR (1886) 8 All. 149

(Sir Comer Petheram, Kt., C.J., Straight, Oldfield, Brodhurst, and Tyrrell, JJ.)

Decided on 21 January 1886

Issues of law

Nature of marriage; nature of dower; husband's liability to pay dower; restitution of conjugal rights; conflict of opinion among jurists

Case summary and decision

Salima was married to Abdul Kadir on 15 March 1883. Her dower was fixed without specifying whether it was partly or wholly prompt or deferred. Precisely three months after the marriage she left for her father's house and refused to return to the conjugal home. Abdul Kadir filed a suit in the Munsif's court for restitution of his conjugal rights. Salima opposed the suit on three grounds. First, Abdul Kadir had irrevocably divorced her and she was no longer his wife. Second, even if he had not irrevocably divorced her, his suit was not maintainable, because he had not paid her dower. Third, he had treated her with cruelty and she apprehended grave personal injury. At this juncture of the proceedings Abdul Kadir deposited the full dower in court. The court found that Salima's allegations of divorce and cruelty were unfounded. As to the dower, the court was of the opinion that as the nature of dower was not specified at the time of marriage, only a part of the dower became payable on demand; that before the institution of the suit, Salima had never demanded payment of dower; and that when she made the demand, Abdul Kadir paid it in court. Therefore, he was entitled to a decree for restitution of conjugal rights. On appeal by Salima, the District Judge held that in the absence of any specification of the mode of payment, the entire amount of the dower was to be considered prompt; Abdul Kadir had no cause of action at the time of the institution of the suit, and payment of the dower in court after institution of the suit was not sufficient. Accordingly, he set aside the lower court's judgment.

Abdul Kadir appealed to the Allahabad High Court. The judgment of the Full Bench of the High Court was delivered by Mahmood, J., an eminent authority on Muslim law in India. He gave an elaborate exposition of the nature and effects of marriage and dower under Muslim law. Marriage in Islam, he observed, is not a sacrament but purely a civil contract. Though it is generally solemnized with recitation of Qur'anic verses, the law does not positively prescribe any service peculiar to the occasion. Dower is a sum of money or property promised by the husband to be paid to the wife in consideration of the marriage. It is a token of love and respect, and not the price for connubial intercourse. Even where no dower is expressly fixed or mentioned at the time of marriage, the law confers the right of dower on the wife as a necessary effect of marriage. The wife has the right to refuse to cohabit with the husband so long as the dower remains unpaid. But she has no right to refuse cohabitation if the marriage had earlier been consummated with her consent. As in the present case the wife had cohabited with her husband for three months after her marriage, and there was no evidence of demand for her unpaid dower, the husband was entitled to restitution of conjugal rights.

Comments

This is a leading case on marriage and dower, and as Fyzee (1965: 103) points out, a number of observations made by Mahmood, J. have been adopted in the Muslim law of South Asia. But some of them have been challenged in later decisions. Mahmood, J. observes that a Muslim marriage is not a sacrament but purely a civil contract. In *Anis Begum* v. *Muhammad Istafa Wali Khan*, Sulaiman, C.J. approves the view that marriage is not a mere civil contract but also a religious sacrament. In *Sirajmohmed Khan* v. *Hafizunnisa*, the Supreme Court of India describes it as a sacrosanct contract. Fyzee (1974: 89) holds: 'It is a contract, but it is also a sacred covenant.' The decision in this case, that a wife whose prompt dower has not been paid loses her right to refuse herself to her husband if the marriage has been consummated with her consent was followed in *Anis Begum* and *Rabia Khatoon* v. *Mohd Mukhtar Ahmad* (Case 16). But the Lahore High Court held in *Rahim Jan* v. *Muhammad* (Case 34) that consummation of marriage does not deprive the wife of her right to refuse conjugal relations if the prompt dower is not paid.

The social dimension of the present judgment deserves special notice. In explaining the elaborate nature of the judgment, Mahmood, J. observes:

> And I may add that I have considered it my duty to go so fully into this question out of respect for the rulings which were cited on behalf of the respondents, but in which I have been unable to concur, and also because such questions, which usually arise only among the poor classes of the Muhammadan population, seldom come up to this Court for adjudication, but of course affect domestic relations of the Muhammadan community at large. (*Abdul Kadir* v. *Salima*, Case 5. p. 172).

6

Moonshee Buzloor Ruheem v. Shumsoonnissa Begum

Restitution of conjugal rights, *pardanashin* woman

Moonshee Buzloor Ruheem—Appellant

v.

Shumsoonnissa Begum—Respondent

(1867) 11 M.I.A. 551

(The Right Hon. Sir James William Colvile, the Right Hon. Sir Edward
Vaughan Willliams, and the Right Hon. Sir Richard Torin Kindersley.
Assessor: The Right Hon. Sir Lawrence Peel)

Decided on 4 July 1867

Issues of law

Pardanashin woman; restitution of conjugal rights

Case summary and decision

In 1847 the appellant, who was a zamindar, married the respondent, a
wealthy widow. She continued to live with him until 1855 when, alleging
cruelty of conduct, she lodged a complaint against him to the Magistrate
of the twenty-four Parganas, who allowed her to leave his house. The
following year she instituted a suit—described in the court proceedings
as the 'Property suit'—against her husband for recovery of government securities worth Rs. 2,34,800 that she owned, which she alleged
he had detained or made away with. He also filed a suit—described as

the 'Restitution suit'—against his wife, the objective of which was to enforce his marital rights, 'by compelling her to return to his house and control' (Fyzee 1965: 283). Regarding the Property suit, the wife's case was that as she lived in parda or seclusion, the securities had been endorsed and handed over to her husband for the purpose of receiving the interest on them for her and she never meant to transfer the property in them to him. The husband's defence was that he had purchased the securities from her and that, on their endorsement and delivery, he paid their full value to her and she appropriated the proceeds for her own use. The Zillah Judge ordered the husband to restore or replace the securities and the High Court confirmed the decree. On appeal by the husband, the Privy Council held that pardanashin women, being vulnerable to undue pressure and influence from their husbands, were entitled to special protection. Here, although the wife failed to prove affirmatively the precise case she alleged in the plaint, the husband was bound to show something more than mere endorsement and delivery of the government securities, and from the relations subsisting between the parties, the onus was upon him to establish that: (i) the transaction which he set up was a *bona fide* sale and (ii) he gave his wife the full value of the securities he received. This he failed to do. In fact, he had incurred a huge debt and had no means of purchasing the securities.

The Restitution suit was tried by the Principal Sudder Ameen and dismissed with costs; and the High Court confirmed the decision. In the appeal before the Privy Council, the question was whether any suit by a Muslim husband would lie in the civil courts of India to enforce his marital rights under Muslim law, by compelling the wife to return to cohabit with him against her will. The Privy Council admitted that the question was a novel and difficult one. After a searching review of the authorities and principles of Muslim law, the Privy Council held that a suit for restitution of conjugal rights by a Muslim husband to enforce his marital rights would lie in a civil court. Such a suit is in the nature of a suit for specific performance, and being founded on the contract of marriage, which Muslim law regards as a civil contract, the court would enforce all the obligations which flow from such a contract. If, however, cruelty to a degree rendering it unsafe for the wife to return to her husband's domain were established, the court would refuse to send her back to his house. Similarly, if it were proved that the husband grossly failed in performing obligations which the marriage contract imposes on him for the wife's benefit, the court would refuse him relief in such a suit. In the present case, there was no finding of the court below on specific acts of cruelty by the husband to enable it to infer if a defence on the ground of cruelty had been established. Hence the Privy Council declined to make a final decree and remitted the case back to the court below for a new trial in the light of its observations.

Comments

For arguments before the Privy Council, see pp. 518–80 and for the judgment, pp. 581–618, (1867) 11 M.I.A. 551. The text is also available in Fyzee (1965: 282–302). An exhaustive statement of the law on the subject of special protection given to pardanashin women is found in the leading case of *Farid-un-Nisa* v. *Mukhtar Ahmad*.

Professor Tahir Mahmood is of the opinion that the concept of restitution of conjugal rights is foreign to Islamic legal ideology and has been engrafted by Anglo-Indian judicial decisions. 'In the legal culture of Islam,' he forcefully asserts, 'there is no place either for judicial separation or for restitution of conjugal rights' (Mahmood 1997: 380).

7

Mansur v. Azizul

Postnuptial agreements

Mansur—Defendant, Appellant

v.

Azizul—Plaintiff, Respondent

AIR 1928 Oudh 303

(Raza and Nanavutty, JJ.)

Decided on 2 April 1928

Issue of law

Agreement giving maintenance to a wife not residing with husband

Case summary and decision

A week after his second marriage, Mansur Ali agreed to pay his first wife Azizul maintenance if she did not pull on well with the second wife and decided to live separately. She could not pull on well with the second wife and went to live in her father's house. In a suit for recovery of arrears of maintenance by her, Mansur admitted the execution of the agreement but denied his liability to give her maintenance on the grounds that the agreement was without consideration and she was not living with him as his wife. The Munsif held that the deed in question was not without consideration and the first wife was entitled to maintenance even if she did not reside in his house. The Subordinate Judge agreed with him. Mansur's counsel contended before the High Court that the agreement was opposed to public policy and Azizul was not entiled to maintenance from her husband under it. Having examined the document the High Court came to the conclusion that the intention of the parties was that the wife would be entitled to the *guzara* even if she did not reside in her husband's house. The court refused to follow the ruling of the Bombay High Court in *Bai Fatima* v. *Alimahomed Aiyeb* that an agreement which provides for and, therefore, encourages future separation between the spouses is void as being against public policy. The court held that, if a Muslim marries a second time and finds that his first wife cannot pull on well with the second wife and if he does not or cannot provide a separate residence for her exclusive use and, therefore, for preserving family peace, executes an agreement *in her favour* giving her maintenance, even if she lives apart from him, that agreement is not against public policy. As the husband can conveniently visit her in her separate apartment, no question of separation between husband and wife really arises in this case. The court confirmed the decree of the lower courts.

Comments

In *Bai Fatima*, the agreement stipulated that if a man took a second wife and his first wife could not live in harmony with her, she would be entitled to live separately and claim maintenance. The Bombay High Court construed it as providing for and encouraging future separation and following English law pronounced it void as being against public policy. In *Mansur*, the court dissented from this decision. *Sadiqa Begum* v. *Ata Ullah*, which supports the view taken in *Mansur*, upheld the validity of an agreement to the effect that if the husband took another wife, the first wife would be entitled either to divorce him or to live apart from him and receive a monthly maintenance allowance.

8

Saiyid Rashid Ahmad
v. Anisa Khatun
Effects of triple talaq

Saiyid Rashid Ahmad and Another—Appellants

v.

Anisa Khatun and Others—Respondents

AIR 1932 PC 25

(Lords Thankerton and Salvesen and Sir George Lowndes)

Decided on 19 November 1931

Issues of law

Classification of talaq; effects of *talaq-i-bid'at*; remarriage without intervening marriage

Case summary and decision

The dispute related to succession of the estate of Ghiyas Uddin, a Hanafi Muslim, who died in 1920 leaving considerable movable and immovable property. The appellants were a brother and sister of Ghiyas Uddin and the respondents were his widow Anisa Khatun and her five children. Ghiyas Uddin pronounced triple talaq on his wife Anisa Khatun, allegedly at his dying father's request, and executed a deed of divorce stating that he had given the divorce in 'abominable form'. The couple continued to live together for fifteen years until Ghiyas Uddin's death. During this period five children were born and he treated Anisa Khatun as his wife and the five children as legitimate. After his death the wife and children claimed their share of his considerable property. But there was no proof of an intermediate marriage of Anisa Khatun with a third person and a subsequent remarriage of the couple. The Subordinate Judge held that Ghiyas Uddin irrevocably divorced Anisa Khatun and therefore, she was not his wife at the time of his death and the five children, all born after the divorce, were illegitimate.

The High Court came to the contrary conclusion that the divorce was fictitious and inoperative; it was a mock ceremony performed by Ghiyas Uddin to satisfy his dying father and he never intended it to be effective. On further appeal, the Privy Council held that the divorce, being in the *bid'at* and not *ahsan* form, at once became irrevocable, irrespective of the *iddat*. The validity and effectiveness of an irrevocable divorce would not be affected by the husband's mental intention that it should not be a genuine divorce. 'A talak actually pronounced under compulsion or in jest is valid and effective.' Subsequent acknowledgement of the status of the woman and her children was ineffective in the absence of evidence of facts which might have made a remarriage lawful. In reply to the submission of Anisa Khatun's counsel to presume remarriage from the facts of continued cohabitation of the couple and the father's acknowledgement of legitimacy of the children, the Privy Council held that an acknowledgement of legitimacy raises a presumption of marriage but only where there was no legal bar to marriage. In this case there was such a bar, created by the triple divorce, which could only be removed by proof that Anisa Khatun had married another man and that this marriage had been consummated and dissolved by death of the husband or divorce of the wife by him, to enable her to remarry her former spouse. As this was not proved, Anisa Khatun was not his lawful wife, the five children were illegitimate, and they could not inherit Ghiyas Uddin's estate.

Comments

The decision has been roundly criticized by Danial Latifi in his article, 'The Triple Talaq and Fatwa by Ahl E Hadith Maulanas' (1993). Relying on the *Fatawa Alamgiri*, Mulla has stated in Section 336(5) of his *Principles of Mahomedan Law* (1990) that remarriage of a couple without an intervening marriage of the wife with a stranger is irregular (*fasid*) and not void (*batil*). The children of such a marriage are legitimate and entitled to inherit their father's property. However, an irregular marriage does not create mutual rights of inheritance between husband and wife [see section 267 in Mulla (1990)]. In *Khadissa* v. *Muhammed* (Case 15), the Kerala High Court did not follow the Privy Council decision. Section 7 of the MFLO, which applies to both Pakistan and Bangladesh, has abolished the talaq-i-bid'at and allowed remarriage after such a divorce without an intervening marriage with a third person, unless the wife has been divorced for a third time.

9

Ahmad Kasim Molla v. *Khatun Bibi*
Arbitrary talaq

Ahmad Kasim Molla—Plaintiff

v.

Khatun Bibi—Defendant

AIR 1933 Cal. 27

(Costello, J.)

Decided on 14 August 1931

Issues of law

Talaq by husband at his mere whim; talaq by a written instrument without notice to wife

Case summary and decision

In this suit, the plaintiff husband's case was that he married defendant Khatun Bibi on 25 August 1926, divorced her on 20 September 1929, and duly communicated it to her. He sought a declaration that he had validly divorced her. Khatun Bibi denied that he had validly divorced her. Alternately, she said that she had no knowledge of the divorce. She also claimed that under the terms of the *kabinnama* she was entitled to be maintained by the plaintiff for the duration of her life. For her counterclaim she relied on a clause of the marriage contract which provided that if the plaintiff committed any breach of the conditions of the contract, she would be justified in living separately from him and he would be bound to make suitable provision for her residence and maintenance. She also alleged that the plaintiff assaulted her and wrongfully drove her away from his house.

The court formed the following two issues for determination: (i) whether Khatun Bibi was validly divorced and (ii) if so, whether, under the terms of the kabinnama, she was entitled to receive anything more than what was payable to a divorced wife under the general provisions of Muslim law. Khatun Bibi's counsel argued that there was no valid talaq for two reasons. First, a Muslim husband could not divorce his wife without a just cause. But the husband had not shown any reasonable ground for the divorce. It was entirely capricious and arbitrary. Second, the talaq was not brought to the notice of the wife. Costello, J. held that 'any Mahomedan may divorce his wife at his mere whim and caprice' (p. 29). For his views he relied on Macnaughten who said: 'There is no occasion for any particular cause for divorce, and mere whim is sufficient' (p. 29). He also approvingly cited the observation of Batchelor, J. in *Sarabai v. Rabiabai*, (1905) ILR 30 Bom. 537 that a talaq without any just cause or assigning any reason is 'good in law, though bad in theology'. The court further held that a talaq was valid even if it was not pronounced in the presence of the wife or not brought to the knowledge of the wife. Regarding the divorced wife's claim for lifelong maintenance, the court observed that a Muslim marriage is purely a civil contract and, therefore, the terms of the kabinnama must be construed in the same way as the provisions of any other kind of contract. It would have been quite competent for the relations of the wife or for the wife herself to have stipulated in the kabinnama that if there were a divorce, the husband would still be under an obligation to pay the wife an adequate subsistence allowance during the wife's lifetime or for any other specified period. But the conditions mentioned in the kabinnama did not amount to more than an assertion of the normal rights of a wife against her husband and provision of maintenance for life could not be inferred from them. The husband was entitled to the declaration that he sought and the wife was not entitled to any maintenance after she was divorced.

Comments

Krishna Iyer, J. disputed the assumption that a Muslim husband enjoys an arbitrary, unilateral power to inflict instant divorce on his wife [*A. Yousuf Rawther v. Sowramma* (Case 23)]. In *Jiauddin Ahmed v. Anwara Begum*, Baharul Islam, J. disagreed with the view taken in *Ahmad Kasim Molla* and held:

> Costello, J. in 59 Calcutta 833 has not, with respect, laid down the correct rule of talaq. In my view the correct law of talaq as ordained by the Holy Quran is that talaq must be for a reasonable cause and be preceded by attempts at reconciliation between the husband and the wife by two arbiters—one from the wife's family the other from the husband's. If the attempts fail, talaq may be effected.

His view was endorsed in *Rukia Khatun v. Abdul Khaliq Laskar, Zeenat Fatema Rashid v. Md Iqbal Anwar* (Case 19), *Saira Bano v. Mohd Aslam, Dagdu Chotu Pathan v. Rahimbi Dagdu Pathan* (Case 20), and, finally, in *Shamim Ara v. State of U.P.* (Case 21) by the Supreme of Court of India. In Bangladesh and Pakistan, talaq no longer becomes effective as soon as it is pronounced. Section 7 of the MFLO freezes for ninety days the talaq pronounced by a husband, for the purpose of bringing about reconciliation between the spouses. If the reconciliation effort does not succeed, talaq becomes effective after the ninety-day period.

10

Sainuddin v. Latifannessa Bibi

Delegated power of divorce

Sainuddin—Plaintiff

v.

Latifannessa Bibi—Defendant

(1918) ILR 46 Cal. 141

(Fletcher and Shams-ul-Huda, JJ.)

Decided on 3 April 1918

Issues of law

Talaq-i-tafwid or delegated power of divorce; revocation of power; restitution of conjugal rights

Case summary and decision

The parties were married in 1901. In 1905 the husband executed a postnuptial kabinnama in place of an unregistered antenuptial kabinnama in favour of his minor wife. The husband delegated his power of divorce to his wife, to be exercised by her if there was a breach of any of the following conditions: (i) the husband was not to take a second wife without her permission; (ii) he was not to beat or ill-treat her; (iii) he was to allow her to visit her parents; (iv) he had to live with her in any place she desired; and (v) he was to pay her maintenance there at a specified monthly rate. When the husband took a second wife, the first wife left for her mother's house. The husband instituted the suit in issue for restitution of conjugal rights. Thereafter, she executed a *talaqnama* divorcing him in exercise of the delegated power of talaq. The husband's suit was dismissed by the Munsif and this decision was confirmed by the District Judge. In the second appeal, the husband's counsel argued that a postnuptial delegation of the power to divorce was not valid. Second, the rules of *tafwid* require that the option must be exercised immediately on the happening of the contingency. In the present case the option was exercised more than a year after the husband took a second wife. Third, according to the law of agency the delegated power was revocable, and the institution of the suit by the husband for restitution of conjugal rights before the execution of the talaqnama operated as a revocation of that power. The High Court disagreed with the three propositions. It held that a postnuptial delegation of the power to divorce is valid. The delegation is not revocable. It may be immediate or postponed, conditional or unconditional. The institution of a suit for restitution of conjugal rights does not operate as a revocation of the delegated power of talaq given to the wife by a husband. In this case, there was a clear delegation of the right of divorce, which the wife was expressly allowed to exercise 'whenever she chose'. She had exercised that power and put an end to marital relations with her husband. The suit for restitution of conjugal rights could not, therefore, lie and it was rightfully dismissed.

11

Moonshee Buzul-ul-Raheem v. Luteefut-oon-Nissa

Talaq and khula

Moonshee Buzul-ul-Raheem—Appellant

v.

Luteefut-oon-Nissa—Respondent

(1861) 8 M.I.A. 379

(The Right Hon. Lord Kingsdown, Right Hon. Lord Justice Knight Bruce,
Right Hon. Sir Edward Ryan, and Right Hon. Lord Justice Turner.
Assessor: The Right Hon. Sir Lawrence Peel)
Decided on 12 July 1861

Issues of law

Distinction between talaq and khula forms of divorce; legal incidents of both forms; dower

Case summary and decision

This was a suit brought by a wife against her husband for recovery of dower, payable to her in the event of dissolution of their marriage. The facts were that the couple was married in 1842 and the dower was settled at Rs. 26,000. In 1847 the husband took another wife to whom he promised that he would divorce his first wife. To force the first wife to seek a khula divorce from him and thus forfeit her right to dower, he began to treat her with great cruelty, refusing to permit her to see her mother, denying her food and clothing commensurate with her status and standard of living, and, finally, succeeded in forcing her to execute a *khulanama*. The wife filed a suit for recovery of her dower, alleging that her husband had divorced her and by fraud and force obtained from her a deed of khula. The husband claimed that he did not divorce her by talaq but that, by her own initiative, she executed the divorce agreement and as consideration she waived payment of her dower. The Principal Sudder Ameen, who heard the case in the first instance, found that the documents put in evidence by the husband to show khula divorce and waiver of dower were fraudulent and of no effect. As the marriage was admittedly dissolved, the wife was entitled to recover the dower with interest. On the husband's appeal, the *sudder dewanny adawlut* at Calcutta approved this decision, reiterating that the execution of the khulanama was not a voluntary, unrestrained act and was, therefore, a nullity, but it proved the factum of divorce.

When the case came up before the Privy Council, it found that Muslim law recognizes two different kinds of divorce—talaq and khula. A divorce by talaq is an arbitrary act of the husband who may repudiate his wife at his own pleasure, with or without cause. If he adopts this mode, he is liable to pay her dower and also give up any jewels or paraphernalia received from him. A divorce by khula is at the instance of the wife and with the consent of the husband, for which the wife gives or agrees to give some consideration to the husband for her release from the marriage tie. In such a case the terms of the bargain are matters of arrangement between the husband and wife; and the wife may, as consideration, waive her dower and other rights or make any other arrangement for the husband's benefit. In the case under review, since the husband, while denying a divorce by talaq, had set up a divorce by khula, he could not argue that a divorce had not taken place. Therefore, the only question before the court was whether the husband could insist on receiving the consideration which he claimed was stipulated. As he could not prove that the alleged deeds on which his claim was based were validly executed, his claim had to fail and the wife was entitled to the dower.

Comments

Regarding the view of the Privy Council that a talaq is an arbitrary act of the husband who may repudiate his wife at his own pleasure, with or without cause, see our comments in *Ahmad Kasim Molla v. Khatun Bibi* (Case 9).

12

Zubaida Begum v. Sardar Shah

Dissolution of marriage

Zubaida Begum—Plaintiff, Appellant

v.

Sardar Shah—Defendant, Respondent

AIR (30) 1943 Lah. 310

(Harries, C.J. and Abdul Rashid, J.)

Decided on 15 February 1943

Issue of law

Dissolution of marriage under Sections 2(ii) and 2(viii)(f) of DMMA

Case summary and decision

Zubaida Begum applied for dissolution of her marriage with Sardar Shah on account of desertion and cruelty. Her plea was that shortly after her marriage he began to ill-treat her, and six months after the marriage turned her out and married another woman. Thereafter, he went away to South Africa without making any provision for her maintenance. Sardar Shah pleaded that he had never ill-treated her. He had asked her to live with him in Africa but she had refused. The issues before the Additional District Judge were: (i) whether the first wife had been neglected and deserted by the husband; (ii) whether she had been treated cruelly; and (iii) if so, whether she was entitled to dissolution of her marriage. The judge held that no cruelty or desertion had been established. The wife's review petition was heard by the District Judge who held that the husband had failed to provide maintenance for his first wife for more than two years and had not treated her equitably in accordance with the injunctions of the Qur'an. He granted her a decree for dissolution of the marriage. The decree was reversed by a Single Judge of the High Court. In the wife's appeal against this decision, the Division Bench of the Lahore High Court held that it was perfectly clear from the evidence that while the second wife was provided with a home and maintenance, no maintenance was provided for the first wife. He had, indeed, asked her to join him in Africa but sent no money for the passage. In these circumstances it must be held that the husband had neglected or failed to provide for the maintenance of the first wife for a period of two years within the meaning of Section 2(ii) of the DMMA. As he had failed to provide for her maintenance, it could not be said that he had treated her equitably in accordance with the injunctions of the Qur'an within Section 2(viii)(f) of the above Act. Therefore, the court set aside the decision of the Single Judge and restored the decree of the District Judge dissolving her marriage with Sardar Shah.

13

Imambandi v. *Haji Mutsaddi*

Guardianship of minors, legitimacy

Imambandi and Others—Defendants, Appellants

v.

Haji Mutsaddi and Others—Plaintiffs, Respondents

AIR 1918 PC 11

(Lord Shaw, Sir John Edge, Mr Ameer Ali, Sir Walter Phillimore, Bart., and Sir Lawrence Jenkins)

Decided on 23 February 1918

Issues of law

Guardianship of minors; mother's right as de facto guardian to alienate minor's immovable property; standard authorities on Hanafi law; acknowledgement of legitimacy

Case summary and decision

Ismail Ali Khan, who owned considerable landed property, died in 1906 leaving behind three widows and several children. Enayet-uz-Zohra, who had two children, conveyed by a deed of sale her and her children's share of the property to certain purchasers. The plaintiff purchasers filed a suit for possession of the share, claiming that: (i) Zohra was a lawfully wedded wife of Ismail Ali Khan; (ii) her two children were his legitimate issues; and (iii) Zohra, acting on her own and her children's behalf, had lawfully transferred the property to them. The defendants, that is, the other two wives and their children denied Zohra's marriage to Ismail Khan and the legitimacy of her children. The Subordinate Judge of Saran accepted the plaintiffs' contention and awarded them possession of the share in the landed property in issue, and the High Court of Calcutta affirmed the decree. The defendants appealed from this judgment to the Privy Council.

The Privy Council observed that clear and reliable evidence that a Muslim has acknowledged children, whose legitimacy is disputed, as his legitimate issues raises a presumption of a valid marriage between him and the children's mother. The Privy Council was satisfied that there was such evidence in this case, and accordingly, held that both Zohra and her children were entitled to their legal share in the inheritance of Ismail Ali Khan. Therefore, the next question was whether the plaintiff purchasers had acquired any title to the two infants' shares under the sale by the mother. The Privy Council held that the mother had no legal power to alienate their property, for she was not their legal guardian. Ameer Ali, J. who delivered the judgment, laid down the following rules governing the subject of guardianship. Under Muslim law the mother is only entitled to the custody of a minor up to a certain age and is not the legal guardian. The father is the legal guardian of his minor children. After his death, his executor is their legal guardian, or, if there is no executor, their grandfather, or, if he be dead, his executor. If there is no legal guardian, it is the duty of the judge to appoint one. If the mother is the father's executor, or has been appointed by court as executor, she has the powers of a legal executor, but those powers are subject to stringent conditions regarding immovable property. In the absence of any legal guardian, the person in charge of the minor children, for example, the mother, has, as de facto guardian, the power to incur debts, or to pledge the minor's goods and chattel for the minor's urgent necessities, such as food, clothing, nursing, but has no power to deal with the minor's immovable property. The court described the concept of de facto guardian and the limitation of his powers as follows:

> [U]nder the Mahomedan law a person who has charge of the person or property of a minor without being his legal guardian, and who may, therefore, be conveniently called a '*de facto* guardian, ' has no power to convey to another any right or interest in immoveable property which the transferee can enforce against the infant; nor can such transferee, if let into possession of the property under such unauthorized transfer, resist an action in ejectment on behalf of the infant as a trespasser. It follows that, being himself without title, he cannot seek to recover property in the possession of another equally without title.

Comments

This is a leading case on the subject of guardianship of property and the rules enunciated in this case have been reaffirmed in a number of later decisions. As to the expression 'de facto guardian' used in this case, Fyzee finds it curious that a person who intermeddles with the property of another was known by the term *'fazuli'* in early times, and yet is known by 'the undeservedly dignified title of *de facto* guardian' in modern law (Fyzee 1974: 205).

SECTION II

INDIA

14

Noor Mohammad v. Mohammad Jiauddin

Contractual nature of marriage

Noor Mohammad—Petitioner

v.

Mohammad Jiauddin—Respondent

AIR 1992 M.P. 244 (Gwalior Bench)

(Dr T.N. Singh, J.)

Decided on 14 December 1990

Issues of law

Contractual nature of marriage; reimbursement of marriage expenses incurred by bride's father; damages for loss of reputation of bride and her father; Article 51A(e) of Indian Constitution

Case summary and decision

Ruksana, a minor, was given in marriage by her father Jiauddin, plaintiff in the case, to Sher Mohammad, son of Noor Mohammad, the first defendant. The plaintiff's case was that he arranged two meals for the *barat* (bridegroom's party) and paid Rs. 2,000 to the defendant for expenses incurred by him for gaslights, music band, etc., accompanying the barat, but refused to pay for the services of the nautch girl. Getting very angry at this, the first defendant and his son returned home without taking with them the bride and for the next two years took no steps to take her to the matrimonial home. The bride repudiated the marriage on attaining majority and the plaintiff sued the defendants, claiming reimbursement of the expenses incurred by him for serving two meals to the barat, for the gaslights and music band, and damages for loss of reputation. The defendants admitted solemnization of the marriage but denied that any payment was made by the plaintiff for gaslights and music band, or that any demand was made by them for payment to the nautch girl. Their case was that, being dissatisfied with the dowry, the plaintiff insulted them, refused to send the bride with them, and drove away the barat. The trial court found that the plaintiff's case was true and that of the defendant false. The court allowed him Rs. 2,700 for the meals, Rs. 2,000 as refund of barat expenses, and Rs. 3,000 as compensation for loss of reputation, mental pain, and suffering. The defendants appealed against the decision.

The Madhya Pradesh High Court held that an Islamic marriage is a civil contract and among the rights conferred on the bride under a valid marriage are those of maintenance and residence in her husband's house. It is the duty and obligation of the marriage guardian to enforce these rights of a minor bride. The bridegroom is duty-bound in law to take her to his house immediately after marriage. It is no part of a marriage contract that the bride or her father is to bear any expenses incurred by the bridegroom or his father in connection with a marriage solemnized at the bride's house. Payment of expenses for gaslights and band and feeding the barat by the plaintiff was not without consideration. It was evidently a non-gratuitous act, the benefits of which were enjoyed by the defendants. Both the defendants were legally liable for those expenses because the plaintiff had no legal obligation to bear them. The damages awarded by the trial court for defamation was also sustainable in law. The scornful abandonment of the bride after the marriage by the defendants under the full gaze of the guests present, their vulgar exhibition of male chauvinism, and contemptuous disregard for the lawful aspirations of the bride and her marriage guardian in a manner that held them up to ridicule clearly showed their intention to defame the father and his daughter. The court also held that the defendants' demand that the plaintiff must pay for the services of the nautch girl employed by them was evidently intimidatory. As a matter of fact, they carried out the threat by illegally abandoning the bride at the marriage hall in full and complete violation of the injunctions of the law of marriage. From the viewpoint of the Constitution of India, the disgraceful conduct of the defendants was also derogatory to the 'dignity of the women' and, therefore, a clear violation of the fundamental duty contemplated under Article 51A(e) of the Constitution. The court affirmed the trial court's decision.

15

Khadissa v. *Muhammed*

Remarriage of divorced couple

Khadissa—Petitioner

v.

Muhammed—Respondent

1979 KLT 878

(Narayana Pillai, J.)

Decided on 7 November 1979

Issue of law

Effects of remarriage of a couple without an intervening marriage of wife

Case summary and decision

Eighteen years after their marriage and the birth of five children during those years, the husband divorced his wife. Sometime later he remarried her, lived together with her for about four months and then divorced her again. During this period of cohabitation, the wife became pregnant, and a child was born in due course. The wife applied to the Magistrate claiming maintenance for her and the child under Section

125 of the CrPC, 1973. The husband denied the second marriage. It was established that the second marriage had actually taken place, but there was no intermediate marriage of the wife with a third person between the first and second marriage of the couple. The Magistrate granted maintenance at the rate of Rs. 50 per month to the wife and Rs. 40 per month to the child. The Sessions Judge, in revision, set aside the order. Relying on Section 336(5) of Mulla's *Principles of Mahomedan Law* (1990: 276), which states that 'where the husband has repudiated his wife by *three* pronouncements ... it is not lawful for him to marry her again until she has married another man, and the latter has divorced her or died after actual consummation of the marriage', he held that the second marriage was invalid, the wife was living in adultery with the husband during those four months, and the child begotten during that period was illegitimate. Thus neither the wife nor the child was entitled to maintenance.

The Kerala High Court held that a woman who cohabits with a man, who was her previous husband and who has remarried her, cannot, on account of such cohabitation, be said to be living in adultery merely because the remarriage is technically invalid in the eyes of the law. The court held that if a remarriage is solemnized without an intermediate marriage of the wife with a third party, it is only an irregularity. In fact, Mulla himself states in Section 336(5) that a remarriage without fulfilling the condition of an intermediate marriage is irregular and not void. The effect of such an irregular marriage is that, if consummation has taken place, the wife is entitled to dower and the issue of the marriage is legitimate. A divorced wife is entitled to claim maintenance under Section 125 of the CrPC, 1973 unless she has received before or after the divorce the whole of the sum which, under any customary or personal law applicable to the parties, was payable on such divorce. The High Court set aside the order of the Sessions Judge and restored that of the Magistrate granting maintenance to the divorced wife and the child.

Comments

In his judgment Pillai, J. does not refer at all to *Saiyid Rashid Ahmad* v. *Anisa Khatun* (Case 8), where the Privy Council held that remarriage of a couple without an intervening marriage of the wife with a third person is void and the children of such marriage are illegitimate. Tahir

Mahmood (1997: 285) warmly supports the decision and praises 'the judicial wisdom and compassion' of Pillai, J. He also says that the decision can be supported on the ground that 'in a case where the application of the *Hanafi* law would cause hardship, the judge administering it may resort to the provisions of the *Maliki*, *Shafe'i* or *Hanbali* law'. In a major contribution on the subject, Danial Latifi (1993) suggests, as a way out of the grave injustice caused to triply divorced wives and their children by *Saiyid Rashid Ahmad*, the following courses of action:

1. The *nikahnama* should comply with the Qur'anic injunctions regarding dissolution of marriage.
2. The Supreme Court should review the judgment of the Privy Council in *Saiyid Rashid Ahmad*.
3. The above two suggestions can also be implemented by legislation.
4. The DMMA should incorporate the provisions of the Qur'an regarding talaq.
5. Any Hanafi Muslim, who finds himself or herself in difficulties on account of *Saiyid Rashid Ahmad*, should be advised to consult an Ahl-e-Hadith or Shia theologian.
6. The procedure of *halala* should be legally declared constructive rape and should be punished.

In a bold and laudable decision in *Masroor Ahmed v. State*, Ahmed, J. took judicial notice of the extreme misery caused to divorced women by triple talaq and treated such a talaq as one revocable talaq, which is in full consonance with the actual spirit and procedure of talaq and does not require the so-called halala procedure for remarriage of husband and wife. Thanks to the MFLO, this has been the legal position in Pakistan and Bangladesh since 1961.

16

Rabia Khatoon v. Mohd Mukhtar Ahmad

Dower, dissolution of marriage

Rabia Khatoon—Appellant

v.

Mohd Mukhtar Ahmad—Respondent

AIR 1966 All. 548

(D.P. Uniyal and S.D. Khare, JJ.)

Decided on 23 November 1965

Issues of law

Non-payment of prompt dower; restitution of conjugal rights; dissolution of marriage under Sections 2(ii) and 2(viii) of DMMA

Case summary and decision

In this case, shortly after the birth of a child the wife went to her father's house and refused to return to the matrimonial home. She complained that her husband had treated her with cruelty, turned her out of his house, failed to maintain her for more than five years, and in spite of her demand, not paid her prompt dower. She claimed dissolution of the marriage. In his written statement the husband denied the charge of cruelty, alleged that the dower payable to the wife was deferred dower, and filed a counter suit for restitution of conjugal rights. The two lower courts found that: (i) cruelty was not established; (ii) the dower settled was prompt dower which was not paid to the wife; and (iii) the husband had not paid any maintenance allowance to the wife ever since she left his house. On these findings the husband's suit for restitution of conjugal rights was decreed, subject to payment of prompt dower to the wife, and the wife's suit for dissolution of marriage was dismissed on the ground that she could not deny herself to the husband after consummation of the marriage merely because her dower had remained unpaid.

The question that the Allahabad High Court was required to consider was whether a Muslim wife has a right to refuse herself to her husband if her prompt dower is not paid, even though the marriage has been consummated with her consent before the date of the refusal. Where there has been no consummation of the marriage, the courts have unanimously held that failure to pay prompt dower is a complete defence to a husband's suit for restitution of conjugal rights. But where the marriage has been consummated, Imam Abu Hanifa holds that the wife has the right to refuse herself to her husband at any time during the marriage until payment of dower, and his two disciples, Imam Abu Yusuf and Imam Muhammad, hold that the wife loses the right. In *Abdul Kadir* v. *Salima* (Case 5), Mahmood, J. adopted the view of the two disciples, which was followed by Sulaiman, C.J. in *Anis Begum* v. *Muhammad Istafa Wali Khan.* Following these two decisions, the High Court held that, after consummation of marriage, non-payment of prompt dower, even though exigible, cannot be pleaded as a defence to an action for restitution of conjugal rights. The court justified its reliance on the rule laid down in *Abdul Kadir* on the ground that it has held the field for seventy-five years and to reject it as bad law 'would not only create uncertainty in the law but also disturb the domestic peace of Muhammedan families throughout India'. Having regard to prevalent practice, modern conditions of life, and progressive thought of the present time, it would be dangerous to adopt the view of Imam Abu Hanifa. The court also held that, as the suit for restitution of conjugal rights is in the nature of a suit for specific performance, the court has discretion to pass a decree for restitution of conjugal rights, subject to payment of the dower. As the wife had failed to prove cruelty by the husband, the other plausible ground for claming dissolution of her marriage was the husband's failure to maintain her for a period of two years. But the court held that, because the wife had no right to refuse to live with her husband after consummation of her marriage and kept herself away without the husband's fault, she had no right to claim maintenance from him and, therefore, to dissolution of the marriage. The court confirmed the decision of the two courts below.

Comments

B.P. Bhatnagar (1996) has questioned the rule laid down by Mahmood, J. in *Abdul Kadir* and followed by Uniyal, J. in *Rabia Khatoon*, on the following grounds. As authority for his rule Mahmood, J. refers to *Durr al-Mukhtar*, which however supports Abu Hanifa's view. His views are also not supported by classical jurists of repute and weight—they, as Syed Ameer Ali says, recognize the rule laid down by Abu Hanifa as law. The reason given in *Rabia Khatoon* that rejection of the rule in *Abdul Kadir* would create uncertainty in law and disturb the domestic peace of Muslim families is specious. It is the very denial of the wife's right that would threaten domestic peace. Finally, the argument advanced in *Rabia Khatoon* that the rule has held the field for seventy-five years is no good reason to immortalize an error having social consequences. Bhatnagar (1966: 416) submits that the rule should be reconsidered 'to make the law more realistic and to bring it in accord with the Islamic concerns of social justice'. It is interesting to note that neither the Allahabad High Court in *Rabia Khatoon* nor Bhatnagar was aware of an earlier decision in a Pakistani case, *Rahim Jan* v. *Muhammad* (Case 34), where Kaikaus, J. refused to follow the rule in *Abdul Kadir*.

17

Itwari v. *Asghari*

Polygamy, restitution of conjugal rights

Itwari—Appellant

v.

Asghari and Others—Defendants

AIR 1960 All. 684

(S.S. Dhavan, J.)

Decided on 29 August 1959

Issues of law

Restitution of conjugal rights; polygamous marriages; defence of cruelty; discretion of court to grant relief

Case summary and decision

In this case, shortly after the marriage, relations between the husband and wife became sour and the wife left the husband to live with her parents. But he took no steps to bring her back and married another woman. She filed an application for maintenance under Section 488 of the CrPC, 1898. Thereupon, the husband filed a suit against her for restitution of conjugal rights. The wife pleaded that she had been thrown out by her husband, who had formed an illicit union with another woman, whom he subsequently married. He had deprived her of her ornaments, refused to pay her dower, and beaten her, causing physical and mental pain. Holding that the wife had failed to prove that she was really ill-treated, the Munsif decreed the husband's suit for restitution of conjugal rights against her. On appeal, the District Judge was of the opinion that the husband had never really cared for her and filed his suit for restitution of conjugal rights as a counter-blast to the wife's claim for maintenance. Accordingly, he allowed the wife's appeal. In the second appeal, the husband's counsel argued before the High Court that the mere fact that the husband had taken a second wife was no proof of cruelty, as every Muslim had the right to take four wives. Further, to defeat a husband's suit for assertion of his conjugal rights there must be proof of cruelty of such character as to render it unsafe for the wife to return to her husband's house.

In a landmark decision Dhavan, J. held that, in a suit for restitution of conjugal rights by a husband against his first wife after he has taken a second wife, if the circumstances reveal that in taking a second wife the husband has been guilty of such conduct as to make it inequitable for the court to compel the first wife to live with him, it will refuse a restitution order. Muslim law has considered polygamy as an institution to be tolerated but not encouraged and has not conferred upon the husband any fundamental right to compel the first wife to share his consortium with another woman in all circumstances. A Muslim husband has the legal right to take a second wife, but if he does so, and seeks the court's assistance to compel the first wife to live with him against her wishes on pain of severe penalties including attachment of her property, she is entitled to raise the question whether the court, as a court of equity, ought to compel her to submit to cohabitation with such a husband. In such a case the circumstances in which his second marriage took place are material in deciding whether his conduct in taking a second wife was itself an act of cruelty to the first. In considering the question of cruelty in any particular case, the court cannot ignore the prevailing social conditions, the circumstances of actual life, and the change in people's habits and modes of living. The onus will be on the polygamous husband to explain his action and prove that his taking a second wife involved no insult or cruelty to the first. But in the absence of a cogent explanation the court will presume that under modern conditions the action of the husband in taking a second wife involved cruelty to the first and that it would be inequitable for the court to compel her to live with such a husband. On the facts of the present case, the court agreed with the lower appellate court that the husband had never really cared for his first wife and filed his suit for restitution only to defeat her claim for maintenance. Therefore, the husband's suit was mala fide and it would be inequitable to compel the first wife to live with him.

Comments

Academic opinions on this decision vary. B. Sivaramayya, for example, dwelling on its immense potentialities, says: 'An extension of concept of cruelty enunciated by Dhavan J. to cases under the Dissolution of Muslim Marriages Act 1939 will enable a Muslim wife to secure divorce whenever the husband contracts a second marriage against her will' (1983: 281). Khalid Rashid and Arshad Masood, on the other hand, take it as 'an unwarranted attempt to change Muslim Personal Law' (1978: 17). The decision was followed in *Raj Mohammad* v. *Saeeda Amina Begum*. In their book David Pearl and Werner Menski (1998: 275) cite an English case where the High Court, being influenced by the decision in *Itwari*, held that, in modern circumstances, the taking of a second wife without the consent of the first wife, even in Muslim societies, could amount to cruelty.

18

Saifuddin Sekh v. *Soneka Bibi*

Stipulations in marriage contract

Saifuddin Sekh—Defendant, Appellant

v.

Soneka Bibi—Plaintiff, Respondent

AIR 1955 Ass. 153

(Sarjoo Prosad, C.J. and Deka, J.)

Decided on 5 August 1954

Issues of law

Validity of antenuptial agreement giving right of divorce to wife in case of happening of a certain event; application of Section 23 of Contract Act, 1872

Case summary and decision

At the time the defendant contracted to marry the plaintiff he already had two wives who, for reasons not mentioned, were not living with him in the matrimonial home. An antenuptial agreement concluded between the defendant and the plaintiff provided that, in case he brought any of the other two wives to stay with him without her consent, she would be at liberty to divorce him. The defendant did bring one of them to stay with him without the plaintiff's consent and she divorced him duly observing the legal formalities of divorce. The question was whether the condition of the contract was valid. The Munsif held that the two other wives were also entitled to have marital relations with the husband and, as the contract purported to deprive them of their right, it was invalid under Section 23 of the Contract Act, 1872. The Subordinate Judge disagreed with this view. He held that there was absolutely no justification in asking an unwilling wife to stay in the company of other wives with whom she could not pull on well. If the plaintiff was allowed the relief claimed by her under the agreement, it would not interfere in any way with the conjugal rights of the other wives; it would also not curtail the husband's right to marry other women of his choice within the permissible limit of four. The condition, therefore, was quite in accord with reason and public policy and should be enforced. The Assam High Court agreed with the Subordinate Judge and held that a contract which served to ensure peace and domestic happiness should not be treated as invalid and opposed to public policy. Under Muslim law, a husband is entitled to have as many as four wives and these wives are also entitled to the exercise of marital rights with their husband. The term of the contract in question did not in any way militate against this provision of the law. It did not place any impediment on the right of the other two wives to have marital relations with their husband or on the right of the husband to have marital relations with them. All that it said was that in case he brought any of the other wives to stay with him along with the plaintiff without her consent, she would be entitled to exercise the right of divorce. Such a right cannot be said to be opposed to public policy and invalid.

19

Zeenat Fatema Rashid
v. Md Iqbal Anwar
Proof and reasonableness of talaq

Zeenat Fatema Rashid—Petitioner

v.

Md Iqbal Anwar—Respondent

1995 AIHC 416 (Gauhati High Court)

(R.K. Manisana and S.B. Roy, JJ.)

Decided on 5 May 1993

Issues of law

Proof of talaq; reasonable cause of talaq and pre-divorce conference; talaq at husband's whim or caprice; oral or written statement of talaq in maintenance proceedings

Case summary and decision

The case of the petitioner wife was that after the birth of a son she was ill-treated by her husband and other members of his family and she had to leave his house. On 29 August 1990 she filed an application under Section 125 of the CrPC, 1973 claiming maintenance for herself and her minor child. The respondent husband's defence was that he had divorced her on 31 August 1990. The family court held that the wife had been duly divorced and her claim for maintenance would be determined under Section 3 of the MWA. The Gauhati High Court formulated two questions for decision: (i) whether a Muslim husband can divorce his wife at his whim and caprice and (ii) whether talaq has been proved. *Sarabai v. Rabiabai*, which was followed in many cases, had decided that a Muslim husband can divorce his wife at his whim and caprice, and no reasonable ground is necessary for divorce. But in *Jiauddin Ahmed v. Anwara Begum* and *Rukia Khatun v. Abdul Khaliq Laskar*, the Gauhati High Court had held that talaq must be for a reasonable cause and it must be preceded by an attempt at reconciliation between the spouses by their nominees. In the instant case the court held that the Qur'an discourages divorce and permits it only in extreme cases after pre-divorce reconciliation efforts. The modern concept of divorce is also that the matrimonial status should be maintained as far as possible. The Family Courts Act, 1984, aims at reconciliation and persuasion of the spouses to arrive at a settlement. For these reasons, the court held that a Muslim husband cannot divorce his wife at his whim or caprice. Divorce must be for a reasonable cause, and it must be preceded by a pre-divorce conference to arrive at a settlement. The court agreed with the two previous decisions of the Gauhati High Court and dissented from the earlier decisions of the other High Courts.

Regarding the second question whether talaq had been proved, the husband's case was that he had divorced his wife by a written talaq-nama. The court held that he had failed to prove the alleged talaqnama by production of requisite documents, as required by law. In his evidence he stated that he had also orally pronounced talaq three times. The court held that there was no evidence to corroborate his claim. There was also no evidence that there was a pre-divorce conference for reconciliation. The third and last contention of the husband in support of talaq was that in a large number of maintenance cases including *Chand Bi v. Bandesha*, it was held that, where the husband stated in the written statement that he had already divorced his wife and the court came to the conclusion that divorce pleaded was not proved, then the averment in the written statement itself operated as a declaration of divorce by talaq, and the divorce would be held to take effect at least from the date on which his written statement was filed by the husband. The court disagreed with these decisions on the ground that pleading and proof were not the same thing. 'Where the parties are in dispute as regards a material fact, an averment in the pleading does not constitute evidence, as what is stated in the pleading is recital of past event which is required to be proved.' For the reasons stated above, the court held that the husband had failed to prove the alleged talaq. It set aside the family court's order with regard to divorce and sent the matter back for disposal afresh.

Comments

This case, together with *Jiauddin Ahmed* and *Rukia Khatun*, on which it relied, are major milestones in the history of the development of Muslim personal law in South Asia. They restated the true Islamic law of talaq and freed it from the distorted interpretation, given to it by colonial judges in cases like *Sarabai, Ahmad Kasim Molla* v. *Khatun Bibi* (Case 9) and others, that the husband can exercise the power of talaq in an arbitrary, capricious, and irrational manner. The three Gauhati decisions expressly dissented from them.

20

Dagdu Chotu Pathan v. *Rahimbi Dagdu Pathan*

Talaq law, pre-divorce reconciliation

Dagdu Chotu Pathan—Petitioner

v.

Rahimbi Dagdu Pathan and Others—Respondent
2002(3) Mh.L.J. 602 (F.B.)
(B.H. Marlapalle, N.V. Dabholkar, and N.H. Patil, JJ.)
Decided on 2 May 2002

Issues of law

Exposition of the law of talaq; pre-divorce reconciliation efforts and reasonable cause of talaq; proof of factum of talaq; mere plea of talaq and its effectiveness; irrevocable talaq; talaq in presence of witnesses; meaning of iddat

Case summary and decision

Rahimbi filed an application in the magistrate's court under Section 125 of the CrPC, 1973 against her husband Dagdu Pathan for maintenance for herself and her three children, claiming that her husband, after his second marriage, neglected and refused to maintain them. Her husband claimed that he had divorced her before contracting his second marriage and prayed for dismissal of the maintenance application. The Magistrate allowed the maintenance application. He held that the fact of marriage must be proved; it could not be accepted by the court merely on pleadings in the husband's written statement. When the husband's appeal against the Magistrate's order came up for hearing before a Single Judge of the High Court, it was noticed that a Division Bench of the Bombay High Court at Mumbai had held in *Jaitunbi Mubarak Shaikh* v. *Mubarak Fakruddin Shaikh* that, in a Muslim wife's maintenance proceedings, if the husband takes a plea in his written statement that his marriage had been dissolved at an earlier date in the talaq form, even assuming that the fact of such dissolution of marriage at an earlier date is not proved, the filing of the written statement containing such a plea of divorce amounts to a dissolution of the marriage under Muslim law from the date on which such a statement was made. But another Division Bench of the Bombay High Court at Nagpur, without referring to the decision in *Jaitunbi Mubarak Shaikh*, held in *Saira Bano* v. *Mohd Aslam* that mere assertion either in the pleadings or witness box does not by itself amount to divorce in Muslim law. The husband must prove that he has given divorce in accordance with Muslim law some time prior to the date of such assertion. The Single Judge referred the controversy to the Chief Justice, who constituted a Full Bench to settle it.

In a brilliant exposition of the law of talaq, the Full Bench said that if a husband feels that his wife is disobedient, incompatible, unfaithful, uncaring, refuses to cohabit with him, or engages in cruel behaviour, for any of these reasons he has the right to give talaq to her but by following certain procedure. She must be given time to change her behaviour. If she does not change, two arbitrators, one representing the wife and other the husband, are required to be appointed to bring about a settlement between the spouses so that they live together happily. If the attempt at reconciliation fails, the husband has the right to give talaq to his wife. Though it is the husband who pronounces the talaq, he is as much bound by the decision of the arbiters as the wife. This shows that he cannot repudiate the marriage at his will or whim. Mere statements made in writing or in oral depositions before a court that talaq had been pronounced some time in the past is not sufficient to hold that the husband has divorced his wife. All the stages—conveying the reasons for divorce, appointment of arbiters, arbiters conducting conciliation proceedings between the parties, and failure of such proceedings or a situation where it was impossible for the marriage to continue—are required to be proved as conditions precedent to the husband's right to give talaq to his wife. The Full Bench reiterated that the husband must prove that the talaq was given and that it was given after satisfying the conditions precedent, namely, arbitration and valid reasons. The court agreed with the view taken in *Saira Bano, Rukia Khatun* v. *Abdul Khaliq Laskar,* and *Zeenat Fatema Rashid* v. *Md Iqbal Anwar* (Case 19), and overruled *Jaitunbi Mubarak Shaikh.*

Comments

This is an outstanding judgment on talaq. Here the court spells out in minute detail the rules of talaq which must be complied with for effecting a valid divorce. It not only agrees with the view taken by the Gauhati High Court in the cases of *Rukia Khatun* and *Zeenat Fatema Rashid*, but also categorically asserts, contrary to a series of decisions including *Chand Bi* v. *Bandesha*, that a mere statement made in writing before a court or in oral depositions that talaq was pronounced in the past is not sufficient to hold that the husband has divorced his wife.

21

Shamim Ara v. State of U.P.

Conditions precedent to talaq, proof

Shamim Ara—Appellant

v.

State of U.P. and Another—Respondents

(2002) 7 SCC 518

(R.C. Lahoti and P. Venkatarama Reddi, JJ.)

Decided on 1 October 2002

Issues of law

Conditions precedent to effectiveness of talaq; proof of pronounce-ment of talaq; meaning of 'pronouncement'; husband's plea of talaq in a written statement; wife's maintenance under Section 125 of CrPC, 1973

Case summary and decision

Shamim Ara, mother of four sons, filed an application under Section 125 of the CrPC, 1973, complaining of desertion and cruelty by her husband Abrar Ahmed. In his written statement Abrar Ahmed made certain generalized accusa-tions that she was sharp, shrewd and mischievous, and had brought disgrace to his family. Being fed up with her unbecoming conduct he had divorced her on 11 July 1987. Claiming protection of the MWA, he also submitted that he had given her a house in lieu of maintenance and, therefore, she was not entitled to any maintenance. Shamim Ara denied having been divorced at any time. The family court held that the husband's plea for divorce was corroborated by an affi-davit filed by him in a civil suit, to which, however, the wife was not a party. The Allahabad High Court held that, although the divorce had not been given in the wife's presence and communicated to her, the communication stood completed on the date the written statement was filed. After that date she was not entitled to maintenance under CrPC. The issue before the Supreme Court was whether the wife could be said to have been divorced and the said divorce communicated to her so as to become effective from 5 December 1990, the date the written statement was filed by the husband. The Court observed that the rule of talaq stated in the textbooks is that a Muslim husband can divorce his wife by his uni-lateral action and without court intervention. A few decided cases also held that a statement made by the husband during the course of any judicial proceedings, for example, the wife's suit for maintenance or restitution of conjugal rights, or the husband's plea of divorce raised in the pleadings, did effect a talaq. Such a liberal view of talaq terminating the marital relationship between the spouses, which is heavily loaded in favour of husbands, has been strongly disapproved by eminent jurists. The court agreed with the two decisions of the Gauhati High Court in *Jiauddin Ahmed* and *Rukia Khatun*, where that court held that the correct law of talaq, as ordained by the Qur'an, is: (i) that the talaq must be for a reasonable cause; (ii) that it must be preceded by an attempt at reconciliation between the husband and wife by two arbiters; and (iii) that if their attempt fails, talaq may be effected. The Court found that the particulars of the alleged talaq had not been pleaded in the written statement nor had the circumstances under which and the witnesses, if any, in whose presence talaq was pronounced, been stated. No reasons in justification of talaq had been shown, nor any plea or proof that any effort at reconciliation preceded the talaq put forward. There was no proof that talaq took place on 11 July 1987. What the Allahabad High Court upheld as talaq was the plea of previous divorce taken by the husband in written statement. The court categorically asserted that a plea of previous divorce taken by the husband in his written statement in proceedings initiated by the wife cannot at all be treated as pronouncement of talaq by the husband on the date the written statement was filed in court, and expressly overruled the cases where a mere plea of previous divorce taken in the written statement was accepted as proof of talaq, bringing to an end the marital relationship with effect from the date of filing of the written statement. The Court held that neither did the marriage between Shamim Ara and Abrar Ahmed stand dissolved on 5 December 1990 nor did the liability of Abrar Ahmed to pay maintenance come to an end on that day.

Comments

It is interesting to note that a number of cases, which strongly sup-ported the *ratio decidendi* of the case under comment, such as *Zeenat Fatema Rashid* v. *Md Iqbal Anwar* (Case 19), *Matiur Rahaman* v. *Sabina Khatun*, *Saleem Basha* v. *Mumtaz Begum*, *Saira Bano* v. *Mohd Aslam*,

Saheda Khatoon v. *Gholam Sarwar*, and *Dagdu Chotu Pathan* v. *Rahimbi Dagdu Pathan* (Case 20) were not brought to the notice of the Supreme Court. The Supreme Court refused to accept the husband's plea of divorce raised in the pleadings as effecting a talaq. It approved *Jiauddin* v. *Anwara Begum* and *Rukia Khatun* v. *Abdul Khaliq Laskar* and overruled a long line of cases including *Sarabai* v. *Rabiabai, Saiyid Rashid Ahmad* v. *Anisa Khatun* (Case 8), and *Ahmad Kasim Molla* v. *Khatun Bibi* (Case 9). The decision in *Shamim Ara*, is a great landmark in the process of reinterpretation of Muslim personal law to make it more in tune with the ethos of a present-day society. Five years later it was reaffirmed by the Supreme Court in *Iqbal Bano* v. *State of U.P.* Talaq perpetually hangs like the sword of Damocles over the neck of Muslim wives. By giving a rational and pragmatic interpretation to the rules of talaq the Supreme Court has undone the mischief caused by the decisions of the colonial courts.

22

Mangila Bibi v. *Noor Hossain*

Delegated power of divorce

Mangila Bibi—Petitioner

v.

Noor Hossain and Another—Opposite Parties

AIR 1992 Cal. 92

(A.K. Chatterjee, J.)

Decided on 13 March 1991

Issues of law

Conditional and unconditional delegation of power of divorce; maintenance under Section 3 of MWA

Case summary and decision

The wife filed an application against the husband under Section 3(1) of the MWA claiming payment of dower and maintenance, and return of her dowry. She contended that after her marriage she discovered that her husband was not a medical graduate as was represented before the marriage and that he ill-treated her and ultimately drove her away from the matrimonial home. In this situation she dissolved the marriage by virtue of the authority delegated to her by her husband as recorded in the kabinnama. The divorce was communicated to him but he refused to pay her maintenance and dower and return her dowry. The husband resisted the application on the ground that the petitioner was not a divorced woman as there was never any delegation of power to her to give talaq. In any case, even if there was any such delegation of power to give talaq, it could not be unconditional. It could be exercised only in specified contingencies, and since no such contingency had taken place, the petitioner could not lawfully repudiate herself. The Magistrate accepted the husband's contention and held that the marriage was subsisting, and her application as a divorced woman could not be sustained. The question which the Calcutta High Court was required to decide was whether the wife had absolute authority to dissolve the marriage at her will or whether such power could be exercised by her only in certain circumstances. The court found that the power to give divorce, which primarily belongs to the husband, may be delegated by him to his wife either absolutely or conditionally. There is no authority which prohibits the wife to exercise the power of divorce delegated to her *save in certain circumstances*. In the instant case, the husband had unilaterally delegated to his wife the power to divorce herself unconditionally, and since it is not prohibited by the personal law of the parties, it was quite open to the wife to divorce herself at her will, which she had, in fact, done. Therefore, the wife was very much a divorced person at the time of filing the application and was entitled to the reliefs claimed by her under Section 3 of the MWA.

Comments

The decision is in accord with the view held by Shams-ul-Huda, J. in *Sainuddin* v. *Latifannessa Bibi* (Case 10). In a similar decision, the High

Court of Dacca held, in *Aklima Khatun v. Muhibur Rahman*, that unconditional delegation of the right of divorce to a wife is valid and relied on
both the *Hedaya* and the *Fatawa Alamgiri* for the decision.

23

A. Yousuf Rawther v. *Sowramma*

Dissolution of marriage, irreconcilable breach

A. Yousuf Rawther—Appellant

v.

Sowramma—Respondent

AIR 1971 Ker. 261

(V.R. Krishna Iyer, J.)

Decided on 24 June 1970

Issues of law

Rules of interpretation of social legislation; dissolution under
Section 2(ii) of DMMA; non-maintenance of wife and irreconcilable breach

Case summary and decision

Sowramma, a Hanafi girl, about fifteen years old, married Yousuf who
was nearly twice her age. After cohabitation with Yousuf for a month,
she went back to her parents' house and at the end of two years sued
for dissolution of marriage under Section 2(ii) of the DMMA. Yousuf's
defence was that he was anxious to keep her with him but she wrongfully refused to return to the conjugal home owing to her father's

pressure. The concurrent findings of the trial court and the Subordinate Judge's court were that Sowramma had attained puberty; the marriage had been consummated; Yousuf had failed to provide maintenance to Sowramma for a period of two years; and it was through her own conduct that she led her husband to refuse to pay maintenance to her. The trial court dismissed the suit but the Subordinate Judge granted a decree dissolving the marriage. The aggrieved husband challenged the validity of the decree before the Kerala High Court. Section 2(ii) of the DMMA states that where a Muslim husband has 'neglected or failed' to provide maintenance to his wife for a period of two years, she is entitled to a decree for dissolution of her marriage. The question before the High Court was whether the wife is eligible to obtain a divorce only if she has not violated her conjugal duties or she can ask for divorce on mere failure by the husband to provide maintenance to her for two years, irrespective of her fault. According to some decisions, before a husband can be said to have neglected or failed to provide maintenance, it must be shown that he was under a legal obligation to provide such maintenance. Where the wife refuses to discharge her marital obligations, without any reasonable cause, she cannot claim maintenance and is, therefore, not entitled to claim divorce. According to others, the wife is entitled to a decree for dissolution of marriage if the husband fails to maintain her for a period of two years, even though the wife's conduct was responsible for the husband's failure to maintain her. In the present case, Krishna Iyer, J. came to the conclusion that the 'serious realism' of the Islamic law on divorce excludes blameworthy conduct of the wife as a factor in divorce and considers failure to provide maintenance for two years as an index of irreconcilable breach, so that the mere fact of non-maintenance during the statutory period entitles the wife to sue for dissolution of marriage. This secular and pragmatic approach to the Islamic law of divorce is also in harmony with the contemporary concept of divorce in advanced Western countries. Accordingly, he held that 'a Muslim woman, under Section 2(ii) of the Act, can sue for dissolution on the score that she has not as a fact been maintained even if there is good cause for it—the voice of the law, echoing public policy is often that of the realist, not of the moralist'. The court affirmed the decree of the lower appellate court.

The case also formulates the following rule of interpretation of social legislation: 'The interpretation of legislation, obviously intended to protect a weaker section of the community, like women, must be informed by the social perspective and purpose and, within its grammatical flexibility, must further the beneficial object (p.264).'

Comments

For a similar Pakistani decision see *Noor Bibi* v. *Pir Bux* (Case 38). The above decision of Krishna Iyer, J. has aroused a lively debate. Professor Anderson (Mahmood 1972: 41), Fyzee (1974: 172–3), and Afzal Wani (1995: 93) have expressed serious doubt about its soundness. But Pearl and Menski (1998: 306), M.R. Zafer (1971:450), and Danial Latifi (1972: 25) have hailed it respectively as a bold, outstanding, and landmark decision.

24

Khurshid Gauhar v. *Siddiqunnisa*
Mother's right of *hizana*

Khurshid Gauhar—Applicant

v.

Siddiqunnisa—Opposite Party

AIR 1986 All. 314

(Amarendra Nath Varma, J.)

Decided on 22 January 1986

Issues of law

Sections 12 and 25 of Guardians and Wards Act, 1890; mother's right of hizana; interim order of custody

Case summary and decision

In this case the mother of a three-and-a-half-year-old boy applied for his interim custody under Section 12 of the Guardians and Wards Act, 1890. She complained that her husband had divorced her, turned her out from the matrimonial home, taken the child away from her custody, and entrusted him to the care of his second wife. She apprehended that the second wife, who had five children of her own, would grossly ill-treat her only child. The father of the boy contested the application alleging that the mother was a woman of questionable character; had no house and means to support the child; and, being a teacher, had no time to look after him. As she was living away from the husband, she lost the right of hizana, under the personal law. He also pleaded that, being the natural guardian of the minor, he could not be deprived of the custody of the child. The Additional District Judge held that in custody cases the paramount consideration was the interest of the child. There were valid grounds for believing that the child would not be looked after properly by the stepmother. Further, under the personal law of the parties the mother was entitled to the custody of her male child until the age of seven. Accordingly, he made an order for the return of the child to the custody of the mother.

In revision, the High Court observed that the Guardians and Wards Act, 1890 had been enacted primarily for the welfare of minor children. Consequently, in construing its provisions, that interpretation ought to be accepted which promotes the welfare of the minor in preference to one that might prove detrimental to his interest. The basic postulate underlying the theory of the mother's right to hizana is that for rearing a child of tender age, the mother is the best-suited person and this right is not lost by the mere fact that she has been divorced by the husband. This principle is based on practical experience; it is conducive to the proper growth of the child. A child of tender age would feel psychologically more secure in the company of the mother than the father. The amount of love and care which a child receives from the mother cannot be had or expected from any other relation, including the father. The main plank of the father's case was that, as the husband resided in Meerut and the wife worked as teacher in a college in Deoband, Saharanpur, the mother ipso facto forfeited her right of custody. The court held that it is normal and natural for a divorced wife to reside separately and away from the husband. So long as it is not demonstrated that the general supervision of the child to which the father is entitled as the natural guardian has not become impossible, the mother cannot be deprived of the right of custody. The overriding consideration in custody cases is the interest of the child and all other claims of rival parents must be subordinated to it. The court endorsed the decision of the Additional District Judge that it was a fit case in which an interim order should be made for the return of the child to the custody of the mother.

25

Irfan Ahmed Shaikh v. *Mumtaz*

Custody of minors, mother's remarriage

Irfan Ahmed Shaikh—Petitioner

v.

Mumtaz and Another—Respondents

AIR 1999 Bom. 25

(R.J. Kocher, J.)

Decided on 19 June 1998

Issues of law

Custody of minor child; remarriage of mother with a person not related to child within prohibited degrees

Case summary and decision

In this case, the mother of a girl, aged seven or eight, married a person not related to the girl within the prohibited degrees, after her marriage to the girl's father was dissolved. The father applied for the girl's custody on the ground that by marrying a person not related to the girl within the prohibited degrees, the mother had forfeited her right to the custody of the child. He also contended that the child was not being looked after by her mother and stepfather who lived in an area and environment not conducive to her proper upbringing and education. As he was unmarried and living with his own mother and other family members, he would be able to look after the child better. The general rule is that a mother who marries a person not related to the child within the prohibited degrees loses the right to custody of the child. The rule is based on the notion that in the house of the wife's new husband the child may not be treated kindly. But if she marries a person closely related to the child, for example, the child's paternal uncle, the child will be treated kindly. In the present case the Bombay High Court did not disagree with the general rule but pointed out that the law 'does not lay down that in any circumstances and at any cost the mother would be disqualified for the custody of the child the moment she gets remarried' (p. 27). Islamic law has not only laid down a general rule but has also in different matters 'provided for exceptional circumstances' (p. 27) to be met with. In the matter of custody it has never ignored the wishes and preferences of a minor child who is of the age of discretion. The underlying principle of custody law is the welfare of the child. Therefore, it is open to the court to appoint the mother as the guardian even if she has married a stranger, if the court considers it to be in the interest of the minor. In the present case, to ascertain the wishes of the child, the court had a 'very close and natural talk with her in her own language' (p. 29) and found that she wanted to remain with her mother. Earlier, the child had been handed to the custody of the father with a view to assessing his behaviour but he had not properly looked after her during that period. There was also no evidence that the child was being ill-treated by the stepfather or was not properly looked after by him. The court gave the custody of the child to the mother, notwithstanding her remarriage with a man who was a stranger to the child.

Comments

This is one of the few cases where an Indian court referred to a Pakistani decision. In that case the father gave up his claim to the custody of a minor child, and the mother who married a stranger looked after the minor well. On reaching the age of discretion the minor refused to go to the father. Considering the welfare of the minor, the court allowed the mother to retain the child's custody.

26

Gauher Begum v. *Suggi*

Custody of illegitimate child

Gauher Begum—Appellant

v.

Suggi—Respondent

AIR 1960 SC 93

(Sarkar, J.)

Decided on 27 August 1959

Issues of law

Custody law regarding illegitimate children; Section 491 of CrPC, 1898

Case summary and decision

In the case under review the Supreme Court had to deal with the right of a Sunni mother to the custody of her illegitimate daughter, just over seven years old. Gauher Begum, an unmarried singing woman in the keeping of one Trivedi, a Hindu, was the mother of Anjum who was acknowledged by Trivedi as his daughter. She sent Anjum to temporarily stay with Suggi, her mother's sister, who later refused to return Anjum to her. Suggi, herself a singing woman like her niece Gauher, claimed that she was looking after Anjum with great care and solicitude, had put her in a good school, and kept a special ayah for her. She was well off and had sufficient means to look after the child well. Suggi also contended that, as Gauher was living in the keeping of a man, it was not in the interest of the child to live with her. It was held by the Supreme Court that under Muslim law, the mother of an illegitimate female child is entitled to her custody. Refusal to restore such a child to the custody of its mother would result in an illegal detention within the meaning of Section 491 of CrPC, 1898. It was further held that before making the order for custody the court would consider the welfare of the child. On this issue the Supreme Court found:

> Both parties belong to the community of singing girls. The atmosphere in the home of either is the same. The appellant as the mother can be expected to take better care of the child than the respondent. Trivedi has acknowledged the paternity of the child. So in law the child can claim to be maintained by him. She has no such right against the respondent. We have not been able to find a single reason how the interests of the child would be better served if she was left in the custody of the respondent and not with the appellant. (Fyzee 1965:279)

Reversing the order of the High Court of Bombay, the Supreme Court handed over the custody of Anjum to her mother.

27

Mohd Ahmed Khan
v. Shah Bano Begum

Maintenance of divorced women

Mohd Ahmed Khan—Appellant

v.

Shah Bano Begum and Others—Respondent

AIR 1985 SC 945

(Y.V. Chandrachud, C.J., D.A. Desai, O. Chinnappa Reddy,
E.S. Venkataramiah, and Ranganath Misra, JJ.)

Decided on 23 April 1985

Issues of law

Section 125 of CrPC, 1973; meaning of 'wife'; maintenance of
divorced wife; interpretation of Qur'anic verse 2:241; Section
127(3)(b) of CrPC, 1973; nature of *mahr*

Case summary and decision

Shah Bano, mother of three sons and two daughters, was driven out
of the matrimonial home, after forty-three years of married life in
1975 by her lawyer husband Ahmed Khan. In April 1978 she filed an
application against her husband in the court of the Judicial Magistrate
for maintenance under Section 125 of the CrPC, 1973. In November
1978 Ahmed Khan pronounced an irrevocable talaq on her. His defence
to the maintenance petition was that she had ceased to be his wife
by reason of the talaq, that he was, therefore, under no obligation to
provide maintenance to her, and that he had paid maintenance to her

for more than two years including the iddat period and deposited the mahr (dower) in the court. Therefore, her application was liable to be dismissed. The Magistrate ordered him to pay Rs. 25 per month to her as maintenance; and the High Court of Madhya Pradesh enhanced it to Rs. 179.20 per month. Ahmed Khan appealed to the Supreme Court against the decision.

Under Section 125(1)(a) of the CrPC, 1973, a person who having sufficient means neglects or refuses to maintain his wife who is unable to maintain herself, may be ordered to pay a monthly maintenance to her at a rate not exceeding Rs. 500. The Supreme Court held that the Explanation to Section 125(1), which defines 'wife' as including a divorced wife, contains no words of limitation to justify the exclusion of Muslim women from its scope. Therefore, a divorced Muslim woman, so long as she has not married, is a 'wife' for the purpose of Section 125. The statutory right available to her under Section 125 is unaffected by the provisions of the personal law applicable to her. Besides, although under Muslim personal law a wife cannot refuse to live with her husband if he contracts another marriage, the Explanation to Section 125 confers upon the wife that right. It unmistakably shows that Section 125 overrides personal law, if there is any conflict between the two. The Court also claimed that there was, in fact, no such conflict between section 125 and Muslim personal law. Section 125 deals with cases in which a person having sufficient means neglects or refuses to maintain, among others, his wife who is unable to maintain herself. Since Muslim personal law, which limits a husband's liability to provide for the maintenance of the divorced wife to the iddat period, does not contemplate or countenance the situation envisaged by Section 125, it would be wrong to hold that a Muslim husband, according to his personal law, is not under any obligation to provide maintenance, beyond the iddat period, to his divorced wife who is unable maintain herself. Therefore, Ahmed Khan's contrary argument on this issue could not be accepted. The Court laid down the law as follows. If the divorced wife is able to maintain herself, the husband's liability to maintain her ceases with the expiration of the iddat period. If she is unable to maintain herself, she is entitled to take recourse to Section 125 of the CrPC, 1973. In support of the view that there is no conflict between Muslim personal law and the provisions of the CrPC on this question, the court quoted the Qur'anic verse 2:241: 'For divorced women maintenance (should be provided) on a reasonable (scale)', which, the Court said, undoubtedly showed that the Qur'an imposes an obligation on the Muslim husband to provide maintenance for his divorced wife. Section 127(3)(b) of the CrPC, 1973 provides that a divorced wife is not entitled to maintenance if she has received 'the whole of the sum which, under any customary or personal law applicable to the parties, was payable on such divorce'. Ahmed Khan contended that mahr is the amount payable by the husband to the wife on divorce, and as he had paid it, Shah Bano's application was liable to be dismissed on this ground too. The Court maintained that if mahr is an amount which the wife is entitled to receive from the husband in consideration of marriage, it cannot be possibly described as an amount payable in consideration of divorce. Again, if mahr is an obligation imposed upon the husband as a mark of respect for the wife, in that case a sum payable to the wife out of respect cannot be regarded as a sum payable 'on divorce'. The Court held that mahr is not a sum which, under Muslim personal law, is payable on divorce and, therefore, does not fall within the meaning of Section 127(3)(b). Accordingly, the Court confirmed the judgment of the High Court.

Comments

For a proper appreciation of the implications of the decision in *Shah Bano*, it should be read along with *Bai Tahira* v. *Ali Hussain Fissalli*, and *Fuzlunbi* v. *K. Khader Vali*, which preceded it and *Danial Latifi* v. *Union of India* (Case 29), which followed it. Though the decision aroused fierce debate and widespread mass agitation, there was, in fact, nothing legally wrong with the decision itself. As the Supreme Court rightly claimed, the statutory right of maintenance available to Shah Bano under the provisions of the CrPC was unaffected by the provisions of personal law applicable to her. Academic critics were of the opinion that the Court's interpretation of the Qur'anic verses was not only uncalled for, it also ignored the Privy Council ruling directing the courts not to give their own interpretations to the Qur'an in opposition to the express rulings of classical commentators. Second, it was also indiscreet for the Court to urge the government in very strong terms, while dealing with a very sensitive personal law issue, to frame a uniform civil code for the country. In Tahir Mahmood's opinion, the Court's attempt to reinterpret the Qur'anic verses and its admonition to the state to formulate a civil code for all communities overlooked the principle of judicial restraint. For a detailed and critical analysis of the case, see Tahir Mahmood (1997: 338–48).

28

Begum Subanu v. *A.M. Abdul Gafoor*

Wife's maintenance

Begum Subanu alias Saira Banu and Another—Appellant

v.

A.M. Abdul Gafoor—Respondent

AIR 1987 SC 1103

(A.P. Sen and S. Natarajan, JJ.)

Decided on 3 April 1987

Issues of law

Explanation to Section 125(3) of CrPC, 1973; maintenance of Muslim wife whose husband has contracted second marriage or taken mistress

Case summary and decision

On grounds of neglect and failure to provide maintenance, the wife filed a petition under Section 125 of CrPC, 1973 in the magistrate's court, seeking maintenance for herself and her child from the respondent husband. The Magistrate held that the appellant had failed to establish adequate justification for living separately. While the wife's appeal was pending in the court of the Sessions Judge, the respondent took a second wife. The appellant argued that, irrespective of other grounds, the second marriage of the respondent was by itself a just ground for grant of maintenance. The Sessions Judge held that since the respondent had offered to take her back before and after the second marriage, the appellant was not entitled to claim maintenance. When the High Court declined to interfere in the matter, the appellant approached the Supreme Court. The appellant's case was that the second marriage of the respondent entitled her to live separately and claim maintenance. The respondent maintained that since he was permitted by Muslim personal law to take more than one wife, his second marriage could not be treated as a just ground for the appellant to live separately and claim maintenance. The Supreme Court was required to consider three issues: (i) whether the second marriage of the respondent entitled the appellant to live separately and claim maintenance; (ii) whether her rights stood curtailed in any manner because of the husband's right to marry more than one wife under his personal law; and (iii) whether even if the respondent was liable to pay maintenance, his liability ceased after his offer to take the appellant back and maintain her.

Section 125 of CrPC, 1973 provides that if a person having sufficient means neglects or fails to maintain his wife who is unable to maintain herself, the Magistrate may order the person to make a monthly allowance for maintenance of his wife. If a husband offers to maintain his wife on the condition of her living with him and she refuses to live with him on just grounds, the Magistrate may make an order for maintenance. According to the Explanation added to this provision, contracting a marriage with another woman or keeping a mistress would be considered a just ground for the wife's refusal to live with her husband. The Supreme Court held that the purpose of the Explanation is not to affect the right of a Muslim husband to take more than one wife or denigrate in any manner the legal and social status of a second wife, to which she is entitled as a legally married wife, as compared to a mistress, but to place on an equal footing the matrimonial injury suffered by the first wife on account of the husband marrying again or taking a mistress during the subsistence of the marriage with her. It will make no difference to the neglected wife, for whose benefit the Explanation had been provided, whether the woman intruding into her matrimonial life and bed is another wife and not a mistress. In fact, taking another wife portends a more permanent destruction of her matrimonial life than the taking of a mistress by the husband. The view that a wife will be entitled to refuse to live with the husband if he has taken a mistress but not so entitled if he has taken a second wife will lead to discriminatory treatment between wives whose husbands have lawfully married again and wives whose husbands have taken mistresses. In other words, a Muslim wife whose husband has married again will be worse off under the law in terms of maintenance entitlements than a Muslim wife whose husband has taken a mistress. Therefore, the Explanation must be construed from the point of view of the injury to the matrimonial rights of the wife and not with reference to the husband's right to marry again. The court noted that the object of Section 125 is prevention of vagrancy and destitution. The Explanation must apply uniformly to all wives including Muslim wives whose husbands have either married again or taken a mistress. Finally, regarding the respondent's defence that his offer to take the appellant back and maintain her exonerated him from liability to pay maintenance, the court held that the offer was not genuine and sincere, and on the basis of such an offer the appellant's rights could not be negated or defeated. The court fixed the maintenance at Rs. 300 per month for the appellant and Rs. 200 per month for the minor girl.

29

Danial Latifi v. Union of India

Validity and interpretation of MWA

Danial Latifi and Another—Petitioners

v.

Union of India—Respondent

2001 FLC 513

(G.B. Pattanaik, S. Rajendra Babu, D.P. Mohapatra,

Doraiswamy Raju, and Shivaraj V. Patil, JJ.)

Decided on 28 September 2001

Issues of law

Constitutional validity of MWA; interpretation of provisions of legislation involving matrimonial relationship and social justice; meaning of 'a reasonable and fair provision and maintenance to be made and paid'; obligation of relatives to maintain divorced Muslim women

Case summary and decision:

After the passing of the MWA, a number of petitions were filed before the Supreme Court, challenging the constitutional validity of the Act. It was claimed in these petitions that the provisions of the Act offended Articles 14 (equality before law), 15 (prohibition of discrimination on grounds of religion, sex, etc.), and 21 (protection of life and personal liberty) of the Constitution. The Supreme Court observed that, in interpreting the provisions of any legislation involving matrimonial relationships and social justice, the courts must bear in mind the prevailing social conditions and the spirit of the Constitution. The society is male-dominated both economically and socially and women are invariably assigned a dependent role, irrespective of the social class to which they belong. The Court's interpretation of the provisions of social legislation should further the purposes of such legislation and secure the wider and greater objectives of gender and social justice. Section 3(1)(a) of the MWA provides that a divorced woman shall be entitled to a reasonable and fair provision and maintenance to be made and paid to her within the period of iddat by her former husband. The wordings of this vital Section, the Court held, indicated that the husband had two separate and distinct obligations: (i) to make a 'reasonable and fair provision' for his divorced wife and (ii) to provide 'maintenance' for her. Arrangement for payment of provision and maintenance should be made 'within the iddat period'. Therefore, Section 3(1)(a) would mean that on or before the expiration of the iddat period, the husband was bound to make provision for and pay maintenance to the wife and if he failed to do so, then the wife was entitled to recover it by filing an application before the Magistrate. The reasonable and fair provision and maintenance was not limited only for the iddat period. It would extend to the whole life of the divorced wife, unless she got married for a second time. Reasonable and fair provision would include provision for her residence, food, clothes, and other articles and its quantum would be worked out with reference to the needs of the divorced woman, the means of the husband, and the standard of life the woman enjoyed during her marriage. 'There is no reason', the Court held, 'why such provision could not take the form of the regular payment of alimony to the divorced woman.'

As to the constitutional validity of the Act, the Court was of the view that to construe its provisions as less beneficial than the provisions of Section 125 of the CrPC, and hold the husband liable to pay maintenance only for the iddat period would result in unreasonable discrimination against divorced Muslim women and render the Act violative of Articles 14, 15, and 21 of the Constitution. But the interpretation that was being given to the Act by the Court in the present case made the Act equally or more beneficial to Muslim women than Section 125 of the CrPC, 1973. Where the state provided for a particular group of citizens, divorced Muslim women in the present case, a scheme for maintenance and prevention of vagrancy which was equally or more beneficial than that provided in the general law, namely, Section 125 of the CrPC, it could not be said that there was any discrimination against these women and violation of the Constitution. The Court summed up its conclusions as follows:

1. A Muslim husband is liable to make reasonable and fair provision for the future of the divorced wife, which obviously includes her maintenance as well. Such a reasonable and fair provision extending beyond the iddat period must be made by the husband within the iddat period.
2. Liability of a Muslim husband to his divorced wife arising under Section 3(1)(a) of the Act to pay maintenance is not confined to the iddat period.
3. A divorced Muslim woman, who has not remarried and who is not able to maintain herself after the iddat period can proceed as provided under Section 4 of the Act against her relatives who are liable to maintain her under her personal law. If any of the relatives is unable to pay maintenance, the Magistrate may direct the State Wakf Board to pay such maintenance.
4. The provisions of the Act do not offend Articles 14, 15, and 21 of the Constitution of India.

In the result, the petitions challenging the validity of the provisions of the MWA were dismissed. The MWA purported to overcome the view expressed in *Mohd Ahmed Khan* v. *Shah Bano Begum* (Case 27) but the Supreme Court's interpretation of the Act in the present case reiterated that view.

Comments

The MWA was understood to have reversed the decision in *Shah Bano*. But, according to Supreme Court's interpretation of the Act, it actually codified the very *ratio decidendi* of the decision. The Supreme Court affirmed *Shah Bano*; approved *Arab Ahemadhia Abdulla* v. *Arab Bail Mohmuna Aaiyadbhai, Ali* v. *Sufaira, K. Kunhammed Haji* v. *K. Amina, Karim Abdul Rehman Shaikh* v. *Shehnaz Karim Shaikh,* and *Jaitunbi Mubarak Shaikh* v. *Fakruddin Shaikh*; and overruled *Usman Khan Bahmani* v. *Fathimunnisa Begum, Abdul Rashid* v. *Sultana Begum, Md Marahim* v. *Raiza Begum,* and *Abdul Haq* v. *Yasima Talat*. Thus, the decision sets to rest the differences of views among the High Courts regarding the interpretation of Section 3(1)(a) of the MWA.

30

Shabana Bano v. Imran Khan

Divorced women's maintenance under CrPC, 1973

Shabana Bano—Appellant

v.

Imran Khan—Respondent

AIR 2010 SC 305

(B. Sudershan Reddy and Deepak Verma, JJ.)

Decided on 4 December 2009

Issues of law

Section 125 of CrPC, 1973; Sections 4 and 5 of MWA; maintenance petition by divorced Muslim woman under CrPC against husband; exclusive jurisdiction of family courts under Sections 7 and 20 of Family Courts Act, 1984 to adjudicate upon petitions

Case summary and decision

Appellant Shabana Bano was married to respondent Imran Khan in 2001. In a maintenance petition for her and a child, she stated that demanding a big dowry, her husband and members of his family had treated her with cruelty, and when she became pregnant, he had taken her to her parents' home and told her that if his demand for dowry was not met, he would not take her back to the matrimonial home even after the birth of the child. A child was born but he refused to take her back. She was thus constrained to file a maintenance petition under Section 125 of CrPC, 1973 against her husband. The husband admitted his marriage with her but denied all allegations of demanding dowry and treating her with cruelty. He asserted that he had divorced her on 20 August 2004 and under the provisions of the MWA, she was not entitled to any maintenance after the divorce and expiry of the iddat period. The family court granted her maintenance from the date of institution of petition until the date of divorce, that is, from 26 April 2004 to 20 August 2004 and further from 20 August 2004 till the expiry of iddat, but denied any maintenance to her thereafter. This order was substantially upheld by the High Court.

In the appeal by grant of special leave, the question before the Supreme Court was whether a divorced Muslim wife would be entitled to receive maintenance from her husband under Section 125 of the CrPC and if yes, then through which forum. Reaffirming the judgments in *Danial Latifi* v. *Union of India* (Case 29), and *Iqbal Bano* v. *State of U.P.*, the Court held that even if a Muslim woman has been divorced, she would be entitled to claim maintenance from her husband under Section 125 of the CrPC, even after expiry of the period of iddat, as long as she does not remarry. The amount of maintenance to be awarded under Section 125 cannot be restricted for the iddat period only. 'This being a beneficial piece of legislation, the benefit thereof must accrue to the divorced Muslim woman'(p.309). The Court also held that a family court established under the Family Courts Act, 1984 would have exclusive jurisdiction to adjudicate upon applications filed under Section 125 of the CrPC.

SECTION III

PAKISTAN

31

Khurshid Jan v. *Fazal Dad*

Sources and interpretation of Muslim law

Khurshid Jan—Appellant

v.

Fazal Dad—Respondent

PLD 1964 (W.P.) Lah. 558

(Muhammad Yaqub Ali, Anwarul Haq,

Muhammad Daud Khan, Wahiduddin Ahmad,

and Inamullah Khan, JJ.)

Decided on 5 May 1964

Issues of law

Sources of Muslim law; rules of interpretation; conflict of views among different schools of law; competence of courts to differ from the views of *a'imma* and *faqihs* on grounds of public policy, justice, equity, and good conscience; dictum of the Privy Council in *Aga Mahomed*; necessity of *ijtihad*

Case summary and decision

Khurshid Jan filed a suit for a declaration that she had repudiated her marriage with Fazal Dad in exercise of the 'option of puberty'. However, after the institution of the suit she went to live with her husband for a period of fifteen days. The trial court decreed the suit on the ground that repudiation of marriage took effect with the institution of the suit and that there was no subsisting marriage between the parties when cohabitation took place. On appeal, relying on the *Hedaya*, the District Judge held that no declaration for repudiation of marriage can be made if the wife has permitted sexual intercourse after the exercise of option, and reversed the findings of the trial court. In the second petition filed by the wife, the husband's counsel, relying on a number of authoritative texts, contended that a court decree was necessary to give validity to the exercise of 'option of puberty'. According to the rule laid down by the Privy Council in *Aga Mahomed Jaffer Bindaneem* v. *Koolsom Bee Bee* (Case 1), it would be wrong for the courts to depart from this rule. At this, the Division Bench of the Lahore High Court referred the following three questions to the Full Bench: (i) what are the sources of Muslim law; (ii) what are the rules of interpretation of Muslim law and can courts differ from the views of Imams and other jurisconsults on grounds of public policy, justice, equity, and good conscience; and (iii) how are courts to be guided in cases of conflict of views among the founders of the schools of law and their disciples, other Imams and faqihs?

In the leading judgment, Muhammad Yaqub Ali, J. stated that the known sources of Muslim law are the Qur'an, Sunnah, *ijma*, *qiyas*, and ijtihad. The Qur'an is the absolute word of God and if there is a clear injunction in it, that is the rule of decision on the facts of a given case. The Sunnah, that is, the sayings and deeds of the Prophet, is the most authentic source of law after the Qur'an. Ijma is an agreement of the jurists in a particular age on a question of law. Qiyas or analytical deduction is a process by which a rule of law embodied in the Qur'an, Sunnah, and ijma is extended to cases not covered by their texts. Ijtihad is the capacity of a jurist to make decisions in matters of law to which no express text or a rule already determined by ijma is applicable. It is academic research and intellectual effort which, in changing circumstances, makes development and evolution of the legal system of Islam possible. On the second question, Ali, J. held that a clear injunction in the Qur'an or Sunnah is binding. Ijma is binding on all, until changed by another ijma. A court of law may differ with the qiyas of earlier jurists, but only on the basis of interpretation and extension of a rule of decision contained in the Qur'anic or Hadith text or ijma, and not on the basis of what appears to be more agreeable to the judge. If there is no clear rule of decision in these sources, the court may resort to private reasoning in which case it will be guided by the rules of justice, equity, and good conscience.

There can be no disagreement regarding the rules contained in the Qur'an, Hadith, or a subsisting ijma. In the case of qiyas, it is open to a court to adopt any of the conflicting views of earlier jurisconsults. Ijma and ijtihad in the form of laws made by competent legislative bodies, as envisaged by modern reformist jurists, will be binding on the courts; they cannot differ from these laws on the ground that they conflict with the views of classical jurists. In his dissenting judgment, Wahiduddin Ahmad, J. held that nothing has happened since the decisions of the Privy Council to justify any departure from the rules of interpretation adopted by them. Courts are not competent to form independent judgments on intricate questions of Muslim law and reliance must be placed on the opinion of recognized jurists. It is not open to courts to differ from the views of classical jurists, and the differences among them should be resolved according to the doctrine of *taqlid*. However, he conceded that 'most of the difficulties which have arisen in answering the questions referred to the Full Bench can be resolved by proper legislative measures' (p. 606). In a separate judgment, Anwarul Haq, J. held that courts must be given the right to interpret for themselves the Qur'an and Sunnah and to differ from the views of earlier jurisconsults on the grounds of equity and public good in matters not governed by a Qur'anic or Hadith text or ijma or a binding qiyas. The views of Imams and earlier jurists are entitled to utmost respect but the right to differ from them must not be denied to present-day courts. Such denial would be a negation of the constitutional and legal obligations resting on courts to interpret the law they are called upon to administer and apply in cases before them. On the basis of the answers of the Full Bench on the reference, the Division Bench of the Lahore High Court held that a wife, who exercised her 'option of puberty' and repudiated the marriage, did not require a court decree for its validity.

Comments

This is the leading case on the sources and interpretation of Muslim law. In the evolution of this law in South Asia the decision is nothing less than revolutionary. It refuses to follow the rules of interpretation of Muslim law laid down by the Privy Council more than a century ago in *Aga Mahomed* and *Baker Ali Khan* (Case 2), denies the binding character of the principle of taqlid in Islamic jurisprudence, and claims a court's right to exercise ijtihad in matters of Muslim law. In categorically asserting that courts have the right to give their own interpretation to the Qur'an and differ from the views of traditionally authoritative texts, which are not based on any specific injunction of the Qur'an and Sunnah, the Lahore High Court departs from the centuries-old tradition that the principles of law as settled by classical jurists are sacrosanct, immutable, and binding. The dissenting judgment of Wahiduddin Ahmed, J. upholds the traditional view on the issue.

32

Iftikhar Nazir Ahmad Khan v. Ghulam Kibria

Constituents of marriage, legitimacy

Iftikhar Nazir Ahmad Khan and Others—Petitioners

v.

Ghulam Kibria and Others—Respondents

PLD 1968 Lah. 587

(Sajjad Ahmad and Muhammad Akram, JJ.)

Decided on 19 May 1967

Issues of Law

Nature and constituents of marriage; presumption of marriage; marriage with a fifth wife in the presence of four existing wives; classes of women with whom marriage is prohibited; doctrine of *shubh*; legitimacy; succession

Case summary and decision

Raja Ghulam Rasul was a man of substance. Soon after his death, differences arose between several claimants regarding succession to his estate, leading to the present suit. In the presence of his four wives, Ghulam Rasul contracted a fifth marriage with Rafia Begum who gave birth to a son named Ghulam Kibria. He divorced her and contracted another marriage with Mehrun Nisa, in the presence of his four existing wives, and a son named Ahmad Mukhtar was born out of this wedlock. At the time of his death Ghulam Rasul was survived by his five wives and a number of children from the six marriages. The two questions before the court were: (i) whether the successive marriages contracted by Ghulam Rasul with Rafia Begum (deceased) and Mehrun Nisa, in the presence of his four other wives were valid under the Muslim law; if no, what was its effect on the right of inheritance of the concerned parties and (ii) whether Ghulam Kibria and Ahmad Mukhtar were Ghulam Rasul's legitimate heirs under Muslim law?

The court observed that marriage in Islam is a contract *uberima fides*, requiring utmost good faith. It creates a legal relationship or consortium, a partnership in life, securing harmony, happiness, peace of mind, good fellowship, and connubial relations between the couple. No rituals are necessary to enter into the contract of marriage. It is completed by a proposal and acceptance by the competent parties in the presence of witnesses. Before the advent of Islam, there was no limit on the number of wives a man could have. Islam enjoined monogamy as the normal rule of marriage and tolerated polygamy subject only to the extremely rigorous conditions that all the wives, up to the maximum of four, must be treated equally and with justice, without any favours to one or disregard towards the others in all matters including love and affection. There are nineteen categories of women with whom marriage is prohibited. In twelve of them the prohibition is perpetual on account of consanguinity, fosterage, affinity, etc. between the parties. In the other seven, the prohibition is temporary, arising from some impediment in the way of the marriage which is not permanent and is liable to be removed. The Hanafi jurists divide marriage into three categories—*saheeh* or valid, fasid or irregular, and batil or void. A marriage which conforms to all the requirements laid down by the sharia and is free from any defect or infirmity is a saheeh marriage. A marriage which suffers from any defect or infirmity of a radical and vital nature is void *ab initio*. But, where the irregularity or defect in a marriage is not fatal to its existence, such a marriage is fasid or irregular. Marriage with a fifth wife in the presence of four wives is prohibited in Islam. But this prohibition is relative and temporary, it springs from an accidental circumstance—the presence of four wives. Such a marriage with fifth wife is fasid, not batil. The children of such marriage are legitimate and entitled to succeed as lawful heirs of their father. But the wife in the case of a fasid marriage is under no circumstances entitled to succeed to the estate of her deceased husband. Accordingly, the court held that both Ghulam Kibria and Ahmad Mukhtar were entitled to share in the estate left by Ghulam Rasul as his legitimate sons along with the other heirs. But neither Rafia Begum nor Mehrun Nisa was entitled to share in the inheritance under Muslim law.

Comments

This case gives a detailed account of the nature and essential requirements of a Muslim marriage, presumption of marriage, polygamy, classes of women with whom marriage is prohibited, division of marriages into saheeh, fasid and batil, *zina* and its consequences, doctrine of *'shubh'*, marriage with a fifth wife, legal effects of such marriages, and legitimacy of the issues and their succession rights. Thus, it is greatly helpful in forming a good idea about the various constituents of a Muslim marriage.

33

Fazli-E-Subhan v. Sabereen

Remarriage of divorced couple

Fazli-E-Subhan—Petitioner

v.

Sabereen and Three Others—Respondents

PLD 2003 Pesh. 169

(Malik Hamid Saeed and Shah Jehan Khan, JJ.)

Decided on 11 March 2003

Issues of law

Remarriage of a divorced couple; procedure of halala; effects of Section 7(6) of MFLO

Case summary and decision

Sabereen obtained a decree for dissolution of her marriage from the trial court and then agreed to marry her husband, Fazli-E-Subhan again. Fazli-E-Subhan filed a writ petition in the Peshawar High Court praying for permission to remarry her. Sabereen's father opposed remarriage without first observing the procedure of halala as laid down under the traditional Islamic law, that is, marriage of Sabereen with a third person, her subsequent divorce from him, and then remarriage with her first husband. The court found that remarriage of a couple is governed by Section 7(6) of the MFLO which reads as follows: 'Nothing shall debar a wife whose marriage has been terminated by talaq effective under this section from re-marrying the same husband, without an intermediate marriage with a third person, unless such termination is for the third time so effective.' Thus, Section 7(6) nullifies the effects of triple talaq and allows remarriage of a divorced couple after a divorce in any form without the necessity of an intervening marriage of the wife, except where they have been divorced thrice and the third divorce has become effective under Section 7 of the Ordinance. The court further observed that the decree granted to Sabereen by the trial court was of the nature of a khula divorce. Under the traditional Islamic law in case of divorce through khula, 'it is not obligatory on the wife to re-marry a third person before entering into re-marriage tie with her first husband'. The court also cited the views of the celebrated *alim*, Maulana Ashraf Ali Thanvi and fatwas of two other muftis in support of its opinion. The court concluded: 'Hence we see no restraint either in the Muslim Family Laws Ordinance or in the Injunctions of Qur'an and Sunnah, not to allow the prayer of the husband for re-union with his wife when she is ready to live again as wife of the petitioner within the limits of God.' Accordingly, the court directed the Darul Aman at Peshawar to arrange their marriage.

34

Rahim Jan v. Muhammad

Prompt dower, conflicting juristic views

Rahim Jan—Plaintiff, Appellant

v.

Muhammad—Defendant, Respondent

PLD 1955 Lah. 122

(B.Z. Kaikaus, J.)

Decided on 4 October 1954

Issues of law

Prompt dower and consummation of marriage; restitution of conjugal rights; differences of opinion between Abu Hanifa and his two disciples; rules laid down in *Abdul Kadir*; res judicata

Case summary and decision

The parties lived together for a month-and-a-half and then separated. Five months later, the husband filed a suit for restitution of conjugal rights which was decreed. Still later, the wife petitioned for divorce on the grounds that the husband had failed to maintain her for more than two years and that he had not performed his marital obligations for more than three years. The trial court found in her favour on both issues and ordered dissolution of the marriage. The District Judge reversed the judgment on the ground that it was the wife who without sufficient cause had refused to live with him. The wife also raised a new point that, as the husband had not paid her prompt dower, she was entitled to refuse to live with him. The District Judge noted that a decree had been passed in favour of her husband for restitution of conjugal rights but she had refused to go to her husband. In the circumstances her husband was not bound to maintain her. The question before the High Court was whether a Hanafi wife is entitled, even after consummation of the marriage, to refuse to live with her husband on the ground that her prompt dower has not been paid. Imam Abu Hanifa was of the opinion that the wife is entitled at any time to refuse to live with her husband until her prompt dower is paid; and the consummation of the marriage does not make any difference. On the other hand, his two disciples, Imam Muhammad and Imam Abu Yusuf held that the right of the wife to refuse to live with her husband on account of non-payment of prompt dower subsists only till the marriage is consummated. In *Abdul Kadir* v. *Salima*, (Case 5), Mahmood, J. held that where there were differences of opinion between Imam Abu Hanifa and his two disciples, Muslim jurists, as a rule, adopted the opinion of the two disciples. Accordingly, he decided that a wife could not refuse herself to her husband for non-payment of dower after consummation of the marriage. In the present case the Lahore High Court refused to follow *Abdul Kadir*. The court held that the observations of Mahmood, J. in this case were *obiter*. Second, Mahmood, J.'s decision in the case contradicted the view adopted by him. If the wife had really no right of refusing herself to her husband, the husband would be entitled to a decree without payment of dower. But he directed a decree for restitution of conjugal rights against the wife only on condition of payment of prompt dower to her. Third, the most authoritative original authority, called *matan*, adopted the opinion of Abu Hanifa without even mentioning any differences of opinion with his disciples. The vast majority of later jurists also accepted his view. Finally, Sulaiman, C.J. who followed *Abdul Kadir* in *Anis Begum* v. *Muhammad Istafa Wali Khan* as precedent agreed that there was no such rule of interpretation that the view of the disciples was to be preferred to that of Imam Abu Hanifa and he adhered to the view of Mahmood, J. only on the basis of *stare decisis*. Disagreeing with the view of Mahmood, J., Kaikaus, J. observed: 'I do not find any principles of justice or reason by which the right of the wife to refuse the performance of marital obligations on account of non-payment of prompt dower may come to an end by her once surrendering herself' (pp.134–35). He categorically asserted that even after consummation the wife retains the right to refuse performance of marital obligation till prompt dower is paid. The decision was, however, of no help to the wife in the instant case, as her plea regarding her right to refuse to live with the husband for non-payment of prompt dower was barred by res judicata.

Comments

Contrary to the decision in *Rahim Jan*, in *Rabia Khatoon* v. *Mukhtar Ahmad* (Case 16) the Allahabad High Court held that the wife's right to refuse the husband his conjugal rights for non-payment of dower is lost on consummation of the marriage. Fyzee (1974: 141) considers this to be the correct view. The trend in Pakistan is to follow the *Rahim Jan* decision, which is more favourable to women, than the Allahabad decision. [For some later Pakistani decisions see Pearl and Menski (1998: 197).]

35

Muhammad Zaman v. *Irshad Begum*

Stipulations in marriage contract

Muhammad Zaman—Plaintiff, Appellant

v.

Irshad Begum and Others—Defendants, Respondents

PLD 1967 Lah. 1104

(Muhammad Fazle Ghani, J.)

Decided on 1 March 1967

Issues of law

Stipulations in restraint of marriage; agreement allowing wife to live separately if husband takes a second wife; restitution of conjugal rights

Case summary and decision

Muhammad Zaman executed a postnuptial agreement in favour of his wife Irshad Begum to the effect that in case he took a second wife, she would be entitled to receive maintenance in a separate house or in the house of her parents. After his second marriage Irshad Begum began to live separately and Muhammad Zaman filed a suit for restitution of conjugal rights against her. She pleaded that he used to beat her in the presence of the second wife and ultimately turned her out of his house. The suit for restitution of conjugal rights was filed by him as a counter-blast to her application for maintenance under Section 488 of the CrPC, 1898. The husband's suit was dismissed by the two lower courts. In the second appeal the husband's counsel argued that the postnuptial agreement contained a stipulation in restraint of marriage and also encouraged future separation between the husband and wife. Therefore, it was opposed to public policy within the meaning of Section 23 of the Contract Act, 1872. For his contention he relied on *Bai Fatima* v. *Alimahomed Aiyeb*, where a similar agreement was held to be void as being against public policy. The High Court held that marriage in Islam is a contract and a wife is entitled to protect her interests in case of future differences with her husband. Where the agreement is to the effect that the wife will be entitled to live away from her husband and receive alimony in case of disagreement or when he takes a second wife, there is nothing in such an agreement which may be considered as opposed to public policy either under Muslim law or Section 23 of the Contract Act.

The alternative contention of the husband's counsel was that even if the agreement was valid, at the most it would enable the wife to enforce her maintenance claim through a court of law but it could not be a defence to the husband's suit for restitution of conjugal rights against the wife. The court held that the decree of restitution of conjugal rights is in the discretion of the court, and it is the court's duty to find out if there is cruelty of a degree rendering it unsafe for the wife to return to the husband's house. It is true that it is the duty of the wife to live with him wherever he wishes. But the law recognizes circumstances, for example, desertion, cruelty, which justify her refusal to live with him. Under Muslim law bad conduct or gross neglect of the husband is a good defence to a suit brought by him for restitution of conjugal rights.

In the present case, the husband failed to provide any maintenance for the wife and her daughter, and she was compelled to go to the criminal court to enforce the husband's obligation to maintain her under Section 488 of the CrPC. Gross failure of the husband to perform the obligations imposed on him by the agreement is a sufficient ground for refusing him a decree for restitution of conjugal rights.

Comments

In this case the court dissented from the judgment in *Bai Fatima*, where, on a wrong understanding of the nature of Muslim marriage, Batchelor, J. had held:

> It is, as I understand it, as much the policy of the Mahomedan law as of the English law, that people who are married should live together and not apart; and if that is so, it seems to me that there should be no difficulty in applying to Mahomedans the English Rule that any agreement such as this, which provides for, and therefore encourages, future separation between the spouses must be pronounced void as being against public policy. (p.283)

36

Balqis Fatima v. Najm-ul-Ikram Qureshi

Khula divorce, interpretation of Qur'an

Balqis Fatima—Plaintiff, Appellant

v.

Najm-ul-Ikram Qureshi—Defendant, Respondent

PLD 1959 (W.P.) Lah. 566

(Shabir Ahmad, B.Z. Kaikaus, and Masud Ahmad, JJ.)

Decided on 30 March 1959

Issues of law

Khula divorce; Qur'anic verse 2:229; meaning of *hakam*; 'limits of God'; interpretation of Qur'an; opinion of jurists

Case summary and decision

After the *nikah* ceremony of the couple but before the *rukhsati* (taking of bride to the matrimonial home for cohabitation) their families quarrelled and the wife never went to live with her husband. About two years and three months after the nikah ceremony, the wife filed a suit for dissolution of marriage on the grounds that: (i) the husband had failed to provide maintenance to her for a period of more than two years and (ii) that he was associating with women of ill repute. The husband filed a counter-suit for restitution of conjugal rights. The trial court found that the husband had failed to provide maintenance to the wife for more than two years. The court decreed the suit for dissolution of marriage and dismissed the husband's suit for restitution of conjugal rights. On appeal, the District Judge found that it was the wife, and not the husband, who was to blame for the rukhsati not taking place. Therefore, she was not entitled to maintenance and, so, to dissolution of her marriage. He was also of the opinion that relations between the parties had become so strained that it would not be proper to ask the wife to live with her husband.

On second appeal, the Division Bench of the High Court agreed with the findings and decisions of the District Judge. But the wife's counsel raised a new point of law that khula is the right of the wife and she can demand the grant of khula divorce on restitution of any benefits that she may have received from the husband. As there was some force in the counsel's contention, the Division Bench referred the following question to a Full Bench: 'Whether under Muslim law the wife is entitled to *khula* as of right' (p. 572). The answer of the Full Bench was that 'the wife is entitled to dissolution of the marriage on restoration of what she received in consideration of marriage if the judge apprehends that the parties will not observe the limits of God' (p. 593). The Qur'anic verse 2: 229, which is the basis of the right of khula, says: 'then if you fear that they cannot keep within limits of Allah, there is no blame on them for what she gives up to become free thereby' (p. 572). This verse permits termination of a marriage by the wife passing consideration to the husband. But it does not clearly say whether the marriage can be terminated only if the husband consents to it, as held by the Hanafi school, or whether the wife can claim termination of the marriage tie, even if the husband does not agree. The court held that the words 'if you fear' in the verse are addressed to the judge; and the reference to the judge can only mean that he is to determine if the circumstances are such as to make a harmonious and happy married life impossible and that if he so determines, to pass an order dissolving the marriage even if the husband does not agree. Islam does not force on the spouses a life devoid of harmony and happiness, and if the parties cannot live together as they should, it permits dissolution of the marriage. If the dissolution is due to some fault on the part of the husband, the wife does not have to restore the benefits received or waive her claim to dower. But there is an important limitation on the wife's right to khula. The wife cannot have a divorce for every passing impulse. It is only if the judge apprehends that it is no longer possible for the couple to live in harmony and in conformity with their marital obligations that he will grant dissolution of the marriage. The judge will consider whether the rift between the parties is a serious one to justify dissolution of the marriage though he may not ask the reasons for the rift. In response to the question whether it is open to a present-day court to differ from the views of classical jurists—in this case the Hanafi view—the court held that in dealing with a question of interpretation of the Qur'an, the court is not bound by the opinion of classical jurists. If the court is clear as to what exactly is the meaning of a Qur'anic verse, it will be the court's duty to give effect to that interpretation, irrespective of what has been stated by the jurists. On the facts of the case, the court decided that the spouses could not live together as husband and wife should, and dissolved the marriage on restoration of the benefits received by the wife.

Comments

This is the first significant case where a Pakistani High Court gave its own interpretation to Qur'anic verses and refused to accept the classical Hanafi rule that the consent of the husband is necessary for a khula divorce. In the earlier cases of *Umar Bibi v. Muhammad Din*, and *Sayeeda Khanam v. Muhammad Sami*, the court had refused to accept incompatibility of temperament as a valid ground for dissolution of marriage. Conrnelius, A.C.J., speaking for the Full Bench of the Lahore High Court said in *Sayeeda Khanam*: 'Under Muslim law, such matters as incompatibility of temperament, aversion or dislike cannot form a ground for a wife to seek dissolution of her marriage at the hands of a Qazi or Court' [see Fyzee (1965: 169–88)]. In *Balqis Fatima*, Full Bench of the same court dissented from the two cases. Later cases have clarified the legal position regarding restoration of benefits received by the wife in consideration of marriage and decided that, where the fault of the husband, for example, cruelty, is proved, the wife does not have to restore the benefits received or waive her claim to dower. (See *Anees Ahmed v. Uzma* and *Karim Ullah v. Shabana*.)

37

Khurshid Bibi v. Muhammad Amin

Khula divorce

Khurshid Bibi—Appellant

v.

Muhammad Amin—Respondent

PLD 1967 SC 97

(S.A. Rahman, Fazle-Akbar, Hamoodur Rahman,

Muhammad Yaqub Ali, and S.A. Mahmood, JJ.)

Decided on 12 October 1966

Issues of law

Fundamental laws of Islam; concept of marriage; mutual rights of husband and wife; separation by means of khula; Qur'anic verse 2: 229; opinions of commentators of Qur'an

Case summary and decision

Khurshid Bibi was married to Muhammad Amin and, in exchange, her brother was married to his sister. Since there was no offspring of the wedlock, Amin took a second wife. As a result, relations between them became so strained that even the panchayat failed to effect reconciliation. Khurshid Bibi brought a suit for a declaration that she had been orally divorced by Amin, or, in the alternative, for dissolution of her marriage by khula. Her case for khula was that it had become impossible for them to harmoniously live together as husband and wife. Amin denied that he had orally divorced her or that their relations were so strained as to warrant a khula divorce. The trial court did not believe her story of oral divorce but decreed dissolution of the marriage by khula on the ground that a harmonious conjugal life had become impossible. On appeal, the District Judge, Lyallpur (now Faisalabad) took the view that this was not a case in which khula should have been granted, for the wife had not come to the court with clean hands. In the second appeal at the wife's instance, a Single Judge of the West Pakistan High Court agreed with the District Judge and held that the decision of *Balqis Fatima* v. *Najm-ul-Ikram Qureshi* (Case 36) did not apply to this case. Special leave to appeal was granted to consider whether the Single Judge was right in holding that the case was not governed by the principles laid down in *Balqis Fatima*.

The question before the Full Bench of the Supreme Court was, whether a wife is entitled, as of right, to claim khula, despite the unwillingness of the husband to release her from the matrimonial tie, if she satisfies the court that there is no possibility of their living together, consistently with their conjugal duties and obligations. Of the four Sunni schools, only the Hanafi school, to which the parties belonged, required the consent of the husband to the termination of marriage by khula. Endorsing the decision in *Balqis Fatima*, the court unanimously held that the wife is entitled to khula, as of right, if she satisfies the conscience of the court that it will otherwise mean forcing her into a hateful union. The court observed that the Imams never claimed finality of their opinions. But due to various historical causes and circumstances, in the subsequent ages their followers invented the doctrine of taqlid under which a Sunni Muslim must follow the opinion of only one of the four Imams exclusively, irrespective of the reasonableness of his views. Neither the Qur'an nor Hadith sanctions this doctrinaire fossilization of sharia law, and one is at liberty to prefer the opinion of any other Imam to that of Imam Abu Hanifa. Besides, the court said, if the opinions of jurists conflict with the Qur'an and Sunnah, they are not binding on the court, and it is the duty of the judges as true Muslims to obey the word of God and the Holy Prophet. The foundation of the law of khula is the Qur'anic verse 2: 229 which says: 'But, if you fear that they cannot observe the limits prescribed by Allah, then it shall be no sin for either of them in what she gives to get her freedom' (p.115). The words 'if you fear', the court held, refer to the *qadi* or judge. Where khula takes place with the mutual consent of the spouses, it is technically called *mubarat* and no reference to the qadi is necessary here. But where the husband disputes the right of the wife to obtain separation by khula, it is obvious that some third party, that is, the qadi, must decide the matter. 'Any other interpretation of the Qur'anic verse regarding *khula* would deprive it of all efficacy as a charter granted to the wife.' Moreover, the Qur'anic verse 2: 228 declares: 'Women have rights against men, similar to those that the men have against them, according to the well-known rules of equity.' It would, therefore, be surprising if the Qur'an did not provide for the separation of spouses at the instance of the wife in any circumstances. Third, khula is separation and not talaq and is not dependent on the will of the husband alone. As to the Hanafi view that the husband's consent is obligatory for khula, the court pointed out that Hanafi jurists do not discuss a situation where the husband is reluctant to divorce the wife but relations between the spouses have deteriorated so considerably that they cannot be expected to live together within the limits of Allah. In such a situation the Malikis, Shafi'is and Hanbalis allow khula divorce without the husband's consent. There cannot be any valid objection to relying on their opinions which are consistent with the court's interpretation of the Qur'anic verse on khula. In the present case the court came to the conclusion that it was no longer possible for the husband and wife to live together in harmony and conformity with their marital obligations, and decreed dissolution of the marriage subject to the restitution of benefits received by the wife in consideration of the marriage.

Comments

In *Khurshid Bibi*, the Full Bench of the Supreme Court endorsed *Balqis Fatima* and overruled *Umar Bibi* v. *Muhammad Din* and *Sayeeda Khanam* v. *Muhammad Sami*, which had held that incompatibility of temperament is not a ground for dissolution of marriage and that a court cannot grant a khula decree unless the husband consents to it. The legal consequence of the decision in *Khurshid Bibi* is that the courts can allow a wife judicial khula on the ground that the marriage has irretrievably broken down. It is not necessary to establish any fault on the part of the husband. In *Abdul Rahim* v. *Shahida Khan*, the Supreme Court reaffirmed the khula rule: 'In case of dislike by the wife of her husband Islam concedes the right to the wife, in circumstances of extreme discord and where life becomes a torture to both, on account of fixed aversion on the part of the spouses, to seek dissolution of marriage on the ground of khula (p.333).' Judicial khula is the best and most salutary example of judicial ijtihad, judicial creativity, and social engineering in the field of Muslim personal law in Pakistan and Bangladesh. In India, the classical Hanafi law on the subject, as enunciated in *Moonshee Buzul-ul-Raheem* v. *Luteefut-oon-Nissa* (Case 11) still prevails.

38

Noor Bibi v. *Pir Bux*
Dissolution of marriage

Noor Bibi—Plaintiff

v.

Pir Bux—Defendant

AIR (37) 1950 Sind 8

(Tyabji, C.J. and Muhammad Bachal, J.)

Decided on 24 October 1949

Issues of law

Section 2(ii) of DMMA; neglect or failure to maintain wife; wife's conduct; conflicting decisions

Case summary and decision

Noor Bibi, a young woman of about twenty-two, lived with her husband for six months after marriage and then returned to her father's house. Her husband attempted to take her back with him but she refused to go back to him. She claimed dissolution of marriage on the ground that the defendant husband had neglected or failed to provide for her maintenance for more than two years before the suit. A Single Judge of the Sind High Court found that the failure of the husband to maintain his wife was due to her disobedience and refusal to go back to him. Under the circumstances the wife was not entitled to any maintenance from her husband for the period in question under Muslim law. Section 2(ii) of the DMMA provides that a Muslim woman shall be entitled to obtain a decree for dissolution of her marriage on the ground that the husband has neglected or failed to provide for her maintenance for a period of two years. The question before the judge was whether, where the husband's failure to maintain had occurred under circumstances in which, on account of the wife's conduct, the wife could not in law sustain a claim for maintenance, the failure was still a ground for dissolution of the marriage by virtue of Section 2(ii). There were conflicting decisions on this question. According to some, the husband could not be said to have neglected or failed to provide maintenance for his wife unless, under Muslim law, he is under an obligation to maintain his wife. In such a situation, the wife could not obtain a decree for dissolution of her marriage. According to others, once failure on the part of husband to maintain his wife was proved as a fact, it was irrelevant to inquire into the causes of that failure; mere failure was sufficient for a decree of dissolution of the marriage. The judge referred the question to a Division Bench of the Sind High Court.

In delivering the judgment of the court, Tyabji, C.J. held that, for dissolution of marriage under Section 2(ii), all that the wife needs to prove is that her husband has, in fact, failed to maintain her for two years. The fact that under the particular circumstances the wife is not entitled in law to claim maintenance for the period in question is of no consequence when the question is whether she is entitled to dissolution. A Muslim marriage is a covenant, not a sacrament. There is no merit in preserving a marriage when the parties are unable to fulfil their mutual marital obligations, and there is no desecration involved in dissolving a marriage which has failed. When a husband and a wife have been living apart and the husband is not maintaining the wife, in such circumstances the failure to maintain for a prolonged period is regarded as an instance where breakdown of the marriage has occurred. The wife's disobedience or refusal to live with the husband does not affect the principle on which dissolution is allowed. The question whether there is a failure to maintain is a pure question of fact and in no way depends upon the circumstances in which the failure has occurred. 'The principle upon which maintenance is enforced during the subsistence of a marriage, and those upon which a dissolution is allowed, are entirely different. A dissolution of marriage is allowed when a cessation of the state of marriage has in reality taken place, or the continuance of the marriage has become injurious to the wife (p.18).' The answer of the Sind High Court to the question referred to them by the Single Judge was that, as the husband had, in fact, failed to provide for the maintenance of his wife for two years preceding the suit, she was entitled to dissolution of her marriage under Section 2(ii) of the DMMA, in spite of the fact that on account of her conduct she would not have been entitled to enforce any claim for maintenance against the husband in respect of the period during which the husband had failed to maintain her.

Comments

The rule laid down by Tyabji, C.J. in *Noor Bibi*, was followed in *A. Yousuf Rawther* v. *Sowramma* (Case 23), where Krishna Iyer, J. held that the conduct of the wife is not material to the issue of dissolution of marriage under Section 2(ii) of the DMMA.

39

Syed Ali Nawaz Gardezi v. Muhammad Yusuf

MFLO

Syed Ali Nawaz Gardezi—Appellant

v.

Muhammad Yusuf—Respondent

PLD 1963 SC 51

(A.R. Cornelius, C.J., S.A. Rahman, Fazle-Akbar,

B.Z. Kaikaus, and Hamoodur Rahman, JJ.)

Decided on 29 November 1962

Issues of law

Validity of a Shia Muslim's marriage with a *Kitabia* woman; talaq rules in Shia law; objects of MFLO; effects of failure to give notice of talaq under Section 7 of MFLO; marriage during iddat; Sections 497 and 498 of Pakistan Penal Code, 1860 (PPC)

Case summary and decision

In 1951 Syed Ali Nawaz Gardezi, a Shia Muslim domiciled in Pakistan, married Christa Renate Sonntag, a German girl, at a Registrar's office in England. The couple returned to Pakistan where the wife fell in love with Lt Col Yusuf and married him on 2 January 1962 according Muslim rites. Gardezi filed a complaint against Yusuf under Sections 497 and 498 of the PPC for committing adultery with his wife and enticing her away. Yusuf was tried by a Single Judge of the West Pakistan High Court, convicted on both the charges and sentenced to pay fines of Rs. 12,500 and Rs. 7,500, or in default, suffer rigorous imprisonment of one year on the first charge and of six months on the second charge. On appeal, the Appellate Bench of the High Court consisting of three judges acquitted him of both the charges. Gardezi appealed to the Supreme Court. Yusuf's defence was that Gardezi had divorced Sonntag by a divorce deed on 29 December 1961. The Supreme Court found that the genuineness of the divorce deed had not been proved beyond reasonable doubt. The alleged divorce was open to a number of objections. First, Sonntag's assertion that she had become a Muslim was not substantiated by the evidence on the record. She could not have been properly divorced by Gardezi, as she was not a Muslim on the relevant date. Second, a talaq in Shia law must be pronounced orally by the husband in the presence of two witnesses in a set form of Arabic words. The written talaq, alleged to have been pronounced by Gardezi, was not recognized as valid in Shia law. Third, Gardezi had not given notice of the alleged pronouncement of talaq to the Chairman of the Union Council as was required by Section 7 of the MFLO. In response to the defence argument that MFLO was applicable only where both parties to a marriage were Muslim citizens of Pakistan, the Supreme Court held that its provisions were attracted even where the husband alone was a Muslim citizen.

In what may be regarded as a classic exposition on the purposes and objectives of Section 7 of MFLO, the Supreme Court held that the object of Section 7 is to prevent a hasty dissolution of marriage by talaq, pronounced by the husband unilaterally, without making an attempt to prevent disruption of the matrimonial status. Accordingly, it provides for a machinery of conciliation, involving representatives of the spouses, to resolve the differences between them and enable the husband to reconsider his decision. The talaq pronounced by the husband is to remain ineffective for a period of ninety days from the date of service of notice of pronouncement of talaq to the Chairman of the Union Council and this period is to be utilized for reconciliation. If the husband abstains from giving notice to the Chairman, he should perhaps be deemed, in view of Section 7, to have revoked the pronouncement of talaq. As the talaq remains ineffective during the ninety-day period, the marital status of the parties remains unchanged. So, when Sonntag went through a form of marriage with Yusuf, she was still the wife of Gardezi, as the divorce, even if granted by Gardezi, could not have become effective without recourse to the provisions of Section 7 of the MFLO. Since the marriage between Gardezi and Sonntag subsisted the court held that Yusuf had committed adultery with Sonntag but the court acquitted him of the charge on the ground that Gardezi had connived at it. The court found Yusuf guilty of enticing and taking away Sonntag from the house of her husband and restored the order of the trial judge but reduced the fine to Rs. 2,000.

Comments

The gist of the decision is that service of notice to the Chairman under Section 7(1) of the MFLO is mandatory and non-compliance amounts to revocation of the talaq pronounced by the husband. One unintended consequence of this decision is to make Section 7(2) of the MFLO, which provides for imprisonment or fine or both for contravention, ineffective or redundant. The decision has been followed by the courts in Pakistan and Bangladesh. For example, see *Abdul Mannan* v. *Safurun Nessa, Ghulam Fatima* v. *Abdul Qayyum Muhammad Salahuddin Khan* v. *Muhammad Nazir Siddiqui,* and *Junaid Ali* v. *Abdul Qadir,* all decisions of the Supreme Court.

40

Kaneez Fatima v. Wali Muhammad
Effects of non-service of notice of talaq

Kaneez Fatima—Appellant

v.

Wali Muhammad and Another—Respondents

PLD 1993 SC 901

(Shafiur Rahman, Abdul Qadeer Chaudhry,
Saleem Akhtar, Saeeduzzaman Siddiqui,
and Wali Muhammad Khan, JJ.)

Decided on 1 August 1993

Issues of law

Mandatory nature of Section 7 of MFLO; effects of failure to give notice of talaq; applicability and interpretation of Section 7; constitutional restraints regarding legality of MFLO

Case summary and decision

In this case the marriage deed provided for a prompt dower of Rs. 30,000, twenty *tolas* of gold, and a monthly maintenance of Rs. 200 for the wife. Following matrimonial discord between the couple, the wife filed a petition before the martial law authorities complaining of non-payment of prompt dower and maintenance. On the basis of a written compromise mediated by the martial law authorities, the husband divorced the wife on 1 November 1977; she received Rs. 10,000 and five tolas of gold from him and renounced further claims in future against him. On 6 April 1978 the wife filed a suit for recovery of the remaining amount of dower, and also maintenance in the family court, claiming that she had been coerced into signing the compromise document by the martial law authorities, and as no notice of dissolution of marriage was given to the Chairman of the Union Council, the marriage between the parties was subsisting. The Family Judge decreed the suit but the Additional District Judge set it aside. The High Court held that both the parties contracted out of the provisions of Section 7 of the MFLO and agreed not to have recourse to arbitration proceedings before the Arbitration Council. Therefore, both of them waived the compulsory proceedings aimed at restoring the marriage and the wife could not claim the benefit of Section 7 for the purpose of claiming maintenance. On appeal, a Full Bench of the Supreme Court held that the High Court's view was not in conformity with the law laid down by the Supreme Court in *Syed Ali Nawaz Gardezi* v. *Muhammad Yusuf* (Case 39), *Abdul Mannan* v. *Safurun Nessa, Muhammad Salahuddin Khan* v. *Muhammad Nazir Siddiqui*, and *Junaid Ali* v. *Abdul Qadir*, and reaffirmed that the provisions of Section 7 of the MFLO have to be observed even where the parties have arrived at settlement for dissolution of marriage. As to the observations made in *Syed Ali Nawaz Gardezi* that husband's failure to give notice would be deemed revocation of talaq, the court said that 'failure to send notice of Talaq to the Chairman of the Union Council does not by itself lead to the conclusion that Talaq has been revoked. It may only be ineffective but not revoked'. The court held that applicability and interpretation of Section 7 of the MFLO has to be construed in light of the facts of each case. In the present case, with the consent of both the parties divorce was effected and confirmed in writing under their undisputed signatures. In such a situation Section 7 should not be strictly construed, particularly in cases where penal provisions of Section 7(2) are to be enforced, for in such cases, the parties do not wilfully commit breach and bona fide believe that they have been divorced with the consent of each other and sending of notice to the Chairman is merely a formality. The notice can be sent at any time thereafter to comply with the provision of Section 7. The court dismissed the wife's appeal but on grounds different from that of the High Court.

Comments

In this case the Supreme Court was also required to define the object, scope, and applicability of Article 2A of the Constitution of Pakistan.

This part of the judgment has not been given in Part II of the book. Regarding the repugnance of Section 7 of the MFLO to the injunctions of Islam, the Court made the following observations. The MFLO is an existing law, which has not so far been declared by the Federal Shariat Court or the Shariat Appellate Bench of the Supreme Court as repugnant to the injunctions of Islam. In view of the constitutional restraints, said the Court, it cannot give any verdict on the conflicting claims about its legality.

However, in *Allah Rakha* v. *Federation of Pakistan*, the Federal Shariat Court held that talaq takes effect from the date of its pronouncement by the husband, and the iddat or waiting period also commences from this date and not from the date of delivery of notice to the Chairman. The period of iddat prescribed by the Qur'an is also different in different situations. In the case of an unconsummated marriage there is no period of iddat at all. In the case of a talaq during pregnancy, the waiting period stands terminated on the delivery of the child. But Section 7 has fixed ninety days' iddat for all situations. Hence, Section 7(3) providing that talaq shall not be effective until the expiration of ninety days from the day of delivery of notice, and Section 7(5) fixing ninety days' waiting period for pregnant women clearly violate Qur'anic injunctions, and shall cease to have effect from 31 March 2002. Ever since, an appeal against the decision has been pending in the Shariat Appellate Bench of the Supreme Court.

In the meantime, though the Karachi High Court has followed *Allah Rakha* in *Batool Tahir* v. *Province of Sind*, the Supreme Court has upheld the validity of Section 7 of the Ordinance in *Manzoor Ahmad* v. *Nargis Mirza*, and *Farah Naz* v. *Judge Family Court*.

41

Bashiran v. *Muhammad Hussain*

Zina offence

Bashiran and Another—Appellants

v.

Muhammad Hussain and Another—Respondents

PLD 1988 SC 186 (Shariat Appellate Bench)

(Nasim Hasan Shah, Pir Muhammad Karam

Shah, and Maulana Taqi Usmani, JJ.)

Decided on 27 January 1988

Issues of law

Sections 4 and 10(2) of Offence of Zina (Enforcement of Hudood) Ordinance, 1979; interpretation of 'wilfully'

Case summary and decision

Muhammad Hussain was already married when he contracted marriage with Bashiran. Shortly after the marriage, their marital relations became extremely strained and she returned to her parents' house. There she fell seriously ill and underwent kidney surgery but Muhammad Hussain showed no concern for her. Eventually, he was persuaded to pronounce an oral divorce and execute a divorce deed. Thereafter, Bashiran contracted a second marriage with Abdur Rahman. Muhammad Hussain filed a private complaint against the couple under Offences of Zina (Enforcement of Hudood) Ordinance, 1979 ('Ordinance'). Zina is defined in the Ordinance as follows: 'Zina: A man and a woman are said to commit "zina" if they wilfully have sexual intercourse without being validly married to each other.' The trial court found that the talaqnama did not bear Muhammad Hussain's signature. Hence the earlier marriage between him and Bashiran subsisted; her second marriage with Abdur Rahman was invalid; and she and Abdur Rahman were guilty of committing the offence of zina under the Ordinance. The trial court sentenced them under Section 10(2) of the Ordinance to five years' rigorous imprisonment, ten stripes and Rs. 1,000 as fine and under Section 494 of the PPC to two years' rigorous imprisonment and Rs. 1,000 as fine. The Federal Shariat Court upheld the conviction and sentence. Against this decision the couple appealed to the Shariat Appellate Bench of the Supreme Court. The apex court was of the opinion that, even if the divorce deed was a forged document and Bashiran contracted the second marriage while she was still the wedded wife of Muhammad Hussain, 'the question would still remain as to whether the appellants can be found guilty of committing "zina", in all the circumstances of the case' (*Bashiran and Another* v. *Muhammad Hussain and Another*, Case 41, p.188). The court maintained that an act is done 'wilfully' if it is done intentionally or deliberately to disobey or disregard a law but if it is not done with an evil purpose or criminal intent but inadvertently it will not have been done wilfully. The court held that Bashiran had taken no part in fabricating the divorce deed. She believed bona fide that it was a genuine document and there was no impediment in her contracting a second marriage. As the appellants had entered into a marriage believing that they could validly do so, and even if they had been having sexual intercourse (which is only a presumption as there was no offspring of this marriage), they could not be held guilty of the offence of zina as defined in Section 4 of the Ordinance. The conviction and sentence were set aside and they were released forthwith.

Comments

The ameliorative provision of Section 7 of the MFLO rebounded against women under the Ordinance. Where the husband failed to give notice of talaq to the Chairman of Union Council under Section 7 of the MFLO the marriage legally subsisted. Due to ignorance of law, if a woman, bona fide believing that the marriage had been dissolved, contracted a second marriage, she was liable to punishment for the offence of zina under the Ordinance. The decision in *Bashiran*, prevented the perpetration of such glaring injustices.

42

Zohra Begum v. Latif Ahmad Munawwar

Hizana of minor children

Zohra Begum—Appellant

v.

Latif Ahmad Munawwar—Respondent

PLD 1965 (W.P.) Lah. 695

(Muhammad Yaqub Ali, J.)

Decided on 17 June 1965

Issues of law

Sections 17 and 25 of Guardians and Wards Act, 1890; mother's hizana of minor children; conflicting rules in textbooks; welfare of minors

Case summary and decision

Following matrimonial discord the wife left her husband's house along with the two children of the marriage. After eight years the husband divorced her, and she instituted suits against him for payment of dower, recovery of dowry, and maintenance of children. In reply, the husband filed an application under Section 25 of the Guardians and Wards Act, 1890 for the custody of the boy who was over seven years of age and the girl who was below the age of puberty. The Guardian Judge gave the custody of the boy to the father and the girl to the mother. The decision conformed to the Hanafi rule that the father is entitled to the custody of a son over seven years of age and the mother of a daughter until she attains puberty. Both the parties preferred appeals against this order in the High Court. The counsel for the mother submitted before the Single Judge of the High Court that there is no definite rule of decision as to the age of a minor son and a daughter at which the mother loses the right of their custody. Textbooks on Muslim law and courts have expressed conflicting views on the question, and the views expressed by the Imams and other jurisconsults of Islam are not sacrosanct. In the absence of a universally accepted rule of decision it is for the courts to ascertain it in each case on the basis of ijma, qiyas, *istihsan, istidlal,* etc. In the light of this submission, the Single Judge referred the following question for a Full Bench decision: in cases where textbooks on Muslim law, such as the *Hedaya* and *Fatawa Alamgiri,* have expressed conflicting views, how are the courts to determine which of the views is correct? The answer given by the Full Bench was that where there is no Qur'anic or traditional text or an ijma on a point of law and there is a difference of views between a'imma and faqihs, a court may form its own opinion on the matter.

The court of the Single Judge found that there is no Qur'anic or traditional text on the subject of hizana, and the rules propounded in different textbooks are not uniform. Therefore, held the court, it would be permissible to depart from the rule stated in the textbooks on the facts of a given case, if its application is against the welfare of a minor. The court claimed that its view is supported by cases in which a qadi, finding that the application of a rule of law to which the parties belonged caused hardship, sent the case to the qadi of another school of law which took a liberal view of the matter. Turning to the merits of the case, the court found that the mother did not have any shortcomings and had, for the last nine years, brought up the two children properly. During all these years the father had not contributed a single penny towards their maintenance. In fact, he had not even seen them once since 1953. In the circumstances, if their custody was given to the father, they would find themselves choked in the custody of a stranger who had had such a long-drawn and bitter litigation with the mother. It would retard their emotional and mental growth. The court further held that the suit instituted by the father was a counter-blast to their mother's suits and was not motivated by affection and genuine concern for their welfare. It was, therefore, in the welfare of the two minors to remain in the custody of their mother.

Comments

This is one of the earliest cases where the Pakistani courts refused to follow the rigid rules of interpretation of the sources of Muslim law laid down by the Privy Council in *Aga Mahomed Jaffer Bindaneem* v. *Koolsom Bee Bee* and *Baker Ali Khan* v. *Anjuman Ara Begum* (Cases 1 and 2) and differed from the views of traditionally authoritative texts which were not based on any specific injunctions of the Qur'an or Sunnah. In the custody case of *Abu Baker Siddique* v. *S.M.A. Bakar* (Case 58) the Appellate Division of the Supreme Court of Bangladesh cited with approval the rule laid down in *Zohra Begum*.

43

Irfana Shaheen v. *Abid Waheed*

Custody of adopted children

Irfana Shaheen—Petitioner

v.

Abid Waheed—Respondent

PLD 2002 Lah. 283

(Muhammad Nawaz Abbasi, J.)

Decided on 2 October 2001

Issues of law

Section 491 of CrPC, 1898; custody of adopted children; custody of abandoned children; female partner in adoption

Case summary and decision

In this case, the Lahore High Court, in a single judgment, decided two suits involving common questions of law and facts. In the first suit, a childless couple adopted a forty-two-day-old female child. As relations between the couple became strained, the husband drove the wife away with the child. The wife filed a suit for dissolution of her marriage and obtained a decree. The husband forcibly took the child away from her and she moved the court under Section 491 of the CrPC, 1898 against the husband for recovery of custody. The court was required to decide the question of right of custody of the adopted child in light of the concept of adoption of a child in Islam. The foster-mother claimed custody of the child on the ground that the foster-father, not being the real father of the child, would have no special or preferential right over the foster-mother to retain custody of the minor girl. The foster-father claimed that he had taken the responsibility of bringing the girl up as his daughter and her welfare demanded that he should retain her custody. The *amicus curiae* contended that the principle of custody of an adopted minor should not be different from that of a biological child, except limitations relating to inheritance. The court held that the mother accepted the duty and responsibility of bringing up the child with motherly love and care. She was the most essential partner in the adoption and in light of the concept of an adopted child in Islam she was exclusively entitled to custody of the child. The welfare of the child also demanded that she should remain in the custody of the female partner in the adoption. In a nutshell, having enjoyed the status of mother to the child, she would be entitled to retain custody in exercise of the right of hizana.

In the second suit, a newborn child was found lying in an open space near a mosque in Taxila. The petitioner, a childless woman, obtained custody of the infant as an adopted child with the consent of the local people and police. She applied to the Judicial Magistrate for regularization of the custody. But the Magistrate handed over the child to Gehwara, an institution authorized to regulate adoption matters, run under the control of the government of Punjab. The petitioner moved an application to the High Court under Section 491 of the CrPC, questioning the legality of the Magistrate's order. The court held that Gehwara was, no doubt, rendering a noble service for the settlement of destitute and abandoned children. But the petitioner had voluntarily adopted the abandoned child with the consent of the people of the area and accepted the responsibility of bringing the child up as her son/daughter. Therefore, she would have the exclusive right to retain custody and Gehwara or any private person except the child's real parents would have no right to deprive her of its custody. However, in the interest of the child's welfare, the court asked the petitioner to give an undertaking to Gehwara to bestow motherly love and affection to the child and abide by the rules and regulations of Gehwara relating to adoption of children.

44

Muhammad Haneef v. *Abdul Samad*
Guardianship of minor's property

Muhammed Haneef—Petitioner

v.

Abdul Samad and Others—Respondents

PLD 2009 SC 751

(Khalil-ur-Rahman Ramday, Faqir Muhammad Khokhar, and Mahmood Akhtar Shahid Siddiqui, JJ.)

Decided on 26 May 2009

Issues of law

Guardianship in Muslim law; persons entitled to be guardians of minor's property; de facto guardian and alienation of immovable property of a minor; Section 41 of Transfer of Property Act, 1882

Case summary and decision

Petitioner Muhammad Haneef, subsequently represented by his legal heirs, alleged that Ghulam Fatima, respondent No. 7, who was the original owner of the suit land, had alienated it by way of exchange in favour of her mother Rabia on 30 May 1967, and the latter sold it to him on 12 June 1967. Later, Ghulam Fatima had obtained an ex parte court decree setting aside the exchange mutation of 30 May 1967, also an order of the Assistant Commissioner cancelling the petitioner's sale agreement with Rabia and sold the suit land to respondents Nos. 1–5. Haneef prayed for a declaration that by virtue of the sale mutation of 12 June 1967 he was the owner of the suit land and the court order obtained by Ghulam Fatima and her sale deeds in favour of respondents Nos. 1–5 were illegal, ex parte, collusive, and void. Respondents Nos. 1–5 also filed a civil suit for a declaration of their title over the suit land on the basis of registered sale deeds by Ghulam Fatima in their favour. The petitioner argued that Rabia was the ostensible owner of the suit land by the exchange mutation, dated 30 May 1967. Therefore, the transaction of sale of the suit land by her to the petitioner could not be set aside on the ground that she was not authorized to sell the suit land. The sale was protected by Section 41 of the Transfer of Property Act, 1882. The respondents took the position that Ghulam Fatima was a minor girl at the time of the exchange mutation dated 30 May 1967, and that her mother, having not been appointed guardian of her property by any court, was not competent to alienate the suit land. The trial court dismissed the suit of the petitioner and decreed the one filed by the respondents. The District Judge reversed the decision of the trial court, but the High Court upheld it. Then the petitioner came to the Supreme Court.

The Supreme Court held that under Muslim law the mother is entitled only to custody of the person of her minor child up to a certain age but she is not the natural guardian. The following persons are entitled in the order mentioned here to be the guardians of a minor's property: (i) the father; (ii) his executor; (iii) the father's father; and (iv) his executor. In default of those de jure guardians the duty of appointing a guardian for the protection and preservation of the minor's property devolves on the judge. It is only when the mother is the father's executrix or is appointed by the court as a minor's guardian that she has all the powers of a de jure guardian. A person who may have voluntarily placed himself in charge of the person and property of a minor is called a de facto guardian. He is merely a custodian of the person and property of the minor and has no power to transfer any right or interest in the immovable property of the minor.

The Court found that the legal position of alienation of immovable property of a minor by his mother, brother, uncle, and other close relatives as de facto guardians of the minor has been examined by superior courts of Pakistan and India in a number of cases, for example, *Ahmed Khan* v. *Rasool Bakhsh, Haji Abdullah Khan* v. *Nisar Muhammad Khan, Imambandi* v. *Haji Mutsaddi,* (Case 13), *Muhammad Ejaz Hussain* v. *Muhammad Iftikhar Hussain, Methiyan Siddqu* v. *Muhammad Kanju, Mahboob Sahab* v. *Ismail,* etc., and in all these cases there was unanimity of views that a de facto guardian of a minor has no power to transfer any immovable property of the minor. The Court found that at the time of effecting the exchange mutation Ghulam Fatima was a minor and at no stage was her mother Rabia appointed by any competent court to be the guardian of her property. Therefore, the exchange mutation of the suit land by Rabia in her own favour was invalid. The petitioner being the transferee of the suit land would not acquire or claim any title to the suit land. The petitioner belonged to the same village where the suit land was situated and was not ignorant of the factual and legal position of the transaction. So he could not be said to have taken reasonable care or acted in good faith to find out whether Rabia had the power to transfer the suit land. The Court upheld the judgment of the High Court and dismissed the petition.

45

Sardar Muhammad v. Nasima Bibi

Wife's maintenance

Sardar Muhammad—Petitioner

v.

Nasima Bibi and Others—Respondents

PLD 1966 (W.P.) Lah. 703

(Anwarul Haq and Muhammad Afzal Cheema, JJ.)

Decided on 5 May 1966

Issues of law

Section 9 of MFLO; meaning of 'fails to maintain the wife adequately'; law of maintenance of wife; arrears of maintenance

Case summary and decision

After their marriage in 1957, the spouses lived happily for a year and a quarter and a daughter was born to them. Then the husband left the wife and child with the wife's parents and never bothered himself about them again. On 7 February 1962 the wife applied to the Union Council Chairman for granting her and her child maintenance under Section 9 of the MFLO, which had come into effect on 15 July 1961. On the husband's failure to participate in the proceedings of the Arbitration Council, the Council granted the wife and child maintenance of Rs. 70 per month with effect from 15 July 1961. The Collector dismissed the husband's revision petition as time-barred. The husband filed a writ petition challenging the maintenance order on the following grounds:

1. The allegations against the husband were those of total neglect and refusal to maintain. Therefore Section 9 of the MFLO, which dealt with only cases of inadequate maintenance, could not be invoked. The court held that a case of inadequate maintenance also included a case of total absence of maintenance.

2. The proceedings against him were heard ex parte by an Arbitration Council which was not properly constituted. The court held that, once notice had been served properly, the proceedings of the Council were not vitiated by the failure of any party to participate in the proceedings.

3. Although there was no provision in the MFLO for children's maintenance, yet the court granted maintenance to the child. The court conceded that the child was not entitled to maintenance under the MFLO.

4. Though the wife applied for maintenance on 7 February 1962, she was granted maintenance from 15 July 1961, and as no decree could be passed for past maintenance under the rule of Hanafi law, this was illegal. On this point the question before the court was: 'from what date could an allowance be allowed to a neglected wife; from the date when the cause of action arises or the date when she makes the application before the Arbitration Council or the date on which the order is made in her favour'.

Relying on Baillie's *Digest* and the *Hedaya*, the husband's counsel argued that maintenance can only be paid to the wife from the date of the decree and not even from the date of making the application. The court observed that the Hanafi rule is inconsistent with the fact that the husband's obligation to maintain his wife commences with the performance of marriage. Second, there was a consensus of opinion among jurists that maintenance of a wife is the bounden duty of a husband, irrespective of his minority, illness, imprisonment, or the means of the wife. Therefore, the argument of the *Hedaya* that arrears of maintenance cannot be claimed because it is an ex gratia payment by way of sympathy and charity is untenable. Third, although the Hanafis do not allow the wife to recover past maintenance, the Shafi'is, Hanbalis, and Malikis are unanimously of the view that arrears of maintenance, being a just charge, can be realized from the husband. Finally, the mere fact that a neglected wife has hesitated to promptly approach the court for relief or has been pursuing alternative remedies out of court cannot be a justification to deprive her of the right of maintenance from the day the cause of action accrued to her. Accordingly, the court held that past maintenance was payable to the wife.

Comments

In *Muhammad Nawaz* v. *Khurshid Begum*, a Full Bench of the Supreme Court of Pakistan endorsed *Sardar Muhammad*. Thus, judicial creativity has restored to the Hanafi wife the right to past maintenance, which was denied to her by traditional Hanafi law. The court rightly observed that the Shafi'i, Maliki, and Hanbali schools of law allow the neglected wife to recover arrears of maintenance from the day the cause of action arises. [For a Shafi'i decision, see *Kozhikati Khadir Mohamed Haji* v. *Moideen Kalimabi.*]

46

Gul Bibi v. *Muhammad Saleem*

Arrears of wife's maintenance

Gul Bibi—Petitioner

v.

Muhammad Saleem and Another—Respondents

PLD 1978 Que. 117

(Abdul Hayee Kureshi, Acting C.J. and Zakaullah Lodhi, J.)

Decided on 1 June 1978

Issues of law

Contractual nature of marriage in Islam; wife's maintenance; Section 9 of MFLO; arrears of maintenance

Case summary and decision

In June 1970 the wife left her husband's house on the ground that he had contracted a second marriage without her consent. She filed a suit on 23 May 1974 in the family court of Quetta for recovery of maintenance from June 1970 onwards at the rate of Rs. 150 per month. On 31 May 1975 the family court decreed the suit, granting maintenance as prayed for. On appeal by the husband, the District Judge set aside the order for past maintenance and allowed the wife maintenance from the date of decree. The wife assailed this order through a constitutional petition in the Quetta High Court. The High Court held that marriage in Islam is not a sacrament but it is a pure and simple contract between a man and a woman legally capable of contracting marriage, and one of its incidents is that the husband is liable to make provision for his wife's maintenance according to his means as long as the marriage subsists. Once a legal obligation comes into existence, it is enforceable through the courts the moment it is violated, and in maintenance cases the cause of action accrues to a wife on the date the husband starts neglecting to maintain her. It is not reasonable to argue that where for some reason the wife delays approaching the court for relief, the period of delay would not be counted towards the total period for which maintenance is payable. Second, although the Hanafi school does not allow arrears of maintenance prior to the date of the court decree, the Shia and the Shafi'i schools do. Since all the schools agree that marriage in Islam is a contract, there should have been unanimity among them on the incidents of such a contract as well. Again, since the main sources of Muslim law, the Qur'an and Sunnah, are silent on arrears of maintenance, some difference of opinion on the matter is not unlikely. But the positive view of other schools is more consonant with reason, logic, and common sense, and its adoption would not be unjustified in view of the consensus amongst jurists that these schools are only different schools of thought and not different religions so as to prohibit the adoption of each other's views in some matters of principle. One should also keep in mind 'the need of times, pattern and structure of the society in which different jurists worked' (p.119). The court adopted the view of the Shia and Shafi'i schools as more akin to reason, set aside the order of the District Judge, and restored the order of the family court granting maintenance to the wife from June 1970.

Comments

Sardar Muhammad v. *Nasima Bibi* (Case 45) is concerned with arrears of maintenance under Section 9 of the MFLO. But *Gul Bibi*, deals with past maintenance under traditional Hanafi law. Here the court specifically emphasized the contractual character of marriage and the husband's legal obligation to maintain his wife under the contract. The contractual obligation to maintain the wife was further elaborated in *Hajiran Bibi* v. *Abdul Khaliq*, where the court held: 'If it is found that the husband has been negligent in maintaining her in spite of being obliged under the law to do so then the wife would be entitled not only to future maintenance but even to past maintenance for the period during which she has not been maintained' (p. 764).

SECTION IV

BANGLADESH

47

A.L.M. Abdulla v. Rokeya Khatoon

Requisites of marriage, registration

A.L.M. Abdulla—Appellant

v.

Rokeya Khatoon and Another—Respondents

21 DLR (1969) 213

(Abu Md Abdullah, J.)

Decided on 11 December 1967

Issues of law

Essentials of a valid marriage: Section 5 of MFLO; effects of non-registration of marriage; prolonged and continuous cohabitation

Case summary and decision

Appellant Abdulla brought a suit against respondent Rokeya Khatoon for restitution of conjugal rights and a permanent injunction restraining her from marrying any other person. His case was that there was close intimacy and love between them leading to marriage, and he produced witnesses to that effect. But there was no kabinnama of the alleged marriage. On an analysis of the evidence the Munsif came to the conclusion that marriage between Abdulla and Rokeya was established and decreed the suit on contest. The Subordinate Judge held that Abdulla had failed to establish solemnization of the alleged marriage with Rokeya and was not entitled to a decree for the reliefs prayed for. On second appeal the High Court held that nothing short of clear, direct, and specific evidence that the woman gave her consent to the marriage would establish marriage. The essential requirements of a valid Muslim marriage are that there should be a proposal, made by or on behalf of one of the parties to the marriage, and acceptance of the proposal by or on behalf of the other, in the presence and hearing of two male or one male and two female witnesses who must be sane adult Muslims, at one meeting. In the present case there was no evidence of who proposed the marriage and who accepted the proposal. Therefore, there was no valid marriage. Moreover, Section 5 of the MFLO makes it absolutely necessary for marriage solemnized under Muslim law to be registered. Here there was no evidence that the alleged marriage was registered. The court said: 'The solemnization of marriage if validly effected might not be affected for non-registration of the marriage. But the non-registration of the marriage causes a doubt on the solemnization of the marriage itself' (p.217). The court further observed that intimacy, however close, between a man and a woman does not prove marriage. Marriage may be presumed from prolonged and continued cohabitation. But this was also not the case here. The court upheld the decision of the Subordinate Judge.

48

Momtaz Begum v. *Anowar Hossain*

Nature and presumption of marriage

Momtaz Begum—Appellant

v.

Anowar Hossain—Respondent

VIII ADC (2011) 855

(Surendra Kumar Sinha, Nazmun Ara Sultana, Syed
Mahmud Hossain, Muhammad Imman Ali,
Muhammad Momtaz Uddin Ahmed, and
Md Shams-ul-Huda, JJ.)

Decided on 31 July 2011

Issues of law

Nature of Muslim marriage; requirements of valid marriage; no religious rites; proof of marriage; marriage without kabinnama; effects of non-registration of marriage; absence of witnesses; irregular or invalid marriage; evidence of conduct and reputation; retirement of couple and consummation of marriage; prolonged and continuous cohabitation raising presumption of marriage

Case summary and decision

Momtaz Begum sued Anowar Hossain for prompt dower of Tk. 25,000 and maintenance at Tk. 500 per month. Her case was that, though there was no kabinnama, her marriage with Anowar Hossain was duly solemnized according to Muslim law. They lived together as husband and wife for a considerable time and the marriage was consummated. On account of her inability to meet his demand for dowry, he drove her away from the matrimonial home. Anowar Hossain denied any marriage between the two of them. On proper assessment of the evidence the family court found that Anowar Hossain had married Momtaz Begum and they had lived together as husband and wife and decreed the suit. The court of appeal below agreed with its findings of facts and affirmed the judgment. The High Court reversed the judgment of the two courts below and dismissed the suit. It held that compliance with the requirements of a valid marriage had not been proved. Mere living together does not bring the couple within the marriage bond. The Appellate Division of the Supreme Court was required to consider the following three points: (i) whether non-registration of marriage under Muslim law makes it illegal or irregular or non-existent; (ii) whether continuous cohabitation by the parties over a period of three years as husband and wife coupled with their conduct raises a presumption that there was a valid marriage; and (iii) whether the High Court, in exercise of its revisional jurisdiction, was justified in interfering with the concurrent findings of facts arrived at by the courts below.

The Appellate Division observed that marriage among Muslims is not a sacrament but purely a civil contract. Marriage brings about a relationship based on and arising from a permanent contract for intercourse and procreation of children between a man and a woman. A marriage contract, as a civil institution, rests on the same footing as other contracts. The parties retain their personal rights against each other as well as against strangers and according to the majority of the schools, have power to dissolve the marriage tie, should circumstances render it desirable. Though generally solemnized with recitation from the Qur'an, no specific ceremonies or religious rites are necessary for contracting a valid marriage, nor is evidence in writing required. All that the law insists on is a declaration or proposal by one party and acceptance by the other, that is, consent of the contracting parties, before competent witnesses. Though the presence of witnesses is considered necessary for the validity of a marriage, their absence only renders it invalid, which is cured by consummation. Even in the absence of formal proof of a valid marriage, a marriage can be presumed by evidence of conduct and reputation and the question of consummation forms an important element in the status of a valid marriage. Where there has been prolonged and continuous cohabitation as husband and wife, in the absence of direct proof, a presumption arises that there was a valid marriage, provided that the parties were not prohibited from inter-marrying.

The Appellate Division held that the High Court had not dislodged the findings of the courts below that the appellant and respondent had lived together for a considerable time as husband and wife, but had dismissed the suit mainly on the ground of absence of a registered kabinnama. The High Court had totally overlooked the presumption of a Muslim marriage. Therefore, its decision was based on a misconception of the basic principles of Muslim law. The evidence on record sufficiently proved that a legal marriage existed between the appellant and the respondent. The High Court had exceeded its power in interfering with concurrent findings of facts of the two courts below.

49

Makbul Ali v. *Manwara Begum*

Criminal liability for polygamy

Makbul Ali and Others—Petitioners

v.

Manwara Begum and Others—Opposite Parties

39 DLR (1987) 181

(Anwarul Hoque Chowdhury and Abdul Bari Sarker, JJ.)

Decided on 15 January 1987

Issues of law

Section 6(5) of MFLO; previous permission of Union Council for taking a second wife; husband's criminal liability under the section; maintainability of proceedings against second wife

Case summary and decision

Manwara Begum, a mother of two children, filed a complaint in the Upazila Magistrate's court, Chhatak against her husband Makbul Ali and his second wife, also named Manwara Begum, under Section 6(5) of the MFLO. Her case was that she was married to Makbul Ali in 1974. Makbul Ali, who was a wage-earner working in London, came home occasionally, and on one such visit in 1984 he sent her to her father's house and in her absence took a second wife in violation of the provisions of Section 6 of the MFLO. The husband claimed that he had divorced her, duly sent notice of the pronouncement of divorce to her and the Chairman of the Union Council, and subsequently married the second wife. Therefore, he had not committed any offence under Section 6.

The Magistrate initiated proceedings against both the bigamous husband and the second wife. They applied to the High Court under Section 561A of the CrPC for quashing the proceedings. The High Court agreed to quash the proceedings in respect of the second wife but not the husband. The court observed that Section 6 of the MFLO did not prohibit polygamy altogether but allowed it under certain conditions. Thus, a man can contract a second marriage provided he has taken permission of the Arbitration Council for it. In his application for such permission he must state the reasons for the proposed marriage and whether he has obtained the consent of the existing wife or wives for this marriage. If the Arbitration Council is satisfied that the proposed marriage is necessary and just, it may grant permission. In deciding whether the proposed marriage is necessary and just, the Arbitration Council may take into consideration such circumstances as sterility, physical infirmity, physical unfitness for conjugal relations, insanity, etc. on the part of an existing wife. Subsection (5) of Section 6 of the MFLO provides that any man who contracts another marriage without such permission during the continuance of his existing marriage or marriages will be liable to: (i) pay forthwith the entire amount of the dower, whether prompt or deferred, due to the existing wife or wives and (ii) punishment with imprisonment or fine or both. Thus, criminal liability will be incurred by the husband as being the man referred to in this subsection and not by the woman whom he marries. The MFLO does not impose any obligation on her to: (i) apply for permission to marry her husband; (ii) suffer any imprisonment for the husband's fault in taking her as a wife without Arbitration Council permission; or (iii) undergo any punishment as an abettor. Accordingly, the court held that the proceedings against the second wife were unwarranted and must be quashed.

Comments

On the matter of the second wife's criminal liability, there are different views. The decision to exempt the second wife from any criminal liability has been welcomed by Pearl and Menski (1998: 270). But, on the ground that inclusion of the second wife in the criminal case will help the first wife prove her case easily, it has been suggested that abetment of the offence by the second wife should be made punishable under Section 6(5)(b) of the MFLO (40 DLR 1988 *Journal* 24). In an earlier case, *Abdul Halim Pattadar* v. *Rahmat Ali*, the Marriage Registrar, witnesses, and second wife were prosecuted for taking part in the second marriage, but as abetment had not been specifically made an offence under Section 6 of the MFLO, proceedings against them were quashed. To restrain the practice, it is desirable that aiding and abetting of such marriages by the second wife, her parents, the Marriage Registrar, and witnesses should also be made a punishable offence under Section 6(5)(b) of the MFLO.

50

Hosna Jahan v. Md Shahjahan

Restitution of conjugal rights

Hosna Jahan (Munna)—Petitioner

v.

Md Shahjahan (Shaju) and Others—Respondent

4 BLC (AD) (1999) 117

(A.T.M. Afzal, C.J., Mustafa Kamal, Latifur Rahman,
Md Abdur Rouf, and B.B. Roy Choudhury, JJ.)

Decided on 6 August 1998

Issues of law

Restitution of conjugal rights; Article 102 of the Constitution; Section 115(1) of Civil Procedure Code, 1908 (CPC)

Case summary and decision

Shahjahan married Hosna Jahan through a registered kabinnama on 28 August 1995 at a dower of Taka one lakh and they began to live together as husband and wife. But Hosna's parents did not accept the marriage. After a while the parents informed Shahjahan that they had decided to accept the marriage and hold a wedding reception at their house. Accordingly, Hosna was taken to her parents' house. Once she was under their control, they confined her, put pressure on her to disown the marriage, and physically tortured her. When his efforts to bring her back to his house failed, Shahjahan instituted a suit in the family court for restitution of conjugal rights. The defendants filed a joint statement denying the marriage, claiming the kabinnama to be collusive and forged, and prayed for rejection of the plaint. The family court rejected their prayer. They preferred a revisional application before the High Court. Relying on *Nelly Zaman* v. *Giasuddin Khan*, their counsel submitted that a direction for restitution of conjugal rights is opposed to the principles laid down in Articles 27 (equality of all citizens before law) and 31 (right to enjoy the protection of the law and to be treated in accordance with law). The High Court division found that Section 5B of the Family Courts Ordinance, 1985 specifically mentions restitution of conjugal rights as a subject matter for trial and disposal by a family court. The Ordinance came into force in 1985 and *Nelly Zaman* was decided by a Single Judge in 1982. Therefore, the subsequent conscious policy of the legislature would prevail over the earlier decided case. The counsel for the defendants also cited the case of *Sharmin Hossain* v. *Mizanur Rahman*, where a Single Judge went a step further and held that the law of restitution of conjugal rights is void. The High Court division held that a Single Judge exercising jurisdiction under Section 115(1) of the CPC had no jurisdiction to strike down a piece of legislation, which is the absolute and exclusive jurisdiction of a properly constituted court exercising jurisdiction under Article 102 of the Constitution. The court summarily dismissed the revisional application. When the case came up for the consideration of the Appellate Division of the Supreme Court, a Full Bench of the court approved the reasonings given by the High Court division, held that a Single Judge has no jurisdiction to decide any question affecting the interpretation of the Constitution and overruled the cases of *Nelly Zaman* and *Sharmin Hossain* as not validly given decisions.

Comments

It is interesting to note that the Full Bench of the Appellate Division of the Supreme Court did not give any opinion on the issue of the constitutional validity of the law of restitution of conjugal rights. The bench preferred to base its decision on technical grounds. However, the outcome of the decision is that, like in India, though not for the same reason, restitution of conjugal rights is a valid law in Bangladesh. In India, it was held, in *T. Sareetha* v. *Venkata Subbaiah*, that Section 9 of the Hindu Marriage Act, 1955 which provides for restitution of conjugal rights is a savage and barbarous remedy violating the right of privacy and human dignity guaranteed by Article 21 of the Constitution and, therefore, constitutionally void. But in *Harvinder Kaur* v. *Harmander Singh Choudhry*, it was decided that the leading idea of Section 9 is to preserve the marriage and hence it is not violative of Articles 14 and 21 of the Constitution. In *Saroj Rani* v. *Sudarshan Kumar Chadha*, the Supreme Court overruled the Andhra Pradesh decision and approved the Delhi view.

51

Hosne Ara Begum v. *Alhaj Md Rezaul Karim*

Cruelty of conduct

Hosne Ara Begum—Petitioner

v.

Alhaj Md Rezaul Karim and Others—Opposite Parties

43 DLR (1991) 543

(F.H.M. Habibur Rahman and Kazi Ebadul Hoque, JJ.)

Decided on 13 August 1990

Issues of law

Claim of dower and maintenance; restitution of conjugal rights; cruelty of conduct; Section 17 of Family Courts Ordinance, 1985

Case summary and decision

The wife left the matrimonial home with her children and filed a petition in the family court claiming her prompt dower and maintenance for herself and the three children. As a counter-blast, the husband brought a suit against her for restitution of conjugal rights. The family court found that the husband did not allow his wife to visit her parents' house, forced her to do menial work, which women of affluent families were not used to do, subjected her to physical and mental torture, and made no attempt to bring her back from her father's house. The court granted maintenance to her and the children, allowed her claim for payment of prompt dower, and dismissed the husband's suit for restitution of conjugal rights. The court of appeal below came to the conclusion that the wife was not entitled to maintenance on the ground of physical and mental cruelty. She was also not entitled to recover prompt dower, as she had never demanded it from her husband. It observed that the family court had, in effect, given the wife the right to reside in her father's house permanently and deprive the husband of his conjugal rights. The family court had also not considered the question of restitution of conjugal rights subject to payment of prompt dower. Accordingly, both the suits were remanded to the trial court for fresh hearing.

A Division Bench of the High Court severely criticized the lower appellate court for its archaic ideas of absolute dominion of the husband over the wife, cruelty of conduct, and restitution of conjugal rights. It held that, in the context of present-day social realities and norms, and the mode of living of the families of the husband and the wife, who were wealthy business people, compelling the wife to do menial work constituted cruelty under Section 2(viii)(a) of the DMMA, which defines cruelty as physical assault or making the life of the wife miserable by cruelty of conduct even if such conduct does not amount to physical ill-treatment. Physical and mental cruelty by the husband is not only an offence under the Cruelty to Women (Deterrent Punishment) Ordinance, 1983, punishable with imprisonment and fine, but also a valid ground for refusing restitution of conjugal rights to the husband and for allowing maintenance to the wife. The suit by the wife for prompt dower was sufficient demand for the same. Thus the lower appellate court was wholly wrong to set aside the decree for recovery of prompt dower and maintenance. Under the Family Courts Ordinance, 1985 the lower appellate court was also not competent to remand a suit to the trial court. The High Court set aside the decree of the court of appeal below and restored that of the family court.

Comments

In this case the court construed compelling a wife to do menial work in the household of wealthy families as cruelty under Section 2(viii)(a) of the DMMA. This is, no doubt, a judicial extension of the meaning of cruelty as envisaged in the DMMA. The decision is certainly an enlightened and welcome one in the context of present-day social realities.

52

Gul Newaz Khan v. *Maherunnesa Begum*

Delegated power of divorce, prompt dower

Gul Newaz Khan—Appellant

v.

Maherunnesa Begum—Respondent

17 DLR (1965) 199

(M.R. Khan, J.)

Decided on 19 June 1964

Issues of law

Non-payment of prompt dower on demand; delegated power of divorce

Case summary and decision

Maherunnesa was married to Gul Newaz Khan on a dower of Rs. 5,000. Gul Newaz executed a kabinnama by which he delegated to her the right to repudiate the marriage on the happening of any of the contingencies mentioned in the deed including non-payment of prompt dower on demand and non-payment of maintenance. In a suit by the wife for a declaration that the marriage between the parties was legally dissolved, her plea was that her husband did not give her prompt dower on demand and in exercise of the right delegated to her in the kabinnama she repudiated the marriage and got a talaqnama registered. Gul Newaz contended that Maherunnesa had not made any demand for prompt dower and, therefore, the right to exercise talaq-i-tafwid (delegated divorce) did not really accrue to her and the marriage was not dissolved according to law. The courts below came to a concurrent finding that the wife had, in fact, made demand for prompt dower and the husband did not pay it. Therefore, the marriage between the parties was legally dissolved by the due exercise of talaq-i-tafwid by the wife. In the second appeal, Gul Newaz argued before the High Court that once marriage is consummated, mere non-payment of prompt dower cannot be a valid ground for repudiating the marriage by talaq-i-tafwid. The High Court held that dower is an essential condition of marriage. When non-payment of maintenance by a husband to a wife for two years is a valid ground for dissolution of a Muslim marriage, there is no reason why a marriage cannot be lawfully repudiated by the wife in exercise of the delegated power in cases of non-payment of prompt dower on demand. The exercise of such power by the wife does not appear to be against public policy or the principles of Muslim law. The appeal, therefore, failed.

Comments

In a similar legal situation in *Tahazzad Hossain Sikdar* v. *Hossneara Begum*, the Dhaka High Court upheld the right of a wife to exercise the delegated power of divorce on the ground of non-payment of prompt dower, although the demand for payment was made after consummation of the marriage. Thus, on the issue of exercising the right of talaq-i-tafwid after consummation of marriage, for non-payment of prompt dower, Bangladeshi law agrees with the view taken in *Rahim Jan* v. *Muhammad* (Case 34) and differs from that in *Rabia Khatoon* v. *Mohd Mukhtar Ahmad* (Case 16).

53

Hasina Ahmed v. Syed Abul Fazal

Khula divorce

Hasina Ahmed—Appellant

v.

Syed Abul Fazal—Respondent

32 DLR (1980) 294

(S.M. Husain, J.)

Decided on 13 June 1978

Issues of law

Section 2(viii)(a) of DMMA; law of *li'an* or imprecation; khula divorce; ijtihad and application of Muslim personal law in changing society

Case summary and decision

The wife instituted a suit for dissolution of marriage with her husband on a number of grounds including physical and mental ill-treatment, failure to maintain her, sale of her property and ornaments, false allegations against her moral character, and husband's immoral conduct and association with women of bad repute. Both the lower courts came to a concurrent finding that no ground was established which could entitle the wife to a divorce against her husband. She preferred a second appeal. One of her complaints was that the husband had consistently made false allegations that she had illicit relations with her cousin, which caused her great mental agony. Her husband did not deny this allegation; on the contrary, he reiterated it in his written statement and deposition before the court. The High Court held that this unsubstantiated allegation definitely constituted cruelty within the meaning of Section 2(viii)(a) of the DMMA, entitling the wife to obtain a decree for dissolution of her marriage. Second, under the law of *li'an* or imprecation, the wife is entitled to sue for divorce on the ground that her husband has falsely charged her with adultery. Third, a Muslim wife can claim khula divorce with the consent of the husband. If the husband does not agree, according to the Full Bench decision of the Pakistan Supreme Court in *Khurshid Bibi* v. *Muhammad Amin* (Case 37) she can still obtain dissolution of her marriage from the court, provided that: (i) she agrees to surrender the dower money and other benefits received from the husband and (ii) satisfies the conscience of the court that there is no possibility of their living together consistently with their conjugal duties and obligations and that if a divorce is refused it will mean forcing her into a hateful union. In the present case the wife had consistently claimed that she could not live with her husband and agreed to give up her dower money in consideration of her release from the marriage bond. For the reasons stated above, the court was of the opinion that the wife had successfully established her right to obtain a divorce against her husband. It further held that, while adjudicating on family disputes, the courts should take into consideration not only the factual and legal position but also changes in social attitudes and values. The court set aside the judgments of the lower courts and dissolved the marriage.

Comments

Like in Pakistan, judicial khula where the marriage has irretrievably broken down has been firmly established in Bangladeshi law, dispensing with the Hanafi requirement of husband's consent to a khula divorce. The Muslims of India however continue to follow the traditional law.

54

Sheerin Alam Chowdhury v. Shamsul Alam Chowdhury

Khula divorce

Sheerin Alam Chowdhury—Petitioner

v.

Shamsul Alam Chowdhury—Opposite Party

48 DLR (1996) 79

(Kazi A.T. Manowaruddin, J.)

Decided on 1 August 1995

Issues of law

Dissolution of marriage by khula; restitution of conjugal rights

Case summary and decision

The wife's case was that her husband's ill-treatment and cruelty made her life unbearable and following an attempted assault by him upon her in 1984 she had to leave his house. She asserted that it was not possible on her part to live with her husband and she wanted dissolution of marriage by khula. She agreed to surrender her right to the unpaid dower of Tk. 25,000. The husband denied the wife's allegations and filed a counter-suit for restitution of conjugal rights. The family court held that there was not enough evidence that the wife was treated with cruelty entitling her to claim dissolution of the marriage, and decreed the husband's suit for restitution of conjugal rights. The lower appellate court affirmed the decision. The High Court held that there was sufficient direct evidence of husband's cruel conduct. However, for dissolution of marriage by khula, the question whether the husband treated his wife with cruelty is not of prime importance. The most important consideration is whether the parties can live together in peace and amity. The lower courts have found that the husband and the wife had not been living together since 1984 and the wife was absolutely determined not to live with her husband. The two Pakistani cases, *Balqis Fatima* v. *Najmul-ul-Ikram Qureshi* (Case 36) and *Khurshid Bibi* v. *Muhammad Amin* (Case 37) decided that the wife is entitled to dissolution of marriage on restoration of what she had received in consideration of marriage, if the judge apprehends that the parties will not observe the limits of God, that is, they will not behave towards each other as husband and wife should, in accordance with the Muslim concept of marriage. Relying on these two cases the court dissolved the marriage.

Comments

Oddly enough, the earlier decision of the High Court in *Hasina Ahmed* v. *Syed Abul Fazal* (Case 53), which is the foundation of the law of judicial khula in Bangladesh, was not brought to the notice of the court in this case.

55

Amena Khatun v. *Sherajuddin Sardar*

Dissolution of marriage, irreconcilable breakdown

Amena Khatun—Appellant

v.

Sherajuddin Sardar—Respondent

17 DLR (1965) 687

(Morshed, C.J.)

Decided on 29 July 1962

Issues of law

Sections 2(ii) and 2(viii) of DMMA; irretrievable breakdown of marriages and khula divorce

Case summary and decision

Allured by Amena Khatun's considerable property, youth, and physical beauty, the much older Sherajuddin Sardar, who was already married with children, married her and undertook to stay with her in her house and look after her property. (In this kind of matrimonial arrangement, the husband is known as *ghar jamai*, which is translated by the judge, in the absence of a better expression, as a 'domesticated son-in-law'.) He also undertook to give her Rs. 12 per month for her maintenance in case he lived in some other house. About six years after the marriage he left her house and began to live separately with his first wife. She instituted a suit against him for dissolution of marriage on the following grounds:

(i) negligence and failure to maintain her for more than two years; (ii) failure to perform marital obligations for more than three years; (iii) cruelty; (iv) unequal treatment to her; (v) violation of the conditions of the marriage contract; and (vi) non-payment of dower. The Munsif who tried the suit directed dissolution of the marriage subject to payment of Rs. 200 by the wife to the husband. The District Judge reversed the judgment and decree passed by the trial court. The wife appealed to the High Court. Having considered the evidence before the court, the High Court held that: (i) the husband had failed to maintain her for more than two years, contrary to the specific stipulation in the marriage contract; (ii) that he had failed to perform his marital obligations for more than three years; (iii) that he was unable to offer equal treatment to her in relation to the first wife; (iv) that he had used physical violence against her; and (v) that the discord and bitter relations between the parties, as made out by them, brought it within the ambit of the decision in *Balqis Fatima* v. *Najm-ul-Ikram Qureshi* (Case 36). That case decided that a wife can claim khula divorce as of right, if the court is satisfied that it is no longer possible for the husband and the wife to live together in harmony and in conformity with their marital obligations. The court, however, preferred to dissolve the marriage on the ground that the husband had failed to provide for the wife's maintenance for a period of two years in breach of the terms of the kabinnama. The court also observed that the husband was not absolved of his duty to maintain his wife because the wife was a woman of means.

Comments

Where the wife obtains divorce under the DMMA, she retains her dower and no financial consideration for the divorce is due to the husband. But in judicial khula she has to give up her dower and other financial benefits received from her husband. Therefore, where the husband's fault is proved, the wife's interest is best protected by a dissolution decree under the DMMA. But the courts tend to grant khula decrees even in those cases where grounds for dissolution of marriage under the DMMA, for example, cruelty or non-maintenance, have been established. The present decision is a welcome departure from this trend.

56

Abdul Aziz v. Rezia Khatoon
Ineffectiveness of talaq

Abdul Aziz—Petitioner

v.

Rezia Khatoon—Opposite Party

21 DLR (1969) 733

(A.M. Sayeem, J.)

Decided on 4 June 1969

Issues of law

Section 7(1) of MFLO; Ineffectiveness of talaq due to non-compliance with Section 7(1); effects of non-compliance with Section 7(4) enjoining formation and function of Arbitration Council

Case summary and decision

Rezia Khatoon's case was that her husband Abdul Aziz took a second wife and drove her out of the matrimonial home. She claimed maintenance under Section 488 of the CrPC, 1898. The husband's defence was that Rezia Khatoon was a disobedient and impertinent woman of loose morals and as marital life became absolutely intolerable he divorced her, duly served notice of divorce on the Chairman of the Arbitration Council, and sent a copy to his wife, as required under Section 7(1) of the MFLO. As she was no longer his wife, her application was not maintainable. Rezia Khatoon denied having received any such notice. As service of notice was not established in evidence, the court held that the alleged talaq, if it was pronounced by the husband, was not effective in law, so that the marriage subsisted and Rezia Khatoon was, therefore, entitled to maintenance.

The case is also important for deciding the issue of non-compliance with Section 7(4) of the MFLO. Section 7(4) makes it obligatory on the Chairman of the Union Council to constitute an Arbitration Council within thirty days of the receipt of notice of talaq and directs the Council to take all necessary steps to bring about reconciliation between the wife and husband. But it does not say what would be the consequences of non-compliance with the provision. In the present case one of the arguments on behalf of the wife was that unless an Arbitration Council was constituted and it failed to bring about reconciliation between the parties, a talaq could not be legally effective. The court held that if the Chairman fails in his duty to constitute an Arbitration Council or the Arbitration Council fails to take necessary steps for reconciliation, the talaq, if otherwise valid, will be effective in law on the expiry of ninety days from the date of receipt of notice of talaq by the Chairman.

Comments

The decision of the court regarding the effects of non-service of notice of divorce is in consonance with the leading case of *Syed Ali Nawaz Gardezi* v. *Muhammad Yusuf* (Case 39). There is however, no reference to *Syed Ali Nawaz Gardezi* in the Dacca High Court decision.

The law on the issue of formation of Arbitration Council and reconciliation procedure was further clarified in *Abdul Sobhan Sarkar* v. *Md Abdul Gani*. Here the court held that failure of either the Chairman of the Union Council to constitute an Arbitration Council or the duly constituted Arbitration Council to take necessary steps to bring about reconciliation between the spouses is 'inconsequential'; the talaq, if otherwise valid, will be effective on the expiry of ninety days of delivery of the notice.

57

Sirajul Islam v. *Helana Begum*

Notice of talaq, wife's maintenance

Sirajul Islam—Petitioner

v.

Helana Begum and Others—Opposite Parties

48 DLR (1996) 48

(Syed J.R. Mudassir Hussain and

M. Bazlur Rahman Talukdar, JJ.)

Decided on 27 July 1994

Issues of law

Effects of non-service of notice and effectiveness of talaq under Section 7 of MFLO; past maintenance of wife

Case summary and decision

Sirajul Islam married Helana Begum in 1983. Dower money was fixed at Tk. 39,999, of which half was prompt dower, and maintenance at Tk. 500 per month. Towards the end of 1987 he assaulted his wife and threw her and two minor children out of the matrimonial home. On 11 April 1990 he swore an affidavit pronouncing talaq and sent a copy of the affidavit to the Nikah Registrar for registration of talaq under the Muslim Marriages (Registration) Act, 1974, but gave no notice of the talaq to the Chairman, Union Council, or his wife. In a suit filed by the wife on 3 June 1990 the family court allowed her claim for prompt dower and maintenance. The husband appealed to the lower court against the decision and disclosed the matter of talaq by affidavit. In addition to maintenance, the lower court awarded his wife the entire dower, both prompt and deferred. In the second appeal, the husband's counsel contended before the High Court that, as no notice was served on the Chairman and the wife, the talaq was ineffective and the wife was not entitled to the entire dower. The wife's counsel argued that swearing the affidavit by the husband and registration of the talaq showed that he definitely intended to sever the marriage tie with his wife and not to revoke it. Mere non-service of notice in such a case could not render the talaq ineffective and the decree for the entire dower was valid in law. The court agreed with the wife's counsel and held that where the conduct of the husband showed that he had no intention to revoke the talaq, non-giving of the notice does not render the talaq ineffective. Therefore, the divorce was valid and effective and the wife was entitled to a decree for the entire dower money. For the decision, the court relied on two Pakistani cases, *Chuhar* v. *Ghulam Fatima* and *Parveen Chowdhury* v. *VI*th *Senior Civil Judge, Karachi*.

The case also deals with the problem of past maintenance of wives and children. For no fault of the wife, the husband neglected and refused to maintain her for two-and-a-half years preceding the institution of the suit. The lower courts granted the wife and the children past maintenance for this period. The husband's counsel argued before the High Court that there was no specific agreement between the parties for claiming past maintenance and there was also no provision for past maintenance in the MFLO and the Family Courts Ordinance, 1985. The question before the court was whether maintenance was payable: (i) from the date of the institution of the suit; (ii) from the date of court decree; or (iii) from the time when the husband started neglecting his wife without any reasonable cause. The court found that it was the duty of the husband to maintain his wife, and for no fault of the wife the husband neglected and refused to maintain her for two-and-a-half years prior to the institution of the suit. The court agreed with the following statement of law in *Sardar Muhammad* v. *Nasima Bibi* (Case 45): 'The mere fact that a neglected wife has been hesitant in promptly coming to the Court or has been pursuing alternative remedies out of Court cannot in all fairness be so construed as to deprive her of the right of maintenance from the day when the cause of action accrued to her.' The court held that courts have the jurisdiction to pass a decree for past maintenance in appropriate cases and the two lower courts had committed no illegality in awarding past maintenance to the wife.

Comments

On the husband's final appeal, in a brief judgment in *Sirajul Islam* v. *Helana Begum*, a Full Bench of the Appellate Division of the Supreme Court upheld the High Court decision. The Full Bench held that the husband could not take advantage of his own wrong and claim the benefit of non-service of notice by him to the Chairman. He was bound by his admission. In *Kazi Rashid Akhter Shahid* v. *Rokshana Chowdhury*, a Division Bench of the High Court said that the facts and circumstances in *Sirajul Islam* were quite distinguishable from the case before them and reiterated the rule that 'a talaq will not be effective even after the expiry of 90 days if any of the conditions of effectiveness of talaq, i.e., pronouncement as per Mohamadan law, service of notice on Chairman and a copy thereof to the wife is not complied with' (*Kazi Rashid Akhter Shahid* v. *Mst. Rokshana* Chowdhury, p. 618).

The court's decision on past maintenance of wives was also approved by a Full Bench of the Appellate Division of the Supreme Court in *Jamila Khatun* v. *Rustom Ali* (Case 60).

58

Md Abu Baker Siddique v. S.M.A. Bakar

Rules of hizana

Md Abu Baker Siddique—Appellant

v.

S.M.A. Bakar and Others—Respondents

38 DLR (AD) (1986) 106

(F.K.M.A. Munim, C.J., Badrul Haider Chowdhury, and Shahabuddin Ahmed, JJ.)

Decided on 3 December 1985

Issues of law

Section 25 of Guardians and Wards Act, 1890; rules of hizana not based on Qur'an or Sunnah; differences among principal jurists; welfare of minor

Case summary and decision

Following dissolution of her marriage, the mother had the custody of her minor son. When the boy was about eight years old, the father filed an application under Section 25 of the Guardians and Wards Act, 1890 for custody of the boy. Under the Hanafi law a father is entitled to the custody of a boy above seven. The boy was suffering from a serious illness called 'Hirshtring'. It was contended on behalf of the mother that she, being a doctor, would be able to look after him better. Both the District Judge and the High Court turned down the father's claim. On appeal, the father reiterated before the Appellate Division of the

Supreme Court that in law he was entitled to the boy's custody. He was a senior engineer and had sufficient means to provide for his son's medical treatment. Besides, the mother might remarry at any time. Therefore, the refusal of the two courts to give him custody of the boy had been arbitrary. The mother submitted that she had been looking after the boy with utmost care and providing him all necessary treatment in Bangladesh and abroad. She alone could give him tender affection and take proper care, both emotional and medical, which the critically ill boy needed. For the sake of love and affection for the boy she had given up her highly remunerative job in Saudi Arabia and come back to Bangladesh to live with him and take care of him. The boy himself had expressed his preference to live with her and her relations.

The court observed that case law, while recognizing the principles of Islamic law as to who is entitled to custody of a minor child with reference to his or her sex and age, also took into consideration the welfare of the minor in determining the question. As to the binding nature of Islamic law regarding custody of a minor child, as pleaded by the father's counsel, the court held that there is absolutely no reason to differ from this position if the particular rule of law to be applied is found in the Qur'an or Sunnah. But custody rules are only juristic views and not based on the Qur'an or Sunnah. No consensus having been established among jurists regarding these rules, they differ from school to school. Therefore, they cannot claim immutability, and departure from them would be permissible if circumstances justified it. The court cited with approval the rule laid down in *Zohra Begum* v. *Latif Ahmad Munawwar* (Case 42), that it would be permissible for present-day courts to differ from the rules of hizana as stated in textbooks such as the *Hedaya*, and held that in custody cases the paramount consideration is the child's welfare, and the welfare of the boy required that his custody should be given to his mother.

Comments

This is the leading case on the subject of custody of children in Bangladesh. It is also the first case where the Appellate Division of the Supreme Court asserted the right to differ from the rules of Muslim personal law laid down by classical jurists and found in the distinguished classical compilations, *Hedaya* and *Fatawa Alamgiri*, which are not based on the Qur'an or Sunnah.

59

Abdul Jalil v. Sharon Laily Begum Jalil

Welfare doctrine of custody

Abdul Jalil and Others—Appellants

v.

Sharon Laily Begum Jalil—Respondent

50 DLR (AD) (1998) 55

(A.T.M. Afzal, C.J., Mustafa Kamal, Latifur Rahman,

Md Abdur Rouf, and

B.B. Roy Choudhury, JJ.)

Decided on 30 March 1997

Issues of law

Section 17 of Guardians and Wards Act, 1890; Article 102 of Constitution of Bangladesh; welfare principle in matters of custody of minors

Case summary and decision

Sharon, a young Bangladeshi mother, born in Britain and holding British citizenship, had married Abdul Jalil, a Bangladeshi citizen in England. She filed a writ petition in the High Court, alleging that her four minor children, all British citizens, were being held in custody by Abdul Jalil without lawful authority, and seeking an order for the custody of the children. Her case was that she agreed to visit Bangladesh with the children on the clear understanding that they would not settle in Bangladesh under any circumstances. During their stay in Bangladesh he deceitfully and illegally removed the children from her custody and divorced her. She claimed that it was in the best interest and welfare of the children to be in the custody of their mother, particularly in view of the facts that Abdul Jalil was prone to recurring violence and abuse, and the youngest child was a breastfeeding infant. Abdul Jalil pleaded before the court that the couple felt that it would not be in the best interest of the children to grow up in the lax and immoral social environment of London. So they decided to settle at Dhaka. As the wife led an immoral life at Dhaka, he divorced her and took custody of the children. In view of the facts that: (i) she was leading an immoral life; (ii) she was a Christian who would rear the four Muslim children as Christians in England; and (iii) she had neither any ostensible source of income nor proper education to earn a livelihood for herself, she was not entitled to the custody of the children. Following traditional Hanafi law, the High Court gave provisional custody of the children below the age of seven to the mother and the eldest child who was above seven to the father. The father appealed against this judgment on the ground that the High Court had not considered at all the welfare of the children in the light of his allegations against the mother. The Appellate Division of the Supreme Court held that in matters of custody the paramount consideration is the welfare of the minor, not the legal right of the parties. The term welfare must be read in the largest sense, meaning that every circumstance must be taken into consideration and the court must do what under the circumstances a wise parent acting for the true interest of the child would do or ought to do. The moral and religious well-being of the child must be considered as well as physical well-being. Nor can ties of affection be disregarded. Normally the minor children should be with their mother as long as she does not earn any disqualification for such custody and if, by any unilateral act, the father violates this rule, the aggrieved mother has the right to move the High Court under Article 102 of the Constitution for immediate custody of the children. Relying on the welfare doctrine of custody, the Appellate Division gave provisional custody of the three younger children to the mother and that of the eldest to the father.

60

Jamila Khatun v. Rustom Ali
Wife's past maintenance

Jamila Khatun—Appellant

v.

Rustom Ali—Respondent

48 DLR (AD) (1996) 110

(A.T.M. Afzal C.J., Mustafa Kamal, Latifur Rahman, and Md Abur Rouf, JJ.)

Decided on 7 March 1996

Issues of law

Wife's past maintenance; judicial ijtihad; Article 120 of First Schedule of Limitation Act, 1908

Case summary and decision

Following the birth of a son whom the husband suspected to be illegitimate, he mercilessly assaulted his wife, drove her and the son out of the conjugal home, and refused to provide maintenance for them. After waiting for more than ten years she applied to the family court for dissolution of her marriage and for maintenance for herself and her minor son from the date of her expulsion from the conjugal home. The family court granted dissolution of marriage and past maintenance to her and the minor son, and the Subordinate Judge upheld the decision. The husband challenged the decision on past maintenance in the High Court [*Rustom Ali* v. *Jamila Khatun*]. Relying on section 278 of Mulla's *Principles* (1990) and the old case of *Abdool Futteh Moulvie* v. *Zabunnessa Khatun*, which stated that past maintenance was not payable unless the claim was based on a specific agreement, the High Court allowed the wife maintenance from the date of the institution of the suit before the family court till three months after the decree of dissolution of the marriage. On appeal, the wife's counsel submitted before the Appellate Division of the Supreme Court that the views expressed in *Abdool Futteh Moulvie*, Mulla's *Principles*, the *Hedaya*, and Baillie's *Digest*, relying on which the High Court denied past maintenance to the wife, are traditional views on the subject. In *Sardar Muhammad v. Nasima Bibi* (Case 45) the Lahore High Court reconsidered these views with reference to the Qur'an, Hadith, and other relevant law and literature on the subject, and held that the wife was entitled to maintenance from the date the cause of action arose. The decision has not only been affirmed by the Supreme Court of Pakistan in *Muhammad Nawaz* v. *Khurshid Begum*, and *Ghulam Nabi* v. *Muhammad Asghar*, but also followed by a Division Bench of the Bangladesh High Court in *Sirajul Islam* v. *Helana Begum* (Case 57). Though traditional Hanafi law does not allow past maintenance, the Shafi'i law does. The Appellate Division of the Supreme Court held that in these cases 'the advance by way of ijtihad has been made in the right direction, with strong reason so far undisputed and of course within the bounds of Sunni law'. Therefore, past maintenance was payable to the wife and the child. But because of the law of limitation, she was entitled to past maintenance for only six years prior to the institution of her suit.

Comments

The legal position regarding arrears of maintenance may be summed up as follows. As a result of judicial intervention, in Pakistan and Bangladesh, a Hanafi wife can now claim maintenance from her husband from the date when the cause of action arose, that is, from the date he wrongfully refused or neglected to maintain her. In India, where traditional Hanafi law on the issue still prevails, a Hanafi wife can claim maintenance only from the date of the court decree. She is not entitled to claim maintenance from the date of her husband's wrongful refusal or neglect to maintain her, unless her claim is based on a specific agreement (*Abdool Futteh Moulvie*).

61

Md Hefzur Rahman v. Shamsun Nahar Begum

Maintenance of divorced wife

Md Hefzur Rahman—Appellant

v.

Shamsun Nahar Begum and Another—Respondents

4 MLR (AD) (1999) 41

(A.T.M. Afzal, C.J., Mustafa Kamal, Latifur Rahman, Mohammad Abdur Rouf, and Bimalendu Bikash Roy Chowdhury, JJ.)

Decided on 3 December 1998

Issues of law

Maintenance of divorced wife; marriage; civil contract, not sacrament; purpose and duration of iddat and maintenance during iddat; maintenance of divorced wife until remarriage meaning of *mataa* in Qur'anic verse 2:241; rule of interpretation of Qur'an; basic sources of Islamic law; legislative provisions for destitute divorced women; Order 7, Rule 7 of CPC; Section 3 of Contempt of Court Act, 1926; Section 2 of Muslim Personal Law (Shariat) Application Act, 1937

Case summary and decision

Three months after divorce the wife filed a suit in the family court claiming unpaid dower and maintenance for herself and a minor son at Tk. 1,000 per month for each. The family court directed the husband to pay the wife Tk. 48,000 as unpaid dower, Tk. 1,000 per month as her maintenance for the iddat period and Tk. 1,000 per month for her son's maintenance. On husband's appeal, the District Judge reduced the maintenance rate for each to Tk. 600 per month. On second appeal for further reduction, the High Court refixed it at Tk. 1,000. After giving this decision, the court took up *sou moto* the legal query whether the divorced wife could have claimed maintenance beyond the iddat period. Abdullah Yusuf Ali has translated the word *mataa* of the Qur'anic verse 2:241 as maintenance and the verse as: 'For divorced women maintenance (should be provided) on a reasonable (scale). This is the duty on the righteous' (Ali, 1938: 96). Relying on this translation of the verse the court held that a person after divorcing his wife is bound to maintain her on a reasonable scale until she remarries another person. Accordingly, Shamsun Nahar Begum, the divorced wife would get maintenance at Tk. 1,000 per month from her former husband Hefzur Rahman until she remarried.

The Appellate Division of the Supreme Court held that the word mataa in the Qur'anic verse was never understood as maintenance or 'provision' in the sense of legal, formal, and regular supply of necessaries of life and livelihood to the wife. It is a 'consolatory offering' or parting gift to a divorced woman as a comfort and solace for the trauma she suffers from divorce. Being a gift, it has never been judicially enforceable. Legislative provisions have been made in several Muslim countries, providing mataa to divorced women. But in these legislations mataa was never considered as maintenance but as a recompense for some blame on the part of the husband. There is not a single judgment in any Muslim country, where the verse has been interpreted to mean that maintenance is to be provided to the divorced wife till remarriage. A divorced woman is entitled to maintenance from her husband during the iddat period only. However, the Appellate Division agreed with the wife's counsel that statutory provisions obligating husbands to maintain their unjustly treated and destitute divorced wives would not be against Muslim personal law.

Comments

Though the ruling of the Indian Supreme Court in the celebrated case of *Mohd Ahmed Khan v. Shah Bano Begum* (Case 27) is very similar to the decision in *Hefzur Rahman*, the Bangladesh High Court did not refer to it all. The Appellate Division of the Bangladesh Supreme Court distinguished it from *Hefzur Rahman* on the ground that it was a limited one given in the context of Section 125 of the CrPC, 1973 and the *Hefzur Rahman* decision was a general and unique one. Section 125 was restricted to the class of cases concerned with vagrancy or destitution arising out of the indigence of the divorced wife, but *Hefzur Rahman* was concerned with the broad and general question whether a husband was liable to maintain his wife, which included a divorced wife, *in all circumstances and at all events*. [For a detailed analysis of *Hefzur Rahman*, see A.M. Serajuddin (2011: 222–32). The book suggests that, within the Islamic legal framework, a strong case can be made out for post-divorce maintenance of distressed Muslim wives.]

PART II

TEXT OF CASES

SECTION I

COLONIAL INDIA

Aga Mahomed Jaffer Bindaneem v. Koolsom Bee Bee

JUDGMENT

LORD DAVEY. This appeal and cross-appeal from the Court of the Recorder of Rangoon deal with questions which have arisen in the administration of the estate of Hadji Hoosain Bindaneem, a Mahomedan of the Shiah sect. The testator died in February, 1890, leaving one widow, Koolsom Bee Bee (respondent in the principal appeal and appellant in the cross-appeal), and no children.

The contents of the will, so far as material, may be shortly stated. The testator appointed his nephew Aga Mahomed Jaffer Bindaneem (the appellant in the principal appeal) his sole executor and trustee, and directed him to sell his property and deduct from the proceeds of sale all costs and charges and a commission of 3 per cent. He devoted one fifth part of the remainder (called khooms) and a sum of Rs. 3000 to religious purposes, and directed his executor and trustee to divide the remainder, after deduction of the said sum of Rs. 3000 and Rs. 2500 due to his wife Koolsom Bee Bee for dower, into three equal shares, and to retain one-third share and divide the remaining shares between his heirs, who were his said wife and brother, Aga Abdool Hadee Bindaneem, in the shares and proportions in which they would be entitled to the same according to Mahomedan law, and made a particular provision of the reserved one-third share. The testator declared that his executor and trustee should have power to charge a commission of 3 per cent, on the proceeds of sale of his property, real and personal, and cash.

Part of the testator's property consisted of land with buildings on it. Several questions were raised on taking the accounts of the executor, four of which are submitted for decision in these appeals. 1st. Whether the commission of 3 per cent, to the executor and trustee is payable out of the entire estate, or only out of this one-third which alone the testator could bequeath by his will? 2nd. Whether the widow was entitled to maintenance for any and what period after the testator's death? 3rd. Whether she ought to be charged with an occupation rent for the time during which she continued to reside in the testator's house after his death? 4th. Whether the widow can by Shiah law take any share by inheritance in the land on which the buildings stand as well as in the value of the buildings.

The widow also claimed adversely to the estate to be entitled to a sum of Rs. 30,000 owing to the testator on deposit notes of the Bank of Bengal, which she alleged the testator had given to her on the Monday preceding the Friday on which he died.

To deal with the last-mentioned question first. The deposit notes signed by the agent of the bank are in the form of receipts from the testator of the sum mentioned in them as a deposit bearing interest at the rate mentioned to remain till notice of twelve months on either side expires. They contain in the margin the words 'not transferable', and are not in a form which would entitle the bearer of the notes to the debts created thereby as transferee thereof. The respondent Koolsom Bee Bee in her evidence stated that on the day in question the testator, being then indisposed (but not apparently in contemplation of his early death), handed her the notes with certain formalities, and added, 'after taking a bath I will go to the bank and transfer the papers to your name.' Her story to this extent is confirmed by two witnesses, who said they were present. The testator never did transfer the notes in the bank, or do any act to complete Koolsom Bee Bee's title.

The learned Recorder has expressed doubts as to the truth of the story told by Koolsom Bee Bee and her witnesses, but he has also held that, even if evidence be accepted, the gift was incomplete, and that she is not therefore, entitled to the money on deposit.

As their Lordships entirely agree with the Recorder on the latter point, it is unnecessary for them to express any opinion on the value of the evidence. It is quite clear that the effect of handing the notes was not to transfer the debts on to give the widow the dominion over them, or enable her to recover the moneys secured by the notes. At most the evidence shows an intention to make such a transfer, but the gift is incomplete, and no legal effect can be given to it. There is no question here of a donatio mortis causa in the English sense, even if such a mode of passing property were known to the Mahomedan law.

Their Lordships also agree with the learned Recorder that the executor's commission can be paid only out of the one-third part of the testator's estate which passed by his will. It is given no doubt, by way of remuneration, but it is a gratuitous bequest, and nothing more than a legacy to the executor, and certainly not in any sense a debt.

The learned Recorder has decided that the widow is entitled to maintenance at the rate of Rs. 150 per mensem for one year after the testator's death, and he has done so on the authority of a passage of the Koran quoted by Ameer Ali J. in his work on the Personal Law of Mahomedans, in which the text-writer makes the observation that several jurists have held that a wife has a right to be maintained out of her husband's estate for a year, independently of any share she may obtain in the property left by him. Unfortunately the writer does not give any references in support of his statement, and counsel have not been able to furnish their Lordships with any. On the other hand, the Hedaya (book iv, ch. Xv, s.3) says expressly, 'Maintenance is not due to a woman after her husband's decease,' and gives reasons for so holding. The Imameea (Baillie 1869 p. 171), after saying that it would seem that, after the death of her husband, the widow has no right to a residence except in the single case of her being pregnant, says: 'A widow has no right to maintenance even though she be pregnant.'

Their Lordships on these authorities must hold that a Mahomedan widow is not entitled to maintenance out of her husband's estate in addition to what she is entitled to by inheritance or under his will. They do not care to speculate on the mode in which the text quoted from the Koran which is to be found Sura II., vv.241–242, is to be reconciled with the law as laid down in the Hedaya and by the author of the passage quoted from Baillie's Imameea. But it would be wrong for the Court on a point of this kind to attempt to put their own construction on the Koran in opposition to the express ruling of commentators of such great antiquity and high authority.

The executor in his accounts charged the widow with an occupation rent for the period of eleven months during which she continued to occupy the testator's house after his death. She objected to the charge on the ground that she had never contracted to pay a rent, and the learned Recorder has decided in her favour. Their Lordships do not disagree with the Recorder. It is quite true that when one occupies the house of another with his permission there is prima facie an implied contract to pay an occupation rent. But this implication may be rebutted by shewing the circumstances under which possession was taken, e.g., that the house was lent to the occupier, or that he was a caretaker. In this case the widow's occupation is referable to the previous occupation by her husband and herself, and as one of the heirs and one of the residuary legatees she had an interest in the house (apart from the land). No notice appears to have been given her that she would be charged a rent, and their Lordships think that in the circumstances of the case they cannot imply a contract on her part to pay a rent, but they must treat her as having occupied the house until sale on behalf of herself and the other parties interested as caretaker.

There only remains the question raised on the widow's behalf that she is entitled to share in the land on which the buildings stand as well as in the value of the buildings themselves. The argument urged by Mr. Branson was that the text from Baillie's Imameea, p. 295, quoted by the learned Recorder, refers only to agricultural land, and that a childless widow is, according to the proper construction of that text, entitled by Shiah law to share in land forming the site of buildings. The argument is characterised by novelty and boldness. It is unsupported by any authority, and is contrary to the accepted doctrine on the subject. Their Lordships have no hesitation in agreeing with the learned Recorder in rejecting it.

Their Lordships, therefore, will humbly advise Her Majesty that the final decree of the learned Recorder, dated 14 September, 1893, be reversed so far as it decrees, '7. That the plaintiff Koolsom Bee Bee is entitled to be paid maintenance out of the estate at the rate of Rs. 150 per month for twelve months', and, instead, thereof, it be declared, 'that the plaintiff Koolsom Bee Bee is not entitled to maintenance out of the estate after the date of the testator's death', and in other respects, that the decree be affirmed. As the appeal of the appellant Aga Mahomed Jaffer Bindaneem has partly failed and partly succeeded, there will be no order as to the costs of that appeal. The appellant Koolsom Bee Bee must pay to Aga Mahomed Jaffer Bindaneem the costs of her appeal. The other respondents in each appeal have not appeared, and there are no costs.

4

Ghulam Kubra Bibi v. Mohammad Shafi

JUDGMENT

Mohammad Shafi sued Mt. Ghulam Kubra for restitution of conjugal rights. He also impleaded her parents and asked that an injunction should be issued against them to restrain them from interfering in his marital relations with his wife. The defence taken by Mt. Ghulam Kubra was that she was never married to Mohammad Shafi. There was also a question whether the woman was of age at the time when she was married. Evidence was led by either side. The Mullah appeared and he said that he read the nikah at the instance of the grandfather of the girl. He categorically denied that anyone was sent to the girl to enquire from her whether she agreed to the marriage. One Mistri Abdul Karim, on the other hand, vaguely deposed that there were two witnesses of the nikah. He did not give their names. Two witnesses, Mohammad Ramzan and Mohammad Din were produced who alleged that they were the witnesses of the nikah. They were again laconic, because they stopped at that, and did not give any detail as to what was done by them. Mohammad Ramzan admitted that he was the neighbour of the plaintiff. Mohammad Din did not deny that the plaintiff was working with him for the last 8 or 9 years.

The trial Judge held that the girl was of age when she was married. He was of the view that the marriage had been proved. He, therefore, granted a decree as prayed for against all the defendants. An appeal was preferred to the District Court. It was admitted by both the parties before the learned Additional Judge that the girl was of age when the marriage was held. The Judge maintained the decree for restitution of conjugal rights. But he did not think it necessary to issue an injunction to the parents of the girl. He, therefore, accepted the appeal to this extent, that he set aside the portion of the order relating to injunction. Mt. Ghulam Kubra has come upon further appeal to this court against the decree granting restitution of conjugal rights. Mohammad Shafi has also come up on appeal with a request that the order issuing injunction should be restored. This judgment will cover both the cases.

According to Mohamedan law, it is absolutely necessary that the man or someone on his behalf and the woman or someone on her behalf should agree to the marriage at one meeting, and the agreement should be witnessed by two adult witnesses. As women are in pardah in this part of the country it is customary to send a relation of the woman to her inside the house accompanied by two witnesses. The relation asks the girl within the hearing of the witnesses whether she authorizes him to agree to the marriage on her behalf for the dower money offered by the husband. He explains to her the detail of the dower proposed. When the girl says 'yes' or signifies her consent by some other method, the three persons come out. The future husband and those three persons are then placed before the Mullah. The Mullah asks the boy whether he offers to marry the girl on payment of the specified dower. He says 'yes'. Then the relation, who had gone inside, tells the Mullah that he is the agent of the girl. The Mullah asks him whether he agrees to the marriage on payment of the specified dower. The relation says 'yes'. The witnesses are present there so that if the Mullah has any doubt he should question them as to whether the relation is a duly authorized agent of the girl. Directly both sides have said 'yes' the Mullah reads the scriptures and the marriage is complete.

I have been at pains to describe the method which is usually adopted in this part of the country for effecting a marriage in order to show that the vague allegation that there were two witnesses of the nikah has no value and that it should be proved that the whole procedure has been gone through: in particular when the man who read the nikah is positive that no one was sent to the girl to enquire from her whether she was a willing party. It is on the record that the girl was 17 years of age when her marriage was solemnised. It appears that the parties did not know then that according to Mohamedan law a girl becomes major for the purposes of marriage when she reaches the age of puberty, which is presumed to be the age of 15 years. I think they were under the impression that she could not be major upto 18 years of age, as is the general law, and I guess that the girl was, therefore, given away by the grandfather and not personally consulted. For when a girl is minor it is permissible in Mohamedan law that her father or grandfather or other paternal relations should give her away. The marriage is valid and is called a nikah all the same.

It is interesting in this connexion to point out that such nikah also requires two adult witnesses. The witnesses produced in this case have only said that they were the witnesses of the nikah. Who knows whether they were not the witnesses of the giving away of the girl by the grandfather. For the reasons given above I hold that no valid marriage has taken place in this case, and that the plaintiff has, therefore, no right to sue for restitution of conjugal rights. The appeal of Mt. Ghulam Kubra is accepted and the suit of Mohammad Shafi is dismissed with costs throughout. The appeal of Mohammad Shafi is dismissed. No costs in this appeal as the contesting defendants-respondents did not appear.

Suit dismissed.

7

Mansur v. *Azizul*

JUDGMENT

This is an appeal from a decree of the Subordinate Judge, Partabgarh, dated 13th October 1927, affirming a decree of Munsif, Partabgarh, dated 20th July 1927. The facts of the case so far as it is necessary to state them for the purpose of disposing of this appeal are as follows: The plaintiff Mt. Azizul is the first wife of the defendant Mansur Ali. Mansur Ali married a second wife in September 1925. The two wives could not pull on well and the agreement, Ex. 1, was then executed by Mansur Ali on 25th September 1925. It was executed about a week after Mansur Ali married his second wife. The plaintiff went to live in her father's house some time after the execution of the agreement. The plaintiff brought the present suit for recovery of Rs. 58-7-0 arrears of maintenance, against the defendant on the basis of the agreement dated 25th September 1925. The defendant admitted the execution of the agreement but denied his liability to give maintenance to the plaintiff on the ground that the agreement was without consideration and that the plaintiff was not living with him as his wife. The learned Munsif found that it was unsafe for the plaintiff to live in the same house with the defendant's second wife. He found also that the plaintiff had once gone to the defendant's house after the agreement was executed by the defendant, but she had to leave the place and to return to her father's house as she could not pull on well with the defendant's second wife. He held that the deed dated 25th September 1925 was not without consideration and that the plaintiff was entitled to the maintenance even if she did not reside in the defendant's house. He, therefore, decreed the claim. The defendant appealed, but his appeal was dismissed by the learned Subordinate Judge. It was contended before the learned Subordinate Judge that the agreement was without consideration and against public policy. The point that the agreement was against public policy was not expressly taken in the first Court. It was taken in appeal before the learned Subordinate Judge. The learned Subordinate Judge agreed with the learned Munsif that the agreement was not without consideration. He held also that the agreement was not opposed to public policy. He, therefore, dismissed the appeal. The defendant has now come to this Court in second appeal. We think there is no substance in this appeal. The contention cannot be supported. The defendant is bound to maintain his wife during the subsistence of marriage. So long as the right to maintenance lasts, the contract in question subsists and it cannot be treated as devoid of consideration. We should like to note also that this plea was not pressed before us by the appellant's learned counsel.

The appellant's learned counsel has contended before us that the agreement in question is opposed to public policy and the plaintiff is not entitled to maintenance from the defendant under the agreement. We are not prepared to accept this contention.

We have examined the agreement carefully. We are not prepared to hold that the lower Courts were wrong in construing the agreement. It was of course stated in the agreement that the defendant would provide his wife, plaintiff, with food and clothing if she would live with him in his house, but it was expressly provided by the agreement that the plaintiff would be entitled to guzara at Rs. 5 per mensem even if she would not live with him in his house. It was stated at the end of the agreement that if the plaintiff would leave the defendant's house without any sufficient reason and without any fault of the defendant and others, the persons named in the agreement would manage to send her to his (defendant's) house. It has been found in this case that the plaintiff had not left the defendant's house without a sufficient reason. Besides, that statement in the agreement is not binding on the plaintiff. Having examined the whole document carefully we have come to the conclusion that the intention of the parties was that the plaintiff would be entitled to the guzara even if she did not reside in the defendant's house.

The appellant's learned counsel has referred to the ruling of the Bombay High Court in the case of *Bai Fatima* v. *Ali Mahomed Ayub* [1913] 37 Bom. 280 in support of his argument that the agreement is opposed to public policy. It was held in that case that an agreement which provides for, and, therefore, encourages, future separation between the spouses (Mahomedans), is void as being against public policy. The agreement in that case was an agreement made between a Mahomedan husband and his wife providing for certain maintenance to be given to the wife in the event of a future separation between them. With great respect, we find great difficulty in following the view adopted in that case. Moreover, the point raised in that case is not similar to that which arises in this case. No question of separation between husband and wife really arises in this case.

Under the Mahomedan law the maintenance (nafkah) of a wife includes everything connected with her support and comfort such as food, raiment, lodging etc.; and must be provided in accordance with the social position of the parties. The wife is not entitled merely to maintenance in the English sense of the word, but has a right to claim a habitation for her own exclusive use to be provided consistently with the husband's means. It is incumbent on the husband to provide a separate apartment for his wife's habitation to be solely and exclusively appropriated by her, because this is essentially necessary to her and is, therefore, her due, the same as her maintenance, and the word of God appoints her a dwelling house as well as a subsistence.

See Ameer Ali's Mahomedan Law, Vol. 2, p. 449, 3rd edn.

It is incumbent upon a husband to provide a separate apartment for his wife's habitation to be solely and exclusively appropriated to her use so that none of the husband's family, or others may enter without her permission and desire, because this is essentially necessary to her and is, therefore, her due the same as maintenance, and the word of God appoints her a dwelling house as well as a subsistence, and as it is incumbent upon a husband to provide a habitation for his wife, so he is not at liberty to admit any person to a share in it, as this would be injurious to her, by endangering her property, and obstructing her enjoyment of his society; but if she desire it, the husband may then lawfully admit a partner in the habitation as she by such a request voluntarily relinquishes her right; neither is the husband at liberty to intrude upon his wife, his child by another woman, for the same reason. If the husband appoints his wife an apartment within his own house giving her the lock and key, it is sufficient, as the end is by this means fully obtained.

See Hamilton's Hedaya, Vol. 1, pp. 401-2.

If a Mahomedan marries a second wife and finds that his first wife cannot pull on well with his second wife and if he does not or cannot provide a separate apartment or habitation for her exclusive use, and for the sake of preservation of the family peace executes an agreement in her favour giving her maintenance, even if she does not reside in the same house with him and his second wife that agreement is not in our opinion against public policy. This arrangement does not necessarily result in separation between husband and wife. The husband may conveniently manage to visit her in the house which she occupies after leaving his house. By occupying another house she does not necessarily refuse 'herself' to her husband. We think the Courts should not lightly take upon themselves in such cases to declare agreements to be void on the ground of public policy. It should be borne in mind that it is the highest policy of the law that contracts should be enforced. The plaintiff in this case is residing in her father's house. The defendant may conveniently visit her there, if he cares for her. We are not, therefore, prepared to disagree with the finding of the learned Subordinate Judge on the point under consideration. The result is that the appeal fails and must be dismissed. We dismiss the appeal with costs. The decree of the lower appellate Court is confirmed in all respects.

Appeal dismissed.

8

Saiyid Rashid Ahmad v. Anisa Khatun

JUDGMENT

LORD THANKERTON. This is an appeal from a decree of the High Court at Allahabad, dated 1st February 1927, which reversed a decree of the Court of the Subordinate Judge of Bijnor at Moradabad, dated 15th December 1923. The dispute relates to the succession to the estate of Ghiyas Uddin, a Mahomedan, who died on 4th April 1920, leaving considerable movable and immovable property.

The appellants are plaintiffs in the suit, which was instituted on 28th June 1922, and are a brother and sister of Ghiyas Uddin, and, along with respondents 10 to 12, who were impleaded as pro forma defendants, would be heirs to Ghiyas Uddin according to Mahomedan law, if respondents 1 to 6 (who were defendants 1 to 6), are unable to establish their claim to be the widow and legitimate children of Ghiyas Uddin.

The main controversy turns on four stages in the matrimonial history of Anisa Fatima, respondent 1, viz. (1) her marriage to Manzur Husain in 1901; (2) her divorce by Manzur Husain early in 1905; (3) her marriage to Ghiyas Uddin on 28th August 1905; and (4) her divorce by Ghiyas Uddin on or about 13th September 1905. It is admitted that Anisa Fatima was married to Manzur Husain in 1901, but the respondents maintain that the marriage was invalid on the ground that both parties were minor at the time. The Subordinate Judge held the marriage to be valid on the ground that Anisa Fatima was then adult, and Manzur's marriage was contracted through his mother as his guardian, and this conclusion appears to have been accepted by the High Court.

The alleged divorce by Manzur Husain early in 1905 was challenged by the appellants on the grounds that it was not proved, and that, even if proved, it was invalid in respect that Manzur had not then attained the age of discretion. Manzur himself was the only witness as to the fact of divorce, and his evidence was rejected by the Subordinate Judge, but was accepted by the High Court as proving the fact. On consideration of the conflicting evidence as to Manzur's age, the Subordinate Judge held that he had not then reached the age of discretion, but the High Court reached the opposite conclusion. The Subordinate Judge held that the marriage of Ghiyas Uddin to Anisa Fatima was not proved, but this finding was reversed by the High Court, and the appellants acquiesced in the decision of the High Court, and merely maintained the invalidity of this marriage in the event of it being held that Anisa Fatima was then the undivorced wife of Manzur.

The fourth stage was the alleged divorce by Ghiyas Uddin in September 1905. The appellants' case was that on 13th September 1905, Ghiyas Uddin pronounced the triple talak of divorce in the presence of witnesses, though in the absence of the wife, and that the latter received Rs. 1,000 in payment of her dower on the same day, for which a registered receipt is produced; there was also produced a talaknama, or deed of divorce, dated 17th September 1905, which narrates the divorce, and which is alleged to have been given to Anisa Fatima. The respondents denied the fact of the divorce, and in any event, they challenged its validity and effect for reasons which will be referred to later. They maintained that the payment of Rs. 1,000 was a payment of prompt dower, and that the deed of divorce was not genuine, in that it was not written or signed by Ghiyas Uddin. There are concurrent findings by the Courts below that Ghiyas Uddin did pronounce the triple talak of divorce, and that the deed of divorce is genuine, and their Lordships have seen no reason to depart in this case from their usual practice of not disturbing such findings.

The Subordinate Judge held that Ghiyas Uddin irrevocably divorced Anisa Fatima, and that she was therefore not his wife at the date of his death in 1920, and also that respondents 2 to 6, who were admittedly their offspring but all born after the date of divorce, were not legitimate. The High Court came to the contrary conclusion on the ground that the divorce was fictitious and inoperative, because it was a mock ceremony performed by Ghiyas Uddin to satisfy his father, but without any intention on his part that it should be real or effective.

As it was obvious that, in the event of their Lordships agreeing with the conclusion of the Subordinate Judge on this stage of the case, consideration on the earlier stages of the case would be rendered unnecessary, counsel were requested to confine their arguments to this stage in the first instance, and after full consideration of these arguments, their Lordships are of opinion that the decision of the Subordinate Judge was right, and therefore it will be sufficient to deal with this stage alone.

There is nothing in the case to suggest that the parties are not Sunni Mahomedans governed by the ordinary Hanafi law, and in the opinion of their Lordships, the law of divorce applicable in such a case is correctly stated by Sir R.K. Wilson, in his Digest of Anglo-Mahomedan Law (5th Edition) at p. 136 as follows:

> The divorce called 'talak' may be either irrevocable (bain) or revocable (raja). A talak bain, while it always operates as an immediate and complete dissolution of the marriage bond, differs as to one of its ulterior effects according to the form in which it is pronounced. A talak bain may be effected by words addressed to the wife clearly indicating an intention to dissolve the marriage, either (a) once, followed by abstinence from sexual intercourse, for the period called the iddat; or (b) three times during successive intervals of purity, i.e., between successive menstruations, no intercourse taking place during any of the three intervals; or, (c) three times at shorter intervals, or even in immediate succession; or, (d) once, by words showing a clear intention that the divorce shall immediately become irrevocable. The first named of the above methods is called ahsan (best), the second hasan (good), the third and fourth are said to be bidaat (sinful), but are, nevertheless, regarded by Sunni lawyers as legally valid.

In the present case the words of divorce addressed to the wife, though she was not present, were repeated three times by Ghiyas Uddian as follows: I divorce Anisa Khatun for ever and render her haram for me, which clearly showed an intention to dissolve the marriage. There can be no doubt that the method adopted was the fourth above described, and this is confirmed by the deed of divorce, which states that the three divorces were given 'in the abominable form,' i.e., bidaat. The learned Judges of the High Court have erred in treating the divorce as in the ahsan form, instead of the bidaat form.

The talak was addressed to the wife by name, and the case is not affected by the decision of the High Court of Calcutta in *Farzund Hossein v. Janu Bibee* (1878) 4 Cal 588, where the words of divorce were alone pronounced. In the bidaat form the divorce at once becomes irrevocable, irrespective of the iddat (Baillie's Digest, Edn. 2, p. 206). It is not necessary that the wife should be present when the talak is pronounced, *Ma Me v. Kallander Ammal* A I R 1927 P C 15 at p. 65 (of 54 I. A.) : *Full Chand v. Nawab Ali Chowdhry* (1909) 36 Cal 184, *Asha Bibi v. Kadir Ibrahim Rowther* (1910) 33 Mad 22 at p. 23 and though her right to alimony may continue until she is informed of the divorce.

Their Lordships are of opinion that the pronouncement of the triple talak by Ghiyas Uddin constituted an immediately effective divorce, and, while they are satisfied in such a conclusion on the evidence in the present case, they are of opinion that the validity and effectiveness of the divorce, would not be affected by Ghiyas Uddin's mental intention that it should not be a genuine divorce, as such a view is contrary to all authority. A talak actually pronounced under compulsion or in jest is valid and effective: Baillie's Digest, Edn.2, p. 298; Ameer Ali's Mahomedan Law, Edn. 3, Vol. II, p. 518; Hamilton's Hidaya, Vol. I, p. 211.

The respondents sought to found on the admitted fact that for about fifteen years after the divorce Ghiyas Uddin treated Anisa Fatima as his wife and his children as legitimate, and on certain admissions of their status said to have been made by appellant I and respondent pro forma 10, who are brothers of Ghiyas Uddin; but once the divorce is held proved such facts could not undo its effect or confer such a status on the respondents.

While admitting that upon divorce by the triple talak, Ghiyas Uddin could not lawfully remarry Anisa Fatima until she had married another and the latter had divorced her or died, the respondents maintained that the acknowledgment of their legitimacy by Ghiyas Uddin, subsequent to the divorce raised the presumption that Anisa Fatima had in the interval married another who had died or divorced her, and that Ghiyas Uddin had married her again, and that it was for the appellants to displace that presumption. In support of this contention, they founded on certain dicta in the judgment of this Board in *Habibur Rahman Chowdhury v. Altaf Ali Chowdhury*, AIR 1922 PC 159. Their Lordships find it difficult to regard this contention as a serious one, for these dicta directly negative it. The passage relied on, which related to indirect proof of a

Mahomedan marriage by acknowledgment of a son as a legitimate son, is as follows (p. 120 of 48 *I.A.*):

> It must not be impossible upon the face of it, i.e., it must not be made when the ages are such that it is impossible in nature for the acknowledger to be the father of the acknowledgee, or when the mother spoken to in an acknowledgment, being the wife of another, or within prohibited degrees of the acknowledger, it would be apparent that the issue would be the issue of adultery or incest. The acknowledgment may be repudiated by the acknowledgee. But if none of these objections occur, then the acknowledgment has more than evidential value. It raises a presumption of marriage—a presumption which may be taken advantage of either by a wife-claimant or a claimant. Being however a presumption of fact, and not juris et de jure, it is, like every other presumption of fact, capable of being set aside by contrary proof.

The legal bar to remarriage created by the divorce in the present case would equally prevent the raising of the presumption. If the respondents had proved the removal of that bar by proving the marriage of Anisa Fatima to another after the divorce and the death of the latter or his divorce of her prior to the birth of the children and their acknowledgment as legitimate, the respondents might then have had the benefit of the presumption but not otherwise.

Their Lordships are therefore of opinion that the appeal should be allowed, that the decree of the High Court should be reversed, and that the decree of the Subordinate Judge should be restored, the appellants to have the costs of this appeal and their costs in the High Court. Their Lordships will humbly advise His Majesty accordingly.

Appeal allowed.

10

Sainuddin v. *Latifannessa Bibi*

JUDGMENT

SHAMS-UL-HUDA, J. This appeal arises out of a suit brought by plaintiff for restitution of conjugal rights against his wife the defendant No.1. The facts of the case are shortly these: The parties were married in 1308[1908] when a *kabinnamah* was executed but not registered. This document was subsequently lost. A dispute then arose between the parties which was settled by the execution and registration of a second *kabinnamah* in 1313[1913] Among other matters the new *kabinnamah* provided that the plaintiff would not take a second wife without the defendant's permission. The document concluded as follows: 'Be it noted that if I violate any of the aforesaid conditions or any portion thereof, I delegate to you my own power of giving three *talaqs* such as is possessed by males. Whenever you choose you may talaq or repudiate your person three times and then take another husband.'

It is found that between 1313[1913] and 1320[*sic*] the plaintiff appellant took a second wife without obtaining the permission of the defendant. When the present suit for the restitution of conjugal rights was instituted the wife gave herself three divorces in accordance with Mahomedan Law under the authority given to her by the husband. Both the lower Courts have dismissed the plaintiff's suit and hence this appeal.

It has been contended before us that a post-nuptial delegation of the power of divorce or *tufweez-i-talaq*, as it is called by Musalman lawyers, is not valid. No authority has been cited for such a proposition. A reference to books on Mahomedan Law makes it abundantly clear that such delegation is valid. In fact most of the instances of *tufweez* given in the books are postnuptial and refer to authority given by a person to another who is already his wife. Reference may be made to Baillie's Digest of Mahomedan Law, p. 211. The more difficult questions, however, that have been raised before us are the following:

I   That the authority given to the wife could only be exercised immediately in the *majlis* in which it was given and was lost, not being so exercised.

II   That the authority should have been exercised immediately on the happening of the event upon which it was contingent.

III   That the delegation was revocable and the institution of the suit amounted to such revocation.

Before proceeding to a discussion of these questions it would be convenient to refer to certain well-established principles of Mahomedan Law with reference to which the law on the subject of 'delegation' has been discussed in the text books. Mahomedan lawyers make a distinction between *isbatat* or acts which create rights and *isqatat*, i.e., acts which only extinguish existing rights. Mr. Justice Abdur Rahim refers to the distinction in his extremely valuable work on Mahomedan Jurisprudence at p. 195. *Tumleek* which means making another the *malik* or owner of a thing and includes ordinary cases of sale, gift and similar other transactions, belongs to the former. The *isqatat* include release, divorce, emancipation of slaves, etc. Leaving aside exceptions to the general rule, it is a well-established rule of Mahomedan Law that in cases of *tumleek*, *taleeq* is not valid, i.e., it is not valid to make the transaction dependent on any condition or contingency....

All *tumleeks* must as a rule be unconditional, they must be accepted immediately in the *majlis* (sitting) itself and it is open in such cases to the *mumallik*, (i.e., the person making another the malik of his rights) to revoke the *tumleek* before acceptance whereas in *isqatat* (i.e., acts causing extinction of rights) *taleeq* is valid, i.e., these may be made dependent on conditions and generally, acceptance in the *majlis* is not necessary, nor is the authority revocable. Mahomedan lawyers have found it difficult to apply to cases of delegation of divorce all the incidents of a *tumleek*. They argue that this is a special kind of *tumleek*, for the reason that in ordinary cases of *tumleek* on the transference of a right, the transferor is completely deprived of his right which after the transfer, vests in the transferee, but in the case of a delegation of the authority to divorce, the husband is not deprived of his right and both husband and the wife have in their hands the power of divorce. It is also not strictly included in the *isqatat* because the delegation does not by itself extinguish any rights, though the exercise of the delegated authority does. They hold that the delegation of an authority to divorce partakes only partially of the character of *tumleek*. It therefore admits of *taleeq*, that is, it may be made dependent on conditions. Accordingly they lay down special rules for cases of this class. These may be stated thus:

(1) That where the delegation is unconditional and the woman is present in the *majlis*, the delegated authority must be accepted and exercised then and there, or as the Mahomedan lawyers call it in the *majlis* as in ordinary cases of *tumleek*.

(2) That unlike ordinary *tumleeks*, acceptance in the *majlis* is not essential, so that if the woman is absent she may accept the delegation in the *majlis* in which she hears of it and must exercise the authority then and there, unless any time is fixed, or she is expressly allowed to exercise the power at any time she chooses.

(3) That there is no power of revocation in such cases.

(4) That the delegation may be contingent or be subject to conditions, and in such cases the contingency must have happened and the conditions must have been fulfilled before the delegated authority could be exercised. This is unlike *tumleek* in which when coupled with any condition, either the condition becomes void or it vitiates the transaction. In cases of conditional or contingent delegation the power must be exercised as soon as the contingency has happened or if the fulfilment of the condition is not in the immediate power of the wife, when the condition is fulfilled, unless as in the case of conditional delegation, words are used to indicate that the power is to be exercised within a particular period or at any time the wife chooses.

The following passages translated from text books on Mahomedan Law amply establish these propositions. The original texts are quoted in the Appendix to this judgment.

(i) 'It is stated in the Zakhira that this *tumleek* (i.e. delegation of the right of divorce) is different from other *tumleeks* inasmuch as it continues after the *majlis*, when the woman is absent, and is not dependent on acceptance. It is therefore clear that this kind of *tumleek* does not require the acceptance on which the validity of other *tumleeks* depend, because it is a *tumleek* which ends alone with the person giving it without acceptance and capable of being revoked': *Fathul-Qadeer, a commentary on the Hedaya by Shaikhul-Islam Ibn-i-Haman*, Vol. III, p. 411, Cal. Ed.

(ii) 'The woman is authorized (to exercise the power of divorce that may be delegated to her) in the *majlis* in which she comes to know of the delegation either by being present when the delegation is made or (if absent) when she hears of it. But if she allows one or more days to pass, she is not entitled to exercise the authority after the *majlis*, except where the husband adds to the expression 'Divorce yourself' or similar expressions, words such as 'when you desire' or 'whenever you desire', in which case the exercise of the authority will not be confined to the *majlis* and the husband has no right to revoke the authority given': *Durrul-Mukhtar*, Book 2, p. 475, 476 (Egyptian Ed.).

(iii) 'The use of the words "when" or "whenever" embraces all times as if the man had said "at any time you desire" and the delegation is not confined to the *majlis*': *Raddul-Muhtar*, Vol. II, p. 487 (Egyptian Ed.).

(iv) 'A delegation is confined to the *majlis*, but where words "when you choose" are added, the woman is authorized to divorce either in the *majlis* or after it': *Bahrur Raiq*, Vol. III, p. 354 Egyptian Ed. (Exactly the same language is used in *Hedaya*, Egyptian Ed., p. 435.)

(v) 'If a man says to his wife "your business is in your hand when or whenever you desire" it is open to her to divorce herself at once in the *majlis* or outside it at any time she desires': *Fatawa-i-Alamgiri*, Vol. I, p. 562, Cal. Ed.

(vi) 'A man left the business of his wife in her hand on this condition that when he beat her without fault she could divorce herself whenever she wished. Then she went out of the house without her husband's permission. The husband then beat her. Would her business be in her hand? It is said it would not be in her hand if her prompt dower has been paid, but if it is not paid, it is open to her to go to her father's house without his permission, or to refuse her person to him for the realization of her prompt dower. In that case her going out of the house will not be a fault (and the beating being without fault she would have the right to divorce herself)': *Fatawa-i-Alamgiri*, Vol. I, p. 559, Cal. Ed.

In this case there was a clear delegation of the right of divorce which the defendant was expressly allowed to exercise 'whenever she chose.' She has exercised that power and thus has put an end to the marital relation between her and her husband. The suit for restitution of conjugal rights cannot therefore lie, and has been rightly dismissed. The appeal fails and is dismissed with costs.

FLETCHER, J. I agree.

11

Moonshee Buzul-ul-Raheem v. *Luteefut-oon-Nissa*

JUDGMENT

Judgment was postponed and now delivered by The Right Hon. Lord KINGSDOWN.

This suit was instituted in the Civil Court of the Twenty-four *Pergunnahs* by the Respondent, *Luteefut-oon-Nissa*, suing as a pauper against the Appellant, *Moonshee Buzul-ul-Raheem*, to whom she had been married, to recover her *dyn-mohr*, consisting of the sum of Rs. 10,000 and of 1,000, gold *mohurs* valued at Rs. 16,000, amounting together to Rs. 26,000.

This sum was payable by the Appellant to the Respondent in the event of the dissolution of the marriage, and she alleged in her plaint that the Appellant had dissolved the marriage by divorcing her. She further stated, that two instruments by which she was alleged to have given up her *dyn-mohr* had been obtained from her by the force or fraud of the Appellant, and were of no avail to bar her rights.

The Appellant, in his answer, denied the divorce as stated by the Respondent, but alleged that two instruments, one a *Khoolanamah*, had been executed by her, by which she released her *dyn-mohr*, and which deeds he insisted were binding upon her.

The *Zillah* Judge was of opinion, that no divorce except by *Khoola* had been proved by the Respondent, but he held that the plea of the Appellant admitted a divorce by *Khoola*, and that the instruments set up by him as containing a release of the *dyn-mohr* were fraudulent and void, and that, therefore, the marriage being dissolved, the Respondent was entitled to recover her claim, and he decreed accordingly.

This decision by the *Zillah* Court was confirmed by the *Sudder*, and from the order of the *Sudder* the present appeal is brought.

Upon the facts, we think, that there is little doubt. The question is mainly one of Mahomedan law, and we should not lightly in such a case disturb the concurrent decision of two Courts. But we are quite satisfied that the decision is conformable both to law and to justice. It appears that by the Mahomedan law divorce may be made in either of two forms; *Talak or Khoola*. A divorce by *Talak* is the mere arbitrary act of the husband, who may repudiate his wife at his own pleasure, with or without cause. But if he adopts that course he is liable to repay her dowry, or *dyn-mohr*, and, as it seems, to give up any jewels or paraphernalia belonging to her. A divorce by *Khoola* is a divorce with the consent, and at the instance of the wife, in which she gives or agrees to give a consideration to the husband for her release from the marriage tie. In such a case the terms of the bargain are matter of arrangement between the husband and wife, and the wife may, as the consideration, release her *dyn-mohr* and other rights, or make any other agreement for the benefit of the husband.

It seems, that according to existing usage, a divorce by *Talak* is not complete and irrevocable by a single declaration of the husband: but a divorce by *Khoola* is at once complete and irrevocable from the moment when the husband repudiates the wife and the separation takes place.

In these particulars the two modes of divorce differ. But there is one condition which attends every divorce, in whichever way it takes place, namely, that the wife is to remain in seclusion for a period of some months after the divorce, in order that it may be seen whether she is pregnant by her husband, and she is entitled to a sum of money from her husband, called her *iddit*, for her maintenance during this period.

At the hearing of this case, two points were made by the Appellant's Counsel. They insisted, first, that the instruments releasing the Respondent's claim under her settlement were valid; and, secondly, that if the *Khoolanamah* executed by the wife were laid out of the case, there was no evidence at all of divorce, and then the marriage was not shown to be dissolved; that the Respondent could not approbate and reprobate the same deed—insist that it was good for the purpose of establishing a divorce, and bad for the purpose of securing to the husband the price which he was to receive for consenting to it.

This objection, however plausible, is founded on a misconception of the real nature of the divorce. The divorce is the sole act of the husband, though granted at the instance of the wife, and purchased by her. The *Khoolanamah* is a deed securing to the husband the stipulated consideration but it does not constitute the divorce. It assumes it, and is founded upon it. The divorce is created by the husband's repudiation of the wife, and the consequent separation. The law might have provided that non-payment of the consideration should invalidate the divorce, but it is clear, as well from the opinion of the Law Officers of the Indian Courts as from the authorities cited at our Bar, that the law is otherwise. The non-payment by the wife of the consideration for the divorce no more invalidates the divorce than in England the non-payment of the wife's marriage portion invalidates the marriage.

In this case the husband, while denying a divorce by *Talak*, not only did not deny but set up a divorce by *Khoola*. He alleged distinctly, in his answer, that the Respondent took from him a *Furuckuttee* (which is a deed of divorcement), that she took from him also the subsistence money or her *iddit*, and gave him a receipt for it, and that she then quitted his house with the assent and under the care of her mother. That a divorce, therefore, had taken place, was the common case of both parties, and the only question was, whether the husband could insist on receiving the consideration for which he says that he had stipulated. This must depend on the validity of the deeds which he sets up in bar of the Respondent's demand. The dissolution of the marriage being admitted, it is for the Appellant to make out that the Respondent has given up the rights which *prima facie* result from the dissolution, and upon this part of the case their Lordships have never felt the least doubt.

Two instruments are relied on by the Appellant: one an *Ibranamah*, or instrument by which the wife is made, out of regard and affection for her husband, voluntarily to release to him all claim to her *dyn-mohr*. This instrument purports to have been made on the 16th April, 1847. It states that the settlement by which the *dyn-mohr* is secured is in the possession, not of the wife, but of her mother; that the wife, therefore, cannot give up the instrument, and is not aware of what the *dyn-mohr* consists.

There is nothing like satisfactory proof that the Respondent ever gave her assent to this deed with a knowledge of its contents, and the admitted facts of the case make it in the highest degree improbable, almost impossible, that she should have done so.

At the time at which this instrument purports to have been made, the husband had married, or was on the point of marrying, a second wife, as by law he was entitled to do. The evidence of one of the witnesses states, that the marriage took place either in *April*, 1847, or in the following *October*; and from the time of the marriage, and indeed from the time when it was decided upon, their Lordships are quite satisfied from the evidence that the Appellant and the Respondent were equally desirous of a divorce. Indeed, it appears that the second wife stipulated as a condition of her consent to the marriage, that her husband should divorce his first wife. He had the power to do so by *Talak*, but this would not answer his purpose; he desired to get rid of his wife, but to retain her dowry, and he prepared this deed in order that, having procured a release of the dowry, he might exercise his power of divorce. The mother of the wife, however, had possession of the settlement, and refused to give it up, and it seems to have been thought by the husband that it would be impossible for him to establish the *Ibranamah* unless he could procure a confirmation of it, and a surrender of the settlement by the mother, and a divorce by *Khoola*. For this purpose he had recourse to measures of great cruelty; he refused to permit the mother to see her daughter, and by a long series of ill-usage, unless there be much exaggeration in the evidence, injured the health and even endangered the life of the Respondent. The mother, after repeated applications to the *Foujdary* Court for the protection of her daughter, at last yielded, and gave up the settlement; under such circumstances the *Khoolanamah* was obtained, which professed to confirm the *Ibranamah*.

The Courts below have most properly held that instruments so obtained can have no legal effect. They can be of no more avail, when used as a defence against the claims of the wife, than they would have had if the husband were suing upon them as Plaintiff to enforce rights secured to him.

Their Lordships are quite satisfied that the judgment complained of is correct, and they will humbly advise Her Majesty to affirm it, with costs.

12

Zubaida Begum v. Sardar Shah

JUDGMENT

ABDUL RASHID, J. This is a Letters Patent appeal from a decision of a learned Single Judge of this Court reversing the judgment and the decree of the District Judge of Gujranwala. The facts of the case are few and simple. On 26th May 1938, Mt. Zubaida Begum presented a petition under S. 5, Muslim Personal Law (Shariat) Application Act, 1937, against her husband, Sardar Shah, praying that her marriage with the respondent may be dissolved on account of desertion and cruelty. It was alleged in the plaint that the appellant had been married to the respondent about 3½ years ago, that two or three months after the marriage the respondent began to ill-treat her because he was not on good terms with her father. Six months after the marriage the respondent turned out the petitioner and married a second wife. As the respondent had failed to maintain the petitioner and had gone away to Africa, she was entitled to a decree for dissolution of marriage in accordance with the provisions of S. 5 of the Act. The respondent pleaded, inter alia, that he had never ill-treated his wife, that she had been asked to come out to Africa and live with him but had refused to do so. On these pleadings, Mr. Mukerji, Additional District Judge, framed the following issues: (1) Has the plaintiff been neglected and deserted by the defendant? (2) Has she been treated cruelly? (3) If so, is the plaintiff for these reasons entitled to have her marriage dissolved according to her personal law?

The learned Additional District Judge came to the conclusion that no cruelty and desertion on the part of the respondent had been established. In coming to this conclusion the learned Judge relied on a Single Bench ruling of this Court reported in A.I.R. 1931 Lah. 721 and on certain passages in Ameer Ali's Mohammadan Law and Mohammadan Law by Mulla. The petition of Mt. Zubeida Begum was dismissed by the Additional District Judge on 31st March 1939. On 25th March 1939, however, the Dissolution of Muslim Marriages Act, 1939, had come into force. The new Act is intended to consolidate and clarify the provisions of the Muslim law relating to suits for dissolution of marriage and to remove doubts as to the effects of the renunciation of Islam by a married Muslim woman on her marriage tie. S. 2 of the Act does not alter or profess to alter the Muslim law. It merely declares what the provisions of the Muslim law have always been.

A petition for review was filed in the Court of the Additional District Judge, Gujranwala, to the effect that as the judgment has been pronounced on 31st March 1939, the learned judge ought to have taken the provisions of Dissolution of Muslim Marriages Act, 1939, into account. According to the petition for review, the petitioner was entitled to a decree for the dissolution of marriage under cls. (ii) and (viii)(f) of S. 2 of the new Act. Notice of the petition for review was issued to the other side by the learned Additional District Judge. The case was however ultimately heard by the learned District Judge of Gujranwala. The learned Judge came to the conclusion that on the evidence produced by the respondent himself it was established that he had failed to provide for his wife for a period of over two years and that he had married another wife and had not treated the petitioner equitably in accordance with the injunctions of the Quran. The learned judge accepted the petition for review and granted the petitioner a decree for dissolution of marriage. This judgment, as mentioned already, was upset by a learned Single Judge of this Court. The first point urged by Mr. Abdul Karim was that as a petition for review had been accepted by the learned District Judge of Gujranwala, an appeal lay to this Court under O. 43, R. 1(w), Civil P.C. The learned counsel contended that in the appeal preferred by Sardar Shah against the order passed on review only three grounds were open to him. These three grounds are enumerated in R. 7 of O. 47, Civil P.C. The learned counsel maintained that the learned Single Judge had erred in taking other grounds into account in disposing of the appeal. In my opinion, this contention is devoid of all force. Sardar Shah preferred an appeal to this Court not only under O. 43, R. 1(w), Civil P.C., but also under S. 38, Punjab Courts Act. He therefore preferred an appeal on merits also against the decree passed by the learned District Judge in favour of Mt. Zubeida Begum. In that appeal, it was open to him to challenge the decree of the learned District Judge on every ground on which a decree can be challenged in a first appeal.

The next point urged by Mr. Abdul Karim was that it had been established from the evidence of Sharif Shah, Mukhtar of the respondent, that appellant had not been treated equitably in accordance with the injunctions of the Quran. It is laid down in the surat-un-nissa of the Quran that a Muslim is permitted to marry two, three or four wives provided he treats them with equality, but if he is apprehensive that he will not be able to do justice between them, he is enjoined to marry one wife only. The words of the holy Quran leave no room for doubt in this respect. They are as follows: *Fankihoo ma Taba Lakum minannisai masna wa Sulsa wa Ruba; Fain khiftum alla Taadiloo Fawahidatum.* In other words, if a man cannot treat his two wives with perfect equality, he is enjoined to marry only one wife. Some commentators have taken a very strict view of this injunction of the Quran. They state that the husband must not only treat his two wives with perfect equality so far as provision for worldly goods, such as clothes, jewellery, house, etc., is concerned; but that he must also treat them with perfect equality so far as love, affection and sentiment are concerned. It would be a nice question for consideration when it arises whether it is possible for a human being to treat two wives with perfect equality as far as love is concerned. That question, however, does not arise in the present case. In the present case, the evidence makes it perfectly clear that while the other wife is being provided with a home and maintenance, no maintenance has been provided for the appellant. The statement of Sharif Shah, the Mukhtar of the respondent, was recorded before the framing of the issues. He stated as follows:

> My son the respondent married a second wife two years after his marriage with the plaintiff. As the defendant had no child by her and he wanted to go to Africa he was anxious to marry another wife and have a child before migrating. I as a step-father of the defendant did try to dissuade him from adopting this course but he would not listen. Defendant left for Africa in Chet two years ago. Defendant has not sent any money to the plaintiff but he has been writing to her to follow him to Africa. I have not contributed anything to the plaintiff as I am not on visiting terms with her father who called me a cheat.

It is clear, therefore, that during the last two years the respondent has not sent any money either to the appellant directly or through his father. He has written to her from Africa to go out to him. He has however, as pointed out by the learned District Judge, not sent her any money for the passage. In these circumstances, it must be held that the husband has neglected or has failed to provide for the maintenance of the wife for a period of two years. Mr. Khurshadi Zaman contended that her refusal to go out to Africa was unreasonable and had she gone out to Africa with her husband he would have maintained her. In my opinion, the letter of the husband asking the appellant to go out to Africa is merely a subterfuge. Had he been anxious to get her to Africa, he would have made arrangements to pay for her passage. In his statement as a witness Sharif Shah, the Mukhtar of the respondent, has not given any indication that any provision has been made for housing and feeding the appellant in a suitable manner. She is not bound to go and live with her father-in-law especially as he is not on good terms with her own father. In these circumstances, it was incumbent of the respondent to provide for the maintenance of his wife either by remitting a part of his salary directly to her or by sending her an allowance through his father. As he has failed to do this, it cannot be said that he has treated her equitably in accordance with the injunctions of the Quran referred to above. For these reasons, I would accept this appeal, set aside the decision of the learned Single Judge and restore the judgment and the decree of the learned District Judge granting the appellant a decree dissolving her marriage with the respondent Sardar Shah. The respondent will pay the costs of the appellant throughout.

HARRIES, C.J. I agree.

Appeal accepted.

13

Imambandi v. Haji Mutsaddi

JUDGMENT

MR AMEER ALI. This is an appeal from a judgment and decree of the High Court of Calcutta, dated the 30th August, 1911, which affirmed the decree of the Subordinate Judge of Saran awarding to the plaintiffs possession of a share in certain landed property situated in that district.

The property in suit belonged originally to one Ismail Ali Khan, a wealthy Mahomedan inhabitant of the subdivision of Siwan in the Saran district. The plaintiffs allege that on his death in March, 1906, he left him surviving three widows and several children, and that from one of these widows, named Enayet-uz-Zohra, acting for herself and for her two minor children, they purchased the share in suit for the possession of which they brought the present action.

It appears that shortly after Ismail Ali Khan's death, the contesting defendants 1 to 7 applied to the Revenue Courts for mutation of names (as proprietors) in the Collector's records, and, as usually happens in these cases in India, especially in Mahomedan families, immediately this application was made, a claim was put forward on behalf of Enayet-uz-Zohra and her children that they were equally entitled with the other heirs of Ismail Ali Khan to have their names entered as co-sharers in the estate by right of inheritance, the allegation being that Zohra was one of his lawfully wedded wives and that her children were his legitimate issue. The Revenue Courts rejected her claim, holding that it was not established to their satisfaction that she was Ismail Ali Khan's married wife or that the children were his lawful issue. They accordingly made an order directing the registration of the contesting defendants' names in succession to Ismail Ali Khan.

It should the mentioned here that the defendants 1 and 5 are admittedly Ismail Ali Khan's married wives, defendants 2, 3 and 4 are his issue by defendant 1, and defendants 6 and 7 his daughters by defendant 5.

The plaintiffs are dealers in hide and live also at Siwan. There seems to have been litigation between them and Ismail Ali Khan in his life time, and since his death they seem to have espoused Zohra's cause. The deed executed by Zohra bears date the 10th June, 1906, and purports to convey to the plaintiffs the shares of both herself and her minor children, and in the suit they are included as defendants Nos. 8 to 10. The reliefs sought are of a twofold character: *first*, a declaration of the title and status of the plaintiffs' vendors; and *secondly*, a decree in favour of the plaintiffs for possession of the shares covered by the deed of sale.

The contesting defendants denied, as they had done in the Revenue Courts, that Zohra was one of Ismail Ali Khan's married wives or that her children were his legitimate issue, and they further contended that the shares the plaintiffs claimed to recover did not pass under the sale. The sixth issue framed by the Subordinate Judge seems to relate to this point.

The plaint was filed on the 25th March, 1909, but it does not appear to have been admitted until the 2nd April. The contesting defendants filed their written statements in July, 1909; after that the case dragged its slow length along until the 18th June, 1910, when the actual trial began. In the interim, however, various interlocutory orders were made, including an order for the appointment of Zohra as guardian *ad litem* for her children (though her interest in the suit was clearly adverse to theirs).

Admittedly she was never appointed under the Guardians and Wards Act (VIII. Of 1890) a guardian of their property.

The examination in Court of the plaintiffs' witnesses commenced on the 16th June 1910; on the 18th June (the date given in the judgment of the High Court does not appear to agree with the date in the order sheet) they applied for a summons against the defendants for the production of certain *bahis* or account books, belonging to Ismail Ali Khan for the Fasli years 1294 to 1313 (1887-1906). The order on this application was as follows:- 'I decline to issue summons at this stage.' And there, so far as the plaintiffs were concerned, the matter was allowed to rest.

As a large part of the judgments of both the Courts in India is occupied with an examination of these *bahis*, viz., whether they are reliable or not, it is necessary to mention that these very books had been produced and filed in Ismail Ali Khan's life time on his behalf in the litigation between him and the plaintiffs; after his death they were returned to the contesting defendants' pleader, when it was discovered that a large number of leaves were abstracted from several of the books. This was represented to the presiding officer of the Court where the books were filed, but there is nothing to show the result of the representation. The plaintiffs' case appears to have closed on the 26th June, and on the following day the defendants commenced to examine their witnesses. On the same day they produced the *bahis*. The Subordinate Judge's order on their petition is in these terms: 'On the defendants' application filing therewith the *bahis* from 1294 to 1311 *Fasli*, it is ordered that they be kept with the records, and that the plaintiffs' pleader be informed accordingly.' About this time the missing leaves turned up mysteriously. The trial Judge says he received them by post from some unknown source; and apparently after receipt, he handed them to the proper officer. Upon becoming aware of this fact the defendants applied to the Court that the torn out leaves thus re-discovered might be admitted in evidence; and on the 29th June, whilst the trial was proceeding and evidently in the presence of the pleader for the opposite party, the Subordinate Judge ordered that the leaves in question should be used as evidence, and marked them as Exhibits F 1 to F 5.

It is hardly likely that the leaves were originally abstracted by the defendants and that this roundabout way was adopted for the purpose of getting the books admitted as evidence. On the face of it, the suggestion appears to be absurd.

The use the contending defendants wished to make of the account books, contain regular entries of payments by Ismail Ali Khan to his admitted wives, defendants 1 and 5, under the honorific designation of *Haveli Kalan* ('senior mansion') and *Haveli Khurd* ('junior mansion'), being euphemisms for wives. There is no entry, however, of any payment to Zohra. The defendants accordingly asked the Court to draw from the absence of any such entry in her name the inference that she was not Ismail Ali Khan's wife and did not hold the same position as the other ladies. Counsel for the plaintiffs seems to have been greatly impressed by the argument; in fact he appears to have conceded that, if the books were to be relied upon Zohra's claim must fail. He was thus driven to challenge their genuineness. The Subordinate Judge appears to have taken the same view; he thought that the books must be first eliminated before the direct evidence could be properly appraised and this reasoning runs through the judgments of both the Courts in India.

The trial Judge on certain grounds came to the conclusion that the *bahis* must be put aside from consideration as unreliable. He then proceeded to discuss the oral testimony; and in the result found that Zohra was, in fact, a wife of Ismail Ali Khan, and that the defendants Nos. 9 and 10 were his children by her. He accordingly decreed the plaintiffs' claim. And his decree has been affirmed by the High Court of Calcutta. The learned Judges of the High Court also felt impressed with the absence of entries in the *bahis* in Zohra's name, and therefore proceeded to deal with them first. This mode of treatment has been strongly assailed, not without reason, before this Board. It seems to their Lordships that the true criterion for the determination of the question at issue was missed by both the Courts. The onus of establishing the title of their vendors lay primarily on the plaintiffs; the evidence furnished by the books was negative and inferential and in substance directed to the corroboration of the defendants' witnesses, who denied that Zohra was one of Ismail Ali Khan's wives. Rule 1, Order XIII of the Civil Procedure Code requires the parties or their pleaders to produce at the first hearing of the suit all the documentary evidence of every description in their possession or power 'on which they intend to rely.' But it does not exclude the discretion of the Court to receive any such documentary evidence at any subsequent stage. In the present case the books had been filed previously in another Court, and when produced on the 27th June they were in fact received and ordered to be placed with the records. There seems to have been no objection to their reception for non-compliance with the provisions of the Code. If the plaintiffs had taken notes of certain entries in the books, as is alleged they had done when the *bahis* were in the other Court, they could surely, have cross-examined the defendants' witnesses, who were called to prove the books, as to the discrepancies. Their Lordships are not satisfied that the books are not the genuine account books of Ismail Ali Khan. What effect the absence in them of entries in Zohra's name may have in the consideration of the general evidence is another matter.

In the absence of any statutory provision making compulsory the registration of Mahomedan marriages, the Indian Courts, in case of a dispute as to the *factum* of a marriage, are usually left to discover, or attempt to discover, the truth from a mass of conflicting and often very unsatisfactory evidence of witnesses. Such has been the burden cast on the Courts in the present instance. The plaintiffs have endeavoured to prove in two ways that Zohra was one of Ismail Ali Khan's wives, viz., *first*, by direct evidence of an actual marriage; and *secondly*, by the acknowledgment by him of her children as his legitimate issue, and by the presumption of marriage, arising from such acknowledgment. The defendants, on the other hand, tried to show that Zohra was a woman of loose character, with the object apparently of establishing that it was most unlikely a man in Ismail Ali Khan's position would marry such a person. They also called a number of witnesses, who are said to have been on terms of intimacy with him, to state that they never heard him speak of Zohra as his wife. Including the inference from the account books, all the evidence on the defendants' side is purely and naturally negative. In their Lordships' opinion, the oral testimony regarding the solemnization of a marriage accompanied by ostentatious ceremonies and high dower is by no means satisfactory, and if the case had stood there, the absence of Zohra's name in Ismail Ali Khan's account books might have weighed heavily against her. But their Lordships find clear evidence of a reliable character regarding his acknowledgment of her children. Her case, therefore, comes within the rule of Mahomedan law to which Garth, C.J., and Wilson, J., (afterwards Sir Arthur Wilson,) gave expression in *Mahatala Bibee* v. *Prince Ahmed Haleem-oozooman* (1881) 10 C.L.R. 293.

In their Lordships' opinion, the legal presumption arising in favour of Zohra from the acknowledgment of the children is not displaced by the mere inference the defendants seek to draw from the absence of entries in her favour in Ismail Ali Khan's account books. Such absence is capable of explanation, and it is possible she could have explained it had her attention been called to the matter. One explanation, however, is on the surface: on the facts proved in the case it is quite clear that this lady's father, though belonging to the same clan as Ismail Ali Khan, was a man considerably inferior in social status; it is not at all unlikely that the deceased was not particularly proud of his connection with his daughter. This would explain both the absence of the entries and his reticence about her to ordinary acquaintances and even friends. On the whole, their Lordships are of opinion that both Zohra and her children are entitled to their legal shares in the inheritance of Ismail Ali Khan. But the Courts in India have awarded to the plaintiffs, on the basis of the deed of purchase from Zohra a decree for possession of her share and the shares of defendants Nos. 9 and 10. And the question is whether they have acquired any title to the infant's shares under the sale by the mother. The defendants objected in the High Court to the decree of the Subordinate Judge on the ground that she had no power to convey her children's interest to the plaintiffs. The learned Judges overruled the objection on the ground that the question did not arise in the present case. Their Lordships regret to have to differ from this view. This is an action in ejectment; the defendants are in possession; the plaintiffs if they are to obtain possession of the minors' shares, must do so on the strength of their own title. It is essential, therefore, to consider whether the title they allege to have acquired under the conveyance by Zohra is well-founded.

The question how far, or under what circumstances according to Mahomedan law, a mother's dealings with her minor child's property are binding on the infant has been frequently before the Courts in India. The decisions, however, are by no means uniform, and betray two varying tendencies; one set of decisions purports to give such dealings a qualified force; the other declares them wholly void and ineffective. In the former class of cases, the main test for determining the validity of the particular transaction has been the benefit resulting from it to the minor: in the latter, the admitted absence of authority or power on the part of the mother to alienate or encumber the minor's property.

In this conflict of opinion, their Lordships think it desirable that a definite rule should, if possible, be laid down; and with this object they propose to review briefly the provisions and principles of the Mahomedan law, as they apprehend it, governing the subject.

It is perfectly clear that under the Mahomedan law the mother is entitled only to the custody of the person of her minor child up to a certain age according to the sex of the child. But she is not the natural guardian; the father alone, or, if he be dead, his executor (under the Sunni law) is the legal guardian. The mother has no larger powers to deal with her minor child's property than any outsider or non-relative who happens to have charge for the time being of the infant. The term— '*de facto* guardian' that has been applied to these persons is misleading; it connotes the idea that people in charge of a child are by virtue of that fact invested with certain powers over the infant's property. This idea is quite erroneous, and the judgment of the Board in *Mata Din* v. *Ahmad Ali* (1912) 34 All. 213 clearly indicated it. There, an infant's share was sold by the elder brother, in whose charge the child was along with his own share, to pay a joint ancestral debt. The vendee at the time of the sale was in possession of the whole property under a mortgage executed by the ancestor. On attaining majority the younger brother, ignoring the sale, brought a suit against the vendee mortgagee for the redemption of his own share. The defence set up was that the sale by the infant's *de facto* guardian, made for a valid necessity, was binding on the infant. The lower Courts decreed the plaintiff's claim; on appeal to this Board, the arguments proceeded on the same lines as in the present case, though in reverse order.

Lord Robson, in delivering the judgment of the Board, observed as follows:

> It is urged on behalf of the appellant that the elder brothers were *de facto* guardians of the respondent, and, as such, were entitled to sell his property, provided that the sale was in order to pay his debts and was therefore necessary in his interest. It is difficult to see how the situation of an unauthorized guardian is bettered by describing him as a '*de facto*' guardian. He may, by his *de facto* guardianship, assume important responsibilities in relation to the minor's property, but he cannot thereby clothe himself with the legal power to sell it.

And he went on to add:-

> There has been much argument in this case in the Courts below and before their Lordships, as to whether, according to Mahomedan law, a

sale by a *de facto* guardian, if made for necessity, or for the payment of an ancestral debt affecting the minor's property, and if beneficial to the minor, is altogether void or merely voidable. It is not necessary to decide that question in this case.

And he then proceeded to state the reason why that was not considered necessary.

This latter passage in Lord Robson's judgment has created the impression that their Lordships' decision was confined to the special facts of that case and left open the general question regarding the validity of alienations by unauthorized guardians of the property of the minors.

As already observed, in the absence of the father under the Sunni law, the guardianship vests in his executor. If the father dies without appointing an executor (*wasi*) and his father is alive, the guardianship of his minor children devolves on their grandfather. Should he also be dead, and have left an executor, it vests in him. In default of these *de jure* guardians, the duty of appointing a guardian for the protection and preservation of the infants' property devolves on the Judge as the representative of the Sovereign (Baillie's *Digest*, ed. 1875, P. 689; Hamilton's *Hedaya*, Vol. IV, p. 555). No one else has any right or power to intermeddle with the property of a minor except for certain specified purposes, the nature of which is clearly defined. But the powers of even the *de jure* guardians are confined within legal limits. For example whilst an executor-guardian (*wasi*) may 'sell or purchase movables on account of the orphan under his charge either for an equivalent or at such a rate as to occasion an inconsiderable loss,' dealings with his immoveable property are subjected to strict conditions (Baillie's *Digest*, p. 687). The reason for the restrictions is thus given in the *Hedaya* (Vol. IV, p. 553):-

> The ground of this (the difference in the power of dealing with the two kinds of property) is that the sale of moveable property is a species of conservation, as articles of that description are liable to decay, and the price is much more easily preserved than the article itself. With respect, on the contrary, to immoveable property, it is in a state of conservation in its own nature whence it is unlawful to sell it unless, however, it be evident that it will otherwise perish, or be lost, in which case the sale of it is allowed.

In fact, the Mussulman law appears to draw a sharp distinction between moveable and immoveable property (*a'kar*) in respect of the powers of guardians, as will be seen from the following passage in Baillie's *Digest*, p. 689:-

> With regard to the executor of a mother or brother, when a mother has died leaving property and a minor son, and having appointed an executor, or a brother has died leaving property and a minor brother, and having appointed an executor, the executor may lawfully sell anything but *a'kar* belonging to the estate of the deceased, but can neither sell the *a'kar*, nor lawfully buy anything for the minor but food and clothing, which are necessary for his preservation. The executor of a mother has no power to sell anything that a minor has inherited from his father, whether the property be moveable or immoveable, and whether the property be involved in debt or free from it. But what he has inherited from herself when it is free from debts and legacies, the executor may sell what is moveable, but he cannot sell *a'kar*. If the estate is involved in debt or legacies, and the debt is such as to absorb the whole, he may sell the whole, the sale of *a'kar* coming within his power; and if the debt does not absorb the whole, he may sell as much of it as is necessary to defray the debts, and to his power to sell the surplus there is the same differences of opining as has been stated above.

When the mother is the father's executrix, or is appointed by the judge as guardian of the minors, she has all the powers of a *de jure* guardian. Without such derivative authority, if she assumes charge of their property to deal with it, she does so at her own risk, and her acts are like those of any other person who arrogates an authority which he does not legally possess. She may incur responsibilities, but can impose no obligations on the infant. This rule, however, is subject to certain exceptions provided for the protection of a minor child who has no *de jure* guardian. A fatherless child is designated in the law books an 'infant orphan' (*yeteem saghir*). The *Hedaya* classifies the acts that may have to be done for an infant under three heads. It says:-

> Acts in regard to infant orphans are of three descriptions, *viz.*, (i) acts of guardianship, such as contracting an infant in marriage, or selling or buying goods for him, a power which belongs solely to the *walee*, or natural guardian, whom the law has constituted the infant's substitute in those points: (ii) acts arising from the wants of an infant, such as buying or selling for him on occasions of need, or hiring a nurse for him, or the like, which power belongs to the maintainer of the infant, whether he be the brother, uncle, or (in the case of a foundling) the *mooltakit* or *taker-up*, or the mother, provided she be the maintainer of the infant : and as *these*

are empowered with respect to such acts, the *walee*, or natural guardian, is also empowered with respect to them in a still superior degree ; nor is it requisite, with respect to the *guardian*, that the infant be in his immediate protection : (iii) acts which are *purely advantageous* to the infant, such as accepting presents or gifts, and keeping them for him a power which may be exercised either by a *mooltakit*, a brother, or an uncle, and also by the infant himself, provided he be possessed of discretion, the intention being only to open a door to the infants' receiving benefactions of an advantageous nature. (Vol. IV, p. 124, Book XLIV)

The examples given under the second head indicate the class of cases in which the acts of an unauthorized person who happens to have charge of a child are held to be binding on the infant's property. They also help to explain and illustrate the extent of such *de facto* guardian's powers. The permissibility of these acts depends on the emergency which gives rise to the imperative necessity for incurring liabilities without which the life of the child or his perishable goods and chattels may run the risk of destruction. For instance, he may stand in immediate need of aliment, clothing, or nursing: these wants must be supplied forthwith. He may own 'slaves' or live-stock; food and fodder must be immediately procured. And these imperative wants may recur from time to time. Under such circumstances power is given to the lawful guardian to incur debts or to raise money on the pledge of the minor's goods and chattels (*mata*) (*Majmaul-Anhar*, Vol. II, p. 571). And this power in the absence of a *de jure* guardian, the law extends to the person who happens to have charge of the child and of the child's property, though not a constituted or authorized guardian.

There is no reference to the pledge or sale of immoveable property (*a'kar*) as the power of dealing with that class of property is confined to the *de jure* guardians, and is treated in the *Fatawai Alamgiri* in a separate chapter (Baillie's 'Mahomedan Law of Sale,' Chapter XVI). It is to be observed that under the third 'description' of acts that may be needful for an infant, a person in charge of a child, although not a *de jure* guardian, may validly accept on behalf of his ward an unburdened bounty, it being an act 'purely advantageous' to the child, to use the expression of the *Hedaya*.

The reasoning on which it is sought to give to persons who happen to have charge of the person and property of a child, and are, therefore called '*de facto*' guardians, the same powers as are possessed by *de jure* guardians is purely inferential. It proceeds on the analogy of a dealing by an outsider who purports to sell another's property without any authority from the real owner. Such a person in the *Hanafi* law is called a *fazuli*, or, as Mr. Hamilton spells it, *fazoolee* which expression is defined by Richardson to mean a person 'busying himself in things not belonging to him or acting without authority.' With the effect of the acts of a *fazuli* their Lordships will deal presently. Before doing so, they wish to refer briefly to the state of the decisions in the Indian Courts.

The Calcutta High Court, in sustaining transactions entered into by *de facto* guardians, has proceeded mainly on considerations of necessity for and benefit to the infant. The other High Courts, generally speaking, have cut the Gordian knot by holding that all such dealings with a minor's property were void.

Their Lordships do not feel called upon to examine in detail either set of decisions. But the last case on the subject in the Madras High Court requires their careful and respectful consideration: *Ayderman Kutti v. Syed Ali* [1912] 37 Mad. 514. In their judgment in this case the learned Judges have examined the law at considerable length and their decision appears to divide itself into three broad propositions: *first*, that as regards the powers of guardians, De *jure* as well as *de facto*, the Mahomedan law recognizes no distinction as to the nature or kind of property, viz., whether it is immoveable or moveable: *secondly*, that in substance the powers of an unauthorized person who has charge of an infant are co-extensive with those of a lawfully constituted guardian except in so far that the acts of the former are subject to considerations of necessity or benefit to the infant: and *thirdly* (and this seems to form the essence of the judgment), that dealings by 'a *de facto* guardian' are neither void nor voidable, but are suspended until the minor on attaining majority exercises his option of either ratifying the transaction or disavowing it.

With regard to the first of the above propositions, their Lordships have already indicated their views. In their opinion, the Mahomedan law, for obvious reasons makes a distinction, between 'goods and chattels' (*mata* and immoveable property (*a'kar*) with regard to the powers of dealing by guardians.

The second proposition, speaking with respect, appears to their Lordships to lose sight of the fact that the acts of *de jure* guardians also are subject to the conditions of necessity for or benefit to the infant. So that upon the reasoning of the Madras judgment the powers of 'a *de facto* guardian' would, to all intents and purposes, be co-extensive with those of a *de jure* guardian. This conclusion would wipe out one of the most important safeguards provided by the Mahomedan law for the protection of the interests of infants. The learned Judges say that:-

> The law as regards the effect of dealings with a minor's property by a *de facto* guardian otherwise than in a case of absolute necessity or clear advantage to the minor is but a corollary of the general rule relating to sales by a person professing to deal with another's property, but without having legal authority to do so, i.e., by a fazuli, as he is technically called; such sales generally are treated as *mauquf*, or dependent.

Then, after referring to various authorities, they continue as follows:-

> The result of the above discussion is that, according to Mahomedan jurists, in cases of urgent and imperative necessity, such as those mentioned, the *de facto* guardian can alienate the property of the minor, no distinction being made between moveable and immoveable property.

It would have been an advantage to their Lordships if they had been placed in a position to judge for themselves, on the actual texts, the meaning of the Arabian text-writers and commentators. However, the *Hedaya* and the *Fatawai Alamgiri* are recognized as standard authorities in India on the *Hanafi* branch of the Sunni Law. Of the *Hedaya* there is a rendering in English made by Mr. Hamilton under the orders of Warren Hastings; and a large part of the *Fatawai Alamgiri* has been paraphrased into English by Mr. Neil Baillie, which is commonly known as Baillie's *Digest (Hanafia Law)*. Both Mr. Hamilton and Mr. Neil Baillie in their renderings have, with the object of elucidation occasionally added phrases which do not exist in the original, but on the whole the English versions of the *Hedaya* and of the *Fatawai Alamgiri* are valuable works on Mahomedan Law.

The subject of sales by unauthorized persons is treated in the *Hedaya* in a separate section entitled 'of *Fazoolee Beea*, or the sale of the property of another without his consent' (Book XVI, Vol. II, p. 508). It says:-

> If a person were to sell the property of another without his order the contract is complete, but it remains with the proprietor either to confirm or dissolve the sale as he pleases. Shafei is of opinion that the contract, in this case, is not complete, because it has not issued from a lawful authority, for that is constituted only by property or permission, neither of which exists in this case.

It then proceeds to give the arguments of the *Hanafi* doctors in support of their view that the unauthorized contract is 'complete.' And then it adds:-

> If the proprietor should die, then the consent of the heirs is of no efficacy in the confirmation of the *Fazoolee* sale, in either case, that is, whether the price have been stipulated in money or in goods : because the contract rested entirely on the personal assent of the deceased.

In other words, the so-called sale remains wholly ineffective until it receives the confirmation of the owner, to whom alone belongs the power of confirming it. If he dies before he had 'confirmed' it, the transaction falls to the ground, as the right to adopt the *fazuli's* act does not pass to his heirs.

In the *Fatawai Alamgiri* the subject is treated under the designation of 'dependent sales' (Vol. III, p. 245; Baillie's 'Mahomedan Law of Sale,' pp. 218-219):

> When a person sells the property of another, the sale is suspended, according to us (i.e., the *Hanafis*), for the sanction or ratification of the proprietor; and the existence of both the parties to the contract, and of the subject of sale, is a necessary condition to the validity of his sanction.... If the owner should die before sanctioning the sale, sanction by his heir would not suffice to give it operation. Sanction by an owner himself renders a sale operative.

The word in the above passage translated as 'suspended' is derived from the same root as the word that has been translated in the heading as 'dependent upon'; also the words 'or ratification' have been introduced by Mr. Baillie by way of explanation. The word *ijazat* in the original is rightly rendered into 'sanction.'

The *Majma-ul-Anhar* states the rule relating to a sale by a *fazuli* in similar terms; it says in substance that such a sale is 'established' (takes effect) on the sanction of the *malik* (owner), subject to four conditions, which it specifies. And then it adds significantly that according to Shafei (the founder of the second great Sunni school of law) all dealings by an unauthorized person are absolutely void (*batil*); Vol. II, p. 88.

In their Lordships' opinion, the Hanafi doctrine relating to a sale by an unauthorized person remaining dependent on the sanction of the owner refers to a case where such owner is *sui juris*, possessed of the capacity to give the necessary sanction and to make the transaction operative. They do not find any reference in these doctrines relating to *fazuli* sales so far as they appear in the *Hedaya* or the *Fatawai Alamgiri*, to dealings with the property of minors by persons who happen to have charge of the infants and their property—in other words, the '*de facto* guardians'.

The Hanafi doctrine about *fazuli* sales appears clearly to be based on the analogy of an agent who acts in a particular matter without authority, but whose act is subsequently adopted or ratified by the principal which has the effect of validating it from its inception. The idea of agency in relation to an infant is as foreign, their Lordships conceive, to Mahomedan Law as to every other system.

In this connection it should be noted that whilst Chapter XII deals exclusively with the effect of 'dependent sales,' in Chapter XVI the rules relating to the powers of guardians are discussed at considerable length (Baillie's 'Mahomedan Law of Sale,' p. 243, *Fatawai Alamgiri*, Vol. III, p. 229). The following rule lays down the conditions governing sales by the executor (i.e., the appointed guardian) of the immoveable property of an infant:-

> And according to modern decisions, the sale of immoveable estate by an executor is lawful only in one of the three cases following ; that is, where there is a purchaser willing to give double its value, or the sale is necessary to meet the minor's emergencies, or there are debts of the deceased, and no other means of paying them. (Baillie's 'Mahomedan Law of Sale,' p. 247; *Fatawai Alamgiri*, Vol. III, p. 233)

Having regard to the object in view, this dictum appears to their Lordships to apply to all forms of property which, like *a'kar*, combine both security and permanency. But it does not exclude the discretion of the Judge to sanction any alteration of investment in the interests of the infant.

The following case affords a further illustration of the limitations on the powers of '*de facto* guardians':-

> A woman after the death of her husband sells property that belonged to him, supposing herself to be his executrix, and her husband having left minor children ; she after some time declares that she was not the executrix, her assertion, however, is not to be credited as against the purchaser, but the sale remains in suspense till her children arrive at puberty. If they should admit that she was the executrix, the sale by her is lawful: but if they deny the fact ; the sale is void: and though the purchaser should have manured the purchased land, he has no recourse for reimbursement

against the woman. What has been said is on the supposition that the woman sues for a cancellation of the sale, on the ground that she was not executrix; but if the minor sues on that ground, his claim is to be heard. (Baillie, p. 249; *Alamgiri*, Vol. III, p. 231)

The rest of the passage is immaterial for the purposes of this judgment.

The above case shows that even where the mother believes she is vested with authority as her husband's executrix, and in that belief purports to deal with the minor's property, a purchaser let into possession by her is liable to be ejected at the instance of the minor. Her own subsequent denial of authority does not affect the purchaser's position; but if the transaction is impugned by the rightful owner—viz., the infant—the *onus* is on the vendee to establish the foundation of his title, that is, that his vendor possessed in fact the authority under which she purported to act.

A further rule, which is given in the 'Book on Pledges' (Mortgages) (Kitab-ur-Rahn) of the *Fatawai Alamgiri*, which does not appear to have been translated by Mr. Baillie, is equally explicit. After stating the principle applicable to the powers of the father to pledge or mortgage his minor child's property, it goes on to say:

> The mother, if she pledges (mortgages) the property of her infant child, it is not lawful unless she be the executrix (of the father) or be authorized therefor by the guardian of the minor ; or the Judge should grant her permission to pledge the infant's property. Then it is lawful and the right to possession and user is established in the murtahin (pledgee or an mortgagee) without power of sale. (*Fatawai Alamgiri*, Vol. V, p. 638)

It seems to their Lordships that the power to sell cannot be wider than the power to mortgage.

For the foregoing considerations, their Lordships are of opinion that under the Mahomedan law a person who has charge of the person or property of a minor without being his legal guardian, and who may, therefore, be conveniently called a '*de facto* guardian,' has no power to convey to another any right or interest in immoveable property which the transferee can enforce against the infant; nor can such transferee, if let into possession of the property under such unauthorized transfer, resist an action in ejectment on behalf of the infant as a trespasser. It follows that, being himself without title, he cannot seek to recover property in the possession of another equally without title.

Their Lordships are accordingly of opinion that the decree of the High Court, in so far as it awards to the plaintiffs' possession of the shares of the defendants Nos. 9 and 10, should be discharged, and, subject to this variation, it should be affirmed and the appeal be dismissed with costs and their Lordships will humbly advise His Majesty accordingly.

Their Lordships cannot help deprecating the practice which seems to be growing in some of the Indian Courts of referring largely to foreign decisions. However useful in the scientific study of comparative jurisprudence judgments of Foreign Courts, to which Indian practitioners cannot be expected to have access, based often on considerations and conditions totally differing from those applicable to or prevailing in India, are only likely to confuse the administration of justice.

Decree varied.

SECTION II

INDIA

15

Khadissa v. Muhammed

ORDER

In a proceeding under S. 125 of the Criminal Procedure Code maintenance was granted to the wife by the trial Magistrate at the rate of Rs. 50/- and to her youngest child at the rate of Rs. 40/- per month. The Sessions Judge in revision set aside that order on the ground that the wife was leading an immoral life and the child was illegitimate.

2. The parties are Muslims. They were first married 18 years before. After five children were born to them they quarrelled. The husband took the wife to her house and divorced her. Thereafter he remarried her and took her to his house, they lived together there for about four months and the wife became pregnant. There was again quarrel between them. The husband took her to her house again, and again divorced her. It was thereafter that the last child was born. The award of Rs. 40/- as maintenance by the trial Magistrate was for that child. This revision petition is by the wife.

3. The Sessions Judge was greatly influenced by the failure to conduct an intermediate marriage between the first and second marriage of the petitioner as cutting at the root of the validity of the second marriage. In Mulla's Mahomedan Law, 17th Edition, it is stated as follows at page 319:

> Where the husband has repudiated his wife by three pronouncements...
> it is not lawful for him to marry her again until she has married another

man, and the latter has divorced her or died after actual consummation of the marriage.

There is no doubt about that proposition. In the present case it has come out from the evidence of the wife, Pw. 1, the Mullah who officiated at the second marriage, Pw. 2 and an invitee of the respondent who attended the second marriage, Pw. 3, that there was really no intermediate marriage between the first and second marriages of the parties. That was why the Sessions Judge said that the second marriage was invalid. The results following from that were also serious. Argument regarding the same by counsel for the husband was of elemental simplicity. He argued that as the husband by such second marriage was no better than a stranger the wife had to be taken as having led an immoral life when she lived with him for about four months after the first divorce and the child begotten during that period had to be taken as illegitimate.

4. Maintenance was disallowed to the wife on account of her leading an immoral life. The Judge in doing that had evidently the provision in S. 125 (4) of the Code in view. For that provision to apply the wife should be living in adultery. If the second marriage was invalid then after the dissolution of the first marriage the wife should be taken as not having a husband at the time and her cohabitation with any man during that period cannot be termed adultery, as held in *Mariyumma* v. *Mohammed Ibrahim* 1978 KLT 573. So the provision in S. 125 (4) cannot be applied for refusing maintenance to the wife.

5. As for immorality, what is immoral has to be judged by the current standards of morality of the community. What was apparently regarded with pious horror in good old days would today hardly draw a raised eyebrow or even a gentle tut-tut. The wife in this case had at no time a husband other than the respondent. I doubt whether in the present day Indian Muslim Society such a woman who cohabits with a man who was her previous husband and who has married her a second time can on account of such cohabitation be said to be immoral merely because the second marriage is technically invalid in the eye of law. I am conscious that by leaving that matter at that, I am leaving it unresolved and open for decision in the future but that is inevitable in the development of law.

6. The respondent, Rw. 1, denied the second marriage. But except his interested statement, which was rightly not believed by the trial Magistrate, there is nothing to show that what he said was true. The

Sessions Judge thought that as there was no part played by the mosque in the second marriage that remarriage was not probable. A mosque has no part to play in a Muslim marriage which is purely contractual. The evidence of the wife, Pw. 1, which is reliable and which is corroborated by that of Pws. 2 and 3 proves that the second marriage actually took place. There was no justifiable reason for the Sessions Judge to interfere in revision with the finding of fact entered by the trial Magistrate after proper appreciation of the evidence adduced in the case that the second marriage between the parties in fact took place.

7. If a remarriage, as is proved in the case, was conducted without conducting an intermediate marriage it is only an irregularity. At page 319 of Mulla's Mahomedan Law after saying that it was not lawful for a Muslim to marry his divorced wife again until she is remarried by another man and that is consummated it is stated as follows: 'A marriage without fulfillment of the above conditions is irregular, not void.' The effect of an irregular marriage is mentioned at page 263 of that book as follows: 'If consummation has taken place—

(i) The wife is entitled to dower...
(ii) The issue of the marriage is legitimate....'

It is clearly proved in the case that the youngest child was born to the petitioner through the respondent after the remarriage. So there was consummation of the remarriage, the petitioner is entitled to dower and the youngest child is legitimate.

8. A divorced wife is also entitled to claim maintenance under S. 125 (1) of the Code unless she has received after the divorce the whole amount which was payable on such divorce. The respondent in the present case even denies the remarriage. There was no justifiable reason whatsoever for the Sessions Judge to interfere in revision with the order passed by the trial magistrate granting maintenance to the wife and child of the respondent after proper consideration of the evidence adduced in the case.

In the result this revision petition is allowed by setting aside the order passed by the Sessions Judge and restoring that passed by the trial Magistrate.

16

Rabia Khatoon v. Mohd Mukhtar Ahmad

JUDGMENT

UNIYAL, J. These three connected second appeals have been referred to us by a learned single Judge as he was of the view that the opinion expressed by Mahmood, J. in the case of Abdul Kadir v. Salima, (1886) ILR 8 All 149 (FB) that a Mohammedan wife has no right to refuse herself to her husband if her prompt dower is not paid when the marriage has been consummated with her consent, is in the nature of an obiter dictum and requires reconsideration.

2. The facts giving rise to these appeals may now be stated. Two suits were filed, one by Smt. Rabia Khatoon against her husband for dissolution of marriage and the other by Mohammad Mukhtar Ahmad against the wife for restitution of conjugal rights. Parties were married in 1948. The marriage was consummated with the consent of the wife and a son was born of the wedlock in 1951. The wife went to her father's house shortly after the birth of the child in 1951. Mohammad Mukhtar, the husband, went to bring his wife Smt. Rabia Khatoon some time in April or May 1951 but she refused to come back. No maintenance allowance was paid by the husband to the wife since 1951, and the suit giving rise to these appeals came to be filed in 1956.

3. In the suit filed by the wife it was alleged that in spite of demand the husband had not paid her prompt dower which was settled at Rs. 5,000; that she continued to perform her marital relations with her

husband for over two years and a child was born to them; that the husband treated her cruelly and beat her and turned her out of the house, with the result that she was obliged to take shelter in her father's house and was living there ever since. She alleged that her husband had failed to maintain her during all these years and had not paid her prompt dower to which she was entitled.

4. In his written statement the husband denied that he treated his wife cruelly or that she was forced to leave his house due to ill treatment. He alleged that the dower payable to the wife was deferred dower and that it was only Rs. 500. In the counter suit filed by the husband for restitution of conjugal rights similar pleas were raised by the parties.

5. Both the Courts below held that it was not established that the husband committed physical cruelty upon his wife or that she was forced to leave her husband's house due to his ill treatment. The Courts below further found that the dower settled was prompt dower and that it was Rs. 5,000 and that the husband had not paid the said dower to the wife. On the question whether the husband had neglected or failed to provide maintenance to his wife for a period of two years, it was found as a fact that the husband had not paid any maintenance allowance to the wife ever since she left his house.

The lower appellate Court was, however, of the opinion that the wife having admitted the husband to sexual intercourse she was not entitled to refuse to live with him as wife and that non-payment of dower could not be a good defence to the suit for restitution of conjugal rights. On these findings the suit of the husband for restitution of conjugal rights was decreed subject to the payment of Rs. 5,000 as prompt dower, while the suit of the wife for dissolution of marriage was dismissed on the ground that she could not deny herself to the husband after consummation of the marriage merely because her dower had remained unpaid.

6. The vital question which arises for consideration is whether a Mohammedan wife has a right to refuse to go to her husband if her prompt dower is not paid, even though the marriage had been consummated with the consent of the wife before the date of the refusal. A similar point arose for consideration in the Full Bench case of (1886) ILR 8 All 149 (FB) (supra). Mahmood, J. whose judgment was adopted by the Full Bench observed that:

> The right of dower does not precede the right of cohabitation which the contract of marriage necessarily involves but that the two rights come

into existence simultaneously and by reason of the same incident of law. The right of the wife to claim maintenance from her husband arises in the same manner as one of the legal effect of marriage, and to say that any of those effects are not simultaneously created by the contract of marriage amounts, in my opinion, to a violation of the fundamental notions of jurisprudence regarding correlative rights and obligations arising from one and the same perfected legal relation.

7. Mahmood, J. referred to a passage in the Hedaya to make his point that the Mohammedan Law entitles the wife to resist the claim of the husband for cohabitation with her by pleading non-payment of her prompt dower, but it proceeds essentially upon the assumption that his right to put forward such a claim is antecedent to the plea. The same is the effect of the passage from the Durrul Mukhtar and the view expressed in the Fatawa Qazi Khan and the Fatawa Alamgiri. Mahmood, J. went on to say that the opinion of Imam Abu Hanifa to the contrary was not shared by his two eminent disciples Qazi Abu Yusaf and Imam Muhammad so far as the question of cohabitation was concerned and said:

> Wherever there is a difference of opinion, the opinion of the two will prevail against the opinion of the third. Now, bearing this in mind, it is clear that the two disciples of Imam Abu Hanifa, regarding the surrender of the wife to her husband as bearing analogy to delivery of goods in sale, held that the lien of the wife for her dower, as a plea for resisting cohabitation, ceased to exist after consummation. According to the ordinary rule of interpreting Muhammadan law, I adopt the opinion of the two disciples as representing the majority of 'the three Masters', and hold that, after consummation of marriage non-payment of dower, even though exigible, cannot be pleaded in defence of an action for restitution of conjugal rights; the rule so laid down having, of course, no effect upon the right of the wife to claim her dower in a separate action.

The view expressed by Mahmood, J. that whenever there is a difference of opinion between Imam Abu Hanifa, the Master, and his two disciples Imam Muhammad and Qazi Abu Yusaf, who was Qazi of Baghdad, the opinion of the latter must prevail over that of the former, was regarded as obiter by Sir Sulaiman, C. J. in the case of Mt. Anis Begum v. Mohammad Istafa, AIR 1933 All 634. Sir Sulaiman pointed out that it was not possible to accept the view that in all matters relating to Mahommedan Law the majority opinion of the disciples was preferable to that of the master. The correct position, according to the learned Chief Justice, was as follows:

> Different doctors have followed different rules of preference. Those who were more orthodox and generally speaking, more ancient, in many cases preferred the solitary opinion of Abu Hanifa to even the joint opinion of his disciples. There are later text-book writers who have preferred the opinion of two as against that of one. But such rules are helpful only when their is no clear consensus.

8. After quoting from Ruddul Mukhtar the learned Chief Justice observed:

> there is no accepted rule that when there is a difference of opinion amongst the founders of schools and their disciples, opinion or ruling of a lawyer ought to be given according to the opinion of Abu Hanifa, even if all his disciples differ from him: and in the absence of any dictum of his in accordance with the opinion of Abu Yusaf, then Muhammad, then Zafar and then Hasan Ibn Ziad. If the authorities were examined it will generally be found that in some matters the solitary view of Abu Hanifa has been preferred whereas in other matters the view of Abu Yusaf, Muhammad or Zafar has been followed. According to Alhawi the correct rule was that in cases of difference of opinion regard should be had to the authority and reasons in support of each view and the one which has the strongest support should be followed.

9. The point for decision in the case of Mt. Anis Begum, AIR 1933 All 634 was whether the suit of the husband for restitution of conjugal rights was liable to be dismissed on the ground that prompt dower had remained unpaid even though the marriage had been consummated with the consent of the wife prior to the refusal of the wife to live with the husband. On this point Sir Sulaiman delivering the judgment of the Division Bench followed the view expressed by Mahmood, J. in (1886) ILR 8 All 149 (FB), and emphasised that:

> The two considerations which might well justify the acceptance of the view of the disciples in India, are: first that owing to the prevalent practice, the amounts of dower fixed in this country are often unduly high and beyond the means of the husband. To allow to the wife the right of refusing to live with her husband even after consummation, so long as any part of the prompt dower remains unpaid would, in many cases, where the husband and wife quarrel, amount to an absolute option of

the wife to refuse to live with her husband and yet demand a maintenance allowance. This would dislocate domestic life. Secondly, as will be shown hereinafter, under the Anglo-Mahommedan Law as administered in this country a suit for restitution of conjugal rights though brought for the enforcement of a right under the Mahommedan Law, is in the nature of a suit for specific performance, and there is accordingly a certain amount of discretion in the Courts of justice which can impose a condition of previous payment of the dower debt, or, at any rate a portion of it, in the decree.

10. The learned Chief Justice went on to say that the view expressed by Mahmood, J. had held the field for nearly 40 years (now 75 years) and had been followed by all the High Courts in India, excepting Oudh. In the result, he held that there was no right in the wife to refuse to return to the husband after the marriage had been consummated on the ground that her dower had remained unpaid.

11. Reference was made by the learned counsel to the case of Mohammad Yasin v. Rahmat Ilahi, AIR 1947 All 201 (FB). That was a case in which the point for consideration was whether according to the Hanafi school of Mahomedan Law a valid waqf could be created by a mere declaration by the waqif, or whether it was necessary for the completion of the waqf that the person appointed mutwalli should be given possession of the dedicated properties. The question debated in that case was whether the opinion of the two disciples of Abu Hanifa was to be preferred to the opinion of the Master. The Full Bench was of the opinion that the observation of Mahmood, J. in (1886) ILR 8 All 149 (FB), that the opinion of the disciples was always to be preferred was obiter and did not bind the Court. Justice Wali Ullah pointed out that the principle of stare decisis was not applicable to a case where the decision was based on an erroneous view of the law if the reversal of the old view of the law would not unsettle transactions entered into on the faith of the pre-existing law.

12. In Tricomdas Cooverji v. Gopinath Jiu Thakur, ILR 44 Cal 759: (AIR 1916 PC 182), the Privy Council observed that a long series of decisions based upon a construction not free from doubt should not be disregarded. In the case of Mohammad Yasin, AIR 1947 All 201 (FB), the point was one which did not have the effect of disturbing titles and unsettling transactions decided on the basis of old decisions; whereas the view of Mahmood, J., which was followed and approved by a

Division Bench of this Court in the case of Mt. Anis Begum, AIR 1933 All 634, has been accepted as the correct view for nearly 75 years. If the decision in (1886) ILR 8 All 149 (FB), were to be held as bad law it would not only create uncertainty in the law but also disturb the domestic peace of Muhammedan families throughout India. According to one school of Mahomedan Law a Muhammedan wife governed by Hanafi law has the right to refuse to go to her husband even after the consummation of marriage with her consent if her dower remains unpaid, but it would be dangerous to adopt this view at the present time having regard to the prevalent practice and the modern conditions of life. The Courts of law, as was pointed out by Sir Sulaiman, have certain discretion in this matter because a suit for restitution of conjugal rights is in the nature of a suit for specific performance and it is open to the Court to impose conditions on the husband to ensure the right of the wife to secure her prompt dower. A contrary view has been expressed in Mst. Noor Bibi v. Pir Bux, AIR 1950 Sind 8, but it is not consistent with progressive thought and has not found acceptance in the Courts in India except Oudh.

13. The suit of the wife Smt. Rabia Khatoon for dissolution of her marriage was based on Section 2(ii) of the Dissolution of Muslim Marriages Act (VIII of 1939). S. 2, so far as material is as follows:-

> A woman married under Muslim Law shall be entitled to obtain a decree for the dissolution of her marriage on any one or more of the following grounds:-
>> ... (ii) That the husband has neglected or has failed to provide for her maintenance for a period to two years
>> ... (vii) That the husband treats her with cruelty, that is to say
>> (a) habitually assaults her or makes her life miserable by cruelty of conduct even if such conduct does not amount to physical ill treatment.

14. The two grounds upon which dissolution of marriage was sought were (a) that the husband had neglected or had failed to provide for her maintenance for a period of two years, and (b) that he habitually assaulted her or made her life miserable, which conduct amounted to physical ill treatment. Both the Courts below held that the wife had failed to prove physical or legal cruelty on the part of the husband. As regards the failure of the husband to maintain her for a period two years, the Courts below were of opinion that this was due to the fact that the

wife refused to go back to the husband in spite of his best efforts and it could not therefore, be said that he had neglected or had failed to provide for her maintenance.

15. In Mst. Badrulnisa Bibi v. Mohammad Yusuf, AIR 1944 All 23 it was held that the word 'neglect' in S. 2 of Dissolution of Muslim Marriages Act, implied wilful failure, and the words 'has failed to provide', though not happily worded, implied an omission of duty. Where the wife through her own conduct led the husband to stop the maintenance, the Court would not allow dissolution of marriage for that would be giving her a benefit—if benefit it could be called—arising from her own wrongful acts.

16. The view expressed in the above case was followed in Zafar Hussain v. Akbari Begum, AIR 1944 Lah 336, and it was held that it is not correct to say that S 2(ii) casts upon the husband an absolute duty to maintain his wife in all cases and any failure in that duty would be a ground for divorce, even if the wife herself was at fault and was really the cause of the husband refusing to maintain her. The learned Judges observed that:

> Before a husband can be said to have neglected or failed to provide maintenance for his wife, it must be held that the husband was under a legal duty to provide such maintenance. If the husband was not under Mahomedan or Anglo-Mahomedan Law bound to maintain his wife, how can it be said that he had neglected or failed to maintain her if he sent her no money or other maintenance?

The learned Judges went on to say: 'The plaintiff for no valid reason has refused to live with her husband and to perform her marital obligations. That being so, it must be held that the defendant husband was not liable to maintain the plaintiff as there was no duty to maintain.'

17. A Division Bench of the Peshawar Judicial Commissioner's Court in Fazal Mahmud v. Mst. Umatur Rahim, AIR 1949 Pesh 7, adopted the reasoning of the Allahabad High Court in AIR 1944 All 23, and that of the Lahore High Court in AIR 1944 Lah 330, and observed that under the Mahomedan Law no wife can claim maintenance unless she resides with the husband and is ready to perform the marital duties.

18. The learned counsel for Smt. Rabia Khatoon vehemently contended that under the Hanafi law she was entitled to refuse herself to the husband so long as her dower was not paid and inasmuch as her

living away from the husband was due to the wrongful act of the husband in not paying her prompt dower, the latter was bound to maintain her. If he did not do so, it amounted to have neglected or to have failed to provide for her maintenance. In our opinion there is no force in this contention. There is no right in the wife to refuse to live with her husband after the marriage has been consummated with her consent. So long as she keeps herself away without the fault of the husband she has no right to claim maintenance from him. If maintenance is not provided by the husband on account of the wife's wrongful refusal to live with him he cannot be considered guilty of negligence in maintaining her.

19. We may point out that in this case there is no reliable evidence in support of the plea of the wife that she had demanded dower from her husband, soon after she left his house she sent a letter Ex. A-4 dated 9th February 1954 [*sic*]to her husband in which she expressed feelings of affection and cordiality towards him. It was for the first time on the 26th May 1951 that a letter Ex. A-13 was sent by her father to the father of her husband saying that he was not prepared to send his daughter as the husband was still immature. As regards the allegation of the wife that she had demanded her prompt dower from her husband when he came to call her the evidence adduced on her behalf is contradictory. While she stated that she did not go to the husband because his people were not prepared to give an undertaking that they would treat her well and also refused to pay her prompt dower, the statement of her father was to the effect that the demand for dower was made at the time when the panchayat was convened and not when her husband's people came to call her. In this state of the evidence the Courts below were right in holding that it was not established that the wife had really made a demand for her prompt dower.

In the view we have taken of the case we are of the opinion that the Courts below were justified in dismissing the suit of the wife for the dissolution of marriage and in decreeing the suit of the husband for restitution of conjugal rights conditional upon his paying a sum of Rs. 5,000 as dower of the wife.

For the reasons given above we see no force in these appeals which are accordingly dismissed. In the circumstances of the case we direct that the parties will bear their own costs throughout.

Appeals dismissed.

18

Saifuddin Sekh v. Soneka Bibi

JUDGMENT

SARJOO PROSAD, C.J. This Second Appeal involves an interesting question of law which, we are advised, is not covered by any precedent or authority. It arises out of a suit for dissolution of marriage instituted by the plaintiff-respondent.

(2) The plaintiff and the defendant who are Muslims by religion, were married on the 25th of Bysak, 1356 B.S., corresponding to 8-5-1949. Before this marriage, admittedly the defendant had two other wives, this being permissible under the Muhammadan law. It appears that these other wives were not living with the defendant. At the time of the marriage, a 'kabinnama' was executed, under the terms of which the parties agreed that in case the defendant would bring any of his formerly married wives to stay with him, without the consent of the plaintiff, the plaintiff would be at liberty to divorce the defendant after performance of the ordinary legal formalities. In Bysak, 1357 B.S., corresponding to April or May 1950, the defendant brought one of his former wives to stay with him without the plaintiff's consent, and when the plaintiff objected to this, it was alleged she was ill-treated, assaulted and driven out of the house. Thereafter the plaintiff observed the formalities of divorce on the 23rd of Ashar 1357 B.S., which corresponds to 4-7-50; and then instituted the present suit.

(3) The substantial defence now is that the agreement in the kabinnama giving the plaintiff the right to divorce the defendant in case the latter brought his former wives to stay with him without the consent of

the plaintiff, was illegal and could not be enforced, and, therefore, the suit for dissolution of marriage should be dismissed.

(4) Both the Courts below have concurrently found that the kabin-nama was a genuine document and by virtue of it the defendant had delegated to the plaintiff the right to divorce the defendant in the circumstances mentioned therein. It was also found that the plaintiff had observed the necessary formalities leading to a divorce. The Munsiff, however, who tried the suit, held that the contract was an invalid contract and opposed to public policy. He was of opinion that the two former wives of the defendant were entitled to conjugal association with him and to have marital relations with their husband and inasmuch as this contract purported to put an impediment in their way, it was an invalid contract under S. 23, Contract Act. He accordingly dismissed the suit. The lower Appellate Court has disagreed with this view and held that the contract was valid, there being nothing illegal or opposed to public policy in the terms thereof; and, accordingly that Court has decreed the suit.

(5) There is no doubt that the Muhammadan law permits divorce. There is no doubt that it is open to the husband to delegate this power of divorce to the wife under certain contingencies. Besides, it is well known that a Muslim marriage is a contract, and not a sacrament and, therefore, the validity or invalidity of the conditions in the kabinnama entitling the plaintiff to exercise the right of divorce, will depend upon the fact whether the condition specified in the document is or is not against the provisions of the Indian Contract Act. It is difficult to see how a contract of this nature can be opposed either to law or to public policy. It is true that under the Muhammadan law, a husband is entitled to have as many as four wives, and those wives are also entitled to the exercise of marital rights with their husband; but the contract in question does not in any manner militate against this provision of the law. All that it says is that in case the husband brings any of his other wives to stay with him along with the plaintiff, without her consent, in that event the plaintiff will be at liberty to exercise this right of divorce. This does not place any impediment on the rights of the other two wives to have marital relations with their husband. It does not even put any such impediment on the right of the husband to have marital relations with those two other wives, all that it does is that if it is without the consent of the plaintiff, she would be entitled to live away from them and to claim divorce.

The learned Subordinate Judge is certainly right in observing that it is of the utmost importance that everyone should be allowed to live in peace and happiness and that even if the plaintiff is allowed the relief claimed by her under the agreement, the other two wives would be free to enjoy their lives. Even the defendant would be free to marry any other woman he chooses provided he does not go beyond the permissible limit; and there is absolutely no meaning in asking an unwilling partner to stay in company, with those other wives with whom she may not, after all, agree. The condition, therefore, is quite in accord with reason and public policy and in my opinion, it should be enforced.

(6) Reliance has been placed on behalf of the respondent upon a decision of the Bombay High Court in Bai Fatima v. Ali Mahomed, 37 Bom 280, wherein it has been held that an agreement for future separation arrived at between husband and wife who are Mahomedans, is void as being opposed to public policy, under S 25, Contract Act. This case has no application to the present facts. Besides, it is doubtful whether the law propounded there can be of universal application, to all cases of agreement for future separation. The view taken in some later decisions, including a decision of this court in Mirjan Ali v. Mt. Maimuna Bibi, AIR 1949 Assam 14, does not seem to be in accord with the above view. The decision of this Court, as expressed in Mirjan Ali's case has been followed in Buffatan Bibi v. Sheikh Abdul Salim, AIR 1950 Cal 304, wherein it was laid down that an antenuptial agreement by a Muhammadan husband in a kabinnama that he would pay separate maintenance to his wife in case of disagreement and that the wife would have power to get herself divorced in case of failure to pay maintenance for a certain period, is not opposed to public policy and is enforceable under the Muhammadan law.

These decisions are evidently based upon the principle that a contract which serves to ensure peace and domestic happiness should not be disregarded as invalid and opposed to public policy. There are several other decisions from which it appears that a contract embodied in a kabinnama, both ante and post nuptial, under which the husband authorizes the wife to divorce herself in the event of the husband taking a second wife, has been held to be valid; see Maharam Ali v. Ayesa Khatun, AIR 1916 Cal 761 and Mahammad Amin v. Mt. Aimna Bibi, AIR 1931 Lah 134 and Mt. Sadiqua Begam v. Ata Ullah, AIR 1933 Lah 885.

The real question here is not whether the other wives were restrained from coming to stay with the defendant and having marital relations with him, but the real question was—what is the effect under the terms of the kabinnama, if they come and stay, without the plaintiff's consent, with the defendant? They may be welcome to stay with the defendant, but the plaintiff is given the right to seek divorce, if she chooses, under those conditions. Such a right cannot be said to be invalid. Mr. Sen argues that those cases which follow the Calcutta view, all relate to cases of prohibition against other marriages, while in the present case, the defendant had already been married, to two other women who, under the law, were entitled to their marital rights. He contends that the effect of the agreement was to deprive those women of their rights. He also points out that in the above cases, mainly S. 26, Contract Act was considered, while, in the present case, according to the learned advocate, the contract comes within the mischief of S. 23. Contract Act. According to him, the consideration or object of the agreement is unlawful and forbidden by law.

These contentions are, in my opinion, quite unsound. Those cases may not apply, but as I have said, the contract in the present case is not hit by the provisions of S 23, Contract Act; it is a valid and reasonable contract because all that it seeks to do is to give a right to the plaintiff to seek divorce and live apart from the defendant and other co-wives in case they choose to live together. I am unable to see how any exception can be taken to such a contract. In my opinion the decision of the learned Subordinate Judge directing dissolution of marriage and granting decree to the plaintiff, is quite correct and the appeal must be dismissed. In the circumstances, however, I would not make any order as to costs.

(7) DEKA, J. I agree.

Appeal dismissed.

19

Zeenat Fatema Rashid v. Md Iqbal Anwar

JUDGMENT

MANISANA, J. This revision petition arises from an order of the Principal Judge of the Family Court at Guwahati made on 7-8-92 in Case No. FC (Cril) No. 111/92/74-M/90.

2. Facts–The case of the petitioner, in brief, is thus. The petitioner Zeenat Fatema Rashid married Md Iqbal Anwar on 2-12-87, according to Muslim rites. After the marriage they lived as husband and wife at husband's residence. She had borne him a son on 3-11-89. After that she was ill-treated by her husband and her in-laws. She, therefore, instituted a criminal case on 13-8-90 being case No. 87 of 1990. Finding no other alternative, she had to leave her husband's house and had to file a criminal case for getting back her properties and those properties were recovered on 31-8-90. She also filed a case under Section 125, Cr. P. C. against her husband on 29-8-90 claiming maintenance for herself and her minor child. Md Iqbal Anwar (the respondent) contested the case by filing written statement. His main defence was that he had divorced his wife, the petitioner herein, on 31-8-90.

3. The Family Court has held that there had been a divorce duly effected and, therefore, claim for maintenance would be determined under section 3 of the Muslim Women (Protection of Rights on

Divorce) Act, 1986. With regard to maintenance of child, the Family Court has directed that interim maintenance granted would continue pending final disposal of the case. Hence this petition.

4. The question which arises for consideration is whether there had been a divorce duly effected. Under the Mahomedan Law, divorce by talak may be effected either orally (by spoken words) or by a written document called a talaknama. No particular form of words is prescribed for effecting a talak, but the words of divorce must indicate an intention to dissolve the marriage (see Mulla's Principles of Mahomedan Law).

5. Mr. Phukan, the learned counsel for the petitioner, has contended that a Mahomedan husband cannot divorce his wife at his whim and caprice. The next question which therefore, arises for consideration is whether a Mahomedan husband can divorce his wife at his whim and caprice. In Sarabai v. Rabiabai, (1906) ILR 30 Bom 537, it has been held that there may not be a particular cause for divorce, and mere whim is sufficient. It is good in law, though bad in theology. In Asha Bibi v. Kadir Ibrahim, (1910) ILR 33 Mad 22, it has been held that, although an arbitrary or unreasonable exercise of divorce of marriage is strongly condemned in the Quran and is treated as spiritual offence, it does not affect the legal validity of a divorce duly effected by husband. In *Ahmed Kasim Molla v. Khatun Bibi*, (1932) ILR 59 Cal 833, the Calcutta High Court has held that 'any Mahomedan husband may divorce his wife at his mere whim and caprice' (p. 29). However, a Single Judge of this Court has, in Jiauddin Ahmed v. Anwara Begum, (1981) 1 GLR 358, held that divorce must be for a reasonable cause, and that must be preceded by an attempt at reconciliation between the husband and wife by two arbiters, one chosen by the wife from her family and the other by the husband from his side. Learned Single Judge, after considering the cases cited above, the observations of some of the High Courts, the mandates of the Quran, and the treatises on Mahomedan Law of various authors and scholars, came to the above conclusion. This decision of the learned Single Judge was approved by a Division Bench of this Court in Rukia v. Abdul Khalique, (1981) 1 GLR 375.

6. Mr. Barua, learned counsel for the respondent has submitted that in view of the earlier decisions of other High Courts that a Mahomedan husband may divorce his wife at his whim and caprice, the decisions of this Court are required to be reviewed for the settled position of law prevailing for a considerable long period, that is to say, long standing

legal position, should not be disturbed. Mr. Barua has further submitted that the matter may be referred to a larger Bench.

7. We are not inclined to accept the submission made by Mr. Barua. We approach the matter as follows. Under the Quran, the marriage state is to be maintained as far as possible and there should be conciliation before divorce (see note 254 of Vol 1 of Holy Quran by A Yusuf Ali). Therefore, the Quran discourages divorce and it permits only in extreme cases after pre-divorce conference. Therefore, a Mahomedan husband cannot divorce his wife at his whim and caprice. The question then is–whether, if divorce by talak is made arbitrarily, it should be treated as spiritual offence only? Under the Mahomedan Law, marriage though regarded as a civil contract between a man and a woman, they become husband and wife after solemnization of the marriage and their respective rights and obligations are regulated by the rules under relevant law. This being the position, marriage is the basis for social organization and foundation of legal rights and obligations. The modern concept of divorce is also that the matrimonial status should be maintained as far as possible. Under Section 7 of the Family Courts Act, 1984, cases relating to matrimonial status of any person are within the jurisdiction of the Family Court. The Family Court aims at reconciliation and persuasion of parties to arrive at a settlement. For these reasons, if a Mahomedan husband divorces his wife at his whim and caprice, it would not only be a spiritual offence but it would also affect the divorce. In the above view of the matter, a Mahomedan husband cannot divorce his wife at his whim or caprice, that is, divorce must be for a reasonable cause, and it must be preceded by a pre-divorce conference to arrive at a settlement. Therefore, we are in agreement with the decision of this Court, and we respectfully are unable to agree with the view taken by the other High Courts that divorce can be made at whim and caprice of the husband. The decisions of this Court were made by the Single Judge in the year 1978 and by the Division Bench in the year 1979, before 14/15 years ago. Therefore, the question of unsettling the settled position of law does not arise.

The next question which arises for consideration is whether divorce by talak has been proved. The case of the husband is that he had divorced his wife by a written document in presence of the witnesses and had handed over talaknama to his wife. Thereafter, a photostat copy of the talaknama was made over to Sadar Kazi of Guwahati for registration of the divorce. A photostat copy of talaknama has been filed. It is settled that a photostat copy of a document is admissible as secondary evidence, if it is proved to be genuine (see Ashok Dulichand v. Madhavlal Dube, AIR 1975 SC 1748). In the present case, the foundation for admission of the photostat copy as secondary evidence has not been laid. No attested copy of the entry of registration of divorce has been produced. Therefore, the husband has failed to prove alleged talaknama. However, in the evidence of the husband, he has stated that he also made pronouncement of the word 'talak' three times. There is no evidence or material to corroborate that talak was effected orally. That apart, the written statement indicates that the case is solely based on talaknama. Under the circumstances, it is held that the talak pleaded has not been proved. Further, we have concluded that the divorce must be for reasonable cause and it must be preceded by pre-divorce conference to arrive at a settlement. There is no evidence that there was a pre-divorce conference. In that view of the matter, the husband has failed to prove the alleged divorced by talak.

8. Mr P.K. Barua, learned counsel for the respondent, has contended that, even if talak pleaded is not proved the husband has stated that she had been divorced not only in his written statement; but also in his deposition and, therefore, the divorce would be deemed to have been effected from the date of filling of the written statement or from the date of statement on oath. The learned counsel has, in order to support his contention, relied on the decisions reported in Asmat Ullah v. Mst Khatun Unnisa, AIR 1939 All 592; Wahab Ali v. Qamro Bibi, AIR 1951 Hyd 117; Chand Bi v. Bandesha, AIR 1961 Bom 121; Abdul Shakoor v. Kulsum, 1962 (1) CrLJ 247; and Mohammed Ali v. Fareedunnisa, AIR 1970 AP 199.

9. In the above cited cases, wife made claim for maintenance under Section 488 (old) 125 (new), Cr. P. C. In those cases, it has been held that, where in proceedings started under Section 488 (old): 125 (new): Cr. P. C., by a Mahomedan wife against her husband for her maintenance, the husband states in written statement that he had already divorced his wife and the Court comes to the conclusion that divorce pleaded is not proved, then such a statement in the written statement itself operates as an expression or declaration of divorce by talak, and the divorce would be held to take effect at least from the date on which the written statement was filed by the husband. The reason for the decision is that the statement made by the husband orally in his deposition or in his written statement that he had divorced his wife is an acknowledgement of

talak alleged to have effected by him already and, therefore, the divorce would be held to have effect at least from the date upon which the acknowledgement is made.

10. We respectfully submit that we are unable to agree with the decisions in the above-referred cases for the following reasons. Written statement is a pleading. Pleading is one thing and proof is another. Pleading is formal allegations by the parties of their respective claims and defences to provide notice of what is to be expected at trial. Proof is establishment of a fact by evidence of matters before the Court or legal tribunal. Where the parties are in dispute as regards a material fact, an averment in the pleading does not constitute evidence, as what is stated in the pleading is recital of past event which is required to be proved. Under the Evidence Act, if a material fact pleaded is not proved, it follows that the Court considers or believes that the fact does not exist. Therefore, averment in the pleading cannot be used in favour of the maker. This being the position, statement made by the husband in his pleading or deposition that he has divorced his wife is recital of past event, and, if talak pleaded is not proved such statement shall be of no consequence. In that view of matter, if statement made by the husband that he had divorced his wife in his pleading or deposition is considered as an acknowledgement of divorce by talak, it will be against the policy of law, and it would also amount to furnishing or providing evidence of talak, which is against the rule of pleading and proof. That apart, in view of our conclusion above that divorce must be for a reasonable cause and it must be preceded by a pre-divorce conference, if the statement made orally in evidence or in the written statement that the husband has divorced his wife in a proceeding under Section 125, Cr. P. C., will be a valid talak from the date of making statement cannot be sustained as it would be contrary to our conclusion, For the reasons stated above, the contention of Mr. Barua is rejected.

11. In the result, the order of the Family Court made on 7-8-92 in Case No. FC (Cril) No. 111/92/74-M/90 in so far as findings with regard to divorce is set aside. The matter is sent back for disposal afresh in accordance with law.

12. The revision petition is allowed.

S.B. ROY, J. I agree.

Revision allowed.

21

Shamim Ara v. State of U.P.

JUDGMENT

R.C. LAHOTI, J. Shamim Ara, the appellant and Abrar Ahmed, Respondent 2 were married sometime in 1968 according to Muslim Shariat law. Four sons were born out of the wedlock. On 12-4-1979, the appellant, on behalf of herself and for her two minor children, filed an application under Section 125 CrPC complaining of desertion and cruelty on the part of Respondent 2 with her. By order dated 3-4-1993 the learned Presiding Judge of the Family Court at Allahabad refused to grant any maintenance to the appellant on the ground that she was already divorced by the respondent and hence not entitled to any maintenance. However, maintenance at the rate of Rs 150 per month was allowed for one son of the appellant for the period during which he remained a minor; the other one having become a major during the pendency of the proceedings.

2. Respondent 2 in his reply (written statement) dated 5-12-1990, to the application under Section 125 CrPC, denied all the averments made in the application. One of the pleas taken by way of additional pleas is that he had divorced the appellant on 11-7-1987 and since then the parties had ceased to be spouses. He also claimed protection behind the MWA, 1986 and submitted that Respondent 2 had purchased a house and delivered the same to the appellant in lieu of *mehar* (dower), and therefore, the appellant was not entitled to any maintenance. No particulars of divorce were pleaded excepting making a bold statement as already stated hereinabove.

3. The appellant emphatically denied having been divorced at any time. Respondent 2, when he appeared in the witness box, stated having divorced the appellant on 11-7-1987 at 11 a.m. in the presence of Mehboob and other 4-5 persons of the neighbourhood. He further stated that since 1988 he had not paid anything either to the appellant or to any of the four sons for their maintenance. The divorce said to have been given by him to the appellant was a triple *talaq* though such a fact was not stated in the written statement.

4. The Family Court in its order dated 3-4-1993 dealt with and upheld a strange story of divorce totally beyond the case set up by Respondent 2. The learned Presiding Judge referred to some affidavit dated 31-8-1988 said to have been filed by Respondent 2 in some civil suit details whereof are not available from the record of the present case but certainly to which litigation the appellant was not a party. In that affidavit it was stated by Respondent 2 that he had divorced the appellant 15 months before. The learned Judge held that from such affidavit the plea of Respondent 2 found corroboration of his having divorced the appellant. The learned Judge concluded that the appellant was not entitled to any maintenance in view of her having been divorced.

5. The appellant preferred a revision before the High Court. The High Court held that the divorce which is alleged to have been given by Respondent 2 to the appellant was not given in the presence of the appellant and it is not the case of the respondent that the same was communicated to her. But the communication would stand completed on 5-12-1990 with the filing of the written statement by Respondent 2 in the present case. Therefore, the High Court concluded that the appellant was entitled to claim maintenance from 1-1-1988 to 5-12-1990 (the later date being the one on which reply to application under Section 125 CrPC was filed by Respondent 2 in the Court) whereafter her entitlement to have maintenance from Respondent 2 shall cease. The figure of maintenance was appointed by the High Court at Rs 200.

6. The appellant has filed this by special leave. The singular issue arising for decision is whether the appellant can be said to have been divorced and the said divorce communicated to the appellant so as to become effective from 5-12-1990, the date of filing of the written statement by Respondent 2 in these proceedings.

7. None of the ancient holy books or scriptures of Muslims mentions in its text such a form of divorce as has been accepted by the High Court

and the Family Court. No such text has been brought to our notice which provides that a recital in any document, whether a pleading or an affidavit, incorporating a statement by the husband that he has already divorced his wife on an unspecified or specified date even if not communicated to the wife would become an effective divorce on the date on which the wife happens to learn of such statement contained in the copy of the affidavit or pleading served on her. Mulla on *Principles of Mahomedan Law* (19th Edn., 1990) states vide para 310:

310. *Talak may be oral or in writing.*—A talak may be effected (1) orally (by spoken words) or (2) by a written document called a *talaknama (d)*.

(I) Oral talak.—No particular form of words is prescribed for effecting a talak. If the words are express (*saheeh*) or well understood as implying divorce no proof of intention is required. If the words are ambiguous (*kinayat*), the intention must be proved (*e*). It is not necessary that the talak should be pronounced in the presence of the wife or even addressed to her (*f*). In a Calcutta case the husband merely pronounced the word '*talak*' before a family council and this was held to be invalid as the wife was not named (*g*). This case was cited with approval by the Judicial Committee in a case where the *talak* was valid though pronounced in the wife's absence, as the wife was named (*h*). The Madras High Court has also held that the words should refer to the wife (*i*). The talak pronounced in the absence of the wife takes effect though not communicated to her, but for purposes of dower it is not necessary that it should come to her knowledge (*j*); and her alimony may continue till she is informed of the divorce (*k*). As the divorce becomes effective for purposes of dower only when communicated to the wife, limitation under Article 104 for the wife's suit for deferred dower ran from the time when the divorce comes to her notice (*l*), under the Act of 1908. See also the Limitation Act, 1963.

Words of divorce—The words of divorce must indicate an intention to dissolve the marriage. If they are express (*saheeh*), e.g., 'Thou are *divorced*'; 'I have *divorced thee*' or 'I divorce my wife forever and render her haram from me' (*Rashid Ahmad* v. *Anisa Khatun*) (*h*), they clearly indicate an intention to dissolve the marriage and no proof of intention is necessary. But if they are ambiguous (*kinayat*), e.g., 'Thou art my cousin, the daughter of my uncle, if thou goest' (*Hamid Ali* v. *Imtiazan* ILR (1878) 2 All 71) or 'I give up all relations and would have no connection of any sort with you' (*Wajid Ali Khan* v. *Jafar Husain Khan* ILR (1932) 7 Luck 430 : 136 IC 209 : AIR 1932 Oudh 34), the intention must be proved.

Pronouncement of the word *talak* in the presence of the wife or when the knowledge of such pronouncement comes to the knowledge of the wife, results in the dissolution of the marriage. The intention of the husband is inconsequential. *Ghansi Bibi* v. *Ghulam Dastagir* 3 (1968) 1 Mys LJ 566.

If a man says to his wife that she has been divorced yesterday or earlier, it leads to a divorce between them, even if there be no proof of a divorce on the previous day or earlier.

(*d*) See *Ma Mi* v. *Kallander Ammal*. AIR 1927 PC 15: 100 IC 1: (1927) 54 IA 61: ILR 5 Rang 18 affirming *Kalenther Ammal* v. *Ma Mi*, ILR (1924) 2 Rang 400.

(*e*) *Ma Mi* v. *Kallander Ammal*, supra: *Asha Bibi* v. *Kadir Ibrahim Rowther*, ILR (1909) 33 Mad 22 : 3 IC 730; *Wahid Khan* v. *Zainab Bibi*, ILR (1914) 36 All 458: 25 IC 387; *Ibrahim* v. *Syed Bibi* ILR (1888) 12 Mad 63.

(*f*) *Ma Mi* v. *Kallander Ammal*, supra: *Ahmad Kasim Molla* v. *Khatun Bibi*, ILR (1932) 59 Cal 833: 141 IC 689: AIR 1933 Cal 27: *Ful Chand* v. *Nazab Ali Chowdhary*, ILR (1909) 36 Cal 184: 1 *Sarabai* v. *Rabiabai*, ILR (1905) 30 Bom 537: 8 Bom LR 35.

(*g*) *Furzund Hossein* v. *Janu Bibee*, ILR (1878) 4 Cal 588.

(*h*) *Rashid Ahmad* v. *Anisa Khatun*, (1931-32) 59 IA 21: ILR (1932) 54 All 46: 135 IC 762: AIR 1932 PC 25.

(*i*) *Asha Bibi* v. *Kadir*, supra.

(*j*) *Ful Chand* v. *Nazab Ali*, supra.

(*k*) *Ma Mi* v. *Kallander Ammal*, supra: M.M. *Abdul Khader* v. *Azeeza Bee*, (1944) I MLJ 17: 214 IC 38: AIR 1944 Mad 227.

(*l*) *Kathiyumma* v. *Urathe Marakkar*, (1931) 133 IC 375: AIR 1931 Mad 647.

The statement of law by Mulla as contained in para 310 and footnotes thereunder is based on certain rulings of the Privy Council and the High Courts. The decision of the A.P. High Court in (1975) 1 APLJ 20 has also been cited by Mulla in support of the proposition that the statement by the husband in pleadings filed in answer to petition for maintenance by the wife that he had already divorced the petitioner (wife) long ago operates as divorce.

8. We will offer our comments on this a little later. Immediately we proceed to notice a few other authorities.

9. In Dr. Tahir Mahmood's *The Muslim Law of India* (2nd Edn., at pp. 113-19), the basic rule stated is that a Muslim husband under all schools of Muslim law can divorce his wife by his unilateral action and without the intervention of the court. This power is known as the power to pronounce a *talaq*. A few decided cases are noticed by the learned

author wherein it has been held that a statement made by the husband during the course of any judicial proceedings such as in the wife's suit for maintenance or restitution of conjugal rights, or the husband's plea of divorce raised in the pleadings did effect a *talaq*.

10. Such liberal view of *talaq* bringing to an end the marital relationship between Muslim spouses and heavily loaded in favour of Muslim husbands has met with criticism and strong disapproval at the hands of eminent jurists.

11. V. Khalid. J., as His Lordship then was, observed in *Mohd Haneefa* v. *Pathummal Beevi*, 1972 KLT 512, p. 514, para 5,

> ...I feel it my duty to alert public opinion towards a painful aspect that this case reveals. A Division Bench of this Court, the highest court for this State, has clearly indicated the extent of the unbridled power of a Muslim husband to divorce his wife. I am extracting below what Their Lordships have said in *Pathayi* v. *Moideen* 1968 KLT 763:
>
> 'The only condition necessary for the valid exercise of the right of divorce by a husband is that he must be a major and of sound mind at that time. He can effect divorce whenever he desires. Even if he divorces his wife under compulsion, or in jest, or in anger that is considered perfectly valid. No special form is necessary for effecting divorce under Hanafi law.... The husband can effect it by conveying to the wife that he is repudiating the alliance. It need not even be addressed to her. It takes effect the moment it comes to her knowledge.'
>
> Should Muslim wives suffer this tyranny for all times? Should their personal law remain so cruel towards these unfortunate wives? Can it not be amended suitably to alleviate their sufferings? My judicial conscience is disturbed at this monstrosity. The question is whether the conscience of the leaders of public opinion of the community will also be disturbed.

12. In an illuminating judgment, virtually a research document, the eminent judge and jurist V.R. Krishna Iyer, J., as His Lordship then was, has made extensive observations. The judgment is reported as *A Yousuf Rawther* v. *Sowramma*, AIR 1971 Ker 261: 1970 Ker LT 477. It would suffice for our purpose to extract and reproduce a few out of the several observations made by His Lordship: (pp. 264-65, paras 6-7):

> 6. The interpretation of a legislation, obviously intended to protect a weaker section of the community, like women, must be informed by the social perspective and purpose and, within its grammatical flexibility, must further the beneficent object. And so we must appreciate the

Islamic ethos and the general sociological background which inspired the enactment of the law before locating the precise connotation of the words used in the statute.

7.... Since infallibility is not an attribute of the judiciary, the view has been ventured by Muslim jurists that the Indo-Anglican judicial exposition of the Islamic law of divorce has not exactly been just to the Holy Prophet or the Holy Book. Marginal distortions are inevitable when the Judicial Committee in Downing Street has to interpret Manu and Muhammad of India and Arabia. The soul of a culture—law is largely the formalized and enforceable expression of a community's cultural norms—cannot be fully understood by alien minds. The view that the Muslim husband enjoys an arbitrary, unilateral power to inflict instant divorce does not accord with Islamic injunctions.... It is a popular fallacy that a Muslim male enjoys, under the Quoranic law, unbridled authority to liquidate the marriage. The whole Quoran expressly forbids a man to seek pretexts for divorcing his wife, so long as she remains faithful and obedient to him. 'if they (namely, women) obey you, then do not seek a way against them'. (Quoran IV: 34). The Islamic law gives to the man primarily the faculty of dissolving the marriage, if the wife, by her indocility or her bad character, renders the married life unhappy: but in the absence of serious reasons, no man can justify a divorce, either in the eye of religion or the law. If he abandons his wife or puts her away in simple caprice, he draws upon himself the divine anger, for the curse of God, said the Prophet, rests on him who repudiates his wife capriciously'.... Commentators on the Quoran have rightly observed—and this tallies with the law now administered in Muslim countries like Iraq—that the husband must satisfy the court about the reasons for divorce. However, Muslim law, as applied in India, has taken a course contrary to the spirit of what the Prophet or the Holy Quoran laid down and the same misconception vitiated the law dealing with the wife's right to divorce.... After quoting from the Quoran and the Prophet, Dr Galwash concludes that divorce is permissible in Islam only in cases of extreme emergency. When all efforts for effecting a reconciliation have failed, the parties may proceed to a dissolution of the marriage by *'talaq* or *by khola'*.... Consistently with the secular concept of marriage and divorce, the law insists that at the time of *talaq* the husband must pay off the settlement debt to the wife and at the time of *khola* she has to surrender to the husband her dower or abandon some of her rights, as compensation.

13. There is yet another illuminating and weighty judicial opinion available in two decisions of the Gauhati High Court recorded by

Baharul Islam, J. (later a Judge of the Supreme Court of India) sitting singly in *Jiauddin Ahmed* v. *Anwara Begum*, (1981) 1 Gau LR 358 and later speaking for the Division Bench in *Rukia Khatun* v. *Abdul Khalique Laskar*, (1981) 1 Gau LR 375. In *Jiauddin Ahmed* case a plea of previous divorce i.e. the husband having divorced the wife on some day much previous to the date of filing of the written statement in the Court was taken and upheld. The question posed before the High Court was whether there has been valid *talaq* of the wife by the husband under the Muslim law. The learned Judge observed that though marriage under the Muslim law is only a civil contract yet the rights and responsibilities consequent upon it are of such importance to the welfare of humanity, that a high degree of sanctity is attached to it. But in spite of the sacredness of the character of the marriage tie, Islam recognizes the necessity, in exceptional circumstances, of keeping the way open for its dissolution (para 6). Quoting in the judgment several Holy Quranic verses and from commentaries thereon by well-recognized scholars of great eminence, the learned Judge expressed disapproval of the statement that 'the whimsical and capricious divorce by the husband is good in law, though bad in theology' and observed that such a statement is based on the concept that women were chattel belonging to men, which the Holy Quran does not brook. The correct law of *talaq* as ordained by the Holy Quran is that *talaq* must be for a reasonable cause and be preceded by attempts at reconciliation between the husband and the wife by two arbiters—one from the wife's family and the other from the husband's; if the attempts fail, *talaq* may be effected (para 13). In *Rukia Khatun* case the Division Bench stated that the correct law of *talaq*, as ordained by the holy Quran, is: (*i*) that '*talaq*' must be for a reasonable cause; and (*ii*) that it must be preceded by an attempt of reconciliation between the husband and the wife by two arbiters, one chosen by the wife from her family and the other by the husband from his. If their attempts fail, '*talaq*' may be effected. The Division Bench expressly recorded its dissent from the Calcutta and Bombay views which, in their opinion, did not lay down the correct law.

14. We are in respectful agreement with the abovesaid observations made by the learned Judges of the High Courts. We must note that the observations were made 20-30 years before and our country has in recent times marched steps ahead in all walks of life including progressive interpretation of laws which cannot be lost sight of except

by compromising with regressive trends. What this Court observed in *Bai Tahira* v. *Ali Hussain Fidaalli Chothia*, (1979) 2 SCC 316: 1979 SCC (Cri) 473: AIR 1979 SC 362, dealing with the right to maintenance of a Muslim divorce is noteworthy. To quote: (AIR pp. 365 & 366, paras 7 & 12)

> The meaning of meanings is derived from values in a given society and its legal system. Article 15(3) has compelling, compassionate relevance in the context of Section 125 and the benefit of doubt, if any, in statutory interpretation belongs to the ill-used wife and the derelict divorcee. This social perspective granted, the resolution of all the disputes projected is easy. Surely, Parliament, in keeping with Article 15(3) and deliberate by design, made a special provision to help women in distress cast away by divorce. Protection against moral and material abandonment manifest in Article 39 is part of social and economic justice, specificated in Article 38, fulfilment of which is fundamental to the governance of the country (Article 37). From this coignage of vantage we must view the printed text of the particular code.... Law is dynamic and its meaning cannot be pedantic but purposeful.

15. The plea taken by Respondent 2 husband in his written statement may be noticed. Respondent 2 vaguely makes certain generalized accusations against the appellant wife and states that ever since the marriage he found his wife to be sharp, shrewd and mischievous. Accusing the wife of having brought disgrace to the family, Respondent 2 proceeds to state, vide para 12 (translated into English)—'The answering respondent, feeling fed up with all such activities unbecoming of the petitioner wife, has divorced her on 11-7-1987.' The particulars of the alleged *talaq* are not pleaded nor the circumstances under which and the persons, if any, in whose presence *talaq* was pronounced have been stated. Such deficiency continued to prevail even during the trial and Respondent 2, except examining himself, adduced no evidence in proof of *talaq* said to have been given by him on 11-7-1987. There are no reasons substantiated in justification of *talaq* and no plea or proof that any effort at reconciliation preceded the *talaq*.

16. We are also of the opinion that the *talaq* to be effective has to be pronounced. The term 'pronounce' means to proclaim, to utter formally, to utter rhetorically, to declare, to utter, to articulate (see *Chambers 20th Century Dictionary*, New Edition, p. 1030). There is no proof of *talaq* having taken place on 11-7-1987. What the High Court has upheld as

talaq is the plea taken in the written statement and its communication to the wife by delivering a copy of the written statement on 5-12-1990. We are very clear in our mind that a mere plea taken in the written statement of a divorce having been pronounced sometime in the past cannot by itself be treated as effectuating *talaq* on the date of delivery of the copy of the written statement to the wife. Respondent 2 ought to have adduced evidence and proved the pronouncement of *talaq* on 11-7-1987 and if he failed in proving the plea raised in the written statement, the plea ought to have been treated as failed. We do not agree with the view propounded in the decided cases referred to by Mulla and Dr Tahir Mahmood in their respective commentaries, wherein a mere plea of previous *talaq* taken in the written statement, though unsubstantiated, has been accepted as proof of *talaq* bringing to an end the marital relationship with effect from the date of filing of the written statement. A plea of previous divorce taken in the written statement cannot at all be treated as pronouncement of *talaq* by the husband on the wife on the date of filing of the written statement in the Court followed by delivery of a copy thereof to the wife. So also the affidavit dated 31-8-1988, filed in some previous judicial proceedings not inter parties, containing a self-serving statement of Respondent 2, could not have been read in evidence as relevant and of any value.

17. For the foregoing reasons, the appeal is allowed. Neither the marriage between the parties stands dissolved on 5-12-1990 nor does the liability of Respondent 2 to pay maintenance comes to an end on that day. Respondent 2 shall continue to remain liable for payment of maintenance until the obligation comes to an end in accordance with law. The costs in this appeal shall be borne by Respondent 2.

22

Mangila Bibi v. Noor Hossain

ORDER

Stripped of unnecessary detail the petitioner Mangila Bibi was admit-tedly married with the opposite party No. 1 Noor Hossain on the 6th March, 1986, according to Muslim rites when a Kabinnama was executed. She contended that after the marriage she came to know that the said opposite party was not a medical graduate as represented before the marriage and further, she was ill-treated at her husband's place and ultimately driven away. In this situation, she dissolved the marriage by virtue of the authority delegated to her by her husband as recorded in the Kabinnama and executed a divorce deed before the Muslim Marriage Registrar and Kazi on the 27th February, 1988. The divorce was communicated to the said opposite party but as he did not pay any maintenance and dower and other properties given to her at the time of marriage as noted in the Kabinnama, she made an application under Section 3 of the MWA, 1986, before a competent Magistrate for appropriate relief.

2. This application was sought to be resisted on behalf of the said opposite party mainly, on the ground that the petitioner was not a divorced woman as there was never any delegation of power to give talak. He also contended that even if, there was any such delegation of power to give talak, it could be exercised only in specified contingencies and since no such contingency had taken place, the petitioner could not lawfully repudiate herself. He also no doubt denied the allegation of false representation said to have been made by him before the marriage as well as the allegation of ill-treatment. He has also taken a plea that

certain entries in the Kabinnama were made against his will and some others were written subsequently without his knowledge.

3. The learned Magistrate has found on evidence that the petitioner had power to dissolve the marriage but such power could be exercised by her only when any of the conditions specified in the agreement was violated by her husband. He has further, held that since there was no such violation she could not validly give a talak and accordingly the marriage was still subsisting and so the application made by her as a divorced woman could not be sustained. Another ground which weighed with the learned Magistrate in dismissing the application was that in any event it was premature because the talak, even if given, was not communicated to the said opposite party and thus he had no opportunity to make payment of dower etc., or to deliver the goods said to have been given to her at the time of marriage. The learned Magistrate has overruled the plea of the said opposite party that certain entries in the Kabinnama were made against his will or without his knowledge and also disbelieved the petitioner's case regarding the alleged ill-treatment to her.

4. Mr. Habibullah appearing in support of the rule has assailed the finding of the learned Magistrate that the power to dissolve the marriage could be exercised by the petitioner only when any of the conditions specified in the agreement was violated by her husband and it was pointed out that the Kabinnama tendered in evidence as Ext. I did not stipulate that such power could be exercised only on the happening of any contingency. The finding of the learned Magistrate that the evidence did not reveal any ground for giving talak has not been challenged and indeed, it being a pure question of fact could not be challenged in revision. The Kabinnama Ext. I apparently delegates an unrestricted power to the petitioner to give talak and, therefore, the principal question which calls for adjudication is whether she had an absolute authority to dissolve the marriage at her will or whether such power could be exercised by her only in certain circumstances. Mr. Habibullah has drawn inspiration from Article 314 of Mulla's Mahammadan Law to argue that the power to give divorce which primarily belongs to the husband may be delegated to his wife either absolutely or conditionally. The argument is further reinforced by the observation of Ameer Ali in his Mahommadan Law (15th ed.) Volume 11, pages 495–497 to the effect that tafwiz—which means delegation of option by the husband to his wife conferring on her the power of divorcing herself—is of three

kinds including one called Mashiet which leaves the exercise of power absolutely to the pleasure or will of the party to whom the power is delegated. Thus it is abundantly clear from the observation made by these erudite authors that the delegation of the power to divorce can be made either conditionally or without any condition at all. This view also finds support from a Bench decision of this Court is Sainuddin v. Latifannessa Bibi, (1919) ILR 46 Cal 141: (AIR 1919 Cal 631). In this case their Lordships after quoting extensively from texts on Muslim Law have pointed out that the delegation may be unconditional and reference was made to certain passages of various authorities, particularly in Fatawa-i-Alamgiri, Volume 1, p. 562, Cal. ed., whereunder if a man said to his wife that her business was in her hand when or whenever she desired, it was open to her to divorce herself at once at the same place or outside it at any time she chose. Thus there is least difficulty in holding that there is no authority which prohibits the wife to exercise the power of divorce delegated to her by her husband save in certain circumstances.

5. Mr. Roy, the learned counsel for the opposite party has, however, heavily relied upon the decision of the Supreme Court in Mst. Zohara Khatoon v. Mohd. Ibrahim, AIR 1981 SC 1243: (1981 Cri LJ 754) in which it was observed that under the Mohammedan Law, there are three distinct modes for dissolving a marriage one of which was by virtue of an agreement either before or after the marriage by which it was provided that the wife should be at liberty to divorce herself in specified contingencies provided such contingencies were of a reasonable nature and were agreed to by the husband. In that case, Zohara Khatoon obtained a decree for dissolution of marriage under the Dissolution of Muslim Marriages Act, on ground of cruelty and wilful neglect and subsequently made an application before a competent Magistrate under S. 125 of the Code of Criminal Procedure 1973 contending that although divorced she could still claim maintenance, looking to the enlarged meaning of 'wife' as given in Cl. (b) of the Explanation to S. 125 (1) of the Code. The ex-husband Mohd. Ibrahim took the plea that the applicant Zohara Khatoon was not entitled to claim maintenance as she has ceased to be his wife. The Magistrate found against the ex-husband and suitable order was made in favour of Zohara Khatoon, which was also upheld by the Sessions Judge in revision. Mohd. Ibrahim thereafter moved the High Court invoking its inherent jurisdiction under S. 482, Code of Criminal Procedure which held that Cl. (b) of the Explanation to S. 125

(1) of the Code of Criminal Procedure, 1973 would apply only if the divorce proceeded from the husband and not in a case where the dissolution of marriage was brought about by the wife under the Dissolution of Muslim Marriages Act, and as such Zohara Khatoon was not entitled to get any maintenance for herself. There was an appeal in the Supreme Court which was thus seized with the question whether Cl. (b) of the Explanation to S. 125 (1), Code of Criminal Procedure would be attracted in a case where the marriage was dissolved at the instance of the wife under the said Act and not with the question whether a husband could delegate to his wife the power to divorce herself unconditionally or without the happening of any contingency. Therefore, this decision does not appear to be an authority for the proposition that there cannot be any unconditional delegation of the power to divorce.

6. The learned Magistrate has taken the view that since the Kabinnama was executed by both the spouses, it was a bilateral agreement and relying upon certain observations made by Dr. Tahir Mammod in his renowned treatise on the Muslim Law of India (1980 ed.) at page 124, he held that the law demands :-

(a) that the delegation must not be absolute;
(b) the wife should be authorized to pronounce talak only when any of the conditions specified in the agreement is violated by the husband; and
(c) those conditions must be reasonable and must not be opposed to the policy of the Islamic Law.

It appears that the learned author has also observed in the very next paragraph, that the aforesaid requirements do not apply where a husband unilaterally authorizes a wife to divorce herself without an agreement with her in this regard. Thus it is not an inflexible rule of law that the delegation of power to divorce cannot be absolute but must be conditional and the issue will be determined upon the finding whether the delegation was made under a bilateral agreement or by the husband unilaterally. In the instant case, even though the Kabinnama Ext. I bears signature of both the spouses, it does not necessarily follow that the delegation of the power to give talak was made bilaterally. A reference to this document would show that in col. 16 thereof the groom of his own will bound himself with the condition that his wife Mangila Bibi would be in a position to give talak ex parte and at her will. Such a situation, even though contained in an instrument signed by both the spouses, cannot be regarded as a bilateral delegation of the power to give talak. There might be bilateral delegation if it was recorded that both the spouses agreed that the wife would have the power to repudiate herself and in such a case it might be said, on the basis of the observation made by Dr. Mahmood, that the wife would not have unfettered liberty to divorce herself. In the case on hand, however, inescapable conclusion seems to be that the opposite party Noor Hossain the husband had unilaterally delegated to the petitioner a power to divorce unconditionally and since it is not prohibited by the personal law of the parties, as already found, it was quite open to her to divorce herself at her will as she in fact, did. In other words, the petitioner was very much a divorced woman and the finding of the learned Magistrate that the marriage was still subsisting cannot be upheld.

7. The other finding of the learned Magistrate that the application made by the petitioner was in any case premature because the talak, even if given, was not communicated to the said opposite party and so he had no opportunity to make payment of dower etc., is also liable to be struck down, as it is found that Saiyad Noor Alla Khandakar P. W. 2 who was assisting the Marriage Registrar and Kazi, Saiyad Golam Ahiya Khandakar P. W. 1 in the dissolution of marriage by the petitioner, has stated in his examination-in-chief that the opposite party was informed of the talak which was not challenged in his cross-examination. The learned Magistrate has apparently overlooked this unchallenged evidence regarding the communication of talak to the said opposite party and, therefore, his finding that the said opposite party had no opportunity to make payment of dower etc., or for this reason the application made by the petitioner was premature cannot be sustained.

8. For the reason stated above, the order of the learned Magistrate dismissing the application of the petitioner under S 3 of the MWA, 1986 is set aside and he is directed to determine, on the evidence already on record the relief to which the petitioner may be entitled and dispose of the application in accordance with the provisions of law with utmost expedition.

The record be sent down immediately.

                                                Order accordingly.

Khurshid Gauhar v. *Siddiqunnisa*

ORDER

This revision is directed against an order dt. Oct. 4, 1985 allowing an application filed by the mother for the interim custody of a minor child, a son aged about three and a half years at the time of making of the application, having been born on Jan. 12, 1982. The said application was filed by the mother of the child under S. 25 of the Guardians and Wards Act for an order for the return of the child from the custody of the applicant who is his father.

2. The relevant facts are that the applicant and the opposite party were married on May 11, 1980 and on Jan. 12, 1982, a son (the child in question) was born to them. On July 20, 1985 the applicant divorced the opposite party and it is alleged that he turned out the opposite party from the marital home and took the child from her custody and entrusted him to the care of his second wife. Thereafter on July 26, 1985, the opposite party filed an application under the Guardians and Wards Act stating the aforesaid facts and praying that she be appointed the guardian of the child and be given the custody of the child so that he may be reared and taken care of properly. A few days later the mother filed an application under S. 12 of the said Act for the interim custody of the child. In this application it was alleged that her husband has forcibly snatched the child from her and has turned her out of the house. She has only one child whereas her husband has five children from his second wife. She has grave apprehension that the step mother of the child, namely, the second wife of the applicant who has five children of her

own, would grossly ill-treat the child. The child is already living under fear and there is even grave danger to the life of the child. The applicant has not been allowed to meet the child and if the interim custody of the child is not immediately granted, the poor and innocent child would be exposed to grave risk of life. The application for interim custody was contested by the applicant who filed a written objection in which it was alleged that the mother was a woman of loose character. She has no house and means to support the child. She is a school teacher and would have no time to look after the child. It was further pleaded that the applicant was the natural guardian of the minor and hence he could not be deprived of the custody of the child.

3. Both the parties filed affidavit in support of their respective allegations. The Court below has on a consideration of the material on record, recorded a finding that in the interest of the child the interim custody must be granted to the mother and made a direction to that effect. While allowing this application the Court below also observed that if, at any time, the applicant found that the child was not being properly maintained by his mother he may move an application for the recall of order. It also fixed Nov. 1, 1985, for evidence observing that in the interest of justice the case should be decided at the earliest. The parties had exchanged their pleadings and only evidence and argument remained to be adduced and heard. The Court below has referred to the authorities relevant to the issue arising for consideration and thereafter applies [*sic*] the principles emerging therefrom to the facts of the present case. It has concluded that there are valid grounds for believing the case of the applicant that the child would not be looked after properly by the step mother who has five children of her own from the applicant. It has further observed that in view of the settled legal position that a mother governed by the Mohammedan Law is entitled to the custody of her male child until he has completed the age of seven years and further in view of the facts mentioned above the interest of the minor which is of paramount consideration in such cases clearly demanded that the wife be allowed the interim custody of the child.

4. The first contention raised by the learned counsel was that the Additional District Judge who has passed the impugned order was not authorized under the Guardians and Wards Act to entertain an application either under S. 25 or S. 12 of the said Act. This argument was, however, immediately given up when the relevant notification issued

by the High Court in the exercise of powers conferred by S. 4-A of the Guardians and Wards Act on Nov. 27, 1958 was brought to the notice of the Court by the learned counsel for the wife. Under this notification the High Court has empowered all the Additional District Judges in the State to dispose of any proceedings under the Guardians and Wards Act.

5. The second submission in support of the revision was that the application filed by the wife under S. 25 itself is not maintainable and consequently the Court below had no jurisdiction to grant interim custody under S. 12 of the Act. It was urged that in the present case as the mother was living away from the husband the right of Hizanat which she had under the personal law disappeared. In support, learned counsel placed reliance on a decision of this Court reported in AIR 1932 All 215 (Mt. Siddiqunnisa Bibi v. Nizamuddin Khan). The contrary view expressed by this Court in the decision reported in 1983 All WC 572 (Hafizur Rahman v. Smt. Shakila Khatoon) relied on by the Court below, it was submitted, did not lay down the law correctly.

6. Having heard learned counsel for the parties at some length and given the matter a careful consideration I find no merit in the above contention. In my opinion, insofar as the question of the maintainability of the application filed by the opposite party under S. 25 is concerned the same stands squarely covered and concluded by the latest decision of this Court reported in Hafizur Rahman's case (supra). The facts of that case are in pari materia with those of the present case. There also the petition under S. 25 had been filed by a divorced wife who had been expelled from the marital home of her husband and the child was removed from her custody. A similar argument as the one advanced in the present case came up for consideration before the bench which, after a very careful analysis of the law on the subject, as spelled out by leading authorities, both textual and judicial precedents, summed up the legal position at page 576 thus:

(1) the father is the natural and legal guardian of the infant child but the right to the custody of the child is of the mother till he attains the age of seven years.

(2) being entitled to custody of the child the respondent is guardian within the meaning of S. 25 as defined in S. 4(2) of the Act and entitled as such to apply for the purpose. 'Custody' over the child, in our opinion, necessarily imports the element of 'care' referred to in S. 4(2). The

custody entrusted to the mother is with the object namely that the child be reared properly by the person to whom he would naturally be most attached in the early years of his life.

(3) there is no conflict between guardianship of the father and the Hizanat of the mother. The two can co-exist side by side under the law. The mother exercises her right to rear up the child under the supervision and guidance of the father.

(4) the Hizanat of the mother is not lost by the mere fact that she has been divorced by the husband. The Hidaya and the Fatwa Alamgiri are recognized as standard authorities in this country on the Hanafi branch of the Sunni law, Imambandi v. Haji Mutsaddi, AIR 1918 PC 11, p. 18.

Ameer Ali points also that—

'The mother can on no account give up her right of Hizanat; for even if she were to obtain a khula in lieu of her abandoning her right to her child's custody, the khula will be valid, and she will retain the right of Hizanat' (Vol. II page 304).

The appellant in this case does not plead any of the recognized grounds for the loss of the mother's custody.

(5) the right of Hizanat is a personal right which the party entitled can enforce by a judicial proceeding under the Act (Ameer Ali, Vol. II page 303). In Mrs. Annie Besant's case, AIR 1914 PC 41 (supra).

7. The nature of right described under the Mohammedan Law as Hizanat was examined by this Court in considerable depth and it was observed that the basic postulate underlying, the theory of the mother's right of Hizanat is that for rearing the child of that tender age mother is the best suited and this right is not lost by the mere fact that she has been divorced by the husband.

8. This principle spelled out in the Mohammedan Law is based on practical experience based on considerations which are conducive to the proper growth of the child. It cannot be disputed that a child of that tender age would feel psychologically most secure in the company of the mother rather than the father. No one can compete with the mother in that respect ordinarily. The amount of love and care which a child receives from the mother cannot be had or expected from any other relation including the father. It is necessary to dilate on the subject as, in my opinion, the law has been very ably summed up by the Division Bench decision of this Court in the case of Hafizur Rahman (1983 All WC 572) (supra). I, however, cannot resist the temptation of citing a very apposite passage from Hamilton's 'Hidaya' (Vol. 1) page 385:

If a separation takes place between a husband and wife, who are possessed of an infant child, the right of nursing and keeping it rests with the mother because it is recorded that the woman once applied to the prophet, saying 'O prophet of God; this is my son, the fruit of my womb, cherished in my bosom and suckled at my breast, and his father is desirous of taking him away from me into his own care' to which the prophet replied 'thou hast a right in the child prior to that of thy husband, so long as thou does not marry with a stranger.' Moreover, a mother is naturally not only more tender, but also better qualified to cherish a child during infancy, so that committing the care to her is of advantage to the child....

9. With respect, I find myself in total agreement with the law spelled out in the case of Hafizur Rahman (1983 All WC 572) (supra) and hold that the application of the opposite party under S. 25 of the said Act is prima facie maintainable.

10. As regards the decision reported in AIR 1932 All 215, the learned counsel for the applicant contended that in this case it was held that if the lady claiming the right of Hizanat takes away the child from the place of his birth and away from his father at a distance from where the supervision of the child by the father would not be possible the limited right of Hizanat automatically comes to an end. To reinforce this argument learned counsel also placed reliance on a passage from Hamilton's Hidaya at page 139 in which there are some observations to the effect that a mother cannot remove the child to a strange place i.e. out of the city where the husband resides and if she does so the right of Hizanat would be lost to her.

11. I have given the above submission a careful consideration and I am clearly of the view that the above decision cited by the learned counsel is of no assistance in the present case. The sole ground on which learned counsel sought to support this contention was that whereas the husband resides at Daurala, Meerut, the wife is working as a teacher in the Government Girls College at Deoband, district Saharanpur. From this fact alone learned counsel wanted this court to conclude that the mother ipso facto forfeited her right of Hizanat. I am unable to agree. In the facts of the case reported in AIR 1932 All 215 this Court, after having held that considering the circumstances prevailing in that case the interest of the child would be best served if he was allowed to remain with the father and that the education of the child would suffer if he was allowed to remain with his maternal grandmother at Zamania,

ruled that the maternal grandmother had lost the right of Hizanat. The decision is, however, no authority for the proposition that in all circumstances as soon as the wife lives away from the husband she automatically loses her right of Hizanat. In the present case, nothing was brought to my notice beyond the fact that whereas the husband resides at Daurala in the district of Meerut the wife is working at Deoband in the district of Saharanpur to justify the conclusion that the wife has lost the right of Hizanat.

12. Further, Mulla in his commentary on Mohammedan Law has in S. 354 specified the grounds when a female becomes disqualified for the custody of a child. These have been set out as:

(1) if she marries a person not related to the the child within the prohibited degrees (Ss. 260-261) e.g. a stranger, but the right revives on the dissolution of the marriage by death or divorce; or

(2) if she goes and resides, during the subsistence of the marriage, at a distance from the father's place of residence; or

(3) if she is leading an immoral life, as where she is a prostitute; or

(4) if she neglects to take proper care of the child.

13. It will be seen that under the second ground enumerated above the female becomes disqualified only if she goes and resides during the subsistence of the marriage at a distance from the father's place of residence. We are here dealing with the case of a divorced wife. It is normal and natural for a divorced wife to reside separately and away from the husband and so long as it is not demonstrated that the general supervision of the child to which the father is entitled as the natural guardian has not become impossible, in my opinion, the mother cannot be deprived of the right of Hizanat. Moreover, as has been repeatedly stressed in the conflict of rival claims put forward by the father and the mother in regard to the custody of a child of tender age based on their respective rights under the personal law, the interest of the child cannot be sacrificed. The overriding consideration in all such cases and in all circumstances is the interest of the child and all other claims of rival parents must be subordinated to it. (See Mohd. Yunus v. Smt. Shamshad Bano, 1985 All WC 386 : (AIR 1985 All 217) following Dr. Mrs. Veena Kapoor v. Verinder Kumar Kapoor, AIR 1982 SC 792; Rosy Jacob v. Jacob A Chakramakkul, AIR 1973 SC 2090; Imam Bandi v. Haji Mutsaddi, AIR 1918 PC 11 and Mst. Samiunnissa v. Mt. Saida Khatun, AIR 1944 All 202.)

14. I have also not found anything to the contrary in the passage cited by the learned counsel from Hamilton's Hidaya which might lead to the conclusion that Hizanat available to a Mohammadan female is automatically lost as soon as she goes and resides away from the husband after divorce in a different district.

15. In any case, this Court is not finally disposing of the petition under S. 25 of the Act which is still pending in the Court below. That being so, I would prefer to rely on the decision reported in 1983 All WC 572 for the present as against the view expressed in AIR 1932 All 215 though I am clearly of the view that the decision in AIR 1932 All 215 had turned on its own facts and does not derogate from the law laid down in 1983 All WC 572 and hold that prima facie the application filed by the opposite party under S. 25 is maintainable and the impugned order cannot be set aside on the submission of the learned counsel for the revisionist to the contrary.

16. As regards the merits of the findings recorded by the Court below on facts learned counsel for the applicant had hardly any submission to make. However, on going through the conclusion reached by the Court below on facts I find myself in total agreement with the Court below. I am not making detailed comments on facts found by the Court below as the petition under S. 25 is still pending and any observations made by this Court may prejudice a fair trial of the issue arising therein. Suffice it to say that the conclusions reached by the Court below not being vitiated by any error of jurisdiction the same are not being interfered with in this revision.

17. The third and the last submission of the learned counsel was that in a petition under S. 25 of the aforesaid Act an order for interim custody cannot be made under S. 12. It was urged relying on a decision of the Gujarat High Court reported in AIR 1962 Guj 227 (Ruzmaniben Tribhovandas Jethabhai v. Minor Narmada) that the power to make an interlocutory order for production of a minor and interim protection of his person is available only in proceedings for appointment or declaration of a guardian provided under Ch. II of the Guardians and Wards Act. S. 12 which provides for making an order for interim protection of the person and property of a minor appears in Chap. II and must, therefore, necessarily be held to be available only in proceedings initiated for appointment or declaration of a guardian and inasmuch as S. 25 appears in Chap. III dealing with the duties, rights and liabilities of guardians,

S. 12 cannot be invoked in an application filed under S. 25. It was further urged that if S. 12 is held not to apply to an application under S. 25, the Court cannot fall back on any supposed inherent powers to make an order for interim protection or production of the minor.

18. Having given the matter a careful consideration I find it difficult to accept the above submission. It must be borne in mind that the Guardians and Wards Act has been enacted primarily for the welfare of minor children. Consequently in construing the provisions of the enactment that interpretation ought to be accepted which subserves the welfare of the minor in preference to one which might prove detrimental to his interest. That this should be the approach of Courts in construing the provisions of the enactment has been repeatedly stressed by Courts throughout and it does not seem necessary to dilate on the subject further. It is in this background that I shall proceed to consider the validity of the argument.

S. 12 provides:

12. Power to make interlocutory order for production of minor and interim protection of person and property—(1) The Court may direct that the person, if any, having the custody of the minor shall produce him or cause him to be produced at such place and time and before such person as it appoints, and may make such order for the temporary custody and protection of the person or property of the minor as it thinks proper.

(2) If the minor is a female who ought not to be compelled to appear in public, the direction under sub-sec. (1) for her production shall require her to be produced in accordance with the customs and manners of the country.

(3) Nothing in this section shall authorise—(a) the Court to place a female minor in the temporary custody of a person claiming to be her guardian on the ground of his being her husband unless she is already in his custody with the consent of her parents, if any or (b) any person to whom the temporary custody and protection of the property of a minor is entrusted to dispossess otherwise than by due course of law any person in possession of any of the property.

It will be seen that intrinsically there is nothing in S. 12 which might indicate that the power of the Court to make interlocutory order for production of a minor and interim protection of his person or property is available only in proceedings for appointment or declaration of a guardian. The words used in the statute 'the Court may direct that the person, if any, having the custody of the minor shall produce him at such place and time ... and may make such order for the temporary custody and protection of the person and property of the minor as it thinks proper' are words of wide amplitude and insofar as the plain language of the section goes there is nothing to suggest that S. 12 should be read down and be restricted in its application only in respect of proceedings for appointment or declaration of a guardian. Section 12 is part of the same statute of which S. 25 is. Except, therefore, that S. 12 appears in the chapter in which Ss. 15 and 16 dealing with the power and procedure for appointment or declaration of guardian appears, there does not exist any valid ground for limiting its application only to the proceedings initiated under Chapter II of the Act. S. 12 itself does not state that this power to make interlocutory order is exercisable pending the disposal of an application under Ss. 15 to 19 of the Act.

19. The contrary view expressed by the Gujarat High Court in AIR 1962 Guj 227 is founded solely on the juxtaposition of S. 12 and the fact that S. 12 appears in Chap. II which deals with the appointment and declaration of guardians. With profound respect to the decision of the Gujarat High Court, I find it difficult to share the view. As already observed, the language of S. 12 is explicit and unambiguously indicates that the same is not limited to any particular type of proceedings contemplated under the Act. I do venture to think that in no contingency would the exercise of power of making interlocutory order for production of a minor and interim protection of his person be more appropriately warranted than an application under S. 25 which deals with cases where ward [*sic*] removed from the custody of a guardians of his person. To deny the power to make such an order for interim production or protection of the child in a petition filed under S. 25 would undeniably result in irreparable harm to the child and be destructive of the very purpose of the enactment. It is not difficult to imagine a case where an infant or a child of tender years being removed from the custody of a guardian of his person in circumstances which may warrant immediate restoration of the child to the custody of the lawful guardian of his person. For example, an infant or a child of tender years may be seriously ill requiring immediate attention by his mother or the other parent for recovery. If in such circumstances the mother makes an application under S. 25 and it is held that the Court totally lacks any power to give immediate relief to the child, it would be undeniably destructive of the very purpose of the entire enactment. Surely

a person who is already recognized as a guardian of a minor applying to the Court for an order for the return of the ward under S. 25 illegally removed from his custody cannot be legitimately held to be in a less advantaged position than one who is still to be appointed or declared a guardian insofar as the right to apply for an order for production of the minor is concerned.

20. For the reason stated above, I hold that S. 12 of the Act is available even in respect of an application filed under S. 25 of the Act and, with respect to the decisions cited by the learned counsel, namely, AIR 1962 Guj 227 and (1916) ILR 40 Bom 600 : (AIR 1961 Bom 129) (Achrat Lal Jaikisendas v. Chimanlal Prabhudas) on which the Gujrat High Court placed reliance, have taken a view which, in my humble view, is far too restricted and is not warranted by the scheme and purpose of the enactment.

21. In any case, the Gujrat decision itself clearly lays down that even if S. 12 is held not to apply to an application under S. 25 of the Act the Court must be held to have inherent powers to make such an order pending the decision of an application filed under S. 25 of the Act. It was observed in that decision at page 228 of the report:

> The question would, however, still remain whether the petitioner was entitled to maintain the application for interim custody of Narmada under the inherent powers of the Court. I do not agree with Mr. R.C. Mankad that the Court has not inherent powers to make interlocutory order for interim custody of a minor apart from the express provision of S. 12. It is no doubt true that since there is an express provision contained in S. 12 for making of interlocutory order for interim custody in an application for appointment or declaration of a guardian, the inherent powers of the Court cannot be invoked for making any order for interim custody in an application for appointment or declaration of a guardian. The enactment by the Legislature of an express provision would exclude the inherent powers of the Court in the area over which the express provision operates but when the question arises whether interlocutory order for interim custody can be made in a petition under S. 25 to which the provisions of S. 12 do not apply I do not see how the inherent powers of the Court can be excluded. If the Court can under S. 25 order that the minor should be returned to the custody of the guardian on the ground that it is for the welfare of the minor to return to such custody, I do not understand why the Court cannot do so as an interim measure. It may take considerable time before a petition under S. 25 may be disposed of

by the Court and if the Court has no power to make interlocutory order for interim custody of the minor, considerable injury may be caused to the interests of the minor during the period that it may take to dispose of the petition. Surely the Court is not so powerless as to prevent any injury being caused to the welfare of the minor during the period that the petition is not disposed of by it. I am of the opinion that the Court has inherent powers to make interlocutory order for interim custody of a minor in a petition under S. 25. This being the position it is obvious that the application of the petitioner for interim custody of Narmada was maintainable under the inherent powers of the Court.

With respect I completely agree with the law laid down in the passage quoted above.

22. In the premise, I hold that the impugned order does not suffer from any error of jurisdiction warranting interference by this Court under S. 115 of the Civil P.C. On merits, I endorse the conclusions reached by the Court below that it is a fit case in which an order should be made for the return of the child to the custody of the mother. The discretion exercised by the Court below is valid and proper.

23. As a result the revision fails and is dismissed with costs. The interim orders passed by this Court from time to time are vacated.

Revision dismissed.

Mohd Ahmed Khan v.
Shah Bano Begum

JUDGMENT

CHANDRACHUD, C.J. This appeal does not involve any question of constitutional importance but, that is not to say that it does not involve any question of importance. Some questions which arise under the ordinary civil and criminal law are of a far-reaching significance to large segments of society which have been traditionally subjected to unjust treatment. Women are one such segment. 'Na stree swatantramarhati' said Manu, the law giver: The woman does not deserve independence. And, it is alleged that the 'fatal point in Islam is the degradation of woman' 'Selections from Kuran'—Edward William Lane, 1873, Reprint 1982, page xc (Introduction). To the Prophet is ascribed the statement, hopefully wrongly, that 'woman was made from a crooked rib, and if you try to bend it straight, it will break; therefore treat your wives kindly.'

2. The appeal, arising out of an application filed by a divorced Muslim woman for maintenance under section 125 of the Code of Criminal Procedure, raises a straightforward issue which is of common interest not only to Muslim women, not only to women generally but, to all those who, aspiring to create an equal society of men and women, lure themselves into the belief that mankind has achieved a remarkable degree of progress in that direction. The appellant, who is an advocate by profession, was married to the respondent in 1932. Three sons and two daughters were born of that marriage. In 1975, the appellant

drove the respondent out of the matrimonial home. In April 1978, the respondent filed a petition against the appellant under section 125 of the Code in the Court of the learned Judicial Magjistrate (First Class), Indore, asking for maintenance at the rate of Rs. 500/- per month. On November 6, 1978 the appellant divorced the respondent by an irrevocable talaq. His defence to the respondent's petition for maintenance was that she had ceased to be wife by reason of the divorce granted by him, that he was therefore under no obligation to provide maintenance for her, that he had already paid maintenance to her at the rate of Rs. 200/- per month for about two years and that, he had deposited a sum of Rs. 3000/- in the Court by way of dower during the period of iddat. In August 1979 the learned Magistrate directed the appellant to pay a princely sum of Rs. 25/- per month to the respondent by way of maintenance. It may be mentioned that the respondent had alleged that the appellant earns a professional income of about Rs. 60,000/- per year. In July, 1980, in a revisional application filed by the respondent, the High Court of Madhya Pradesh enhanced the amount of maintenance to Rs. 179.20 per month. The husband is before us by special leave.

3. Does the Muslim Personal Law impose no obligation upon the husband to provide for the maintenance of his divorced wife? Undoubtedly, the Muslim husband enjoys the privilege of being able to discard his wife whenever he chooses to do so, for reasons good, bad or indifferent, indeed, for no reason at all. But, is the only price of that privilege the dole of a pittance during the period of iddat? And, is the law so ruthless in its inequality that, no matter how much the husband pays for the maintenance of his divorced wife during the period of iddat, the mere fact that he has paid something, no matter how little, absolves him forever from the duty of paying adequately so as to enable her to keep her body and soul together? Then again, is there any provision in the Muslim Personal Law under which a sum is payable to the wife 'on divorce'? These are some of the important, though agonising, questions which arise for our decision.

4. The question as to whether section 125 of the Code applies to Muslims also is concluded by two decisions of this Court which are reported in Bai Tahira v. Ali Hussain Fidaalli Chothia (1979) 2 SCR 75: (AIR 1979 SC 362) and Fuzlunbi v. K. Khader Vali (1980) 3 SCR 1127: (AIR 1980 SC 1730). Those decisions took the view that the divorced Muslim wife is entitled to apply for maintenance under section 125. But,

a Bench consisting of our learned Brethren, Murtaza Fazal Ali and A. Varadarajan, JJ., were inclined to the view that those cases are not correctly decided. Therefore, they referred this appeal to a larger Bench by an order dated February 3, 1981, which read thus:

> As this case involves substantial questions of law of far-reaching consequences, we feel that the decisions of this Court in Bai Tahira v. Ali Hussain Fidaalli Chothia and Fuzlunbi v. K. Khader Vali require reconsideration because, in our opinion, they are not only in direct contravention of the plain and unambiguous language of S. 127 (3) (b) of the Code of Criminal Procedure, 1973 which far from overriding the Muslim Law on the subject protects and applies the same in case where a wife has been divorced by the husband and the dower specified has been paid and the period of iddat has been observed. The decision also appears to us to be against the fundamental concept of divorce by the husband and its consequences under the Muslim law which has been expressly protected by S. 2 of the Muslim Personal Law (Shariat) Application Act, 1937—an Act which was not noticed by the aforesaid decisions. We, therefore, direct that the matter may be placed before the Hon'ble Chief Justice for being heard by a larger Bench consisting of more than three Judges.

5. Section 125 of the Code of Criminal Procedure which deals with the right of maintenance reads thus:

Order for maintenance of wives, children and parents
125. (1) If any person having sufficient means neglects or refuses to maintain—
(a) his wife, unable to maintain herself ... a Magistrate of the first class may, upon proof of such neglect or refusal, order such person to make a monthly allowance for the maintenance of his wife ... at such monthly rate not exceeding five hundred rupees in the whole as such Magistrate thinks fit....
Explanation....
For the purpose of this Chapter ...
(a) ...
(b) 'Wife' includes a woman who has been divorced by, or has obtained a divorce from her husband and has not remarried....
(3) If any person so ordered fails without sufficient cause to comply with the order, any such Magistrate may, for every breach of the order, issue a warrant for levying the amount due in the manner provided for levying fines, and may sentence such person, for the whole or any part

of each month's allowance remaining unpaid after the execution of the warrant, to imprisonment for a term which may extend to one month or until payment if sooner made:

Provided....

Provided further that if such person offers to maintain his wife on condition of her living with him, and she refuses to live with him, such Magistrate may consider any grounds of refusal stated by her, and may make an order under the section notwithstanding such offer, if he is satisfied that there is just ground for so doing.

Explanation—If a husband has contracted marriage with another women or keeps a mistress, it shall be considered to be just ground for his wife's refusal to live with him.

6. Section 127(3)(b), on which the appellant has built up the edifice of his defence reads thus:

Alteration in allowance

127.– (1) - (2)....

(3) Where any order has been made under section 125 in favour of a woman who has been divorced by, or has obtained a divorce from, her husband, the Magistrate shall, if he is satisfied that ...

(a) ...

(b) the woman has been divorced by her husband and that she has received, whether before or after the date of the said order, the whole of the sum which, under any customary or personal law applicable to the parties, was payable on such divorce, cancel such order ...

(i) in the case where such sum was paid before such order, from the date on which such order was made.

(ii) in any other case, from the date of expiry of the period, if any, for which maintenance has been actually paid by the husband to the woman.

7. Under section 125(1)(a), a person who, having sufficient means, neglects or refuses to maintain his wife who is unable to maintain herself, can be asked by the court to pay a monthly maintenance to her at a rate not exceeding five hundred rupees. By clause (b) of the Explanation to section 125(1), 'wife' includes a divorced woman who has not remarried. These provisions are too clear and precise to admit of any doubt or refinement. The religion professed by a spouse or by the spouses has no place in the scheme of these provisions. Whether the spouses are Hindus or Muslims, Christians or Parsis, pagans or heathens, is wholly irrelevant in the application of these provisions.

The reason for this is axiomatic, in the sense the section 125 is a part of the Code of Criminal Procedure, not of the Civil Laws which define and govern the rights and obligations of the parties belonging to particular religions, like the Hindu Adoptions and Maintenance Act, the Shariat, or the Parsi Matrimonial Act. Section 125 was enacted in order to provide a quick and summary remedy to a class of persons who are unable to maintain themselves. What difference would it then make as to what is the religion professed by the neglected wife, child or parent? Neglect by a person of sufficient means to maintain these and the inability of these persons to maintain themselves are the objective criteria which determine the applicability of section 125. Such provisions, which are essentially of a prophylactic nature, cut across the barriers of religion. True, that they do not supplant the personal law of the parties but, equally, the religion professed by the parties or the state of the personal law by which they are governed, cannot have any repercussion on the applicability of such laws unless, within the framework of the Constitution, their application is restricted to a defined category of religious groups or classes. The liability imposed by section 125 to maintain close relatives who are indigent is founded upon the individual's obligation to the society to prevent vagrancy and destitution. That is the moral edict of the law and morality cannot be clubbed with religion. Clause (b) of the Explanation to section 125(1), which defines 'wife' as including a divorced wife, contains no words of limitation to justify the exclusion of Muslim women from its scope. Section 125 is truly secular in character.

8. Sir James Fitz James Stephen who piloted the Code of Criminal Procedure, 1872 as a Legal Member of the Viceroy's Council, described the precursor of Chapter IX of the Code in which section 125 occurs, as 'a mode of preventing vagrancy or at least of preventing its consequences'. In Jagir Kaur v. Jaswant Singh, (1964) 2 SCR 73 at p. 84: (AIR 1963 SC 1521 at p. 1525) Subba Rao, J. speaking for the court said that Chapter XXXVI of the Code of 1898 which contained section 488, corresponding to section 125, 'intends to serve a social purpose'. In Nanak Chand v. Chandra Kishore Agarwala, (1970) 1 SCR 565: (AIR 1970 SC 446), Sikri, J., while pointing out that the scope of the Hindu Adoptions and Maintenance Act, 1965 [*sic*] and that of section 488 was different, said that section 488 was 'applicable to all persons belonging to all religions and has no relationship with the personal law of the parties'.

9. Under section 488 of the Code of 1898, the wife's right to maintenance depended upon the continuance of her married status. Therefore, that right could be defeated by the husband by divorcing her unilaterally as under the Muslim Personal Law, or by obtaining a decree of divorce against her under the other systems of law. It was in order to remove this hardship that the joint Committee recommended that the benefit of the provisions regarding maintenance should be extended to a divorced woman, so long as she has not remarried after the divorce. That is the genesis of clause (b) of the Explanation to section 125(1), which provides that 'wife' includes a woman who has been divorced by, or has obtained a divorce from her husband and has not remarried. Even in the absence of this provision, the courts had held under the Code of 1898 that the provisions regarding maintenance were independent of the personal law governing the parties. The induction of the definition of 'wife' so as to include a divorced woman lends even greater weight to that conclusion. 'Wife' means a wife as defined, irrespective of the religion professed by her or by her husband. Therefore, a divorced Muslim woman, so long as she has not remarried, is a 'wife' for the purpose of section 125. The statutory right available to her under that section is unaffected by the provisions of the personal law applicable to her.

10. The conclusion that the right conferred by section 125 can be exercised irrespective of the personal law of the parties, is fortified, especially in regard to Muslims, by the provision contained in the Explanation to the second proviso to section 125(3) of the Code. That proviso says that if the husband offers to maintain his wife on condition that she should live with him, and she refuses to live with him, the Magistrate may consider any grounds of refusal stated by her, and may make an order of maintenance notwithstanding the offer of the husband, if he is satisfied that there is just ground for passing such an order. According to the Explanation to the proviso:

> If a husband has contracted marriage with another woman or keeps a mistress, it shall be considered to be just ground for his wife's refusal to live with him.

It is too well-known that 'A Mahomedan may have as many as four wives at the same time but not more. If he marries a fifth wife when he has already four, the marriage is not void, but merely irregular' (see Mulla's Mahomedan Law, 18th Edition, paragraph 255, page 285, quoting

Baillie's Digest of Moohummudan Law; and, Ameer Ali's Mahomedan Law, 5th Edition, Vol. II, page 280). The explanation confers upon the wife the right to refuse to live with her husband if he contracts another marriage, leave alone 3 or 4 other marriages. It shows, unmistakably, that section 125 overrides the personal law, if there is any conflict between the two.

11. The whole of this discussion as to whether the right conferred by section 125 prevails over the personal law of the parties, has proceeded on the assumption that there is a conflict between the provisions of that section and those of the Muslim Personal Law. The argument that by reason of section 2 of the Shariat Act, XXVI of 1937, the rule of decision in matters relating, inter alia, to maintenance 'shall be the Muslim Personal Law' also proceed upon a similar assumption. We embarked upon the decision of the question of priority between the Code and the Muslim Personal Law on the assumption that there was a conflict between the two because, in so far as it lies in our power, we wanted to set at rest, once for all, the question whether section 125 would prevail over the personal law of the parties, in cases where they are in conflict.

12. The next logical step to take is to examine the question, on which considerable argument has been advanced before us, whether there is any conflict between the provisions of section 125 and those of the Muslim Personal Law on the liability of the Muslim husband to provide for the maintenance of his divorced wife.

13. The contention of the husband and of the interveners who support him is that, under the Muslim Personal Law, the liability of the husband to maintain a divorced wife is limited to the period of iddat. In support of this proposition, they rely upon the statement of law on the point contained in certain text books. In Mulla's Mahomedan Law (18th Edition, para 279, page 301), there is a statement to the effect that 'After divorce, the wife is entitled to maintenance during the period of iddat', at page 302, the learned author says:

> Where an order is made for the maintenance of a wife under section 488 of the Criminal Procedure Code and the wife is afterwards divorced, the order ceases to operate on the expiration of the period of iddat. The result is that a Mahomedan may defeat an order made against him under section 488 by divorcing his wife immediately after the order is made. His obligation to maintain his wife will cease in that case on the completion of her iddat.

Tyabji's Muslim Law (4th Edition, para 304, pages 268-269), contains the statement that:

> On the expiration of the iddat of the talaq, the wife's right to maintenance ceases, whether based on the Muslim Law, or on an order under the Criminal Procedure Code.

According to Dr. Paras Diwan:

> When a marriage is dissolved by divorce the wife is entitled to maintenance during the period of iddat... On the expiration of the period of iddat, the wife is not entitled to any maintenance under any circumstances. Muslim law does not recognize any obligation on the part of a man to maintain a wife whom he had divorced. (Muslim Law in Modern India, 1982 Edition, page 130)

14. These statements in the text books are inadequate to establish the proposition that the Muslim husband is not under an obligation to provide for the maintenance of his divorced wife, who is unable to maintain herself. One must have regard to the entire conspectus of the Muslim Personal Law in order to determine the extent, both in quantum and in duration, of the husband's liability to provide for the maintenance of an indigent wife who has been divorced by him. Under that law, the husband is bound to pay Mahr to the wife as a mark of respect to her. True, that he may settle any amount he likes by way of dower upon his wife, which cannot be less than 10 Dirhams, which is equivalent to three or four rupees (Mulla's Mahomedan Law, 18th Edition, para 286, page 308). But, one must have regard to the realities of life. Mahr is a mark of respect to the wife. The sum settled by way of Mahr is generally expected to take care of the ordinary requirements of the wife, during the marriage and after. But these provisions of the Muslim Personal Law do not countenance cases in which the wife is unable to maintain herself after the divorce. We consider it not only incorrect but unjust, to extend the scope of the statements extracted above to cases in which a divorced wife is unable to maintain herself. We are of the opinion that the application of those statements of law must be restricted to that class of cases, in which there is no possibility of vagrancy or destitution arising out of the indigence of the divorced wife. We are not concerned here with the broad and general question whether a husband is liable to maintain his wife, which includes a divorced wife, in all circumstances and at all events. That is not the subject matter of section 125. That section deals with cases in which, a person who is possessed of sufficient

means neglects or refuses to maintain amongst others, his wife who is unable to maintain herself. Since the Muslim Personal Law, which limits the husband's liability to provide for the maintenance of the divorced wife to the period of iddat, does not contemplate or countenance the situation envisaged by section 125, it would be wrong to hold that the Muslim husband, according to his personal law, is not under an obligation to provide maintenance, beyond the period of iddat, to his divorced wife who is unable to maintain herself. The argument of the appellant that, according to the Muslim Personal Law, his liability to provide for the maintenance of his divorced wife is limited to the period of iddat, despite the fact that she is unable to maintain herself, has therefore to be rejected. The true position is that, if the divorced wife is able to maintain herself, the husband's liability to provide maintenance for her ceases with the expiration of the period of iddat. If she is unable to maintain herself, she is entitled to take recourse to section 125 of the Code. The outcome of this discussion is that there is no conflict between the provisions of section 125 and those of the Muslim Personal Law on the question of the Muslim husband's obligation to provide maintenance for a divorced wife who is unable to maintain herself.

15. There can be no greater authority on this question than the Holy Quran. 'The Quran, the Sacred Book of Islam, comprises in its 114 Suras or Chapters, the total of revelations believed to have been communicated to Prophet Muhammed, as a final expression of God's will.' (The Quran Interpreted by Arthur J. Arberry). Verses (Aiyats) 241 and 242 of the Quran show that there is an obligation on Muslim husbands to provide for their divorced wives. The Arabic version of those Aiyats and their English translation are reproduced below:

Arabic version	English version
Aiyat No. 241	
WA LIL MOTALLA QATAY MATAUN	For divorced women Maintenance (should be provided)
BIL MAAROOFAY	On a reasonable (Scale)
HAQQAN ALAL MUTTAQEENA	This is a duty on the righteous.
Aiyat No. 242	
KAZALEKA YUBA IYYANULLAHO	Thus doth God
LAKUM AYATEHEE	Make clear His Signs
LA ALLAKUM TAQELOON	To you: in order that you may understand.

(See 'The Holy Quran' by Yusuf Ali, page 96) The correctness of the translation of these Aiyats is not in dispute except that, the contention of the appellant is that the word 'Mata' in Aiyat No. 241 means 'provision' and not 'maintenance'. That is a distinction without a difference. Nor are we impressed by the shuffling plea of the All India Muslim Personal Law Board that, in Aiyat 241, the exhortation is to the 'Mutta Queena', that is, to the more pious and the more God-fearing, not to the general run of the Muslims, the 'Muslminin'. In Aiyat 242, the Quran says: 'It is expected that you will use your commonsense'.

16. The English version of the two Aiyats in Muhammed Zafrullah Khan's 'The Quran' (page 38) reads thus:

For divorced women also there shall be provision according to what is fair. This is an obligation binding on the righteous. Thus does Allah make His commandments clear to you that you may understand.

17. The translation of Aiyats 240 to 242 in 'The Meaning of the Quran' (Vol. 1, published by the Board of Islamic Publications, Delhi) reads thus:

240-241.
Those of you, who shall die and leave wives behind them, should make a will to the effect that they should be provided with a year's maintenance and should not be turned out of their homes. But if they leave their homes of their own accord, you shall not be answerable for whatever they choose for themselves in a fair way; Allah is All-Powerful, All-wise, Likewise, the divorced women should also be given something in accordance with the known fair standard. This is an obligation upon the God-fearing people.

242. Thus Allah makes clear His commandments for you: It is expected that you will use your commonsense.

18. In 'The Running Commentary of The Holy Quran' (1964 Edition) by Dr. Allamah Khadim Rahmani Nuri, No. 241 is translated thus:

241. And for the divorced woman (also) a provision (should be made) with fairness (in addition to her dower); (This is) a duty (incumbent) on the reverent.

19. In 'The meaning of the Glorious Quran, Text and Explanatory Translation', by Marmaduke Pickthall, (Taj Company Ltd., Karachi), Aiyat 241 is translated thus: 'For divorced women a provision in kindness: a duty for those who ward off (evil).'

20. Finally, in 'The Quran Interpreted' by Arthur J. Arberry, Aiyat 241 is translated thus:

241. There shall be for divorced women provision honourable—an obligation on the God-fearing. So God makes clear His signs for you: Happily you will understand.

21. Dr. K.R. Nuri in his book quoted above: 'The Running Commentary of The Holy Quran', says in the preface:

Belief in Islam does not mean mere confession of the existence of something. It really means the translation of the faith into action. Words without deeds carry no meaning in Islam. Therefore the term 'believe and do good' has been used like a phrase all over the Quran. Belief in something means that man should inculcate the qualities or carry out the promptings or guidance of that thing in his action. Belief in Allah means that besides acknowledging the existence of the Author of the universe, we are to show obedience to His commandments....

22. These Aiyats leave no doubt that the Quran imposes an obligation on the Muslim husband to make provision for or to provide maintenance to the divorced wife. The contrary argument does less than justice to the teachings of the Quran. As observed by Mr. M. Hidayatullah in his introduction to Mulla's Mahomedan Law, the Quran is Alfurqan, that is, one showing truth from falsehood and right from wrong.

23. The second plank of the appellant's argument is that the respondent's application under section 125 is liable to be dismissed because of the provision contained in section 127(3)(b). That section provides, to the extent material, that the magistrate shall cancel the order of maintenance, if the wife is divorced by the husband and, she has received 'the whole of the sum which, under any customary or personal law applicable to the parties, was payable on such divorce'. That raises the question as to whether, under the Muslim Personal Law, any sum is payable to the wife 'on divorce'. We do not have to grope in the dark and speculate as to which kind of a sum this can be because the only argument advanced before us on behalf of the appellant and by the interveners supporting him is that Mahr is the amount payable by the husband to the wife on divorce. We find it impossible to accept this argument.

24. In Mulla's Principles of Mahomedan Law (18th Edition, page 308), Mahr or Dower is defined in paragraph 285 as 'a sum of money or

other property which the wife is entitled to receive from the husband in consideration of the marriage'. Dr. Paras Diwan in his book, 'Muslim Law in Modern India' (1982 Edition, page 60), criticises this definition on the ground that Mahr is not payable 'in consideration of marriage' but is an obligation imposed by law on the husband as a mark of respect for the wife, as is evident from the fact that non-specification of Mahr at the time of marriage does not affect the validity of the marriage. We need not enter into this controversy and indeed, Mulla's book itself contains the further statement at page 308 that the word 'consideration' is not used in the sense in which it is used in the Contract Act and that under the Mohammedan Law, dower is an obligation imposed upon the husband as a mark of respect for the wife. We are concerned to find whether Mahr is an amount payable by the husband to the wife on divorce. Some confusion is caused by the fact that, under the Muslim Personal Law, the amount of Mahr is usually split into two parts, one of which is called 'prompt', which is payable on demand and the other is called 'deferred', which is payable on the dissolution of the marriage by death or by divorce. But, the fact that deferred Mahr is payable at the time of the dissolution of marriage, cannot justify the conclusion that it is payable 'on divorce'. Even assuming that, in a given case, the entire amount of Mahr is of the deferred variety payable on the dissolution of marriage by divorce, it cannot be said that it is an amount which is payable on divorce. Divorce may be a convenient or identifiable point of time at which the deferred amount has to be paid by the husband to the wife. But, the payment of the amount is not occasioned by the divorce, which is what is meant by the expression 'on divorce', which occurs in section 127(3)(b) of the Code. If Mahr is an amount which the wife is entitled to receive from the husband in consideration of the marriage, that is the very opposite of the amount being payable in consideration of divorce. Divorce dissolves the marriage. Therefore, no amount which is payable in consideration of the marriage can possibly be described as an amount payable in consideration of divorce. The alternative premise that Mahr is an obligation imposed upon the husband as a mark of respect for the wife is wholly detrimental to the stance that it is an amount payable to the wife on divorce. A man may marry a woman for love, looks, learning or nothing at all. And, he may settle a sum upon her as a mark of respect. Therefore, a sum payable to the wife out of respect cannot be a sum payable 'on divorce'.

25. In an appeal from a Full Bench decision of the Allahabad High Court, the Privy Council in Hamira Bibi v. Zubaide Bibi, 43 Ind App 294: (AIR 1916 PC 46 at p. 48) summed up the nature and character of Mahr in these words:

> Dower is an essential incident under the Mussulman law to the status of marriage; to such an extent that is so that when it is unspecified at the time the marriage is contracted, the law declares that it must be adjudged on definite principles. Regarded as a consideration for the marriage, it is, in theory, payable before consummation; but the law allows its division into two parts, one of which is called 'prompt' payable before the wife can be called upon to enter the conjugal domicil; the other 'deferred', payable on the dissolution of the contract by the death of either of the parties or by divorce. (pp. 300–301)

26. This statement of law was adopted in another decision of the Privy Council in Syed Sabir Husain v. Farzand Hasan, 65 Ind App 119 at p. 127: (AIR 1938 PC 80 at p. 83). It is not quite appropriate and seems invidious to describe any particular Bench of a court as 'strong' but, we cannot resist the temptation of mentioning that Mr. Syed Ameer Ali was a party to the decision in Hamira Bibi while Sir Shadi Lal was a party to the decision in Syed Sabir Husain. These decisions show that the payment of dower may be deferred to a future date as, for example, death or divorce. But, that does not mean that the payment of the deferred dower is occasioned by these events.

27. It is contended on behalf of the appellant that the proceedings of the Rajya Sabha dated December 18, 1973 (volume 86, column 186), when the bill which led to the Code of 1973 was on the anvil, would show that the intention of the Parliament was to leave the provisions of the Muslim Personal Law untouched. In this behalf, reliance is placed on the following statement made by Shri Ram Niwas Mirdha, the then Minister of State, Home Affairs:

> Dr. Vyas very learnedly made certain observations that a divorced wife under the Muslim law deserves to be treated justly and she should get what is her equitable or legal due. Well, I will not go into this, but say that we would not like to interfere with the customary law of the Muslims through the Criminal Procedure Code. If there is a demand for change in the Muslim Personal Law, it should actually come from the Muslim Community itself and we should wait for the Muslim public opinion on these matters to crystallize before we try to change this customary

right or make changes in their personal law. Above all, this is hardly the place where we could do so. But as I tried to explain, the provision in the Bill is an advance over the previous situation, Divorced women have been included and brought within the ambit of clause 125, but a limitation is being imposed by this amendment to clause 127, namely, that the maintenance orders would cease to operate after the amounts due to her under the personal law are paid to her. This is a healthy compromise between what has been termed a conservative interpretation of law or a concession to conservative public opinion and liberal approach to the problem. We have made an advance and not tried to transgress what are the personal rights of Muslim women. So this, I think, should satisfy Hon. Members that whatever advance we have made is in the right direction and it should be welcomed.

28. It does appear from this speech that the Government did not desire to interfere with the personal law of the Muslims through the Criminal Procedure Code. It wanted the Muslim community to take the lead and the Muslim public opinion to crystallise on the reforms in their personal law. However, we are not concerned with the question whether the Government did or did not desire to bring about changes in the Muslim Personal Law by enacting sections 125 and 127 of the Code. As we have said earlier and, as admitted by the Minister, the Government did introduce such a change by defining the expression 'wife' to include a divorced wife. It also introduced another significant change by providing that the fact that the husband has contracted marriage with another woman is a just ground for the wife's refusal to live with him. The provision contained in section 127(3)(b) may have been introduced because of the misconception that dower is an amount payable 'on divorce'. But, that cannot convert an amount payable as a mark of respect for the wife into an amount payable on divorce.

29. It must follow from this discussion, unavoidably a little too long, that the judgments of this Court in Bai Tahira (AIR 1979 SC 362) (Krishna Iyer J., Tulzapurkar J. and Pathak J.) and Fazlunbi (AIR 1980 SC 1730) (Krishna Iyer J., one of us, Chinnappa Reddy J. and A.P. Sen J.) are correct. Justice Krishna Iyer who spoke for the Court in both these cases, relied greatly on the teleological and schematic method of interpretation so as to advance the purpose of the law. These constructional techniques have their own importance in the interpretation of statutes meant to ameliorate the conditions of suffering sections of the

society. We have attempted to show that taking the language of the statute as one finds it, there is no escape from the conclusion that a divorced Muslim wife is entitled to apply for maintenance under section 125 and that. Mahr is not a sum which, under the Muslim Personal Law, is payable on divorce.

30. Though Bai Tahira was correctly decided, we would like, respectfully, to draw attention to an error which has crept in the judgment. There is a statement at page 80 (of SCR): (at p. 365 of AIR 1979 SC 362) of the Report, in the context of section 127(3)(b), that 'payment of Mahr money, as a customary discharge, is within the cognizance of that provision'. We have taken the view that Mahr, not being payable on divorce, does not fall within the meaning of that provision.

31. It is a matter of deep regret that some of the interveners who supported the appellant, took up an extreme position by displaying an unwarranted zeal to defeat the right to maintenance of women who are unable to maintain themselves. The written submissions of the All India Muslim Personal Law Board have gone to the length of asserting that it is irrelevant to inquire as to how a Muslim divorcee should maintain herself. The facile answer of the Board is that the Personal Law has devised the system of Mahr to meet the requirements of women and if a woman is indigent, she must look to her relations, including nephews and cousins, to support her. This is a most unreasonable view of law as well as life. We appreciate that Begum Temur Jehan, a social worker who has been working in association with the Delhi City Women's Association for the uplift of Muslim women intervened to support Mr. Danial Latifi who appeared on behalf of the wife.

32. It is also a matter of regret that Article 44 of our Consititution has remained a dead letter. It provides that 'The State shall endeavour to secure for the citizens uniform civil code throughout the territory of India'. There is no evidence of any official activity for framing a common Civil Code for the country. A belief seems to have gained ground that it is for the Muslim community to take a lead in the matter of reforms of their personal law. A common Civil Code will help the cause of national integration by removing disparate loyalties to laws which have conflicting ideologies. No community is likely to bell the cat by making gratuitous concessions on this issue. It is the State which is charged with the duty of securing a uniform Civil Code for the citizens of the country and, unquestionably, it has the legislative competence

to do so. A counsel in the case whispered, somewhat audibly, that legislative competence is one thing, the political courage to use that competence is quite another. We understand the difficulties involved in bringing persons of different faiths and persuasions on a common plat-form. But, a beginning has to be made if the Constitution is to have any meaning. Inevitably the role of the reformer has to be assumed by the courts because it is beyond the endurance of sensitive minds to allow injustice to be suffered when it is so palpable. But piecemeal attempts of courts to bridge the gap between personal laws cannot take the place of a common Civil Code. Justice to all is a far more satisfactory way of dispensing justice than justice from case to case.

33. Dr. Tahir Mahmood in his book *Muslim Personal Law* (1977 Edition, pages 200-202), has made a powerful plea for framing a uniform Civil Code for all citizens of India. He says: 'In pursuance of the goal of secularism, the State must stop administering religion-based personal laws.' He wants the lead to come from the majority community but we should have thought that, lead or no lead, the State must act. It would be useful to quote the appeal made by the author to the Muslim community:

> Instead of wasting their energies in exerting theological and political pressure in order to secure an 'immunity' for their traditional personal law from the State's legislative jurisdiction, the Muslims will do well to begin exploring and demonstrating how the true Islamic laws, purged of their time-worn and anachronistic interpretations, can enrich the com-mon civil code of India.

At a Seminar held on October 18, 1980 under the auspices of the Department of Islamic and Comparative Law, Indian Institute of Islamic Studies, New Delhi, he also made an appeal to the Muslim community to display by their conduct a correct understanding of Islamic concepts on marriage and divorce (See Islamic and Comparative Law Quarterly, April-June, 1981, page 146).

34. Before we conclude, we would like to draw attention to the Report of the Commission on Marriage and Family Laws, which was appointed by the Government of Pakistan by a Resolution dated August 4, 1955. The answer of the Commission to Question No. 5 (page 1215 of the Report) is that 'a large number of middle-aged women who are being divorced without rhyme or reason should not be thrown on the streets

without a roof over their heads and without any means of sustaining themselves and their children'. The Report concludes thus:

> In the words of Allama Iqbal, 'the question which is likely to confront Muslim countries in the near future, is whether the law of Islam is capable of evolution—a question which will require great intellectual effort, and is sure to be answered in the affirmative'.

35. For these reasons, we dismiss the appeal and confirm the judgment of the High Court. The appellant will pay the costs of the appeal to respondent 1, which we quantify at rupees ten thousand. It is needless to add that it would be open to the respondent to make an application under section 127(1) of the Code for increasing the allowance of maintenance granted to her on proof of a change in the circumstances as envisaged by that section.

Appeal dismissed.

Danial Latifi v. Union of India

JUDGMENT

R AJENDRA BABU, J.
1. The constitutional validity of the Muslim Women (Protection of Rights on Divorce) Act, 1986 [hereinafter referred to as 'the Act'] is in challenge before us in these cases.

2. The facts in *Mohd. Ahmed Khan Vs. Shah Bano Begum & Ors.*, (1985) 2 SCC 556, are as follows.

3. The husband appealed against the judgment of the Madhya Pradesh High Court directing him to pay to his divorced wife Rs. 179/- per month, enhancing the paltry sum of Rs. 25 per month originally granted by the Magistrate. The parties had been married for 43 years before the ill and elderly wife had been thrown out of her husband's residence. For about two years the husband paid maintenance to his wife at the rate of Rs. 200/- per month. When these payments ceased she petitioned under Section 125 Cr. P. C. The husband immediately dissolved the marriage by pronouncing a triple *talaq*. He paid Rs. 3000/- as deferred *mahr* and a further sum to cover arrears of maintenance and maintenance for the *iddat* period and he sought thereafter to have the petition dismissed on the ground that she had received the amount due to her on divorce under the Muslim law applicable to the parties. The important feature of the case was that the wife had managed the matrimonial home for more than 40 years and had borne and reared five children and was incapable of taking up any career or independently supporting herself at that late stage of her life—remarriage was

an impossibility in that case. The husband a successful Advocate with an approximate income of Rs. 5,000/ per month provided Rs. 200/- per month to the divorced wife, who had shared his life for half a century and mothered his five children and was in desperate need of money to survive.

4. Thus, the principle [*sic*] question for consideration before this Court was the interpretation of Section 127(3)(b) Cr. P. C. that where a Muslim woman had been divorced by her husband and paid her *mahr*, would it indemnify the husband from his obligation under the provisions of Section 125 Cr. P. C. A Five-Judge Bench of this Court reiterated that the Code of Criminal Procedure controls the proceedings in such matters and overrides the personal law of the parties. If there was a conflict between the terms of the Code and the rights and obligations of the individuals, the former would prevail. This Court pointed out that *mahr* is more closely connected with marriage than with divorce though *mahr* or a significant portion of it, is usually payable at the time the marriage is dissolved, whether by death or divorce. This fact is relevant in the context of Section 125 Cr. P. C., even if it is not relevant in the context of Section 127(3)(b) Cr. P. C. Therefore, this Court held that it is a sum payable on divorce within the meaning of Section 127(3)(b) Cr. P. C. and held that *mahr* is such a sum which cannot *ipso facto* absolve the husband's liability under the Act.

5. It was next considered whether the amount of *mahr* constitutes a reasonable alternative to the maintenance order. If *mahr* is not such a sum, it cannot absolve the husband from the rigour of Section 127(3)(b) Cr. P. C. but even in that case, *mahr* is part of the resources available to the woman and will be taken into account in considering her eligibility for a maintenance order and the quantum of maintenance. Thus this Court concluded that the divorced women were entitled to apply for maintenance orders against their former husbands under Section 125 Cr. P. C. and such applications were not barred under Section 127(3)(b) Cr. P. C. The husband had based his entire case on the claim to be excluded from the operation of Section 125 Cr. P. C. on the ground that Muslim law exempted from any responsibility for his divorced wife beyond payment of any *mahr* due to her and an amount to cover maintenance during the *iddat* period and Section 127(3)(b) Cr. P. C. conferred statutory recognition on this principle. Several Muslim organizations, which intervened in the matter, also addressed arguments. Some of the

Muslim social workers who appeared as interveners in the case supported the wife brought in question the issue of *'mata'* contending that Muslim law entitled a Muslim divorced woman to claim provision for maintenance from her husband after the *iddat* period. Thus, the issue before this Court was: the husband was claiming exemption on the basis of Section 127(3)(b) Cr. P. C. on the ground that he had given to his wife the whole of the sum which, under the Muslim law applicable to the parties, was payable on such divorce while the woman contended that he had not paid the whole of the sum, he had paid only the *mahr* and *iddat* maintenance and had not provided the *'mata'* i.e. provision of maintenance referred to in the Holy *Quran*, Chapter II, Sura 241. This Court after referring to the various text books on Muslim law, held that the divorced wife's right to maintenance ceased on expiration of *iddat* period but this Court proceeded to observe that the general propositions reflected in those statements did not deal with the special situation where the divorced wife was unable to maintain herself. In such cases, it was stated that it would be not only incorrect but unjust to extend the scope of the statements referred to in those text books in which a divorced wife is unable to maintain herself and opined that the application of those statements of law must be restricted to that class of cases in which there is no possibility of vagrancy or destitution arising out of the indigence of the divorced wife. This Court concluded that these Aiyats [the Holy *Quran*, Chapter II, Suras 241-242] leave no doubt that the Holy *Quran* imposes an obligation on the Muslim husband to make provision for or to provide maintenance to the divorced wife. The contrary argument does less than justice to the teaching of the Holy *Quran*. On this note, this Court concluded its judgment.

6. There was a big uproar thereafter and Parliament enacted the Act perhaps, with the intention of making the decision in *Shah Bano's* case ineffective.

7. The Statement of Objects & Reasons to the bill, which resulted in the Act, reads as follows:

> The Supreme Court in *Mohd. Ahmed Khan Vs. Shah Bano Begum & Ors.,* [AIR 1985 SC 945], has held that although the Muslim Law limits the husband's liability to provide for maintenance of the divorced wife to the period of *iddat* it does not contemplate or countenance the situation envisaged by Section 125 of the Code of Criminal Procedure, 1973. The Court held that it would be incorrect and unjust to extend the above

principle of Muslim Law to cases in which the divorced wife is unable to maintain herself. The Court, therefore, came to the conclusion that if the divorced wife is able to maintain to herself, the husband's liability ceases with the expiration of the period of *iddat* but if she is unable to maintain herself after the period of Iddat, she is entitled to have recourse to Section 125 of the Code of Criminal Procedure.

2. This decision has led to some controversy as to the obligation of the Muslim husband to pay maintenance to the divorced wife. Opportunity has, therefore, been taken to specify the rights which a Muslim divorced woman is entitled to at the time of divorce and to protect her interests. The Bill accordingly provides for the following among other things, namely:

(a) a Muslim divorced woman shall be entitled to a reasonable and fair provision and maintenance within the period of iddat by her former husband and in case she maintains the children born to her before or after her divorce, such reasonable provision and maintenance would be extended to a period of two years from the dates of birth of the children. She will also be entitled to *mahr* or *dower* and all the properties given to her by her relatives, friends, husband and the husband's relatives. If the above benefits are not given to her at the time of divorce, she is entitled to apply to the Magistrate for an order directing her former husband to provide for such maintenance, the payment of *mahr* or *dower* or the deliver (*sic*) of the properties;

(b) where a Muslim divorced woman is unable to maintain herself after the period of iddat, the Magistrate is empowered to make an order for the payment of maintenance by her relatives who would be entitled to inherit her property on her death according to Muslim Law in the proportions in which they would inherit her property. If any one of such relatives is unable to pay his or her share on the ground of his or her not having the means to pay, the Magistrate would direct the other relatives who have sufficient means to pay the shares of these relatives also. But where, a divorced woman has no relatives or such relatives or any one of them has not enough means to pay the maintenance or the other relatives who have been asked to pay the shares of the defaulting relatives also do not have the means to pay the shares of the defaulting relatives, the Magistrate would order the State Wakf Board to pay the maintenance ordered by him or the shares of the relatives who are unable to pay.

8. The object of enacting the Act, as stated in the Statement of Objects & Reasons to the Act, is that this Court, in *Shah Bano's* case

held that Muslim Law limits the husband's liability to provide for maintenance of the divorced wife to the period of *iddat*, but it does not contemplate or countenance the situation envisaged by Section 125 of the Code of Criminal Procedure, 1973 and, therefore, it cannot be said that the Muslim husband, according to his personal law, is not under an obligation to provide maintenance beyond the period of *iddat* to his divorced wife, who is unable to maintain herself.

9. As held in *Shah Bano's* case, the true position is that if the divorced wife is able to maintain herself, the husband's liability to provide maintenance for her ceases with the expiration of the period of *iddat* but if she is unable to maintain herself after the period of *iddat*, she is entitled to have recourse to Section 125 Cr. P. C. Thus it was held that there is no conflict between the provisions of Section 125 Cr. P. C. and those of the Muslim Personal Law on the question of the Muslim husband's obligation to provide maintenance to his divorced wife, who is unable to maintain herself. This view is a reiteration of what is stated in two other decisions earlier rendered by this Court in *Bai Tahira Vs. Ali Hussain Fidaalli Chothia*, (1979) 2 SCC 316, and *Fuzlunbi Vs. K. Khader Vali & Anr.*, (1980) 4 SCC 125.

10. Smt. Kapila Hingorani and Smt. Indira Jaisingh raised the following contentions in support of the petitioners and they are summarized as follows:

1. Muslim marriage is a contract and an element of consideration is necessary by way of *mahr* or dower and absence of consideration will discharge the marriage. On the other hand, Section 125 Cr P. C. has been enacted as a matter of public policy.

2. To enable a divorced wife, who is unable to maintain herself, to seek from her husband, who is having sufficient means and neglects or refuses to maintain her, payment of maintenance at a monthly rate not exceeding Rs. 500/-. The expression 'wife' includes a woman who has been divorced by, or has obtained a divorce from her husband and has not remarried. The religion professed by a spouse or the spouses has no relevance in the scheme of these provisions whether they are Hindus, Muslims, Christians or the Parsis, pagans or heathens. It is submitted that Section 125 Cr. P. C. is part of the Code of Criminal Procedure and not a civil law, which defines and governs rights and obligation of the parties belonging to a particular religion like the Hindu Adoptions

and Maintenance Act, the Shariat, or the Parsi Matrimonial Act. Section 125 Cr. P. C. it is submitted, was enacted in order to provide a quick and summary remedy. The basis there being, neglect by a person of sufficient means to maintain these and the inability of these persons to maintain themselves, these provision have been made and the moral edict of the law and morality cannot be clubbed with religion.

3. The argument is that the rationale of Section 125 Cr. P. C. is to off-set or to meet situation where a divorced wife is likely to be led into destitution or vagrancy. Section 125 Cr. P. C. is enacted to prevent the same in furtherance of the concept of social justice embodied in Article 21 of the Constitution.

4. It is, therefore, submitted that this Court will have to examine the questions raised before us not on the basis of Personal Law but on the basis that Section 125 Cr. P. C. is a provision made in respect of women belonging to all religions and exclusion of Muslim women from the same results in discrimination between women and women. Apart from the gender injustice caused in the country, this discrimination further leads to a monstrous proposition of nullifying a law declared by this Court in *Shah Bano's* case. Thus there is a violation of not only equality before law but also equal protection of laws and inherent infringement of Article 21 as well as basic human values. If the object of Section 125 Cr. P. C. is to avoid vagrancy, the remedy thereunder cannot be denied to Muslim women.

5. The Act is an un-Islamic, unconstitutional [*sic*] and it has the potential of suffocating the Muslim women and it undermines the secular character, which is the basic feature of the Constitution; that there is no rhyme or reason to deprive the Muslim women from the applicability of the provisions of Section 125 Cr. P. C. and consequently the present Act must be held to be discriminatory and violative of Article 14 of the Constitution; that excluding the application of Section 125 Cr. P. C. is violative of Articles 14 and 21 of the Constitution; that the conferment of power on the Magistrate under sub-Section (2) of Section 3 and Section 4 of the Act is different from the right of a Muslim woman like any other woman in the country to avail of the remedies under Section 125 Cr. P. C. and such deprivement would make the act unconstitutional, as there

is no nexus to deprive a Muslim woman from availing of the remedies available under Section 125 Cr. P. C. notwithstanding the fact that the conditions precedent for availing of the said remedies are satisfied.

11. The learned Solicitor General, who appeared for the Union of India, submitted that when a question of maintenance arises which forms part of the personal law of a community, what is fair and reasonable is a question of fact in that context. Under Section 3 of the Act, it is provided that a reasonable and fair provision and maintenance to be made and paid by her former husband within the *iddat* would make it clear that it cannot be for life but would only be for a period of *iddat* and when that fact has clearly been stated in the provision, the question of interpretation as to whether it is for life or for the period of *iddat* would not arise. Challenge raised in this petition is *dehors* the personal law. Personal law is a legitimate basis for discrimination, if at all, and, therefore, does not offend Article 14 of the Constitution. If the legislature, as a matter of policy, wants to apply Section 125 Cr. P. C. to Muslims, it could also be stated that the same legislature can, by implication, withdraw such application and make some other provision in that regard. Parliament can amend Section 125 Cr. P. C. so as to exclude them and apply personal law and the policy of Section 125 Cr. P. C. is not to create a right of maintenance *dehors* the personal law. He further submitted that in *Shah Bano's* case, it has been held that a divorced woman is entitled to maintenance even after the *iddat* period from the husband and that is how Parliament also understood the ratio of that decision. To overcome the ratio of the said decision, the present Act has been enacted and Section 3(1)(a) is not in discord with the personal law.

12. Shri Y. H. Muchhala, learned Senior Advocate appearing for the All India Muslim Personal Law Board, submitted that the main object of the Act is to undo the *Shah Bano's* case. He submitted that this Court has hazarded interpretation of an unfamiliar language in relation to religious tenets and such a course is not safe as has been made clear by *Aga Mahomed Jaffer Bindaneem Vs. Koolsom Bee Bee & Ors.*, 24 IA 196 particularly in relation to *Suras* 241 and 242 Chapter II, the Holy *Quran*. He submitted that in interpreting Section 3(1)(a) of the Act, the expressions 'provision' and 'maintenance' are clearly the same and not different as has been held by some of the High Courts. He contended that the aim of the Act is not to penalize the husband but to avoid vagrancy

and in this context Section 4 of the Act is good enough to take care of such a situation and he, after making reference to several works on interpretation and religious thoughts as applicable to Muslims, submitted that social ethos of Muslim society spreads a wider net to take care of a Muslim divorced wife and not at all dependent on the husband. He adverted to the works of religious thoughts by Sir Syed Ahmed Khan and Bashir Ahmed, published from Lahore in 1957 at p. 735. He also referred to the English translation of the Holy *Quran* to explain the meaning of 'gift' in *Sura* 241. In conclusion, he submitted that the interpretation to be placed on the enactment should be in consonance with the Muslim personal law and also meet a situation of vagrancy of a Muslim divorced wife even when there is a denial of the remedy provided under Section 125 Cr. P. C. and such a course would not lead to vagrancy since provisions have been made in the Act. This Court will have to bear in mind the social ethos of Muslims, which are different and the enactment is consistent with law and justice.

13. It was further contended on behalf of the respondents that the Parliament enacted the impugned Act, respecting the personal law of Muslims and that itself is a legitimate basis for making a differentiation; that a separate law for a community on the basis of personal law applicable to such community, cannot be held to be discriminatory, that the personal law is now being continued by a legislative enactment and the entire policy behind the Act is not to confer a right of maintenance, unrelated to the personal law; that the object of the Act itself was to preserve the personal law and prevent inroad into the same; that the Act aims to prevent the vagaries and not to make a Muslim woman, destitute and at the same time, not to penalize the husband, that the impugned Act resolved all issues, bearing in mind the personal law of Muslim community and the fact that the benefits of Section 125 Cr. P. C. have not been extended to Muslim women, would not necessarily lead to a conclusion that there is no provision to protect the Muslim women from vagaries and from being a destitute; that, therefore, the Act is not invalid or unconstitutional.

14. On behalf of the All India Muslim Personal Law Board, certain other contentions have also been advanced identical to those advanced by the other authorities and their submission is that the interpretation placed on the Arabic word *'mata'* by this Court in *Shah Bano's* case is incorrect and submitted that the maintenance which includes

the provision for residence during the *iddat* period is the obligation of the husband but such provision should be construed synonymously with the religious tenets and, so construed, the expression would only include the right of residence of a Muslim divorced wife during *iddat* period and also during the extended period under Section 3(1)(a) of the Act and thus reiterated various other contentions advanced on behalf of others and they have also referred to several opinions expressed in various text books, such as:

1. The Turjuman Al-*Quran* by Maulana Abul Kalam Azad, translated into English by Dr. Syed Abdul Latif;
2. Persian Translation of the *Quran* by Shah Waliullah Dehlavi;
3. Al-Manar Commentary on the *Quran* (Arabic);
4. Al-Isaba by Ibne Hajar Asqualini [Part-2]; Siyar Alam-in-Nubla by Shamsuddin Mohd. Bin Ahmed Bin Usman Az-Zahbi;
5. Al-Maratu Bayn Al-Fiqha Wa Al Qanun by Dr. Mustafa As-Sabai;
6. Al-Jamil' Ahkam-II Al *Quran* by Abu Abdullah Mohammad Bin Ahmed Al Ansari Al-Qurtubi;
7. Commentary on the *Quran* by Baidavi (Arabic);
8. Rooh-ul-Bayan (Arabic) by Ismail Haqqi Affendi;
9. Al Muhalla by Ibne Hazm (Arabic);
10. Al-Ahwalus Shakhsiah (The Personal Law) by Mohammad Abu Zuhra Darul Fikrul Arabi.

15. On the basis of the aforementioned text books, it is contended that the view taken in *Shah Bano's* case on the expression 'mata' is not correct and the whole object of the enactment has been to nullify the effect of the *Shah Bano's* case so as to exclude the application of the provision of Section 125 Cr. P. C. however, giving recognition to the personal law as stated in Sections 3 and 4 of the Act. As stated earlier, the interpretation of the provisions will have to be made bearing in mind the social ethos of the Muslims and there should not be erosion of the personal law.

16. On behalf of the Islamic Shariat Board, it is submitted that except for Mr. M. Asad and Dr. Mustafa-as-Sabayi no author subscribed to the view that the *Verse* 241 of Chapter II of the Holy *Quran* casts an obligation on a former husband to pay maintenance to the Muslim divorced wife beyond the *iddat* period. It is submitted that Mr. M. Asad's translation and commentary has been held to be unauthentic and unreliable

and has been subscribed by the Islamic World League only. It is submitted that Dr. Mustafa-as-Sabayi is a well-known author in Arabic
but his field was history and literature and not the Muslim law. It was
submitted that neither are they the theologists nor jurists in terms of
Muslim law. It is contended that this Court wrongly relied upon Verse
241 of Chapter II of the Holy *Quran* and the decree in this regard is to be
referred to Verse 236 of Chapter II which makes paying *'mata'* as obligatory for such divorcees who were not touched before divorce and whose
mahr was not stipulated. It is submitted that such divorcees do not have
to observe *iddat* period and hence not entitled to any maintenance.
Thus the obligation for *'mata'* has been imposed which is a one time
transaction related to the capacity of the former husband. On the basis
of certain texts, it is contended that the expression *'mata'* which according to different schools of Muslim law, is obligatory only in typical case
of a divorce before consummation to the woman whose *mahr* was not
stipulated and deals with obligatory rights of maintenance for observing *iddat* period or for breast-feeding the child. Thereafter, various other
contentions were raised on behalf of the Islamic Shariat Board as to
why the views expressed by different authors should not be accepted.

17. Dr. A. M. Singhvi, learned Senior Advocate who appeared for the
National Commission for Women, submitted that the interpretation
placed by the decisions of the Gujrat, Bombay, Kerala and the minority
view of the Andhra Pradesh High Court should be accepted by us. As
regards the constitutional validity of the Act, he submitted that if the
interpretation of Section 3 of the Act as stated later in the course of this
judgment is not acceptable then the consequence would be that a Muslim
divorced wife is permanently rendered without remedy insofar as her
former husband is concerned for the purpose of her survival after the
iddat period. Such relief is neither available under Section 125 Cr. P. C.
nor it is properly compensated by the provision made in Section 4 of the
Act. He contended that the remedy provided under Section 4 of the Act
is *illusory* inasmuch as *firstly*, she cannot get sustenance from the parties
who were not only strangers to the marital relationship which led to
divorce; *secondly*, Wakf Boards would usually not have the means to support such destitute women since they are themselves perennially starved
of funds and *thirdly*, the potential legatees of a destitute woman would
either be too young or too old so as to be able to extend requisite support. Therefore, realistic appreciation of the matter will have to be taken

and this provision will have to be decided on the touchstone of Articles 14,15 and also Article 21 of the Constitution and thus the denial of right to life and liberty is exasperated by the fact that it operates oppressively, unequally and unreasonably only against one class of women. While Section 5 of the Act makes the availability and applicability of the remedy as provided by Section 125 Cr. P. C. dependent upon the whim, caprice, choice and option of the husband of the Muslim divorcee who in the first place is sought to be excluded from the ambit of Section 3 of the post-*iddat* period and, therefore, submitted that this provision will have to be held unconstitutional.

18. This Court in *Shah Bano's* case held that although Muslim personal law limits the husband's liability to provide maintenance for his divorced wife to the period of *iddat*, it does not contemplate a situation envisaged by Section 125 Cr. P. C. 1973. The Court held that it would not be incorrect or unjustified to extend the above principle of Muslim Law to cases in which a divorced wife is unable to maintain herself and, therefore, the Court came to the conclusion that if the divorced wife is able to maintain herself the husband's liability ceases with the expiration of the period of *iddat*, but if she is unable to maintain herself after the period of *iddat*, she is entitled to recourse to Section 125 Cr. P. C. This decision having imposed obligations as to the liability of Muslim husband to pay maintenance to his divorced wife, Parliament endorsed by the Act the right of a Muslim woman to be paid maintenance at the time of divorce and to protect her rights.

19. The learned counsel has also raised certain incidental questions arising in these matters to the following effect:

1. Whether the husband who had not complied with the orders passed prior to the enactments and were in arrears of payment could escape from their obligation on the basis of the Act, or in other words, whether the Act is retrospective in effect?
2. Whether Family Courts have jurisdiction to decide the issues under the Act?
3. What is the extent to which the Wakf Board is liable under the Act?

20. The learned counsel for the parties has elaborately argued on a very wide canvass. Since we are only concerned in this Bench with the constitutional validity of the provision of the Act, we will consider only such questions as are germane to this aspect. We will decide only the

question of constitutional validity of the Act and relegate the matters when other issues arise to be dealt with by respective Benches of this Court either in appeal or special leave petitions or writ petitions.

21. In interpreting the provisions where matrimonial relationship is involved, we have to consider the social conditions prevalent in our society. In our society, whether they belong to the majority or the minority group, what is apparent is that there exists a great disparity in the matter of economic resourcefulness between a man and a woman. Our society is male dominated both economically and socially and women are assigned, invariably, a dependent role, irrespective of the class of society to which she belongs. A woman on her marriage very often, though highly educated, gives up her all other avocations and entirely devotes herself to the welfare of the family, in particular she shares with her husband, her emotions, sentiments, mind and body, and her investment in the marriage is her entire life—a sacramental sacrifice of her individual self and is far too enormous to be measured in terms of money. When a relationship of this nature breaks up, in what manner we could compensate her so far as emotional fracture or loss of investment is concerned, there can be no answer. It is a small solace to say that such a woman should be compensated in terms of money towards her livelihood and such a relief which partakes basic human rights to secure gender and social justice is universally recognized by persons belonging to all religions and it is difficult to perceive that Muslim law intends to provide a different kind of responsibility by passing on the same to those unconnected with the matrimonial life such as the heirs who were likely to inherit the property from her or the Wakf Boards. Such an approach appears to us to be a kind of distortion of the social facts. Solutions to such societal problems of universal magnitude pertaining to horizons of basic human rights, culture, dignity and decency of life and dictates of necessity in the pursuit of social justice should be invariably left to be decided on consideration other than religion or religious faith or beliefs or national, sectarian, racial or communal constraints. Bearing this aspect in mind, we have to interpret the provisions of the Act in question.

22. Now it is necessary to analyse the provisions of the Act to understand the scope of the same. The Preamble to the Act sets out that it is an Act to protect the rights of Muslim women who have been divorced by, or have obtained divorce from, their husbands and to provide for

matters connected therewith or incidental thereto. A 'divorced woman' is defined under Section 2(a) of the Act to mean a divorced woman who was married according to Muslim law, and has been divorced by, or has obtained divorce from her husband in accordance with Muslim law; '*iddat period*' is defined under Section 2(b) of the Act to mean, in the case of a divorced woman:

(i)   three menstrual courses after the date of divorce, if she is subject to menstruation;

(ii) three *lunar* months after her divorce, if she is not subject to menstruation; and

(iii) if she is enceinte at the time of her divorce, the period between the divorce and the delivery of her child or the termination of her pregnancy whichever is earlier.

23. Sections 3 and 4 of the Act are the principal Sections, which are under attack before us. Section 3 opens up with a *non-obstante* clause overriding all other laws and provides that a divorced woman shall be entitled to:

(a)   a reasonable and fair provision and maintenance to be made and paid to her within the period of *iddat* by her former husband;

(b)   where she maintains the children born to her before or after her divorce, a reasonable provision and maintenance to be made and paid by her former husband for a period of two years from the respective dates of birth of such children;

(c)   an amount equal to the sum of *mahr* or dower agreed to be paid to her at the time of her marriage or at any time thereafter according to Muslim Law; and

(d)   all the properties given to her before or at the time of marriage or after the marriage by her relatives, friends, husband and any relatives of the husband or his friends.

24. Where such reasonable and fair provision and maintenance or the amount of *mahr* or dower due has not been made and paid or the properties referred to in clause (d) sub-Section (1) have not been delivered to a divorced woman on her divorce, she or any one duly authorized by her may, on her behalf, make an application to a Magistrate for an order for payment of such provision and maintenance *mahr* or dower or the delivery of properties, as the case may be. Rest of the

provisions of Section 3 of the Act may not be of much relevance, which are procedural in nature.

25. Section 4 of the Act provides that, with an overriding clause as to what is stated earlier in the Act or in any other law for the time being in force, where the Magistrate is satisfied that a divorced woman has not remarried and is not able to maintain herself after the *iddat* period, he may make an order directing such of her relatives as would be entitled to inherit her property on her death according to Muslim Law to pay such reasonable and fair maintenance to her as he may determine fit and proper, having regard to the needs of the divorced woman, the standard of life enjoyed by her during her marriage and the means of such relatives and such maintenance shall be payable by such relatives in the proportions in which they would inherit her property and at such periods as he may specify in his order. If any of the relatives do not have the necessary means to pay the same, the Magistrate may order that the share of such relatives in the maintenance ordered by him be paid by such of the other relatives as may appear to the Magistrate to have the means of paying the same in such proportions as the Magistrate may think fit to order. Where a divorced woman is unable to maintain herself and she has no relatives as mentioned in sub-Section (1) or such relatives or any one of them has not enough means to pay the maintenance ordered by the Magistrate or the other relatives have not the means to pay the shares of those relatives whose shares have been ordered by the Magistrate to be paid by such other relatives under the second proviso to sub-Section (1), the Magistrate may, by order direct the State Wakf Board, functioning in the area in which the divorced woman resides, to pay such maintenance as determined by him as the case may be. It is, however, significant to note that Section 4 of the Act refers only to payment of 'maintenance' and does not touch upon the 'provision' to be made by the husband referred to in Section 3(1)(a) of the Act.

26. Section 5 to the Act provides for option to be governed by the provisions of Sections 125 to 128 Cr. P. C. It lays down that if, on the date of the first hearing of the application under Section 3(2), a divorced woman and her former husband declare, by affidavit or any other declaration in writing in such form as may be prescribed, either jointly or separately, that they would prefer to be governed by the provisions of Sections 125 to 128 Cr. P. C., and file such affidavit or declaration in

the Court hearing the application, the Magistrate shall dispose of such application accordingly.

27. A reading of the Act will indicate that it codifies and regulates the obligations due to a Muslim woman divorcee by putting them outside the scope of Section 125 Cr. P. C. as the 'divorced woman' has been defined as 'Muslim woman who was married according to Muslim law and has been divorced by or has obtained divorce from her husband in accordance with the Muslim law'. But the Act does not apply to a Muslim woman whose marriage is solemnized either under the Indian Special Marriage Act, 1954 or a Muslim woman whose marriage was dissolved either under Indian Divorce Act, 1969 [*sic*] or the Indian Special Marriage Act, 1954. The Act does not apply to the deserted and separated Muslim wives. The maintenance under the Act is to be paid by the husband for the duration of the *iddat* period and this obligation does not extend beyond the period of *iddat*. Once the relationship with the husband has come to an end with the expiry of the *iddat* period, the responsibility devolves upon the relatives of the divorcee. The Act follows Muslim personal law in determining which relatives are responsible under which circumstances. If there are no relatives, or no relatives are able to support the divorcee, then the Court can order the State Wakf Boards to pay the maintenance.

28. Section 3(1) of the Act provides that a divorced woman shall be entitled to have from her husband, a reasonable and fair maintenance which is to be made and paid to her within the *iddat* period. Under Section 3(2) the Muslim divorcee can file an application before a Magistrate if the former husband has not paid to her a reasonable and fair provision and maintenance or *mahr* due to her or has not delivered the properties given to her before or at the time of marriage by her relatives, or friends, or the husband or any of his relatives or friends. Section 3(3) provides for procedure wherein the Magistrate can pass an order directing the former husband to pay such reasonable and fair provision and maintenance to the divorced woman as he may think fit and proper having regard to the needs of the divorced woman, standard of life enjoyed by her during her marriage and means of her former husband. The judicial enforceability of the Muslim divorced woman's right to provision and maintenance under Section (3)(1)(a) of the Act has been subjected to the condition of husband having sufficient means which, strictly speaking, is contrary to the principles of Muslim law as

the liability to pay maintenance during the *iddat* period is unconditional and cannot be circumscribed by the financial means of the husband. The purpose of the Act appears to be to allow the Muslim husband to retain his freedom of avoiding payment of maintenance to his erstwhile wife after divorce and the period of *iddat*.

29. A careful reading of the provisions of the Act would indicate that a divorced woman is entitled to a reasonable and fair provision for maintenance. It was stated that Parliament seems to intend that the divorced woman gets sufficient means of livelihood, after the divorce and, therefore, the word 'provision' indicates that something is provided in advance for meeting some needs. In other words, at the time of divorce the Muslim husband is required to contemplate the future needs and make preparatory arrangements in advance for meeting those needs. Reasonable and fair provision may include provision for her residence, her food, her cloths [*sic*], and other articles. The expression 'within' should be read as 'during' or 'for' and this cannot be done because words cannot be construed contrary to their meaning as the word 'within' would mean 'on or before', 'not beyond' and, therefore, it was held that the Act would mean that on or before the expiration of the *iddat* period, the husband is bound to make and pay a maintenance to the wife and if he fails to do so then the wife is entitled to recover it by filing an application before the Magistrate as provided in Section 3(3) but nowhere the Parliament has provided that reasonable and fair provision and maintenance is limited only for the *iddat* period and not beyond it. It would extend to the whole life of the divorced wife unless she gets married for a second time.

30. The important Section in the Act is Section 3 which provides that divorced woman is entitled to obtain from her former husband '*maintenance*', '*provision*' and '*mahr*', and to recover from his possession her wedding presents and dowry and authorizes the Magistrate to order payment or restoration of these sums or properties. The crux of the matter is that the divorced woman shall be entitled to a reasonable and fair provision and maintenance to be made and paid to her within the *iddat* period by her former husband. The wordings of Section 3 of the Act appear to indicate that the husband has two separate and distinct obligations; (1) to make a '*reasonable and fair provision*' for his divorced wife; and (2) to provide '*maintenance*' for her. The emphasis of this Section is not on the nature of duration of any such '*provision*' or

'*maintenance*', but on the time by which an arrangement for payment of provision and maintenance should be concluded, namely, 'within the *iddat* period'. If the provisions are so read, the Act would exclude from liability for post-*iddat* period maintenance to a man who has already discharged his obligations of both 'reasonable and fair provision' and 'maintenance' by paying these amounts in a lump sum to his wife, in addition to having paid his wife's *mahr* and restored her dowry as per Section 3(1)(c) and 3(1)(d) of the Act. Precisely, the point that arose for consideration in *Shah Bano's* case was that the husband has not made a 'reasonable and fair provision' for his divorced wife even if he had paid the amount agreed as *mahr* half a century earlier and provided *iddat* maintenance and he was, therefore, ordered to pay a specified sum monthly to her under Section 125 Cr. P. C. This position was available to Parliament on the date it enacted the law but even so, the provisions enacted under the Act are '*a reasonable and fair provision and maintenance to be made and paid*' as provided under Section 3(1)(a) of the Act and these expressions covers different things, *firstly*, by the use of two verbs—'*to be made and paid* to her within the *iddat period*' it is clear that a fair and reasonable provision is to be made while maintenance is to be paid; *secondly*, Section 4 of the Act, which empowers the Magistrate to issue an order for payment of maintenance to the divorced woman against various of her relatives, contains no reference to 'provision'. Obviously, the right to have 'a fair and reasonable provision'' in her favour is a right enforceable only against the woman's former husband, and in addition to what he is obliged to pay as 'maintenance'; *thirdly* the words of the Holy *Quran*, as translated by Yusuf Ali of '*mata*' as 'maintenance' though may be incorrect and that other translations employed the word 'provision', the Court in *Shah Bano's* case dismissed this aspect by holding that it is a distinction without a difference. Indeed, whether '*mata*' was rendered 'maintenance' or 'provision', there could be no pretence that the husband in *Shah Bano's* case had provided anything at all by way of '*mata*' to his divorced wife. The contention put forth on behalf of the other side is that a divorced Muslim woman who is entitled to '*mata*' is only a single or one time transaction which does not mean payment of maintenance continuously at all. This contention, apart from supporting the view that the word 'provision' in Section 3(1)(a) of the Act incorporates '*mata*' as a right of the divorced Muslim woman distinct from and in addition to *mahr* and maintenance for the *iddat* period, also enables 'a reasonable and fair provision' and 'a reasonable and fair provision' as provided under Section 3(3) of the Act would be with reference to the needs of the divorced woman, the means of the husband, and the standard of life the woman enjoyed during the marriage and there is no reason why such provision could not take the form of the regular payment of alimony to the divorced woman, though it may look ironical that the enactment intended to reverse the decision in *Shah Bano's* case, actually codifies the very rationale contained therein.

31. A comparison of these provisions with Section 125 Cr. P. C. will make it clear that requirements provided in Section 125 and the purpose, object and scope thereof being to prevent vagrancy by compelling those who can do so to support those who are unable to support themselves and who have a normal and legitimate claim to support is satisfied. If that is so, the argument of the petitioners that a different scheme being provided under the Act which is equally or more beneficial on the interpretation placed by us from the one provided under the Code of Criminal Procedure deprive them of their right loses its significance. The object and scope of Section 125 Cr. P. C. is to prevent vagrancy by compelling those who are under an obligation to support those who are unable to support themselves and that object being fulfilled, we find it difficult to accept the contention urged on behalf of the petitioners.

32. Even under the Act, the parties agreed that the provisions of Section 125 Cr. P. C. would still be attracted and even otherwise, the Magistrate has been conferred with the power to make appropriate provision of maintenance and, therefore, what could be earlier granted by Magistrate under Section 125 Cr. P. C. would now be granted under the very Act itself. This being the position, the Act cannot be held to be unconstitutional.

33. As on the date the Act came into force the law applicable to Muslim divorced women is as declared by this Court in *Shah Bano's* case. In this case to find out the personal law of Muslims with regard to divorced women's rights, the starting point should be *Shah Bano's* case and not the original texts or any other material—all the more so when varying versions as to the authenticity of the source are shown to exist. Hence, we have refrained from referring to them in detail. That declaration was made after considering the Holy *Quran*, and other commentaries or other texts. When a Constitution Bench of this Court analysed *Suras* 241-242 of Chapter II of the Holy *Quran* and other relevant textual

material, we do not think, it is open for us to re-examine that position and delve into a research to reach another conclusion. We respectfully abide by what has been stated therein. All that needs to be considered is whether in the Act specific deviation has been made from the personal law as declared by this Court in *Shah Bano's* case without mutilating its underlying ratio. We have carefully analysed the same and come to the conclusion that the Act actually and in reality codifies what was stated in *Shah Bano's* case. The learned Solicitor General contended that what has been stated in the Objects and Reasons in Bill leading to the Act is a fact and that we should presume to be correct. We have analysed the facts and the law in *Shah Bano's* case and proceeded to find out the impact of the same on the Act. If the language of the Act is as we have stated, the mere fact that the Legislature took note of certain facts in enacting the law will not be of much materiality.

34. In *Shah Bano's* case this Court has clearly explained as to the rationale behind Section 125 Cr. P. C. to make provision for maintenance to be paid to a divorced Muslim wife and this is clearly to avoid vagrancy or destitution on the part of a Muslim woman. The contention put forth on behalf of the Muslim organizations who are interveners before us is that under the Act vagrancy or destitution is sought to be avoided but not by punishing the erring husband, if at all, but by providing for maintenance through others. If for any reason the interpretation placed by us on the language of Sections 3(1)(a) and 4 of the Act is not acceptable, we will have to examine the effect of the provisions as they stand, that is, a Muslim woman will not be entitled to maintenance from her husband after the period of *iddat* once the *talaq* is pronounced and, if at all thereafter maintenance could only be recovered from the various persons mentioned in Section 4 or from the Wakf Board. This Court in *Olga Tellis Vs. Bombay Municipal Corporation*, 1985 (3) SCC 545, and *Maneka Gandhi Vs. Union of India*, 1978 (1) SCC 248, held that the concept of 'right to life and personal liberty' guaranteed under Article 21 of the Constitution would include the 'right to live with dignity'. Before the Act a Muslim woman who was divorced by her husband was granted a right to maintenance from her husband under the provisions of Section 125 Cr P. C. until she may remarry and such a right, if deprived, would not be reasonable, just and fair. Thus the provision of the Act depriving the divorced Muslim women of such a right to maintenance from her husband and providing for her maintenance to be paid by the

former husband only for the period of *iddat* and thereafter to make her run from pillar to post in search of her relatives one after the other and ultimately to knock at the doors of the Wakf Board does not appear to be reasonable and fair substitute of the provisions of Section 125 Cr P. C. Such deprivation of the divorced Muslim women of their right to maintenance from their former husbands under the beneficial provisions of the Code of Criminal Procedure which are otherwise available to all other women in India cannot be stated to have been effected by a reasonable, right, just and fair law and, if these provisions are less beneficial that the provisions of Chapter IX of the Code of Criminal Procedure, a divorced Muslim woman has obviously been unreasonably discriminated and got out of the protection of the provisions of the general law as indicated under the Code which are available to Hindu, Buddhist, Jain, Parsi or Christian women or women belonging to any other community. The provisions *prima facie*, therefore, appear to be violative of Article 14 of the Constitution mandating equality and equal protection of law to all persons otherwise similarly circumstanced and also violative of Article 15 of the Constitution which prohibits any discrimination on the ground of religion as the Act would obviously apply to Muslim divorced women only and solely on the ground of their belonging to the Muslim religion. It is well settled that on a rule of construction a given statute will become 'ultra vires' or 'unconstitutional' and therefore, void, whereas on another construction which is permissible, the statute remains effective and operative the Court will prefer the latter on the ground that Legislature does not intend to enact unconstitutional laws. We think, the latter interpretation should be accepted and therefore, the interpretation placed by us results in upholding the validity of the Act. It is well settled that when by appropriate reading of an enactment the validity of the Act can be upheld, such interpretation is accepted by Courts and not the other way.

35. The learned counsel appearing for the Muslim organizations contended after referring to various passages from the text books to which we have adverted to earlier to state that the law is very clear that a divorced Muslim woman is entitled to maintenance only upto the stage of *iddat* and not thereafter. What is to be provided by way of '*mata*' is only a benevolent provision to be made in case of divorced Muslim woman who is unable to maintain herself and that too by way of charity or kindness on the part of her former husband and not as a

result of her right flowing to the divorced wife. The effect of various interpretations placed on *Suras* 241 and 242 of Chapter 2 of Holy *Quran* has been referred to in *Shah Bano's* case. *Shah Bano's* case clearly enunciated what the present law would be. It made a distinction between the provisions to be made and the maintenance to be paid. It was noticed that the maintenance is payable only upto the stage of *iddat* and this provision is applicable in case of normal circumstances, while in case of a divorced Muslim woman who is unable to maintain herself, she is entitled to get *'mata'*. That is the basis on which the Bench of Five Judges of this Court interpreted the various texts and held so. If that is the legal position, we do not think, we can state that any other position is possible nor are we to start on a clean slate after having forgotten the historical background of the enactment. The enactment though purports to overcome the view expressed in *Shah Bano's* case in relation to a divorced Muslim woman getting something by way of maintenance in the nature of *'mata'* is indeed the statutorily recognized by making provision under the Act for the purpose of the 'maintenance' but also for 'provision'. When these two expressions have been used by the enactments, which obviously means that the Legislature did not intend to obliterate the meaning attributed to these two expressions by this Court in *Shah Bano's* case. Therefore, we are of the view that the contentions advanced on behalf of the parties to the contrary cannot be sustained.

36. In *Arab Ahemadhia Abdulla and etc, Vs. Arab Bail Mohmuna Saiyadbhai & Ors. etc.*, AIR 1988 (Guj.) 141; *Ali Vs. Sufaira*, (1988) 3 Crimes 147; *K. Kunhashed Hazi Vs. Amena*, 1995 Crl. L. J. 3371; *K. Zunaideen Vs. Ameena Bagum*, (1998) II DMC 468; *Karim Abdul Shaik Vs. Shenaz Karim Shaik*, 2000 Cr. L. J. 3560 and *Jaitunbi Mubarak Shaikh Vs. Mubarak Fakruddin Shaikh & Anr.*, 1999 (3) Mh. L. J. 694, while interpreting the provision of Section 3(1)(a) and 4 of the Act, it is held that a divorced Muslim woman is entitled to a fair and reasonable provision for her future being made by her former husband which must include maintenance for future extending beyond the *iddat* period. It was held that the liability of the former husband to make a reasonable and fair provision under Section 3(1)(a) of the Act is not restricted only for the period of *iddat* but that divorced Muslim woman is entitled to a reasonable and fair provision for her future being made by her former husband and also to maintenance being paid to her for the *iddat* period. A lot of emphasis was laid

on the words 'made' and 'paid' and were construed to mean not only to make provision for the *iddat* period but also to make a reasonable and fair provision for her future. A Full Bench of the Punjab and Haryana High Court in *Kaka Vs. Hassan Bano & Anr.*, II (1998) DMC 85 (FB), has taken the view that under Section 3(1)(a) of the Act a divorced Muslim woman can claim maintenance which is not restricted to *iddat* period. To the contrary it has been held that it is not open to the wife to claim fair and reasonable provision for the future in addition to what she had already received at the time of her divorce; that the liability of the husband is limited for the period of *iddat* and thereafter if she is unable to maintain herself, she has to approach her relative or Wakf Board, by majority decision in *Umar Khan Bahamani Vs. Fathimnurisa*, 1990 Crl. L. J. 1364; *Abdul Rashid Vs. Sultana Bagum*, 1992 Crl. L. J. 76; *Abdul Haq Vs. Yasima Talat*, 1998 Crl. L. J. 3433; *Md. Marahim Vs. Raiza Begum*, 1993 (1) DMC 60. Thus preponderance of judicial opinion is in favour of what we have concluded in the interpretation of Section 3 of the Act. The decision of the High Courts referred to herein that are contrary to our decision stand overruled.

37. While upholding the validity of the Act, we may sum up our conclusions:

1. A Muslim husband is liable to make reasonable and fair provision for the future of the divorced wife which obviously includes her maintenance as well. Such a reasonable and fair provision extending beyond the *iddat* period must be made by the husband within the *iddat* period in terms of Section 3(1)(a) of the Act.

2. Liability of Muslim husband to his divorced wife arising under Section 3(1)(a) of the Act to pay maintenance is not confined to *iddat* period.

3. A divorced Muslim woman who has not remarried and who is not able to maintain herself after *iddat* period can proceed as provided under Section 4 of the Act against her relatives who are liable to maintain her in proportion to the properties which they inherit on her death according to Muslim law from such divorced woman including her children and parents. If any of the relatives being unable to pay maintenance, the Magistrate may direct the State Wakf Board established under the Act to pay such maintenance.

4. The provisions of the Act do not offend Articles 14, 15 and 21 of the Constitution of India.

38. In the result, the writ petition Nos. 868/86, 996/86, 1001/86, 1055/86, 1062/86, 1236/86, 1259/86 and 1281/86 challenging the validity of the provisions of the Act are dismissed.

39. All other matters where there are other questions raised, the same shall stand relegated for consideration by appropriate Benches of this Court.

Petition allowed.

SECTION III

PAKISTAN

Khurshid Jan v. Fazal Dad

JUDGMENT

MUHAMMAD YAQUB ALI, J. The facts of the two appeals out of which this reference to the Full Bench has arisen, may be briefly stated thus:

R. S. A. No. 486 of 1961, has been preferred by *Mst.* Khurshid Jan from the judgment and decree of Mr. Salah-ud-Din Hanif, District Judge, Rawalpindi, dated the 4th of November 1961, by which he has, reversing the judgment and decree of trial Court, dismissed her suit for a declaration of repudiation of marriage in exercise of option of puberty. A peculiar feature of this litigation is that after the institution of the suit for dissolution of marriage, *Mst.* Khurshid Jan appellant went to stay with her husband, Fazal Dad respondent, for a period of 15 days, during which cohabitation is said to have taken place between the parties. The appellant claimed that she was taken away by the respondent with the assistance of the police and that she had not submitted herself to cohabitation with him, but the plea has not found favour with the Courts below. The Court of first instance, following the judgment of this Court in *Mst. Aishan* v. *Jodha Ram* A I R 1938 Lah. 719 and *Mst. Muni* v. *Habib Khan* P L D 1956 Lah. 403 decreed the suit on the ground that repudiation of marriage took effect with the institution of the suit and that there was no subsisting marriage between the parties when the respondent cohabited with the appellant. On appeal by the respondent, the learned District Judge, relying on a note under paragraph 275 of the Principles of Muhammadan Law by Mulla, that according to Hedaya no declaration for repudiation of marriage can be made if the wife has permitted sexual intercourse with her husband after the exercise of option, reversed the finding of the trial court and dismissed the appellant's suit. Dissatisfied with this finding, *Mst.* Khurshid Jan instituted the present appeal and, in addition to the two judgments, referred to above, has relied on *Muhammad Bakhsh* v. *Crown* P L D 1950 Lah. 203.

2. In opposition to the appeal the learned counsel for the defendant relied on the text of Hedaya, Radd-ul-Muhtar, Digest of Muslim Law by Baillie, Amir Ali and Tyabji, in which the view expressed is that the decree of the Qazi is essential to impart validity to the exercise of option of puberty. The dictum of the Judicial Committee in *Agha Mahmood Jaffer Bindanim* v. *Koolsoom Beebee* I L R25 Cal. 9 at p. 18. was also pressed into service that 'it would be wrong for the Courts to put their own construction on the Qur'an in opposition to the express ruling of commentators of great antiquity and high authority', namely, Hedaya and Baillie's Imamiya in which the clear text of Qur'an, 'such of you as shall die and leave your wives ought to bequeath to them a year's maintenance' is not followed. It was accordingly contended that in delivering the aforementioned judgments this Court had acted without authority in departing from the settled rule of Muslim Law that a decree of a Qazi is necessary to effectuate the exercise of option of puberty.

3. The decision of the Judicial Committee had force of law in the Sub-Continent until Independence. The dictum in *Agha Mahmood Jaffer Bindanim* v. *Koolsoom Beebee* had, therefore, considerably lessened the burden on the Courts to determine the rule of law applicable to both Sunni and Shia Muslims, but with the coming into being of Pakistan, the situation has considerably changed.

Firstly, the scope of application of Shariat to disputes of civil nature between Muslims was enlarged by the Punjab Muslim Personal Law (Shariat) Application Act (IX of 1948) since replaced by the West Pakistan Muslim Personal Law (Shariat) Application Act (V of 1962). Section 2, as amended by Punjab Act XI of 1951, provided as under:

> Notwithstanding any rule of custom or usage, in all questions regarding succession (whether testate or intestate), special property of females, betrothal, marriage, divorce, dower, adoption, guardianship, minority, legitimacy or bastardy, family relations, wills, legacies, gifts, religious

usages or institutions including *waqfs*, trusts and trust property, the rule
of decision shall be the Muslim Personal Law (Shariat) in cases where the
parties are Muslims.

Secondly, the Constitution of Islamic Republic of Pakistan (1956) and
present Constitution of 1962 contain express provisions that the Muslims
of Pakistan should be enabled individually and collectively to order their
lives in accordance with the teaching and requirements of Islam as set
out in the Qur'an and Sunnah; that no law should be enacted which is
repugnant to the Qur'an and Sunnah and that all existing laws should
be brought into conformity with the Qur'an and Sunnah. The dictum
of the Judicial Committee in *Agha Mahmood Jaffer Bindanim* v. *Koolsoom
Beebee*, therefore, did not hold good for if a rule in a text book of whatever antiquity and high authority is in opposition to a clear injunction in
Qur'an or an authentic Hadith of the Holy Prophet (may peace be upon
him), then undoubtedly the latter shall prevail and it is the bounden duty
of the Courts to ascertain the correct rule of decision in all the matters
enumerated above. This, in my view, gave rise to the following questions
of fundamental importance to administration of justice in the country—

(i)   what are the sources of Muslim Law;
(ii) what are the rules of interpretation of Muslim Law and can Courts
      differ from the views of Imams and other jurisconsults of Muslim
      Law on grounds of public policy, justice, equity and good con-
      science; and
(iii) in case of conflict of views found in text books on Muslim Law,
      such as Hedaya, Fatawa-i-Alamgiri, Radd-ul-Muhtar, how are the
      Courts to determine which of the views is correct?

5. F. A. O. No. 65 of 1962, has been preferred by *Mst.* Zohra Begum
from the order, dated the 31st of July 1962, of the Guardian Judge,
Lahore, directing her to hand over the custody of her minor son, who
has attained the age of seven years, to his father Sheikh Latif Ahmed
Munawwar, respondent. Mr. A. R. Sheikh learned counsel for the appellant (since elevated to the Bench) maintained that there is no definite
rule of decision in Islamic Jurisprudence as to the age at which the
mother loses the right of custody of her son and that under Section
25 of the Guardians and Wards Act the principal consideration before
the Court in directing that the custody of the minor should be given
to the father is the welfare of the minor. He took me through a large

number of text books of Muslim Law in which conflicting views are expressed about the age of a minor at which the mother loses the right of his custody and strenuously maintained that the views expressed by the faqihs on this point were not of such binding authority as to exclude the discretion of the Court to decide the question of custody in accordance with the welfare of the minor. In support of it, he relied on *Mst. Aishan* v. *Jodha Ram and others* and *Muhammad Bakhsh* v. *Crown* and *Mst. Muni* v. *Habib Khan* in which as seen above, this Court did not follow the view expressed in more than one authoritative text books on Muslim Law that the decree of a Qazi was necessary to impart validity to the exercise of option of puberty. Reference was also made to *Mst. Rashida Begum* v. *Shahab Din and others* P L D 1960 Lah. 1142 in which Mr. Justice Muhammad Shafi did not follow the rule that on remarriage a mother loses the right of custody of her minor daughters. The questions of law raised in the appeal were the same as in R. S. A. No. 486 of 1961, and it was, therefore, directed that both of them be referred together to a larger Bench for an authoritative pronouncement.

6. The known sources of Muslim Law are Qur'an, Sunnah, *i.e.*, precepts and the conduct of the Holy Prophet (may peace be upon him), Ijma', Qiyas and Ijtihad.

Qur'an

Qur'an consists of divine revelations and is divided into chapters and verses. It was compiled by Hazrat Abu Bakr the first Caliph, within two years of the demise of the Holy Prophet and completed in its present form by Hazrat Usman, the third Caliph, ten years later. The arrangement is not the same in which it was revealed but is said to be in accordance with the plan of the Holy Prophet. The rules of law are mostly contained in Surat-ul-Baqara, Surat-un-Nisa, Surat-al-Imran, Surat-ul-Maida, Surat-un-Noor, Surat-ut-Talaq, and Surat-ul-Bani Israel. The ordinances contained in the Qur'an were revealed to settle questions which arose for determination by the Prophet and to repeal the objectionable customs like unforbidden gambling, usury and unlimited polygamy among Arabs and for effecting social reforms like the raising of the status of the women, regulating succession and inheritance on equitable basis, providing protection to minors and persons suffering from disabilities and to provide punishment ... for maintaining law and order. Qur'an is the absolute word of God, and if there is a clear injunction in it that is the rule of decision on the facts of a given case. There are detailed rules for interpretation of the Qur'an. Some them are collected in Chapter IV of Al-Risala by Imam Al-Shafi'i under the heading 'on the Book of God'....

Sunnah

7. But the divine revelations did not cover the facts of every case, the dicta of the Holy Prophet, to whom cases were brought for decision were, therefore, treated as supplementaries to the Divine Ordinances and accorded the same sanctity. In the beginning, there was a controversy as to the authority of Sunnah for, some believed that if later in point of time it repealed the text of Qur'an. The accepted position, however, is that it is the most authentic source of Islamic Law next to Qur'an. This is based on the doctrine that the holy Prophet, as a recipient of the message of God, was guided by Him in his narrative and action (...). These both are, thus, the words of God, one expressed in direct form and the other as the interpretation and application of the word of God by His Prophet. There can, thus, be no contradiction between the two of them, and this is the test to judge the authenticity of a Hadith.

8. Much of the important work on Fiqah is contained in the collection of Ahadith in the form of corpus juris as compared to corpus traditions. Previous to these compilations, Jurists like Imam Abu Hanifa an-Numan ibn Thabit formulated legal theories of speculative character comparable to legal fiction in the modern laws. While he relied on eighteen Ahadith only, Imam Malik (died A. H. 179) relied mainly on Ahadith and he gathered them not for their own sake but to use them in law.

9. The earliest and most authentic *musnaf* is that of Imam Hanbal (died A. H. 240). It contained 30,000 Ahadith narrated by 700 narrators. The first *musnaf* in which Ahadith are arranged in chapters according to their subject-matter is Sahih by Al-Bokhari (died in A. H. 257). Out of 6,00,000 Ahadith, which were prevalent during his age, he selected only 7,000, including 2,000 repetitions, thus, reducing their number to some 5,000. The principal arrangement in Sahih is legal and affords a basis for a complete system of jurisprudence. The next Sahih is that of Muslim (died in A. H. 261). The two Sahihs are known as Jamis. There are four

other collections: (1) by Ibne Maja (died in A. H. 275), (2) Abu-Daud, (died in A. H. 276), (3) Al-Tirmizi (died in A. H. 279), and (4) Al-Nisayee (died in A. H. 303).

By the end of the fifth century of the Hijra, those six compilations came to be regarded the principal and most authentic work on the science of traditions. Ibne Khaldoon, the great historian of Islam (died A. H. 808), speaks of only five while others speak of seven adding Mauta-i-Imam Malik which contains only 300 Traditions....

10. Even in these authentic compilations of Ahadith there are certain contradictions. How are the Courts to reconcile them? The answer is twofold: either the so-called contradiction lies in different rules of decision being laid down for different set off acts or that one or more of them are not authentic. There are numerous rules for determining the authenticity of a Tradition.

Ijma'

11. On the demise of the Holy Prophet (may peace be upon him) in the 12th year of Hijra, the third source of Muslim Law, *viz* Ijma' came into being....

12. On the authority of some Traditions, particularly, 'Whatever the Muslims hold to be good is good before God' (Taudih, p. 298 and Kashaful Israr, Vol. III, p. 258) and certain Qur'anic texts, Dr. Abdur Rahim has defined Ijma' as agreement of the jurists among the followers of Muhammad (peace be upon him) in a particular age on a question of law. (Taudih, p. 498; 'Mukhtasar', Vol. II, p. 29; 'Jam'ul-Jawani', Vol. III, p. 288). The Qur'anic Texts relied in support of this definition are—

(i) 'God does not allow the people to go astray after he has shown them the right path.'
(ii) 'Do not be like those who separated and divided after they have received clear proofs.'
(iii) 'Today we have completed your religion.'
(iv) 'What lies outside the truth is an error.'
(v) 'Obey God and obey the Prophet and those amongst you who have authority.'
(vi) 'If you yourself do not know, then question those who do.'

(vii) 'You are the best of men, and it is your duty to order men to do what is right and to forbid them from practising what is wrong.'

(viii) 'We have made you followers of the middle course so that you may be witnesses (of truth) to others.'

(ix) 'He who breaks away from the Prophet after he has been shown the right path and follows the ways of men other than Muslims, we shall give him what he has chosen and relegate him to hell.'

Besides the Traditional and Qur'anic Texts, the Sunni School of Law recognizes the authority of Ijma' on the basis of unanimity of opinion among the Companions. (Bazdawi, p. 253; Taudih, p. 283, 'Mukhtasar' Vol. II p. 30, 'Jam'ul-Jawani', Vol. III, p. 308). Imam Abu Hanifa an-Numan Ibn Thabit (born A. H. 80), the first of the four great Imams of the Sunni School, recognized Ijma' of the Companions, the successors of the Companions and their successors and extended it to every age.

13. It was not considered valid by Imam Ibne Hanbal, who is known to have said that any claim of unity is a mere lie and that the utmost one could claim is that he does not know of any disagreement on a particular issue. Ibne Hazm considered only the consensus of opinion among the Companions as being a sign of early Prophetic sanction or approval. Professor Abu Zahra says:

> The very validity of al-Ijma' is not a matter of consensus among Muslims. There are prominent jurists who have explicitly denied its very existence. There are others who have admitted its validity, but when an issue came with a claim of a previous Ijma', they denied its very existence

and concludes:

> It was but for the maintenance of national unity and as a check against individual deviations, that al-Ijma' was legalised as an authority after the sacred texts.

14. Ijma' is now an accepted source of law in Islamic Jurisprudence and without it further evolution of law cannot come into being which is absolutely essential to avoid outmoding of many of the laws in the changed situation and facts of the present age. The all important question, therefore, is how can this source of law-making be utilized in the present day. The answer is fraught with religious and political considerations and we are not in a position to give an authoritative pronouncement on the subject. But on a humbler plane we may point out

that Ijma' is not only a source of law-making but also bedrock of unity in Islam. The difficulties in its implementation are, of course, many, particularly the modern trend of a national State which has spread over most of the Muslim countries. Legislation is an important constituent of sovereignty. A national State will, therefore, stand in the way of an Ijma ul-Ummat. Indeed, in the dissolution of the office of Khilafat, the possibility was lost for ever.... The conclusion to be drawn from the above discussion is that Ijma' is an important source of law-making in Islam, but in the present conditions it is not feasible to resort to it in an orthodox sense. The Legislative Assemblies are perhaps the only bodies which may perform this function and the duty of the Courts is to interpret and apply the laws to be enacted by them in conformity with the Qur'an and Sunnah.

[Paragraphs 15–20 are omitted.]

Qiyas

21. The fourth source of law in Islam is Qiyas which is comparable to legal fiction in western jurisprudence. It is based on Qur'an, Sunnah and Ijma'. Fresh facts and situations arose in the ever-growing Muslim world in the early centuries of Hijra. In many cases neither the dicta of Qur'an nor the Sunnah was applicable in terms. Nor was the rule of decision settled by an Ijma'. Qiyas, or analogical deduction, from these sources was, therefore, the only answer. The Companions had applied Qiyas and so did their successors, but Imam Abu Hanifa was the first to treat it as a formal source of law-making in Islam and he gave great latitude to private opinion and in his formulations relied on eighteen Ahadith only....

22. A common place instance of Qiyas is that Qur'an has prohibited only *khumar*, that is, a distilled preparation of dates. The principle underlying the prohibition, however, is intoxication on account of which one is restrained from joining a prayer. Every intoxicant which creates such a state of mind, whether prepared from dates, opium or other drugs, is, therefore, forbidden by analogy.

23. In literal sense, Qiyas means 'measuring', 'accord' and 'equality'. It is a process by which the rule of law embodied in the Qur'an, Sunnah and Ijma' is extended to cases not covered by their text. The reason of the text on which analogy is based is 'effective cause' (...) and the legal

effect is (...). It is to be distinguished from interpretation of Qur'an, Sunnah and Ijma', though in theory Qiyas is a process of discovering the law embodied in them....

25. In the modern state the place of the Qazi is taken by Judges appointed by the authority of the State and their jurisdiction to interpret and apply Laws is derived from the Constitution and the law of the land. The tests laid down by Imam Al-Shafi'i may not, therefore, be strictly applicable to the presiding officers of present day Courts. Qiyas is not the word of God nor Sunnah of the Holy Prophet. It also lacks the authority of Ijma'. The application of Qiyas cannot, therefore, be limited to the early doctors nor their opinion, though entitled to utmost respect, be considered as binding for all times to come. The fact that the great Imams and their disciples have differed among themselves on numerous rules of decision as well as their details also furnishes further warrant for it. Some recent judgments of our own Court furnish instances of application of Qiyas by Courts of law as well as difference of learned judges with the views of the learned A'imma and Faqihs....

Ijtihad

29. While recounting the causes which brought about the decadence of Muslims, Dr. Sobhi Mahmassani, a learned modern jurist states:

> After the fall of Baghdad in the 13th century, the Islamic civilization began to fade, and orthodox or Sunni jurists agreed that the four well-known Sunni Schools i.e., the Hanafi, Maliki, Shafi and Hanbali were sufficient. They, thus, agreed upon the closing of the door of Ijtihad. As a result, new interpretations were prohibited and, consequently, inconsiderate and slavish imitation (*taqlid*) became general.

According to the learned doctor, this resulted in intellectual stagnation, in the history of Islamic jurisprudence and to remedy this evil it is necessary to reopen the door of Ijtihad. In support of it, he relies on the view of the Shiaites and the reformist Sunnites, such as Ibn Taimayya, Ibn Kayyam Al-Jawziyya, Muhammad Ibn Abdul Wahhab, Jamaluddin Al-Afghani and Sheikh Muhammad Abduh.

30. In Islamic Law and Constitution, Abul-ala-Maudoodi has defined Ijtihad as an academic research and intellectual effort which makes the legal system of Islam dynamic and its development and evolution in the

changing circumstances possible. Ijtihad, however, does not, according to him, mean completely independent use of one's opinion. The primary source of Muslim Law being Qur'an and Sunnah, the legislation that human-beings may undertake must, therefore, be derived from this fundamental law. Or it should be within the limits prescribed by it for the use of one's discretion or the exercise of one's opinion. In conclusion, it is observed that Ijtihad that purports to be independent of the Shari'ah can neither be an Islamic Ijtihad nor there is any room for such an incursion in the legal system of Islam.

31. Imam Al-Shafi'i includes Ijtihad in Qiyas. In reply to the question as to what is analogy; is it Ijtihad, or are the two different; at page 288 of Al-Risala he states that they are two terms with the same meaning. When asked as to what is their common basis, he replied that in all matters touching the life of a Muslim there is either a binding decision or an indication to the right answer. If there is a decision, it should be followed and if there is no indication as to the right answer, it should be sought by Ijtihad and Ijtihad is Qiyas (analogy)....

32. Ijtihad may be in the form of determining the rule of decision in a particular case or class of cases and it attains the status of law by (i) consensus of opinion (Ijma') of the learned men of the community, (ii) wide popularity of Ijtihad of an individual or a group of individuals and acceptance of their verdict by the people ... *suo motu*, such as the four Sunni Schools of the Hanbalite and (iii) adoption by a Muslim Government of a particular form of law, just as Ottoman Government adopted the Hanafi Law. Maulana Maudoodi adds that an institution may be empowered in an Islamic State to legislate and it may enact any particular piece of Ijtihad in the form of law. One may presume that the 'institution' means a Legislative body, though this nomenclature appears to have been purposely avoided by the Maulana.

33. At page 168 of the Muhammadan Jurisprudence, Dr. Abdur Rahim has described Ijtihad and Taqlid as follows:

> The word Mujtahid which is a *nomen agentis* means a person who can make *Ijtihad*. Ijtihad literally means striving, exerting and as a term of jurisprudence it means the application by a lawyer (faqih) of all his faculties to the consideration of the authorities of the law (that is Qur'an, the Traditions and the Ijma') with a view to find out what in all probability is the law that is, in a matter which is not covered by the express words of such texts and has not been determined by Ijma'. In other words Ijtihad

is the capacity for making deductions in matters of law in cases to which no express text or a rule already determined by Ijma' is applicable.

34. The next question is what are the qualifications of a Mujtahid? As stated by Dr. Abdur Rahim, Sadru'-sh-Shariat following Fakhru'l Islam says that a jurist should have knowledge of the Qur'an together with its meaning dictionary and legal, and its various divisions, of the traditions including the texts and the authorities thereof, and of the rules relating to analogical deduction....

35. Ijtihad is, thus, a very fruitful source of Muslim Law and all modern reformist jurists are agreed that Taqlid should be discarded and the door of Ijtihad thrown open to help in the evolution of laws necessary for meeting new facts and situations as they arise from time to time in different parts of the Muslim World.

Istihsan, Istislah and Istidlal

36. Istihsan and Istislah are doctrines of equity, while Istidlal is a branch of Qiyas applicable to those cases where no analogy is to be found in the Qur'an, Sunnah and Ijma'. Equity, in English sense, claims to override the elder jurisprudence of the country on the strength of an intrinsic ethical superiority. In Roman Law, it was the Law of Nature (Jus Nature), the part of law which natural reason appoints for all mankind. In spite of the fact that the analogy (Qiyas) clearly points to one course but the legist 'considers it better' (Istihsan), he may follow a different course. Under the same conditions, he may choose a free course 'for the sake of general benefit to the community' (Istislah). The rule of Istihsan was reduced to definiteness by Imam Abu Hanifa. He would say 'analogy in the case points to such and such rule but under the circumstances I hold it for better to rule such and such'. The principle of Istislah enunciated by Imam Malik is when a rule would work general injury it was to be set aside even in the face of valid analogy. It is also called as Musalihul-Mursala Wal-Istislah and has more valid basis than the mere preference of a legist. According to Jam-ul-Jawani, Volume IV, pages 101-102, Imamul-Harmain also held the same view.

37. In literal sense Istidlal means inferring from a thing another thing. The Hanafi jurists used it in this sense in connection with the rules of interpretation, while according to Malikis and Shafi'is it is a distinct method of juristic deduction, not falling within the scope of Qiyas....

38. In the light of the above discussion, a stage has been reached when we may proceed to answer the questions raised in the order of reference.

I.   The first question deals with the sources of Muslim Law:

As seen above, the primary sources of law are Qur'an and Hadith, while Ijma', Qiyas, Ijtihad and Istidlal are the secondary sources; Istihsan and Istihsab being doctrines of equity and not an independent source.

II.   As to the rules of interpretation of Muslim Law:

A clear injunction in Qur'an and Sunnah is binding and no departure is permissible provided that if the effective cause of an injunction has disappeared or an injunction was confined to the facts of a particular case its extension is not warranted.

39. There are, of course, detailed rules for the interpretation of Qur'an and for testing the genuineness of a Hadith, the two principal subjects of Fiqah. For obvious reasons, it is not possible to set out those rules in this order, but we may take advantage of this opportunity to emphasize that it is of utmost necessity to amend the curriculum of legal studies in Pakistan so as to include Fiqah as a compulsory subject in the examination of Degree of Laws.

40. The well-known rules of interpretation have been collected by Dr. Abdur Rahim in Muhammadan Jurisprudence at pp. 77-112....

[Paragraphs 41–44 are omitted.]

45. As to the competence of Courts to differ from the view of earlier A'imma and Faqihs on the grounds of public policy, justice, equity and good conscience, it may be admitted that this part of the question is not properly framed. As seen above, a Qazi or a Court of Law may differ with the Qiyas of earlier A'imma and Faqihs, but that will be on the basis of interpretation and extension of the rule of decision containedin Qur'anic and Traditional Text or Ijma' and not on the basis of what appears to be more agreeable to the Judge. A reference has earlier been made to the rules of Istihsan and Istislah, two distinct doctrines of Muslim Jurisprudence. If there is no clear rule of decision in Qur'anic and Traditional Text nor an Ijma' or a binding juristic analogy (...) a Qazi or a Court may resort to private reasoning (...) and, in that, he will undoubtedly be guided by the rules of justice, equity and good conscience or, in terms of Fiqah, by the doctrines of Istihsan and Istislah.

46. The third question referred to the Full Bench likewise needs amendment: It reads—'In case of conflict of views found in text books on Muslim Law, such as Hedaya, Fatawa-i-Alamgiri, Radd-ul-Muhtar, how are the Courts to determine which of the views is correct?'

In the course of hearing arguments, we found that the more appropriate question which falls for determination under this head is:

'How are the Courts to be guided in case of conflict of views among the founders of different Schools of Muslim Law and their disciples, other A'imma and Faqihs?'

If we are in a position to ascertain with a degree of certainty the opinion of Mujtahidun fish-Shari' who founded the Schools of Law, such as Abu Hanifa, Malik, Shafi, and Ibn Hanbal, Mujtahidun fil-Madhahab as Imam Abu Yusuf, Imam Muhammad, Zufar, Hasan Ibn Ziyad and the opinion of Mujtahidun fil-Masa'l as Khassaf, Tahawi, Sarakhsi, Karkhi, Bazdawi, Halwani and Qadi Khan, who are called the jurists of the first three ranks, ordinarily that would be binding on Courts. And if there is a difference of opinion among them, according to some the Fatwa is that the view of Imam Abu Hanifa shall weigh even if all his disciples differ from him. In the absence of any dictum of his, the decision will be in accordance with the opinion of Abu Yusuf, then Muhammad, then Zufar and then Hasan Ibn Ziyad. In all judicial matters and in questions relating to the duties of the Courts and the Law of Evidence, the Fatwa is based on the opinion of Abu Yusuf because of his experience as the Chief Qazi of Baghdad, and in questions relating to the succession of distant kindred on the opinion of Muhammad. The opinion of Zufar has been accepted only in seventeen cases, according to Radd-ul-Muhtar, Volume 1, page 53.

47. The view of Imam Al-Shafi'i on disagreement (of law) has been reproduced in the earlier part of this order. On all matters concerning which God provided clear textual evidence in His Book or a Sunnah uttered by the Prophet's tongue, disagreement among those to whom these texts are known is unlawful. As to matters that are liable to different interpretations or derived from analogy, so that he who interprets or applies analogy arrived at a decision different from that arrived at by another, Imam Shafi'i did not hold that disagreement of this kind constitutes such strictness as that arising from textual evidence. Lastly, as a doctrine of juristic preference it is permissible that a Qazi belonging to one School of Sunni law such as the Hanafi may decide a case depending

on juristic deduction according to a Shafi'i law, or he may make over the case to a Shafi'i Qazi, if there is one available. In support of this view, Dr. Abdur Rahim has quoted a number of instances. A Hanafi Qazi, following the views of other Sunni Schools, may declare that divorce by a drunken person is not valid, uphold a marriage contracted without two witnesses being present a valid, set aside the marriage of a minor contracted by his father in the presence of profligate witnesses, uphold the sale of a mudabbar. In Fatwa Qazi Khan, Volume 11, pages 451 to 459 and Fatawa-i-Alamgiri, Volume 111, pages 439 to 441, the authorities cited in support of this view are As-Siyaru-l-Kabir, Jamiul Futawa Khazanutul-Muftin, Majma'un-Nawazi, Al-Zakhira, Futawa Rashiduddin, Shaikhul-Islam Abdul Wahabu'sh-Shaibani, Shaikhul-Islam Ata Ibn Hamza and others. In the modern context, Courts who have taken the place of Qazis may, with advantage, apply this rule to mitigate hardship or the rigour of a particular School of Law to which the parties belong, if the facts of the case so merit.

48. The answer to the third question may be summed up thus:

There can be no disagreement in matters which are provided for in the Qur'anic and Traditional Text. Smilarly, Ijma' is binding upon all, until changed or modified by another Ijma'. There is, thus, no room for a Court to disagree with it for, according to the tradition relied upon by Imam Shafi'i, 'whatever the community of Islam may agree upon at any time is of 'God'. In the case of juristic analogy ... and Istidlal ... it is open to Courts to adopt any one of the conflicting view of the earlier A'imma and Faqihs, subject of course to the qualification that they possess the requisite knowledge. Lastly, Ijma' and Ijtihad in the form of law made by the competent legislative bodies, as envisaged by the modern reformist Jurists, will be binding on Courts and it is not permissible for them to differ from those laws on the ground that they conflict with the views of the earlier A'imma and Faqihs....

[The dissenting and concurring judgments of Wahiduddin Ahmed, J. and Anwarul Haq, J. respectively are omitted.]

Reference answered.

Fazli-E-Subhan v. *Sabereen*

JUDGMENT

MALIK HAMID SAEED, J. The matter of divorce between the petitioner Fazli-E-Subhan and the respondent/wife Mst. Sabereen took an advantage step [*sic*] in the earlier writ Petition No. 608 of 2002, when in spite of obtaining a decree for dissolution of marriage from the trial Court, the respondent/wife again came to an agreement of re-union with her husband by making an oral statement at the bar in this regard before this Court on 21-1-2003. The respondent/lady also desired not to go with their parents. This Court therefore ordered that she should be kept in 'Darul-Aman' and the learned counsel for the petitioner was asked to prepare the case keeping in view the Muhammadan Law/Sharia. The learned counsel for the petitioner on the next date of hearing withdrew the said writ petition and has now filed the instant writ petition on the ground that keeping in view the willingness of the respondent/lady, the parties may be allowed to live as husband and wife within the limits of God.

2. The father of Mst. Sabereen, in the peculiar circumstances has, however, raised the question of inability of the spouses to again re-unite the marriage tie without first observing the procedure provided by Islam in the shape of 'Halala'.

3. We have heard the learned counsel for the parties and have also gone through the relevant provisions of law and the Injunctions of Islam on the point.

4. Before discussing the matter in the light of Muhammadan Law/Sharia, we deem it proper to first refer to the relevant provisions of the

Muslim Family Laws Ordinance, 1961 (hereinafter to be referred as the 'Ordinance'). Through enactment of the Ordinance ibid, the Legislature has, to a great extent, trammelled and curtailed the arbitrary power of the husband to divorce his wife. It has abolished the practice of disapproved form of 'Talaq' and the mode prescribed in the Ordinance is that of a 'Talaq-e-Ahsan'. Moreover, it has been made mandatory that the notice of 'Talaq' should be given in writing to the Chairman of Union Council. The 'Talaq' shall be effected only if the efforts of reconciliation finally fails. Along [with] that, under subsection (6) of section 7 of the Ordinance it is also provided that:

> Nothing shall debar a wife whose marriage has been terminated by 'Talaq' effective under this section from re-marrying the same husband, without an intervening marriage with a third person, unless such termination is for the 3rd time so effective.

The law previous to the enforcement of the Muslim Family Laws Ordinance was making it obligatory for couples divorced by any mode of 'Talaq' other than 'Talaq-e-Ahsan' not to re-marry each other again, unless the wife marries another man by a valid contract, and the latter dies or divorces her after actual consummation and she marries her first husband after the period of 'Iddat'. Before re-marriage the parties had to prove that the bar to their marriage was removed by an intermediate marriage, consummation and dissolution, otherwise their marriage was not considered valid.

5. As stated above, the mode of 'Talaq' effected under the provisions of the Ordinance is almost that of 'Talaq-e-Ahsan', so the couples could re-marry without any intervening marriage except where they have been divorced thrice and the third divorce has become effective. In that case they cannot re-marry without an intervening marriage. The plain reading of this section though implies that all kinds of 'Talaqs' have been made revocable without an intervening marriage and may be that its repugnancy to such extent could validly be agitated on the touchstone of the Qur'anic behest and the traditions of the Holy Prophet (peace be upon him), yet neither the vires of section 7 have been challenged nor the matter raised before us pertains to all kinds of 'Talaqs'. In this writ petition, we are only concerned with a 'Talaq' obtained by the wife through Court decree in the shape of 'Khula'.

6. The principle of 'Khula' as laid down in various eminent commentaries on Muslim Law in the light of sayings of the Holy Qur'an

and Sunnah is to the effect that when married parties disagree and are apprehensive that they cannot observe the bounds prescribed by the Divine law the woman can release herself from the tie by giving up some property in return in consideration of which the husband is to give her a 'Khula' and when they have done this, a 'Talaq-ul-Ba'ayen' takes place. Hence 'Khula' is a repudiation with consent and at the instance of the wife in which she agrees to give a consideration to the husband for her release from the marital tie. The decree granted to the respondent/wife in this case is also of the kind of 'Khula' because she was found unable by the trial Court to properly establish her assertion for the dissolution of marriage, but keeping in view the abhorrence shown by the wife towards the husband in her statement as well as her pleadings and the extent of unpleasantness of matrimonial relation between the parties, which even culminated into criminal proceedings, it was held by the trial Court that the relation between the parties has reached to the extent where the re-union between the two is impossible and only separation will be in the interest of both the parties.

7. Maulana Muhammad Ashraf Ali in his book known as 'Bahishti Zaiwar', at page 20 (Fourth Part) has stated on the point as under: ...Two Fatawas; one by Mufti Saifullah Haqqani of Jamia Darul-Uloom Haqqania, Akora Khattak, and the other by Mufti Muhammad Naeem, District Khateeb of Kohat are also on the file, wherein it is stated that....

In view of the above, we are of the considered view that in case of divorce through 'Khula' it is not obligatory on the wife to re-marry a third person before entering into re-marriage tie with her first husband and same is the case here. The re-marriage with same husband of course would be subject to performance of another Nikah. Section 7(6) of the Muslim Family Laws Ordinance also allows such re-union without 'Halala', hence we see no restraint either in the Muslim Family Laws Ordinance or in the Injunctions of Qur'an and Sunnah, not to allow the prayer of the husband for re-union with his wife when she is ready to live again as wife of the petitioner within the limits of God.

8. The writ petition in hand for the aforesaid reasons is allowed. Presently, Mst. Sabereen is in 'Darul-Aman' at Peshawar under the orders of this Court, hence the In-charge of 'Darul-Aman', Peshawar is directed to arrange for performing the Nikah of the petitioner with the

respondent. After Nikah the respondent Sabereen should be allowed to go with the petitioner and needless to say that the minor children shall also accompany their parents. No order as to costs.

Petition allowed.

35

Muhammad Zaman v. *Irshad Begum*

JUDGMENT

The brief facts giving rise to the present second appeal are as follows:

Plaintiff Muhammad was married with *Mst.* Irshad Begum sometime in the year 1949-50. They lived for sometime together and a daughter was born to them out of this wedlock. In 1951 Muhammad Zaman executed an agreement in favour of his wife *Mst.* Irshad Begum to the effect that in case he was to take a second wife she will be entitled to receive maintenance in a separate house and even if she wanted to live with her parents he will be liable to pay maintenance to her in her parental home. On the 11th of October 1960 Muhammad Zaman filed a suit for the restitution of conjugal rights against *Mst.* Irshad Begum and also prayed that a perpetual injunction be issued against Muhammad Bashir, Nawazish Ali and *Mst.* Aziza Begum so as to restrain them from preventing *Mst.* Irshad Begum, his wife, from coming to his house. All the defendants resisted the suit and on behalf of *Mst.* Irshad Begum it was pleaded that the plaintiff Muhammad Zaman had not paid her prompt dower of Rs. 1,000.00 and tha the used to ill-treat her and as such her life was in danger and at any rate, the suit for the restitution of conjugal rights was brought by the plaintiff against her as a counterblast to her application which she had moved before the Criminal Court under section 488, Criminal Procedure Code for the payment of maintenance allowance for herself and for her daughter. Consequent to the above pleadings of the parties the trial Court framed the following issues:

(1) Whether the plaintiff has not paid dower to the defendant, if so what is its effect?
(2) Whether the suit is *mala fide* and has been brought to be saved from the maintenance allowance?
(3) Whether the plaintiff has accused the defendant of theft and misappropriation, if so what is its effect?
(4) Whether the plaintiff has any cause of action against defendants Nos. 2 to 4?
(5) Whether the plaintiff executed an agreement in favour of the defendant Irshad Begum that in case the plaintiff marries a second woman, the defendant would be entitled to reside away from him, if so what is its effect?
(6) Relief.

After recording the evidence of the parties the trial Court found that the prompt dower was not paid by the plaintiff to his wife but the decision of the case rested mainly on the findings on issue No. 5 and it was held that by executing the agreement (Exh. D. 2) the plaintiff unconditionally undertook 'not to take a second wife, and in case he does so, he allows the defendant to live with her parents'. As a result of the above finding the plaintiff's suit was dismissed by the trial Court on the 12th of April 1961. The plaintiff's appeal before the learned District Judge was dismissed on the 13th of July 1961. It was held by the learned lower appellate Court that the plaintiff had admitted that he had taken a second wife and as such he was not entitled to the decree for the restitution of conjugal rights against his wife *Mst.* Irshad Begum.

2. In this second appeal, learned counsel for the appellant mainly relied on one argument. He submitted that both the Courts below had acted contrary to law inasmuch as they relied on agreement (Exh. D. 2) which is a void agreement as it contains a stipulation in restraint of marriage and provides condition for the husband and wife to live separately from each other. This agreement, according to the learned

counsel, is opposed to public policy within the meaning of section 23 of the Contract Act and should not be acted upon. In support of his contention he relied on *Mst. Bai Fatima* v. *Ali Muhammad Aiyeb* I L R 37 Bom. 280 and *Mst. Bibi Fatima* v. *Nur Muhammad* (1921) 60 I C 88. In both these cases it was held that an *iqrarnama* which provides and encourages future separation between husband and wife, must be pronounced as being against public policy. Since the question decided in these two cases involves an important question of law, it needs detailed examination.

3. In the Bombay case *Mst. Bai Fatima* v. *Ali Muhammad Aiyeb*, Batchelor, J., who delivered the judgment of the Division Bench, relied on his earlier judgment which he had given while sitting single in *Meherally* v. *Sakerkhanoobai* (1905) 7 Bom. L. R. 620 and it was held by him that an agreement made by a husband with his wife was bad in English Law and as such was also bad between Muhammadan spouses. The learned Judge concluded his judgment with the following observations:-

> It is, as I understand it, as much the policy of the Muhammadan Law as of the English law, that people who are married should live together and not apart; and if that is so, it seems to me that there should be no difficulty in applying to Muhammadans the English Rule that any agreement such as this, which provides for, and therefore encourages, future separation between the spouses, must be pronounced void as being against public policy.

In the Lahore case *Mst. Bibi Fatima* v. *Nur Muhammad* learned Judges of the Division Bench relied on the judgment of the Bombay High Court and it was held that an agreement by a Muslim husband with his wife that she will live in her parents' house was invalid and cannot be utilized by the wife to defeat the husband's claim for the restitution of conjugal rights. In this case learned Judges examined the statement of law as given in Muhammadan Law, Vol. II, 1917 Edition by Sir Amir Ali and taking into consideration the facts of the case it was found that the right, if any, in the *iqrarnama*, executed by the husband had been waived by the wife because after the execution of the deed the wife had consented to live with her husband. However, in this case also it was held that an agreement between husband and wife to live away from each other was void as being opposed to public policy.

4. The Bombay case came for examination before the Chief Court of Oudh in *Manzoor* v. *Azizul* A I R 1928 Oudh 303. In that case the wife was the first wife of the plaintiff husband and when both the wives could not

pull on well an agreement was executed by the husband for the payment of maintenance in a separate house. On a suit by the wife for the maintenance the husband pleaded that he was not liable to maintain her under the agreement because she was not living with him as a wife. The suit of the wife was decreed up to the first appellate stage and in second appeal before the Chief Court it was urged that the agreement was without consideration and against public policy. The learned Judges repelled the contention and dissenting from the Bombay view, observed as follows:

> If a Muhammadan marries a second wife and finds that his first wife cannot pull on well with his second wife and he does not and cannot provide a separate apartment or habitation for her exclusive use, and for the sake of preservation of the family peace excutes an agreement in her favour giving her maintenance, even if she does not reside in the same house with him and his second wife, that agreement is not in our opinion against public policy. This arrangement does not necessarily result in separation between husband and wife.

The Lahore High Court in a later decision *Muhammad Ali Akbar* v. *Mst. Fatima Begum* A I R 1929 Lah. 660 considered the judgment of the Bombay High Court in a case where the District Judge had made an award of Rs. 900 in favour of wife on account of the arrears of *Kharcha-i-Pandan*. It seems that their earlier decision in *Mst. Bibi Fatima* v. *Nur Muhammad* was not cited but the Bombay case was particularly dissented in the following words:

> With all due deference to the learned Judges (of Bombay High Court) who decided that case, I do not see why a stipulation by the husband to make an allowance to his wife in case of separation should be deemed to offend against the rule of public policy. Such a stipulation encourages their living separate from each other no more than their living together by imposing an obligation on the husband calculated to prevent him from doing any act which would lead to separation.

The obligation of the husband which he had undertaken for the payment of *Kharcha-i-Pandan* at the time of his marriage, was, therefore, enforced.

5. With utmost respect to the learned Judges, who decided the two cases of Bombay and Lahore High Courts, which were cited by the learned counsel for the appellant, I am unable to accept the proposition that an agreement made by the husband with his wife allowing her to

live away from him in case of disagreement or when he takes a second wife can in any way be termed as opposed to public policy either under the Muslim Law or within the meaning of section 23 of the Contract Act. A marriage between Muslim male and female is purely of a nature of civil contract and the wife is entitled to protect herself at the hands of her husband in case of their future differences. In the present case the agreement is to the effect that the wife is entitled to receive alimony in the house of her parents or anywhere else where she chooses to reside in case the husband takes a second wife and there is nothing in such an agreement which may be considered to offend against the term 'public policy' which is very broad and it is not safe to rely upon it in such cases as a ground for legal decision.

6. Meherally's case was decided by Batchelor, J. in 1905 but the position of law has undergone a considerable change after the decision of their lordships of the Privy Council in *Nawab Khawaja Muhammad Khan* v. *Husaini Begum alias Dilbari Begum* 7 I C 237 where it was held that:

> Where the father of the husband by an agreement executed to the father of the wife bound himself to pay to the wife the fixed allowance and there was no condition that it should be paid only whilst the wife is living in the husband's home the wife would be entitled to the allowance even if she refused to live with her husband.

The attention of the learned Judges, who decided the Bombay case in 1912 and the Lahore case in 1925, does not seem to have been drawn to the above-mentioned pronouncement of their Lordships of the Privy Council.

7. The other cases which can be referred in this context are *Saeed Khan* v. *Balatunnisa Bibi* 25 C W N 888, wherein a suit by the husband for the restitution of the conjugal rights it was held by a Division Bench that a stipulation that a Muhammadan wife may leave her husband's house on ill-treatment is not opposed to Muhammadan Law. In this case the husband was given a conditional decree to go and perform his marital obligations in the house of her wife's parents. It was clearly laid down in this case that there is nothing in the Muslim law which can invalidate the agreement of the husband with the wife that wife can live away from the husband in case of disagreement. This case is completely on all fours with the facts of the present case and being directly in point furnishes a complete answer to the argument of the learned counsel for the appellant.

8. In *Mst. Sakina Farooq* v. *Shamshad Khan*, A I R 1936 Pesh. 195 in similar circumstances it was held that a Muslim husband could make a stipulation that he will not remove his wife from her parental home and that such an agreement is a valid contract and not opposed to public policy.

9. Taking into consideration the preponderance of judicial dicta on the subject I am of the opinion that if a Muslim marries a second wife and finds that his first wife cannot keep on well with his second wife and he does not or cannot provide a separate and exclusive habitation for her for the sake of preservation of family peace and, therefore executes an agreement giving her a right to maintenance even if she does not live with him and his second wife and lives in the house of her parents the agreement is not in any way opposed to public policy. In the present case the agreement was executed by the appellant to meet such a situation. The appellant has admitted before the trial Court that he has taken a second wife and has also got children from her and he is living with them. In these circumstances it is obvious that this agreement was executed in order to maintain the harmony between his two wives and such an agreement is legally perfect and valid under the law.

10. Learned counsel for the appellant had also raised an alternative contention. He submitted that in case the agreement is held to be valid there is nothing under the law to prevent a husband for getting a decree for restitution of conjugal rights in his suit because at the most the wife can enforce her maintenance in a separate house through a Court of law but the existence of such an agreement or failure of the husband to fulfil the obligations under the agreement is no defence to the plaintiff's suit for the restitution of the conjugal rights against his wife. I regret I am not able to accept this contention of the learned counsel for the appellant. No doubt it is the duty of the wife to follow the husband wherever he desires her to go. But such an obligation of the wife to live with her husband at all times and in all circumstances is not an absolute one. The law recognises circumstances which justify her refusal to live with him. For instance if he has habitually ill-treated her, if he has deserted her for a long time etc., or he has directed her to leave his house or even connived at her doing so. On all such occasions the husband cannot require his wife to re-enter the conjugal domicile nor the Court of justice can give him assistance to restore him the hand of his wife. The bad canduct or gross neglect of the husband under the

Muslim law is good defence to a suit brought by him for conjugal rights, *Buzloor Rahman v. Shumsoonnisa Begum* (1876) 11 Moore's I A 555; Ameer Ali's Muhammadan Law, Vol. II (1929 Edn.) section II, pp. 442-446.

11. No doubt a husband can maintain a suit for the restitution of the conjugal rights in civil court against his wife, but the decree of restitution of the conjugal rights is in the discretion of the Court whose duty it is to find out, if there be a cruelty of a degree rendering it unsafe for her if she is ordered to return to the husband's house. In the present case I find that the appellant has committed breach of the agreement which he has executed in favour of his wife as early as 14th of May 1951. The defendant has asserted in her statement before the trial Court that she was maltreated by the appellant as he used to beat her in the presence of his second wife and has ultimately turned her out of his house. There is no evidence in rebuttal to these allegations and the appellant did not even care to cross-examine her with reference to the allegations which she had levelled against him about the maltreatment, etc. The appellant has failed to provide any maintenance for the defendant wife and her daughter and she was compelled to go to the Criminal Court to enforce the appellant's obligation of maintenance under section 488, Cr. P. C. In these circumstances, I find that the appellant had been guilty of gross failure on his part to perform his obligations imposed on him by the agreement and these circumstances afford a sufficient ground to refuse to the appellant any relief in his suit. I am clear in my mind that the appellant has brought this suit for the restitution of the conjugal rights *mala fide* and as a counterblast to the application of the respondent for maintenance under section 488, Cr.P.C. I, therefore, do not think that the appellant is entitled to crave for the indulgence of the Court for the grant of the decree for the restitution of the conjugal rights in his favour. Every case, in which the question of conjugal domicile is involved, depends upon its own features and the general principles of the Muslim Law on the subject are that a wife is bound to reside with her husband unless there is a valid reason of her refusal to do so. The sufficiency or validity of the reason in each case is a matter for the consideration of the Court with special reference to the circumstances in which the parties have been residing or they wish to settle in future.

12. In the present case I have no hesitation in saying that the grounds on which *Mst.* Irshad Begum has separated herself justify her in that step and if a decree for restitution of conjugal rights is granted to the

appellant directing the defendant wife to return to the conjugal domicile of her husband I will be perpetuating a grievous injustice by compelling her to live with the appellant in his house with his second wife and her step children.

13. For the aforesaid reasons I do not see any justification to interfere with the judgments and decree passed by the two Courts below. The plaintiff's suit has rightly been dismissed. Since no one appears for the respondent there will be no order as to costs.

Appeal dismissed.

Khurshid Bibi v. Muhammad Amin

JUDGMENT

S. A. RAHMAN, J. This appeal, by special leave, arises out of the following facts. A suit was brought by the appellant *Mst*. Khurshid Bibi, for dissolution of her marriage with the respondent, Baboo Muhammad Amin, in a Civil Court at Khanpur, District Rahimyar Khan. A counter-suit, for restitution of conjugal rights, was brought by the husband. The appellant's suit was dismissed, while that of the husband was decreed by the Senior Civil Judge, Rahimyar Khan, on the 21st January 1960. The plaintiff-appellant then brought a suit on the 19th Fabruary 1960, for a declaration that she had been divorced by the husband or in the alternative for dissolution of marriage by way of *khula*, in the Court of Civil Judge, Toba Tek Singh, District Lyallpur. Her case was that the rift between the parties was so serious that there was no chance of reconciliation, and harmonious relation between the spouses had become an impossibility. She also alleged in her plaint that the respondent had not spent any money on his *Nikah* with her, and that the plaintiff was prepared to give up her dower money in return for her release from the matrimonial tie. The respondent, in his written statement, denied that the relations between the spouses had become strained. He also averred that he had spent a sum of Rs. 2,000 on his marriage with the plaintiff. He declared that even if the plaintiff gave up her dower money, he would not be prepared to divorce her.

On the pleadings of the parties, the trial Court framed the following issues:

(1) Whether this Court has no jurisdiction to try this suit?
(2) Whether the suit of the plaintiff is barred by *res judicata*?
(3) Whether the defendant has divorced the plaintiff by pronouncing oral *talaq*?
(4) Whether the plaintiff is entitled to divorce on principle of *khula*? If so, on what consideration?
(5) Relief.

Issues Nos. 1 and 2 were not pressed on behalf of the defendant. Issue No. 3 was answered in the negative. Issue No. 4 was found in favour of the plaintiff and the suit was, consequently, decreed. The learned Civil Judge, however, did not make it clear on what conditions the decree was being passed.

On appeal, the learned District Judge, Lyallpur, took the view that this was not a case in which *khula* should have been granted. He observed that the plaintiff, as her own witness in the case, had admitted that the defendant's treatment of her was unexceptionable at the outset, but that, subsequently he changed and took a second wife, after which he started subjecting her to physical violence. The learned District Judge, disbelieved her statement that her husband had granted a divorce to her orally, after her first suit had been dismissed. He thought that the divorce might have been expected to be in writing. He was, therefore, not prepared to place reliance on the plaintiff or her witnesses who also deposed to the alleged oral divorce. He then referred to the statement of the defendant, as his own witness, to the effect that a Panchayat had been arranged for requesting the plaintiff's family that she be sent with him but it failed because she had taken offence at his marrying a second wife. The main ground for accepting the appeal that prevailed with the District Judge was that 'the plaintiff had not come with clean hands, or with a straightforward story'. He was of the opinion that there was substance in the defendant's contention that this was a matter of *zid* (obstinacy) on her part. The appeal was allowed and the plaintiff's suit dismissed with costs throughout.

The order, passed by the learned District Judge, was affirmed, in second appeal, by a learned Single Judge of the High Court of West Pakistan. The learned Judge referred to *Balqis Fatima* v. *Najmul Ikram Qureshi*, P L D 1959 Lah. 566, and remarked that the instant case was not one to which this ruling could be applied. The learned Judge observed that the sister of the defendant-respondent was married to the brother of the plaintiff-appellant and, in the circumstances, the defendant could not possibly afford to be inconsiderate or cruel towards the appellant, for fear of reprisal. As regards the plaintiff's demand for a separate residence, it was held that the defendant was unable to make provision in this regard for lack of funds. The learned Judge thought that the plaintiff was not prepared to go and live with the husband, because he had remarried, but that this circumstance could not furnish a ground for *khula* divorce. The learned Judge further went on to say that the plaintiff-appellant nowhere stated that she was prepared to forego her rights to obtain *khula*. The appeal was dismissed *in limine*.

Special leave to appeal was granted in this case to consider whether the learned Single Judge was right in holding that the case was not governed by the principle laid down in Mst. Balqis Fatima's case. In that case, it was held that for *khula* divorce to be granted, it was only necessary that the plaintiff must express seriousness, in support of her demand and the reasonableness or otherwise of that demand was not a relevant question at all.

It would be useful, at the outset, to give a summary of the plaintiff's own statement, made as P. W. 1, in the trial Court. She stated that she had been married when she was only 6 or 7 years old and that she had lived with her husband in Alhar village and in Rahimyar Khan. Initially, she was well-treated by her husband, but later he married another wife, from whom he had children and he then ill-treated her, by not giving her maintenance and even beat her on occasions. He refused to let her go to see her parents. He wanted to marry her forcibly to his own brother. She, however, sent word of this to her parents. Her brother obtained a warrant under section 100, Criminal Procedure Code, and she was then brought to Court from her husband's house and released. She went away to her parents' house. She stated that, in December 1960, the defendant had come to her parents' village and expressed a desire, at the *baithak* of one, Muhammad Ali to take the plaintiff back with him. In the presence of Muhammad Ali and others, the plaintiff asked for an assurance that she would be given proper maintenance and not subjected to any ill-treatment and would not be forced into marriage with his brother. The defendant declined to give these assurances but later gave her an oral divorce and promised to grant a written divorce at Toba Tek Singh. When the plaintiff and her relatives arrived there, the defendant was not to be found. She declared that she could not pull on with the defendant, from whom she apprehended danger to her life. She denied, in her cross-examination, that the defendant had come to the village, merely to realize costs that had been awarded to him in his decree for restitution of conjugal rights and that she had brought the present suit as a counterblast. She admitted that the defendant's sister was married to her own brother and was living with him. It was characterized by her as a false allegation that her brother was ill-treating his own wife and pressing her to obtain divorce for the plaintiff from her brother. Incidentally this suggestion cuts across defendant's plea that plaintiff's brother would resent defendant parting with her and maltreat his sister, in consequence.

It may be noted that the plaintiff did not say is so many words in her statement in Court that she was prepared to relinquish her dower for separation by *khula* or that her husband had spent nothing on her marriage. The omission of the first fact was noted by the learned District Judge, in appeal, but it is pointed out that she had made these allegations in her plaint in paragraph No. 5. In answer to this averment in the plaint, the defendant pleaded in the written statement that she was not entitled to *khula*, as there was no estrangement between them, that he had spent Rs. 2,000 on his marriage with her, and that, even if she was prepared to give up her dower, he was not willing to give her a divorce. On these pleadings, the case for *khula*, as an alternative to a declaration that she had been divorced, must be held to have been definitely set up. The point of *khula* was also the subject-matter of a specific issue between the parties.

In his statement as D. W. 1, the defendant-respondent, stated that he had obtained a decree for restitution of conjugal rights against the plaintiff and he went to realize the costs awarded to him therein, that the plaintiff's relativers concealed themselves and that the plaintiff brought the present suit in retaliation. He denied that he had orally divorced her. He said she had lived with him for three years and then left his house. Her suit for dissolution of marriage had been dismissed. He declared that they could live together even now, amicably and that, if he divorced her, this might recoil on his own sister who was married to the plaintiff's brother. The truth of this assertion is obviously open to question. In cross-examination, he conceded that he had married a second wife before the plaintiff was taken away from his house, on a warrant under section 100 of the Code of Criminal Procedure. His relations with the plaintiff deteriorated after he had married his second wife. He averred that the plaintiff wanted a separate residence and he had promised her this facility but could not carry out his promise, owing to straitened circumstances. His father owned 13 acres of land, whose produce was taken by him. He and his four brothers lived jointly with his father. He acknowledged that he owned two houses in Rahimyar Khan, that he was employed on a salary of Rs. 200 p.m. in the firm of Lever Brothers, and that he was himself living in one house, while he had rented the other house at Rs. 20 p.m. to a tenant. It is thus difficult to credit him with truth when he says that he was unable to provide a separate residence to the plaintiff because of lack of facility. The fact, moreover, that she had to be taken away from the house of her husband on a warrant under section 100, Criminal Procedure Code, shows that their relations had come to such a pass, as to leave little hope for connubial bliss. That she had developed an aversion for her husband who had married another wife, is clear from the record. She made determined efforts to get release from the matrimonial bond, by first bringing a suit for dissolution which was dismissed, and then by bringing a second suit, in which she claimed a declaration that she had been divorced, and, in the alternative, she prayed for release by way of *khula*. On the defendant's own showing, he had not gone personally to bring his wife, to the plaintiff's parents' village, but had tried to realize the costs of a decree against her. The Panchayat was said to have been arranged by his father. His claim, in Court, therefore, that they could still live together amicably, does not appear to me to be sincere or genuine.

This being the state of relations between the parties, the question arises whether the wife is entitled, as of right, to claim *khula*, despite the unwillingness of the husband to release her from the matrimonial tie, if she satisfies the Court that there is no possibility of their living together, consistently with their conjugal duties and obligations.

Learned counsel for the appellant, Mr. Ghazanfar Ali Gondal, strongly relied on *Mst. Balqis Fatima* v. *Najmul Ikram Qureshi*, as authorities for the view that, under Muslim Law, the wife is entitled to *khula* as of right, if she satisfies the conscience of the Court that it will otherwise mean forcing her into a hateful union. A Full Bench of the West Pakistan High Court held, in that case, that the wife is entitled to dissolution of her marriage, on restoration of what she received in consideration of marriage, if the Judge apprehends that the parties will not observe the 'limits of God'. This latter limitation is an important one and it is only in cases where a harmonious married state, as envisaged by Islam, will not be possible, that such a decree for *khula* will be granted. If the rift between the parties is a serious one and there is danger of the wife transgressing the Islamic injunction, in case the dissolution is not ordered, then there would be plain necessity for the grant of *khula*. This conclusion was arrived at, after a review of the Qur'anic injunctions on the subject, the relevant *Ahadith*, previous case-law, and the opinions of legists and commentators of the Qur'an. The view expressed in *Mst. Umar Bibi* v. *Muhammad Din* I L R (1944) 25 Lah. 542, by a Division Bench of the Lahore High Court and endorsed in the Full Bench case of *Mst. Sayeeda Khanam* v. *Muhammad Sami* P L D 1952 Lah. 113, to the effect, that incompatibility of temperament, is not a ground for dissolution of marriage and that it is not possible for a Court to grant a *khula* decree, unless the husband consents thereto, was dissented from.

Besides referring to the quotations from the original sources, relied on in the case of *Mst. Balqis Fatima*, Mr. Gondal also drew our attention to an Urdu translation of 'Badayat-ul Mujtahid' by Allama Ibn-e-Rushud, at p. 158, published by the Idara-tul-Muslimin, Rabwah. After discussing the nature of *khula* and the conditions, in which it would be permissible, the learned author expresses himself as follows:

> And the philosophy of *khula* is this, that *khula* is provided for the woman in opposition to the right of divorce vested in the man. Thus if trouble arises from the side of the woman, the man is given the power to divorce her, and when injury is received from the man's side, the woman is given the right to obtain *khula*.

Allama Ibn-e-Rushud who had been reared in the Maliki school of thought, was born in Cordove in Spain in 1126 A. D., and died in Morroco in the year 1198 A. D. He did not believe in confining himself to the principle of *fiqh*, enunciated by Imam Malik. He was a philosopher and scholar, who formed independent opinions and had no hesitation in accepting views of the other Imams like Imam Abu Hanifa, in several matters.

Mr. Muhammad Almas Ali, who appeared for the respondent, contended before us that, among the followers of the Hanafi sect to which the parties in this case belong, the view prevails that the consent of the husband, to the grant of *khula*, is absolutely necessary and the Court cannot decree *khula*, without such consent. He relied on the cases of

Mst. Sayeeda Khatun v. *Muhammad Sami* and *Mst. Umar Bibi* v. *Muhammad Din*, referred to above, and also invited attention to certain verses of the Qur'an, and the opinions of a number of commentators and legists on the subject.

Learned counsel for the respondent relied on the Hedaya, p. 112 of Hamilton's Translation, Second Edition by Grady, where it is stated as follows:

> Whenever enmity takes place between husband and wife, and they both see reason to apprehend that the ends of marriage are not likely to be answered by a continuance of their union, the woman need not scruple to release herself from the power of her husband, by offering such a compensation *as may induce him* to liberate her, because the word of God says, 'NO CRIME IS IMPUTED TO THE WIFE OR HER HUSBAND RESPECTING THE MATTER IN LIEU OF WHICH SHE HATH RELEASED HERSELF' that is to say, there is no crime in the husband's accepting such compensation, nor in the wife's giving it.

It is further recited in that book that 'where compensation is thus offered and accepted, a single divorce, irreversible, takes place, in virtue of *khoola*; and the woman is answerable for the amount of it, because the Prophet has said that *khoola* effects an irreversible divorce; and also, because the word *khoola* bears the sense of divorce, whence it is that it is classed with the implied expressions of it, and from an implied divorce a divorce irreversible takes place'. Learned counsel fortified his argument by referring us to Qur'anic verse No. 238 in Para II of the Qur'an, which reads as follows:

> And if you divorce them before you have touched them, but have settled for a dowry, then half of what you have settled shall be due from you, unless they remit, or he, in whose hand is the tie of marriage, should remit. And that you should remit is nearer to righteousness. And do not forget to do good to one another. Surely, Allah sees what you do.

In this connection, learned counsel drew our attention to certain commentaries of the Qur'an, which take the view that by the expression 'person in whose hand is the tie of marriage' is meant the husband, in this verse. This is by no means universally accepted. Some commentators have interpreted these words as referring to the guardian of the woman and this interpretation seems to be more consistent with context. Learned counsel cited from Tafseer-i-Mazhari, Inaya, which is a commentary of the Hedaya, Radd-ul-Mukhtar, Tafseer-ul-Madarik, Tafseer-ul-Ahmadya, Tafseer-i-Kabir, in support of the view that *khula* means *talaq-i-bain*, that is, an irreversible divorce. He also drew strength from the language, used in certain *Ahadith*, which showed that the Prophet, while ordering release of the woman by way of *khula*, directed that the husband should give the wife *talaq*.

The fundamental laws of Islam are contained in the Qur'an and this is, by common consent, the primary source of law for Muslims. Hanafi Muslim jurisprudence also recognizes *hadith, ijtehad* and *ijma* as the three other secondary sources of law. The last two really fall under a single category of subsidiary reasoning, *ijtehad* being by individual scholars and *ijma* being the consensus of scholars who have resorted to *ijtehad* in any one age. That this is the order of priority, in their importances, is clear from the well-known *hadith*, relating to Muadh-ibn-e-Jabal who was sent by the Prophet as Governor and Qazi of Yemen. The Prophet asked him, how he would adjudicate cases, 'By the Book of God', he replied. 'But if you find nothing in the Book of God, how?' Then by the precedent of the Prophet'. 'But if there be no precedent?' 'Then I will diligently try to form my own judgment.' On this, the Prophet is reported to have said, 'Praise be to God who hath fulfilled in the messenger sent forth by his apostle that which is well-pleasing to the apostle of Allah'.

The four orthodox schools of *Sunni fiqh* were headed by Imam Abu Hanifa, Imam Malik, Imam Shafei and Imam Ahmad-bin-Hanbal. The learned Imams never claimed finality for their opinions, but due to various historical causes, their followers in subsequent ages, invented the doctrine of taqlid, under which a Sunni Muslim must follow the opinions of only one of their Imams, exclusively, irrespective of whether reason be in favour of another opinion. There is no warrant for this doctrinaire fossilization, in the Qur'an or authentic *Ahadith*. In the *Almital-wan-Nihal* (page 39), it is stated that the great Abu Hanifa used to say 'This is my opinion and I consider it to be the best. If someone regards another person's opinion to be better, he is welcome to it' ('for him is his opinion and for us ours').

A few words may now be said about the concept of marriage in Islam. As is well-settled, marriage among Muslims is not a sacrament, but in the nature of a civil contract. Such a contract undoubtedly has spiritual and moral overtones and undertones, but legally, in essence, it remains a contract between the parties which can be the subject of dissolution for good cause. In this respect, Islam, the *Din-al-Fitrat*, conforms to the dictates of human nature and does not prescribe the binding together of a man and woman to what has been described as 'holy deadlock'.

The husband is given the right to divorce his wife, though, of course, arbitrary divorces are discountenanced. There is a saying of the Prophet to the effect that 'the most detestable of lawful things in Allah's view is divorce'... (Abu Daood). Similarly, the wife is given the right to ask for *khula* in cases of extreme incompatibility though the warning is conveyed by *Ahadith* against the free exercise of this privilege, one of which says that women asking for *khula* will be deprived of the fragrance of paradise ... (Tirmizi). The warning both to man and woman in this regard is obviously placed on the moral rather than the legal plane and is not destructive of their legal rights.

The Qur'an also declares: 'Women have rights against men, similar to those that the men have against them, according to the well-known rules of equity'.... It would, therefore, be surprising if the Qur'an did not provide for the separation of the spouses, at the instance of the wife, in any circumstances. The Qur'an expressly says that the husband should either retain the wife, according to well-recognised custom ... (Imsak-un-bil ma'roof) or release her with grace ... (*Tasree-hun-bi-ihsan*). The word of God enjoined the husband not to cling to the woman, in order to cause her injury.... Another *hadith* declares ... *Lazarar- un wa- la zarar- fil-Islam* 'Let no harm be done, nor harm be suffered in Islam'. In certain circumstances, therefore, if the husband proves recalcitrant and does not agree to release the woman from the marital bond, the Qazi may well intervene to give redress and enforce the Qur'anic injunctions.

As was pointed out by Kaikaus, J. in Mst. Balqis Fatima's case the foundation of the law relevant to *khula* is contained in the Qur'anic verses, which may be translated as follows:

> Such divorce may be pronounced twice; then, either retain them in a becoming manner or send them away with kindness. And it is not lawful for you that you take anything of what you have given them, unless both fear that they cannot observe the limits prescribed by Allah. But, if *you* fear that *they* cannot observe the limits prescribed by Allah, then it shall be no sin for either of them in what she gives to get her freedom. These are the limits prescribed by Allah, so transgress them not; and whoso transgresses the limits prescribed by Allah, it is they that are the wrong-doers.

We may first consider the opinions of the commentators of the Qur'an as to the meaning of these verses, bearing on *khula*. The words ... (if you fear) are addressed to the community or ... (those in authority from among you), and include the *Qazi*, who represents the community, for adjudication of disputes. This is borne out from the commentary of the Qur'an by Qurtabi, known as ... '*Al Ja'me-le-Ahkaam al-Qur'an*'. The learned author says that this is the opinion of Ibn-e-Abbas and Malik-bin-Anas as well as the majority of the legists. Similar opinion is expressed by ... *Zamakhsri* in his well-known commentary ... (*Alkashshaf*), by ... (*Nasafi*) in his Tafseer, called ... (*Madarak-ul-tanzil-wa-Haqaiq-ul-Ta'veel*), by Baizavi... in his *Tafsir...Anwar-ul-Tanzil-wa-Israr-ul-Ta'veel*, by ... (Al-Qastallani) in his ... (*Irshad-us-Sazi*), by ... Jassas in his (*Ahkamul Qur'an*) and by the authors of ... (Tafsir Ibne Kasir) and ... (Tafsir Khazin). Baizavi distinctly says that this is so because the rulers are in a position to give orders when disputes are presented before them. In more recent times, Mufti Muhammad Abduh of Egypt, in his Tafsir Al Manay ... has endorsed this view. For analogy, the cases of ... (li'an) and ... ('Ila) ... (Inin) and *Mafqooedel Khabar* ... may be cited in which cases the Qazi, it is settled, has the authority to separate the spouses, even if the husband is refusing to grant a divorce or is not available. The Hedaya, the ... (*Radd-ul-Mukhtar*) and the ... (*Ahkam-ul- Qur'an*) of ... (*Aljasas*) agree in this respect.

By the phrase 'limits of Allah', according to the above-cited commentators, reference is intended to the injunctions regarding the performance of conjugal obligations while living together. Ibne-Hammam ... in his ... (*Fateh-ul-Qadir*), Vol. III, p. 199 and ... Jassas in his (*Ahkam-ul-Qur'an*). Vol. 1, p. 391 have adopted this view which also finds mention in Sahih Bokhari (Arabic Text), published by Karkhana Tijarat-i-Kutub, Karachi (Vol. II, p. 794). It is explained that incurable aversion to the husband, on the part of the wife would be sufficient justification for *khula*. Shah Wali Ullah of Delhi in ... (*Al-Masawwa-min-Ahadith-al-Muatta* Vol. II, p. 160) goes to the length of saying that 'even if she obtains *khul*' without any reason (apart from personal dislike) it is lawful but not approved. The reason is that the Prophet and the companions never inquired from her the reason for her (seeking) *khul*'.'

The question whether *khula* is to be equated with *talaq*, or it is a form of dissolution of marriage in a category of its own, has been the subject of controversy amongst the jurists. Ibn-e-Rushud, in his

Badayat-ul-Mujtahid, says that most of the *ulema* and Imam Malik and Imam Abu Hanifa are of the opinion that *khula* is equivalent to *talaq*. On the other hand, Imam Shafe'i, Imam Ahmed, Imam Daood and out of the Companions, Ibn-e-Abbas were of the view that *khula* amounts to *fiskh-i-nikah* (cancellation or dissolution of marriage) and not *talaq*. Imam Shafe'i had also stated on another occasion that if the husband intended *talaq*, even in a contract of *khula*, it would operate as *talaq* and if he had the intention of *fiskh-i-nikah*, it will have effect as such. Ibn-e-Hajar Asqlani in his books ... (Alderaya-fi-Takhrija-Ahadith-ul-Hidaya and Fat-hul-Bari) prefers the opinion of Ibn-e-Abbas on this point and casts doubt on the authenticity of the *hadith* which equates it with ... (irreversible divorce). He relies in this connection on a Tradition of the Prophet, which specified that Sabet-bin-Qais's wife, after the grant of *khula*, was ordered to pass one period of menstruation as her *iddat* and this would not be so if *khula* were *talaq*. He reiterates this position in ... (Talkhisul Habir Vol. III, p. 205). On the other hand, the authorities quoted, on behalf of the respondent, including the Hedaya, take the view that there is no difference between *khula* and *talaq*. This question need not detain us further. There are good reasons for the view that *khula* is separation and not *talaq*, as right of the husband to take back the wife after *khula*, does not exist, as it does in the case of *talaq-i-raja'i* and the period of iddat is different in the two cases. The relevant *Ahadith* are discussed by Shaukani in ... (Kitab-ul-Khul Vol. III, p. 260) of his celebrated work ... (Nail-al-Autar) and he reaches the conclusion that *khula* is not a type of *talaq*, but is a category apart from it. If this opinion is accepted, then it is clear that *khula* is not dependent on the will of the husband alone. But even if *khula* be regarded as *talaq* as seems to be the view of some of the orthodox Hanafi jurists, the question arises whether the wife is not entitled, in appropriate cases, to demand a *khula* divorce from the husband, in the face of the latter's opposition. This problem finds no express treatment in the treatises of these Hanafi jurists who content themselves by saying that divorce is the right of the husband.

It must be admitted that this is also a controversial question. Dr. Sabuni has summarized various opinions, bearing on this point, at page 621 of his book.... In particular, he refers to what is related from Umar-ibn-Al-Khattab, through the authority of Behaqi, that he said that 'when women desire *khul*' do not deny it'. Sha'rani in his book, ... (Al-Mizan-ul-Kubra,

Vol. II, p. 117) says: 'Imams agree in that the woman, if she dislikes her husband because of his ugliness or misconduct, she has a right to seek *khul'* by payment of compensation'. Even if there is nothing to cause her dislike and the husband and wife both agree upon *khula;* without any reason, it is lawful and is not condemned.

On the contrary, Zuhri, Ata and Daood refute this stand by saying that '*khul* in this case is futile and what is futile is unlawful and that which is unlawful is condemned'. Dr. Sabuni in his book 'Mada Hurriyat-al-Zaujain' at page 572, says: 'A large section of Muslim jurists believe that *khula* is lawful only with the existence of dislike on the part of the wife, so that the husbands may not start oppressing their wives to make them seek *khul'* so as to get back the property they gave to them.' Badaruddin Ayni in his Umda-tul-Qari, ... Vol. IX, p. 573 says:

> There is difference of opinion in the case when both spouses agree on separation, Malik, Auza'i and Ishaq are of the opinion that no *Hakams* are required and nor (further) permission of spouses. Kufis, Shaf'i and Ahmad have said that their permission is necessary, as the right to divorce is in the hands of the husband. If he permits, well and good, otherwise *the Court will divorce on his behalf.*

This has reference to the well-known verse of the Qur'an, which requires *Hakams* to represent spouses to be appointed in case of *siqaq* which means breach or schism between them, for the purpose of effecting reconciliation if possible and for ordering separation, if that be necessary. Some of the legists have described *Hakams* as merely Attorneys or arbitrators and not Judges, but others have said that they have full powers to decide as they think fit. Some have held that the arbitratiors' opinion is to be submitted to the Qazi, who will decide, in accordance with that opinion. There is also difference of opinion among the legists as to whether reference to the Sultan (Sovereign) or Qazi is necessary, at all, or not. This will be found discussed by Ibn-e-Hazm in ... (Al-Mohalla).

This difference arises owing to the fact that two situations are contemplated by the writers. One is where *khula* takes place as a result of the mutual consent of the spouses, which is technically called *Mubara't.* In such a case it appears that no reference to the Qazi is necessary. But where the husband disputes the right of the wife to obtain separation by *khula*, it is obvious that some third party has to decide the matter and, consequently, the dispute will have to be adjudicated upon by the Qazi, with or without assistance of the *Hakams*. Any other interpretation of the Qur'anic verse regarding *khula* would deprive it of all efficacy as a charter granted to the wife. It is significant that according to the Qur'an, she can 'ransom herself' or 'get her release' and it is plain that these words connote an independent right in her.

The Qur'anic injunctions must be interpreted in the light of well-known *Ahadith*. The classical instance of *khula* is that of the wife of Sabet-bin-Qais-bin-Shamas. That tradition is to be found in various collections of *Ahadith*, including Bokhari, Abu Daood, Nasai, Ibn-e-Maja and Tirmizi. Bur there are two versions, one referring to Jamila, daughter of a sister of Abdullah bin Abi Salool (in some versions, daughter of Abdullah) and the other to Habiba, daughter of Sahl). It is said by some commentators that the two cases relate to two different wives of the same person. Jamila came to the Prophet, according to this tradition, and said that she had no reason to reproach Sabet-bin-Qais, in respect of his morals or his faith, but she disliked him and after going into the fold of Islam, she did not want to commit infidelity. The Prophet asked her whether she was prepared to return the garden given by her husband to her, in dower. She answered in the affirmative. The Prophet then directed the husband to accept the garden and to give her a divorce according to one version. Another version given by Bokhari has it that when she agreed to return the garden to her husband, the Prophet ordered 'Qais and he' separated her.... From still another version given by Hazrat Aisha Siddiqa, (related by Abu Daood) it seems that Habiba was also subjected by her husband to physical violence during the previous night but this fact was not put forward by the woman, apparently, as ground for her release. Abu Daood also talks of two gardens being returned, which had been originally gifted by the husband. The two different versions may be reconciled by the suggestion that, due to her aversion, Habiba was not willing to perform her marital obligations and was beaten by her husband in consequence. The generally accepted account of Jamila's case as well as that of Habiba makes it clear that the only ground on which the Prophet ordered the woman to be released from the marriage bond, was her intense dislike of her husband. According to one text, she clarified that she found him to be ugly and repulsive, and in another that she felt like spitting at him. The Prophet being convinced that the spouses could not live together in conformity with their conjugal obligations, ordered the husband to separate her.

Hakim in Almustadrak ... Ibne-Abdul Barr in ... (*Al-Istiab*), Shaukani in Nail-ul-Autar ... the last-named (relying on Dar Qatani's version), are categorical in saying that it was the Prophet who ordered the separation. As has been observed above, Ibne Hajr Asqalani shares this opinion and doubts the authenticity of the *hadith* which specifies that this was a case of *talaq*. Ibne Hazm in Al-Mohalla upholds the Qazi's right to effect separations by *khula*, after efforts at conciliation through *Hakams* have failed. It is not possible to consider this act of the Prophet, except as one conceding the right of the wife, in circumstances of extreme discord.

The opinion of Allama Ibn-e-Rushud on this point has already been quoted in support of the thesis that *khula* is a right of the wife. Amir Ali in his Muhammadan Law, Vol. 11, p. 466 and M. Muhammad Ali in his Religion of Islam p. 676, express themselves in similar terms. Some other modern opinions will be found collected in Kaikaus, J.'s judgment in Balqis Fatima's case including one by Wilson in his Anglo-Muhammadan Law. Kaikaus, J., has also cited the case of a woman who sought divorce from her husband in Hazrat Umar's time and after testing the seriousness of her demand by confining her in a dirty prison, he ordered her to be separated from her spouse. A modern priest of Egypt, Ali Khafif in his book Furaq-al-Zauj-fi-al Mazahib al Islamia ... strongly supports the wife's right to *khul'* when discord is established. I may add, however, that opinions of living authors are not entitled to as much weight as those who have joined the majority, since the possibility of their changing their views before death cannot be excluded.

The present trend of legislation in Muslim countries which may provide indication of Ijma's in modern times, may also be examined. The right of the wife to obtain separation from her husband on any ground of ... (injury), is recognized in Iraq by section 40 of Qanun-ul-Ahwal-al-Shakhsiya of 1959, in Egypt by section 6 of law No. 25 of 1929, in Tunis by section 25 of Mujalla-tul-Ahwal-ul Shakhsiya, in Morroco by section 56 of Mudawwana-tul-Ahwal-ul-Shakhsiya-al-Maghrib, in Jordan by section 96 of Qanun-o-Huquq-al-Alla-tul-Urdani and in Syria by section 112 of Qanun-ul-Ahwal-ul Shakhsiya-Assuri. In some of these Codes it is provided that the matter will first be referred to *Hakams* and the final decision will rest with the Court.

The argument was raised on behalf of the respondent, that the case should be decided only in accordance with the opinions of Hanafi doctors, who contemplate the grant of a divorce on the part of the husband even in the case of *khula* and not separation such as could be ordered by a Qazi. The authorities referred to, however, do not discuss what would happen in case the husband is reluctant to divorce the wife but the relations between the spouses have deteriorated so considerably that they could not be expected to live together within the limits of Allah. Such a position is expressly dealt with in books of other Sunni sects—the Malikis, the Shafe'is and the Hanbalis. It is permissible to refer to those opinions which are consistent with the Qur'anic injunctions. A certain amount of fluidity exists, even among orthodox Hanafis in certain matters. In the case of a husband who has become *mafqudulkhabar* (absent without news) for instance, Malikis opinion can be resorted to by a Hanafi Qazi, as is mentioned in Radd-ul-Mukhtar.

There is a *hadith* of the Prophet, concerning Barairah who was married to a slave, named Mughis. She did not live with her husband who followed her disconsolate and weeping, in public. The Prophet advised her to go back to her husband, she asked: 'Is this an order?' The Prophet said that it was merely a recommendation. She then declined to go back to her husband, saying: 'I have no need of him.' This shows that a woman cannot be compelled, if she has a fixed aversion to her husband to live with him.

The reasoning that found favour in the cases of *Umar Bibi* and *Sayeeda Khanam* may also be briefly noticed. Those reasons were analysed by Kaikaus, J. in Balqis Fatima's case and with respect, it seems to me, justification was shown to exist for departing from the earlier view. Sir Abdur Rahman, J. in Umar Bibi's case relied on Baillie's Digest of Muhammadan Law, First Part, p. 305, the Hedaya, Book I, Vol. IV, Chapter on *khula* and the corresponding Chapter in Durr-ul-Mukhtar and held that even in *khula* cases, it is the right of the husband to effect separation, by granting a divorce. These authorities, however, do not consider contentious cases, where the husband refuses to release the wife, out of pure obstinacy. The learned Judge also expressed the opinion that even where there was mutual dislike or extreme incompatibility of temperament between husband and wife there can be *muaddat* ... *sukoon* ... and *rehmat* ... in the married life (declared to be objectives of marriage by the Qur'an), with the procreation of children. With respect, it seems to me, that this view is difficult to sustain. In such cases, if there is fixed aversion on the part of the wife or the husband, life becomes a torture for both. The learned Judge also thought that the first condition for separation between the spouses is that *Hakams* should have been appointed, in accordance with the injunctions of the Qur'an, and it would be for them to consider whether the couple should be parted or not. But if the *Hakams* can so decide under authority of an order by the Qazi, I confess, it is difficult to see why a Qazi does not possess a similar capacity in suitable cases. It is said in the Mabsoot of Al-Sarakhsi, Vol. II that the Qazi has the power to remove causes of tyranny by means of *talaq*. It is also in the Radd-ul-Mukhtar that, for this purpose, the Qazi becomes the agent of the husband, if he refuses to give divorce.

In Sayeeda Khanam's case, the verse bearing on the right of *khula*, was not noticed, though the *hadith* in respect of Jamila, wife of Sabet-bin-Qais was discussed. The opinion was expressed in that judgment that the decision of the Prophet in that case was not to be regarded as a decree, awarded by him in the capacity of a Judge or as the Head of the State of Islam. It was thought that as the husband was agreeable to the separation, on the delivery back to him, of his garden, this was a separation by mutual consent, and it was in consequence of this that the Prophet gave his direction. It would be more consistent, in my humble opinion, with the letter and spirit of the Qur'an which places the husband and the wife on an equal footing, in respect of rights of one against the other, to construe this incident as meaning that the person in authority, including the Qazi, can order separation by *khula* even if the husband is not agreeable to that course. Of course the Qur'anic condition must be satisfied that it is no longer possible for the husband and the wife to live together in harmony and in conformity with their obligations.

After a discussion of the original sources, I have, therefore, reached the conclusion that the view, taken by Kaikaus, J. in Balqis Fatima's case, that the relevant verse of the Qur'an gives the right of *khula* to the wife subject to the limitation mentioned therein is correct.

In the present case, on the facts, it has been found that there is no possibility left, of the parties residing together in amity and goodwill. There has been litigation between them. The wife had to be brought away from the husband's house, on a warrant, issued under section 100, Criminal Procedure Code. She may have taken an intense dislike to her husband, after he contracted his second marriage, but ever since that time, she has consistently declined to share the connubial bed with him. In the circumstance, it would be idle to have recourse to the formality of appointing *Hakams* to attempt a reconciliation between them considering that a Panchayat, convened by the defendant's father, also failed, in this respect. I would therefore, hold that the plaintiff is entitled to separation from her husband, by *khula*, in the circumstances of the instant case.

The next question is on what terms, such a decree should be granted to her. Unfortunately, in the trial Court, the question of terms was not gone into, on either side, and the trial Judge also failed to advert to this aspect of the matter. There is no material on the file, from which it can be ascertained how much money, if at all, the husband had given to the wife, on the occasion of the marriage, and on receipt of what compensation he would be willing to grant her *khula*. The pleadings of the parties show that the dower, whatever its amount was, had not yet been paid to the wife. She merely expresses her willingness to relinquish her dower, but the husband said, he was not agreeable even, on this condition, to grant her *khula*. He did not plead that he had actually paid her the dower. Though, according to the Hedaya, it is abominable on the part of the husband to have more than the dower itself, in a case of separation by *khula*, yet if he insists, it is legally permissible for him to demand something more than the dower, and to the extent that he might have been out of pocket, in respect of gifts, given to the wife on marriage, he may, in law, demand restitution. This would necessitate an enquiry into the facts and the final decision as to what compensation must be paid by the wife for her relief, must rest with the Court. I would, therefore, allow the appeal and send back the case to the trial Judge, with the direction the parties may be permitted to lead evidence to what gifts, if any, and of what value, were given by the husband to the wife, on the occasion of the marriage, so that if the husband wants to take more than the dower, the condition may be imposed on the wife, to pay the additional sum, expended by the husband on her, to the grant of *khula*. The parties may be left to bear their own costs throughout in the circumstances of the case. (Some of the original authorities referred to in this judgment have been collected together by me in the form of an appendix to this judgment.)

HAMOODUR RAHMAN, J. I agree.

MUHAMMAD YAQUB ALI, J. I agree.

FAZLE-AKBAR, J. I have had the advantage of reading the judgment prepared by learned brother S.A. Rahman, J. As I entirely agree with the line of reasonings in his judgment, I concur in the order proposed by my learned brother.

[S.A. MAHMOOD, J. gives a concurring judgment, which is omitted.]

39

Syed Ali Nawaz Gardezi v. Muhammad Yusuf

JUDGMENT

S.A. RAHMAN, J. The respondent, Lt.-Col. Muhammad Yusuf, was tried under sections 497 and 498 of the Pakistan Penal Code by a learned Single Judge of the High Court of West Pakistan. He was convicted on both charges and sentenced to pay fines of Rs. 12,500 and Rs. 7,500 thereunder, or in default, to suffer rigorous imprisonment for one year on the first charge and to six months on the second charge. In case the fine was not paid, the terms of imprisonment for default, awarded on the two charges, were directed to run consecutively. The case had been tried on a complaint lodged by the petitioner, Mr. Ali Nawaz Gardezi, (hereinafter referred to as the complainant), in the Court of the A. D. M., Lahore, but it had been transferred, on his application, for trial in the High Court, by the learned Judge, on the ground that the respondent being a Commissioner of a Division, the subordinate Courts would feel embarrassed in dealing with the case.

2. The convict appealed and the Appellate Bench consisting of three Judges of the High Court, set aside the convictions and sentences and acquitted him of both the charges.

3. Mr. Ali Nawaz Gardezi was granted special leave to appeal as a large number of complicated questions of law and fact arose in the case and on nearly all of those questions, the judgment of the Appellate Bench had reversed the findings of the learned trial Judge. A number of the questions thus arising, were sufficiently important to attract the special jurisdiction of this Court in criminal cases.

4. The prosecution case was that the complainant, who is a Shia Muslim and a citizen of Pakistan, married a German girl, Christa Renate Sonntag, at Hull (England), before the Registrar of Marriages, on the 21st of July 1951. She was a Christian at that time. There children were born of the marriage—two sons and a daughter. The couple lived for some time abroad but came to Pakistan in 1953, for the first time. The complainant is a manager of Siemens Engineering Company Ltd., the Mall, Lahore, a German firm. The complainant and his wife were visiting Europe off and on, and in August 1961, they returned therefrom to Pakistan *via* Quetta. There they happened to meet the respondent on the 13th of August 1961. Friendly relations were established between them and the complainant and his wife invited the respondent to stay with them when he visited Lahore. Accordingly, on two occasions, the respondent stayed as the house-guest of the complainant, before the end of September 1961. It appears that Renate and the respondent developed a liking for each other soon after their first meeting and this turned into a mutual infatuation later. They corresponded with each other and the respondent made frequent telephone calls to the lady, from Quetta or Loralai, mostly at times when the husband was away from his house. In or about the middle of November 1961, the complainant is said to have intercepted the letter, Exh. P. I, written by the respondent to his wife. This was dated the 9th of November 1961, and shows that matters had advanced so far between the respondent and the lady that they were thinking of taking active steps to obtain release from their marital ties (both parties being married persons) and to marry each other. The letter is reproduced below....

6. On the 29th of December 1961, after dinner, Renate produced two chits, Exhs. P. 3 and P. 4, before the complainant, setting out drafts of what purported to be a divorce-deed and asked him to sign them....

7. The complainant claims that he refused to sign the chits. On the 30th of December 1961, when he returned from his office to the house at 1-30 p. m., he found that his wife had gone away with her belongings....

8. On the 2nd of January 1962, the respondent and Renate were married at Quetta according to Muslim rites. She was declared to have become a Muslim and was given the name of Ruqayya. On the 5th of January 1962, Mr. Gardezi filed his complaint under sections 497 and 498, P. P. C.....

[Paragraphs 9–29, which review evidences of the parties, are omitted.]

30. This being the state of the evidence on record, it is not possible to accept the assertion made by the respondent in his statement as an accused person, and the evidence of Christa Renate that she had become a Muslim on the 26th of October 1961. If there had been a genuine conversion on that day, it would not have been at all difficult to arrange for some witnesses to be present, when she made her declaration of change of faith. If the intention was to keep the husband in the dark about it, she could have easily accompanied the complainant to a place outside the house, so that she could profess her new faith before a *Moulvi* or even before a lay-witness. The circumstance that such a solemn ceremony was performed *sub rosa* and was attended by the two lovers only, casts doubt on the truth of the allegation.

31. There is then no escape from the conclusion that, on her own showing, Christa Renate had not been properly divorced by the complainant, as she was not a Muslim on the relevant date.

32. The alleged *talaq* could at best be described as *Talaq Bidat*, which is not recognized as valid by Shia Law. (*see* Baillie's Digest of Muhammadan Law, Part 11, p. 118, Tyabji's Muhammadan Law, Third Edition, Ss. 136-142, Mulla's Muhammadan Law, p. 662, Fifteen Edition, Amir Ali's Muhammadan Law, Fourth Edition, Vol. 11, p. 533). These text-books writers, moreover, are unanimous in stating that according to Shia doctors, the *talaq* must be orally pronounced by the husband, in the presence of two witnesses and the wife, in a set from of Arabic words. A written divorce is not recognized, except in certain circumstances which do not exist in the present case. The learned trial Judge took the view that Exh. D. I, even if it was executed by the complainant, was not effective in law to separate the two spouses because of these

provisions of the Shia *Fiqh*. The Appellate Bench of the High Court regarded the provisions of the Shia *Fiqh* with regard to the presence of witnesses and the necessity of an oral pronouncement of divorce, as merely rules of evidence which could be disregarded. The law being, however, laid down in categorical terms, it is open to question whether the view taken by the Appellate Bench can be sustained. The learned Judges do not appear to have adverted to the point that the alleged *talaq* was in the heretical form (*Talaqul Bidat*) which the Shia dispensation of Islamic Law does not sanction.

33. Assuming for the sake of argument, that the technicalities of the Shia *Fiqh* could be ignored in respect of the form of divorce, another obstacle to the document D. I taking effect from the date of its execution, is raised by the provisions of the Muslim Family Laws Ordinance, 1961. This Ordinance came into force with effect from the 15th July 1961, and by subsection (2) of section 1, declares that it extends to the whole of Pakistan and applies to 'all Muslim citizens of Pakistan wherever they may be'. Section 3 *inter alia* declares that the provision of the Ordinance would have effect, 'notwithstanding any law, custom or usage'. Section 7 of the Ordinance is pertinent to this case and may be reproduced *in extenso*:-

> 7. *Talaq*:- (1) Any man who wishes to divorce his wife shall, as soon as may be after the pronouncement of *talaq* in any form whatsoever, give the Chairman notice in writing of his having done so, and shall supply a copy thereof to the wife.
>
> (2) Whoever contravenes the provisions of subsection (1) shall be punishable with simple imprisonment for a term which may extend to one year or with fine which may extend to five thousand rupees or with both.
>
> (3) Save as provided in subsection (2), a *talaq* unless revoked earlier, expressly or otherwise, shall not be effective until the expiration of ninety days from the day on which notice under subsection (1) is delivered to the Chairman.
>
> (4) Within thirty days of the receipt of notice under subsection (1), the Chairman shall constitute an Arbitration Council for the purpose of bringing about a reconciliation between the parties; and the Arbitration Council shall take all steps necessary to bring about such reconciliation.
>
> (5) If the wife be pregnant at the time *talaq* is pronounced, *talaq* shall not be effective until the period mentioned in subsection (3) or the pregnancy, whichever be later, ends.

(6) Nothing shall debar a wife whose marriage has been terminated by *talaq* effective under this section from remarrying the same husband, without an intervening marriage with a third person, unless such termination is for the third time so effective.

It is common ground between the parties that the complainant in the case had failed to give notice to the Chairman of the Union Council concerned, in respect of the alleged grant of divorce by him to his wife, as required by this section. The learned trial Judge, therefore, found that, in the face of this section, the *talaq* failed to operate as such. The learned Judges of the Appellate Bench, however, were of the opinion that the Ordinance itself could not apply to the facts of the case, because Christa Renate was a non-citizen and the Ordinance was meant to apply only to Muslim citizens of Pakistan.

34. A brief examination of the provisions of the Ordinance would seem to be necessary in order to determine its scope. As has been observed above, undoubtedly subsection (2) of section 1 of the Ordinance makes it applicable to all Muslim citizens of Pakistan wherever they may be. The question is whether this means that the provisions of the Ordinance are attracted only if both spouses are Muslim citizens; or even where the husband alone is a Muslim citizen. Mr. Mahmud Ali, on behalf of the respondent, has strenuously argued that the Ordinance would be applicable only where both parties to a marriage are Muslim citizens.

35. Section 5 of the Ordinance provides that every marriage solemnized under Muslim Law, shall be registered, in accordance with the provisions of the Ordinance and for this purpose, the Union Council is authorized to grant licences to one or more persons, to be called Nikah Registrars. Every marriage not solemnized by the Nikah Registrar, is required to be reported to him by the person officiating at the marriage, for the purpose of registration, and contravention of this provision is made punishable with simple imprisonment for a term which may extend to three months, or with fine up to one thousand rupees, or with both. The section appears to be general in character, with the only limitation that the marriage should have been solemnized under Muslim Law. It is impossible to read into it a further limitation that the marriage should necessarily be between two Pakistani Muslims. A marriage entered into by a Pakistan Muslim male with, say, an Indian Muslim woman, would seem to fall within the purview of this section, if it is performed within Pakistan.

36. Section 6 is aimed at restricting polygamy. Subsection (1) thereof reads: 'No man, during the subsistence of an existing marriage, shall, except with the previous permission in writing of the Arbitration Council, contract another marriage, nor shall any such marriage contracted without such permission, be registered under this Ordinance.' The expression 'existing marriage' stands unqualified and would obviously cover the marriage of a Pakistan Muslim male with [a] Muslim non-citizen or even a non-Muslim lady, if it is recognized as valid by the laws of Pakistan. The expression 'another marriage' occurring subsequently in this subsection, should have the same connotation, *prima facie*. The generality of the words cannot be cut down by importing into this subsection any extraneous considerations. The Ordinance of course only penalizes the person in respect of a marriage, celebrated in contravention of the provisions of the Ordinance by making him liable to imprisonment or fine or both but does not invalidate the marriage itself. But that has no bearing on the question we are considering.

37. Coming next to the important section 7 itself, it seems to us that the Legislature had attempted to incorporate the Islamic Law provisions with regard to the two forms of '*Talaq-us-Sunnat*', viz., '*Talaq Ahsan*' and '*Talaq Hasan*', as far as may be, in this section. The first of them is that form in which a single pronouncement of divorce is made during a period of menstrual purity, no intercourse having taken place during that period, and is followed by a period of *iddat*. The second is one in which the first pronouncement made in similar circumstances is followed by two further pronouncements in succeeding periods, no intercourse taking place at any time during the three periods. Such a divorce becomes irrevocable on the third pronouncement. Whether the result achieved is in strict conformity with Islamic Law is a question which does not fall within the province of this Court to determine by reason of Articles 5 and 6 of the Constitution. The section clearly contemplates a machinery of conciliation whereby a husband wishing to divorce his wife unilaterally, may be enabled to think better of it, if the mediation of others can resolve the differences between the spouses. The *talaq* pronounced is to be ineffective for a period of 90 days from the date on which notice under subsection (1) of this section is delivered to the Chairman and this period is to be utilized for the attempt at reconciliation. Subsection (6) makes it clear that even if *talaq* has become effective under the previous subsection, the spouses would not

be prevented from re-marrying, without an intervening marriage with a third person, unless such termination is effective for the third time. All that the section requires is that the marriage in question should be dissolvable by means of a *talaq* and it does not seem necessary to adopt the narrow construction contended for on behalf of the respondent, that the wife mentioned in the section must necessarily be a Pakistani citizen. To suggest, as Mr. Mahmud Ali has done, that unless she is such a citizen she would have no right to appoint an Arbitrator on her behalf, under section 2 (a) of the Ordinance, appears to beg the question.

38. Mr. Mahmud Ali also put forward the suggestion that the word 'effective', occurring in subsection (3) of this section, means 'effective against the husband only' and that if the husband failed to give the required notice to the Chairman, the *talaq* would be effective at once. This interpretation would make the section itself wholly nugatory. All that the husband has to do then is that he should refrain from giving the requisite notice and the *talaq* would automatically take effect. This is exactly the mischief which the section seems designed to remedy. The alternative contention raised by the learned counsel that *Talaq Bidat* is altogether outside the purview of the section is plainly untenable as it takes no account of the words '*talaq* in any form whatsoever' occurring in subsection (1) of section 7.

39. Mr. Mahmud Ali also tried to maintain that in the present case, to permit the complainant to say that by not giving the notice to the Chairman, the divorce granted by him had been robbed of legal effect, would be tantamount to allowing him to take advantage of his own wrong. Learned counsel referred to pages 200-203 of Maxwell's Interpretation of Statutes, Eleventh Edition, in support of the proposition that on the general principle of avoiding injustice and absurdity, any construction would, if possible, be rejected (unless the policy and object of the Act required it) which enabled a person to defeat or impair the obligation of his contract by his own act or otherwise to profit by his own wrong. But here it is obvious that the object of section 7 is to prevent hasty dissolution of marriages by *talaq*, pronounced by the husband, unilaterally, without an attempt being made to prevent disruption of the matrimonial status. If the husband himself thinks better of the pronouncement of *talaq* and abstains from giving a notice to the Chairman, he should perhaps be deemed, in view of section 7, to have revoked the pronouncement and that would be to the advantage of the

wife. Subsection (3) of this section precludes the *talaq* from being effective as such, for a certain period and within that period, consequently, it could not be said that the marital status of the parties had in any way been changed. They would still in law continue to be husband and wife. The result in the present case, so far as the question of legality of the subsequent marriage of the respondent to Christa Renate is concerned, would not be in any way different, even if the period envisaged by this section is deemed to start from time of the pronouncement of *talaq* or as soon as may be thereafter, instead of postponing the start to the date of receipt of a notice by the Chairman, in order to avoid giving the benefit of his own default to the husband. Ninety days had not yet elapsed from the date of alleged pronouncement of *talaq*, when the respondent went through his marriage with the lady.

40. The sphere of attempted conciliation seems to be further extended by section 8 of the Ordinance to cases of '*Talaq Tafviz*' and also to other forms of dissolution of marriage at the instance of either party, *mutatis mutandis*, and this throws further light on the objective aimed at by the Ordinance. It would be idle to speculate what alternative forms of dissolution are contemplated by this section.

41. There is nothing in section 9 of the Ordinance (which relates to maintenance to be provided by the husband for the wife) that could cut down the connotation of the term 'wife' to a Muslim citizen of Pakistan alone.

42. To hold that the Ordinance could not be pressed into service except in cases where both spouses were Muslim citizens, would lead to the result that a male Muslim citizen, could, with impunity, have more than one wife, without recourse to the provisions of the Ordinance, provided that he confines himself to non-citizen Muslim ladies, for marriage purposes. On this interpretation, if a Muslim male citizen of Pakistan, is already married to a Muslim non-citizen, he could marry another wife, whether a Muslim citizen or not, without incurring any penalty under the Ordinance. Similarly, he could go on divorcing non-citizen Muslim ladies, without limit, if he was so minded. Such absurd results would apparently rob the Ordinance of almost all its utility and the narrow interpretation which leads to such results, would not, in all probability, be in consonance with the intention of the Legislature. The policy of the Ordinance seems to be to provide some curbs on too facile pronouncements of divorce and unnecessary or unjustified plural marriages.

43. We are, therefore, disposed to agree with the learned trial Judge that on the 2nd of January 1962, when Christa Renate went through a form of marriage with the respondent, she was still the wife of the complainant as the divorce, even if granted by the latter, could not have become effective, without recourse to the provisions of section 7 of the Muslim Family Laws Ordinance, 1961. It is also fairly clear that by the 2nd of January 1962, even the *iddat* period prescribed by Islamic Law for a divorced wife, had not yet expired....

47. The position that emerges therefore is that the respondent was guilty of enticing or taking away Christa Renate, when she was still the lawfully-wedded wife of the complainant, from the latter's house and he, therefore, committed an offence which fell within the purview of section 498, P. P. C. The circumstances clearly point to the inference that he knew her to be the wife of Mr. Gardezi at the relevant time. The intention to 'marry' her, had no genuine basis as he must have known that there was no legal separation between her and her first husband and no marriage ceremony, even if gone through, could wipe out that fact from his consciousness. The subsequent marriage in the circumstances, must be regarded merely as a disingenuous device to put up a façade of respectability over an illegal union. We, therefore, hold that the acquittal of the respondent, of the charge under section 498, P. P. C., by the appellate Bench, was not justified on the evidence on record. We allow the appeal to that extent, set aside his acquittal on this charge and restore the order of conviction passed by trial Judge, with reference to section 498, P. P. C.

48. With regard to the charge under section 497, P. P. C., it may be observed that although the respondent has apparently committed adultery with Christa Renate, when she was still the wife of the complainant, the charge must fail on the ground that there was connivance on the part of the complainant. In the course of the above discussion, we have referred to circumstances which show that the complainant was performing the role of a somewhat subdued and accommodating husband. On the 30th of December 1961, when he found his wife with the respondent in Gen. Rana's house, after an abortive attempt at persuading her to return, he kept quiet and allowed the couple to proceed to Quetta by train, without further interference. The letter, Exh. D. 3, which he wrote to her when they had reached Quetta, is tell-tale evidence of his connivance to the adultery which he knew was

being committed with his wife and which he took no step to prevent. Of course, mere passive inaction is not enough for a finding of connivance, but as was said by the House of Lords in *Gipps* v. *Gipps* (1864) 11 H L C 3, 'conniving' means 'not merely refusing to see an act of adultery but also wilfully abstaining from taking any step to prevent adulterous intercourse which, from what passed before the husband's eyes, he must reasonably accept, will occur'. In Halsbury's Laws of England, Vol. 12, Third Edition, para. 589, at page 297, it is stated that connivance is not limited to active conduct. 'It includes the case where a spouse acquiesces in the adultery alleged, that is to say, where the spouse is aware that a certain result will follow, if he does nothing and desires the result to come about. On the principle of *volenti non fit injuria*, a person cannot complain of any act, he passively assents to.' It is to be remembered that in the letter, Exh. D. 3, the complainant even wished his wife happiness in her new life, knowing that she was living in adultery with the respondent. In the circumstances, it is difficult to maintain that the respondent was guilty of an offence under section 497, P. P. C. The acquittal of the respondent on that charge, consequently, must stand.

49. The question is then of the sentence. The complainant in the case seems to have allowed things to develop under his very nose, without taking effective restrictive action in respect of his erring wife, or to counteract the conduct of the respondent who was subject to service discipline as an officer of Government. We are also conscious that the conviction might conceivably entail departmental action by Government, against the respondent, in respect of his service. Taking all the circumstances of the case into consideration, we are of the opinion that the ends of justice would be met by sentencing the respondent under section 498, P. P. C. to pay a fine of Rs. 2,000. In default of payment of fine, he will suffer rigorous imprisonment for 3 months. We order accordingly. The fine will be paid within 15 days from date....

40

Kaneez Fatima v. Wali Muhammad

JUDGMENT

SALEEM AKHTAR, J. This appeal by the leave of the Court arises from the judgment of the High Court passed in a Constitution petition whereby the family suit filed by the appellant for recovery of dower and maintenance in the Court of Family Judge was dismissed.

2. Appellant and respondent were married on 14-10-1975 and Nikahnama was registered under the provisions of the Muslim Family Laws Ordinance, 1961 (hereinafter referred as the Ordinance). It provided for a prompt dower of Rs. 30,000 and 20 tolas of gold while monthly maintenance of Rs. 200 was also fixed. As the relationship between the parties became strained the appellant filed a petition before the Martial Law Authorities complaining of non-payment of maintenance and prompt dower. The parties entered into a written compromise on 22-9-1977 before the Martial Law Authorities under which the respondent undertook to make payment of Rs. 10,000 as prompt dower and agreed to give 5 tolas of gold to the appellant. It was also agreed that the divorce between the parties will take effect from 1-11-1977. As a consequence of the compromise appellant received Rs. 10,000 and 5 tolas of gold and she acknowledged that the matrimonial ties between the parties had come to an end. Both the parties agreed that they will have no further claim in future against each other. On 6-4-1978 the appellant filed a suit for recovery of the remaining amount of dower (i.e. Rs 20,000), and maintenance in the Court of Family Judge pleading that the compromise was arrived at due to coercion by Martial Law Authorities

and no notice of dissolution of marriage in pursuance of the agreement was given to the Chairman, Union Council as provided by section 7 of the Ordinance and therefore the marriage between the parties was still subsisting. She claimed maintenance from May, 1977 up to the date of decision. The suit was decreed by the learned Family Judge against which appeal was filed by the respondent before the Additional District Judge. The learned appellate Court held that the divorce had become effective between the parties from 1-11-1977 under the compromise and maintenance was granted up to 1-11-1977. Aggrieved by this judgment the appellant filed a Constitution petition in the High Court. By the impugned judgment the petition was dismissed with the following observation:

> From the resume of the facts of the case it is clear that both the parties contracted out of the provisions of section 7 of the Act and agreed not to have a recourse to arbitration proceedings before the Chairman, Union Council, therefore, both of them waived the compulsory proceedings aimed at to restore the marriage. Therefore, the petitioner cannot claim the benefit of section 7 of the Act for the purpose of claiming maintenance.

The judgment also records that the Advocate for the appellant had contended that he would not dispute the finding of first appellate Court in respect of dower and recovery of the golden ornaments in view of the compromise agreement and that the finding on maintenance was being challenged before the High Court.

3. At the time of granting leave it was noticed that the impugned judgment of the High Court Mst. Kaniz Fatima v. Wali Muhammad PLD 1989 Lah. 490 was in conflict with the judgment in Mirza Qamar Raza v. Mst. Tahira Begum and others PLD 1988 Kar. 169. The controversy seems to be with regard to applicability and interpretation of Article 2A of the Constitution. The main question which has been discussed by these authorities is whether the Court has jurisdiction to strike down any law which is inconsistent with Article 2A in so far as it is held to be in contravention of the Injunctions of Islam and Muslim Law. Till the time the impugned judgment had been passed there were several judgments of the High Court in which conflicting views were expressed. In Habib Bank Ltd. v. Wahid Textile Mills Ltd. PLD 1989 Kar. 371 it was held that as Article 2A was not self-executory, on the touchstone of this provision the Court cannot strike down any law being in

conflict with the principles and Injunctions of Islam. Contrary view was expressed in Ijaz Haroon v. Inam Durrani PLD 1989 Kar. 304. Similarly, same view was reiterated in Shaukat Hussain v. Mst. Robina and others PLD 1989 Kar. 513, in which it was held that section 7 of the Ordinance was not in accordance with Islamic Law and was hit by Article 2A.

4. The effect and interpretation of Article 2A was considered by a Full Bench of this Court in Hakim Khan and others v. Government of Pakistan and others PLD 1992 SC 595 decided on 9-7-1992. In this judgment all the judgments of this Court as well as of the High Courts and the Federal Shariat Court have been noted and considered. Till then in all there were 39 judgments in which Article 2A had directly been referred or observations had been made on its applicability and effect. The main question under consideration in Hakim Khan's case was whether Article 2A which was inserted by President's Order No. 14 of 1985 in the Constitution of Pakistan, 1973 and made its substantive part has resulted in denuding the President of the power of commuting the sentence of death passed on persons guilty of murder despite the power conferred on him by Article 45 to do so and whether the provision of said Article 45 to this extent has become ineffective. This Court did not approve the observation of the Lahore High Court that Article 2A has an 'overwhelming position in the Constitution' and is now 'in control of the Constitution' and ruled that the Objectives Resolution is not a supra-Constitutional document and is not in control of the Constitution....

[Paragraphs 5–9 are omitted.]

10. Now coming to the present case we find that the learned Judge of the High Court has held that in view of the compromise between the parties both of them had waived the compulsory proceedings under section 7 of the Ordinance for the purpose of claiming maintenance. It may first be noticed that the Muslim Family Laws Ordinance is an existing law which has not so far been declared by the Federal Shariat Court or by the Shariat Appellate Bench of the Supreme Court in conflict with the provision of Islamic Injunctions. Nothing has been brought on record to show that the Council of Islamic Ideology has made any recommendation in this regard. The learned counsel for the appellant has referred to Allah Dad v. Mukhtar Ahmad and another 1992 SCMR 1273 where it has been observed that in the absence of notice under section 7 of the Ordinance, talaq becomes effective and reliance was placed

on Mirza Qamar Raza v. Mst. Tahira Begem and others PLD 1988 Kar. 169, where on the basis of Article 2A while exercising Constitutional jurisdiction in a family matter section 7 of the Ordinance was declared to be void and against the Injunctions of Islam. With respect it may be pointed out that the jurisdiction of the Federal Shariat Court and the Shariat Appellate Bench of the Supreme Court does not extend to the Constitution and the Family Laws. Furthermore, Mirza Qamar Raza's case was set aside by a Bench of the Supreme Court on the ground that elucidation on the question of validity of section 7 on the touchstone of Article 2A was not required in the facts and circumstances as it is an accepted principle that if a case can be decided on other issues properly, it is not necessary to enter into Constitutional issues. In Allah Dad's case decision would be made on the basis of Mst. Bashiran and others v. Muhammad Hussain and another PLD 1988 SC 186 which has been noted by the learned Judge in para. 21 of that judgment. As Allah Dad's case could be decided on the principles of Mst. Bashiran's case, there was no need to enter into questions of Constitutional issues particularly so when it did not fall within the jurisdiction of the Court. As regards notice of Talaq reference can be made to the following judgments:

(1) Syed Ali Nawaz Gardezi v. Lt.-Col. Muhammad Yusuf PLD 1963 SC 51 where it was observed that if husband opts not to give notice perhaps he may be deemed to have revoked pronouncement of Talaq.

(2) Abdul Mannan v. Safurun Nessa 1970 SCMR 845 where it was observed that if no notice under section 7(3) of the Ordinance is given divorce 'is yet to be effective'.

These judgments were followed in Muhammad Salahuddin v. Muhammad Nazir Siddiqui 1984 SCMR 583 and Junaid Ali v. Abdul Qadir 1987 SCMR 518. In the last judgment our learned brother Shafiur Rahman, J. observed that the 'statute takes over where the parties by settlement arrive at dissolution'. Section 7 was held to be observed even in such circumstances. The observation in the impugned judgment as contained in para. 55 reproduced above, is not in conformity with the law laid down by this Court which had interpreted section 7 of the Ordinance.

11. So far the observations made in Syed Ali Nawaz Gardezi's case, it may be observed that failure to send notice of Talaq to the Chairman of

the Union Council does not by itself lead to the conclusion that Talaq has been revoked. It may only be ineffective but not revoked. This controversy should be considered from practical and purposive point of view taking into consideration the facts and circumstances of each case. In the present case the appellant having matrimonial disputes particularly relating to payment of prompt dower and maintenance, filed an application before the Martial Law Authorities where both the parties appeared. The stand taken by the respondent was that he had divorced the appellant on 27-8-1976, but she denied having received any copy of the Talaq or notice. The parties settled their dispute and two documents were executed. The appellant admits her signature on these documents. The first document is dated 22-9-1977 in which the respondent has declared that he would pay Rs. 10,000 and also deliver 5 tolas of gold to the appellant on 5-10-1977. This document is signed by the appellant. The other document is dated 1-11-1977 in which the respondent stated that he had divorced the appellant on 27-8-1976 and in pursuance of that divorce he again reiterated to divorce her on 1-11-1977 before the witnesses and further stated that in terms of settlement, dated 22-9-1977 Rs. 10,000 and 5 tolas of gold are delivered to the appellant. It is further stated that the appellant will have no claim against him. The next document is also, dated 1-11-1977 executed by the appellant and also signed by the respondent. It was signed in the presence of a Military Officer and the S.H.O. It is a document and declaration by the appellant in which it has been stated that the respondent had divorced her on 27-8-1976, but it was not received by her. Today on 1-11-1977 'the respondent in the presence of the witnesses has divorced me' and she has received Rs. 10.000 and 5 tolas of gold as agreed in terms of settlement dated 22-9-1977. She also stated that she will have no legal right or institute any legal proceedings against the respondent. The appellant had stated in her evidence that these documents were signed by him [*sic*] without reading them and under force and threat by the Martial Law Authorities. The appellant had herself filed the application before the Martial Law Authorities in pursuance of which proceedings were drawn and documents were executed. When the appellant filed suit for recovery of maintenance in March 1978 it was pleaded that she had made application before the Martial Law Authorities where the respondent pleaded that he had divorced her but she contended that as provisions of section 7 of the Ordinance were not complied with, there was no effective divorce under law. It is significant to note that not a single word has been stated that any settlement was arrived at and her signatures were obtained on those documents by force or threat. The suit had been filed only for maintenance and not for the dower debt. This fact lends support that the appellant had received the dower debt in terms of the settlement and had accepted it and that is why the suit for maintenance was filed ignoring the fact that she had been divorced and without pleading that divorce, dated 1-12-1977 was illegal, not binding and not effective. In these facts it is to be considered whether strict construction should be given to section 7 of the Ordinance. The provisions of section 7 of the Ordinance have remained controversial from the very beginning and there are conflicting views in general about it. In view of the Constitutional restraints the Courts cannot give any verdict on the conflicting claims challenging or justifying the provisions of section 7 of the Ordinance. However, keeping in view the facts of each case the applicability and interpretation of section 7 has to be construed in that light. In a case where with the consent of both the parties divorce is effected and confirmed in writing under their undisputed signatures section 7 should not be strictly construed particularly in cases where penal provision of section 7(2) is to be enforced because in such cases the parties do not wilfully commit breach and bonafide believe that they have been divorced with consent of each other and sending of notice to the Chairman, Union Council is merely a formality. The notice can be sent at any time thereafter to comply with the provisions of section 7. Where such view has been taken but its validity has been challenged, the Court would be justified to refuse to issue writ and exercise its jurisdiction.

We, therefore, dismiss the appeal, but completely on different grounds.

Appeal dismissed.

Zohra Begum v. Latif Ahmad Munawwar

ORDER

The question which falls for determination in this case is whether among Muslims, a father as against the mother is entitled to the custody of his minor son who has attained the age of 7 years. Mr. A. R. Sheikh, learned counsel for the appellant, maintained that, firstly, there is no definite rule of decision as to the age at which the mother loses right of custody of her son and, secondly, that under section 25 of the Guardians and Wards Act the only consideration before the Court in directing that the minor should be given back to the custody of his legal guardian is his welfare and that implying thereby that conditions embodied in section 17 of the Act, for appointment of guardians of minors, were inapplicable to applications under section 25.

2. The learned counsel took me through a large number of text books on Muslim Law in which conflicting views are expressed about the age of minor son at which the mother loses the right of his custody and stressed that the views expressed by Imams and other jurisconsults of Islam are not sacrosanct. In this connection he drew my attention to *Mst. Aishan v. Jodha Ram and others* AIR 1938 Lah. 719, *Muhammad Bakhsk v. Crown and others* PLD 1950 Lah. 203, and *Mst. Muni v. Habib Khan* PLD 1956 Lah. 403, in which this Court did not follow the view expressed in more than one authentic text books on Muslim Law that the decree of a Qazi is necessary to effectuate dissolution of marriage in exercise of option of puberty, *e. g.*, Principles of Muhammadan Law

by Mulla, 14th Edition, page 243, Digest of Muslim Law by Baillie (Pak. Edition) page 75, Hedaya by Hamilton (Pak. Edition) page 35, Fatawa-i-Alamgiri, Volume 11, page 31 and Minhaj Kitab-un-Nikah Sharah-ul-Waqiah. Similarly, in *Mst. Rashida Begum* v. *Shahab Din and others* PLD 1960 Lah. 1142 Mr. Justice, S.M. Shafi did not follow the rule that on remarriage a mother loses the right of custody of her minor daughters. On this premise, the learned counsel urged that in the absence of a universally accepted rule of decision it is for the Courts to ascertain it in each case on basis of *Ijmaa, Qias, Istihsan* and *Istidlal*, etc.

3. In *Mst. Khurshid Jan* v. *Fazal Dad* R. S. A. No. 486 of 1961 a similar question arose as to the interpretation of Muslim Law and in order that it may be decided authoritatively, I have requested the learned Chief Justice to constitute a larger Bench to determine:—

(i) what are the sources of Muslim Law;
(ii) what are the rules of interpretation of Muslim Law and can Courts differ from the views of Imams and other jurisconsults of Muslim Law on grounds of public policy, justice, equity and good conscience; and
(iii) in case of conflicting views expressed in text books on Muslim Law, such as Hedaya, Fatawa-i-Alamgiri, Radd-ul-Mukhtar, Muhammadan Law by Sayyed Ameer Ali, etc., how are the Courts to determine which of the view is correct?

It is, therefore, expedient that this case should also be heard along with R. S. A. 486 of 1961.

JUDGMENT

This will be read in continuation of the order of reference made in these two appeals (F. A. O. 65 of 1962 and F. A. O. 88 of 1962) on the 24th of June 1963, and the opinion of the Full Bench delivered on the 5th of May 1964. [See *Mst. Khurshid Jan* v. *Fazal Dad* PLD (W.P.) Lahore 558.]

2. The dispute relates to the custody of two minor children of Sheikh Latif Ahmad Munawwar and *Mst.* Zohra Begum (parties to the two appeals), namely, Khalid Latif, who attained the age of seven years and Robeena Khatoon, who is yet below the age of puberty. Both the

children are in the custody of the mother, but in pursuance to an application made by the father under section 25 of the Guardians and Wards Act, Mr. Ishaq Rahim Bakhsh, Guardian Judge, Lahore, had directed that the custody of the boy be handed over to the father and the custody of the girl retained by the mother. It is against this order that both the parties have preferred the above-mentioned appeals in this Court.

3. The relevant facts are that Sheikh Latif Ahmad Munawwar and *Mst.* Zohra Begum were married on the 15th of April 1951. The two children named above were born of this wedlock during 1952 and 1953; but as misfortune would have it, the relations between the parents progressively became strained until in 1953 Mst. Zohra Begum felt compelled to leave the house of Sheikh Latif Ahmad Munawwar, along with the two children, and since then has been residing with her parents in Lahore. No repproachment [rapprochement] could be made between the strained spouses during the next eight years until on the 24th of April 1961, the marital ties between them were dissolved by the pronouncement of divorce by Sheikh Latif Ahmad Munawwar. This led to multifarious litigation between the parties. On the 3rd of June 1961, *Mst.* Zohra Begum instituted two civil suits against Sheikh Latif Ahmad Munawwar, one for payment of dower and the other for recovery of her dowry. A little later, she filed a complaint under section 488, Criminal Procedure Code, against Sheikh Latif Ahmad Munawwar for grant of maintenance of the children in the Court of a Magistrate Ist Class, Lahore. In reply, Sheikh Latif Ahmad Munawwar instituted the present application under section 25 of the Guardians and Wards Act for the custody of Khalid Latif and Robeena Khatoon, out of which, as stated above, these two appeals have arisen.

4. The claim for the custody of Khalid Latif and Robeena Khatoon by Sheikh Latif Ahmad Munawwar proceeded on the averments that *Mst.* Zohra Begum was mentally deranged and incompetent to look after the welfare of the minors and was not possessed of independent means of livelihood to bring them up properly. The petition was resisted by *Mst.* Zohra Begum, who in her written statement maintained that the claim put forth by Sheikh Latif Ahmad Munawwar was a counterblast to the suits and the complaint under section 488, Criminal Procedure Code, instituted by her against him. On facts, the respondent pleaded that as a result of maltreatment meted out to her by Sheikh Latif Ahmad Munawwar she had, for a little while, gone out of her mind, but

since then she had fully recovered and was capable of looking after her minor children. As regards the means to bring up the children, it was maintained that Sheikh Latif Ahmad Munawwar up to date had not contributed a single penny for their maintenance and, as such, he was not entitled to claim their custody.

5. On the pleadings of the parties, the learned Guardian Judge framed an issue as to whether it would be for the welfare of the minors to be given into the custody of the father or in their remaining with the mother. The hearing was adjourned to enable the parties to examine evidence in support of their respective claim, in the meantime a change took place in the presiding officer of the Court. Mr. Ishaq Rahim Bakhsh, the new incumbent, on examining the record of the case on the 22nd of April 1962, recorded an order which, for facility of reference, may be reproduced *in extenso*:—

I have examined the file. My learned predecessor rightly converted the application under section 7 into one under section 25 as application under section 7 by father is not competent. The father seeks custody of son of 7 years and of daughter who has not attained puberty. He has levelled two allegations. First, the mother is not in a position to bring up the children for lack of means and secondly she has been a patient in the Mental Hospital. The application is resisted. The contention of the respondent mother is that the petitioner abandoned her after one and-a-half years' conjugal company and has never taken interest in the welfare of the children and that she had to move the Criminal Court under section 488, Cr. P. C. There were no other allegations with respect to the averments in the application under section 25. The father claims to be a gazetted officer. It goes without saying that welfare of the minor is the cardinal principle in dealing with the application for the appointment of the guardian or for restoration of the custody of the minors. His Lordship Mr. Justice Abdul Hamid after canvassing various authorities on the subject, ruled in P L D 1958 Pesh. 26, that the rule of Personal Law proceeds on the welfare of the minors and welfare of the minor does not mean that appointment shall be inconsistent with the rule of Personal Law. His Lordship Mr. Justice Jamil Hussain Rizvi in P L D 1962 Lah. 162 even went to the extent of laying down that where a father takes another wife and neglects the children of first wife notwithstanding the order under section 488, Cr. P. C. cannot be refused the custody of the children under section 25 of Guardians and Wards Act. The allegations in the present case speak for themselves and no evidence apart from physical mental incapacity of the mother is invited. It will be for decision whether she is physically incapable to look after the children. If the decision goes against the petitioner, the allegation that she is not sufficiently possessed of means will not be ground for depriving her of the custody of the girl because under the Muhammadan Law it is the duty of the father to maintain the children even if they are not in his custody. If he thinks that the girl is not receiving proper education, let him put her in a good school of his choice and foot the bill of her education. With this observation, I confine myself only to the evidence of mother's physical capacity in so far as the custody of the girl is concerned.

The welfare of the minors was, thus, not to be inquired into by the Court. The boy who had attained the age of seven years must be given in the custody of the father and the girl to remain in the custody of the mother unless the father succeeded in proving that the mother was mentally unfit to bring up Robeena Khatoon.

6. The evidence produced by Sheikh Latif Ahmad Munawwar in support of the mental incapacity of *Mst.* Zohra Begum consisted of the testimony of Dr. Muhammad Rashid Choudhary, Medical Superintendent of the Government Mental Hospital, Lahore. The substance of his evidence was that *Mst.* Zohra Begum was admitted in the Mental Hospital on the 10th of May 1958. He found her suffering from schizophrenia (split personality), as a result of which she had been aggressive, crying and tearing clothes and breaking utensils; but by the time she was discharged from the hospital the aggressiveness had disappeared. In reply to a Court question the doctor amplified (i) that environmental structure precipitates the ailment from which *Mst.* Zohra Begum suffered though the prerequisites in the form of emotional and mental make-up were either inherited or acquired by her and (ii) that the removal of stresses playing upon the nerves of the patient like *Mst.* Zohra Begum contributes to restoration of normalcy. Appearing as her own witness, *Mst.* Zohra Begum deposed that she was a sensitive and thoughtful person and went off her head as a result of maltreatment by the petitioner; but as a result of treatment of Dr. Muhammad Rashid she had recovered and had had no mental trouble since then. In the light of this evidence the learned Guardian Judge held that *Mst.* Zohra Begum was not mentally incapacitated to look after the welfare of Robeena Khatoon, and in the result directed that Khalid Latif should be given to the custody of the father and Robeena Khatoon should remain with the mother.

7. The order of the learned Guardian Judge, dated the 22nd of April 1962, was based on the view expressed by this Court in *Chand Bibi* v. *Bulbullah* PLD 1958 Pesh. 26 and *Khanamji* v. *Farman Ali* PLD 1962 Lah. 166. In the first case Abdul Hamid, J. expressed the view that

> the language of the pharse 'consistently with the law to which the minor is subject' clearly means that the appointment should be consistent and not inconsistent with the personal law of the minor. If the interests of a minor demand that his person should be in the care of his mother who has remarried a stranger, but the rule of minor's personal law forbids the appointment of such mother, the appointment of the mother will be inconsistent with that law.

In the second case Jamil Hussain Rizvi, J. extended the rule still further by laying down that if a father otherwise neglects the children of the first wife and fails to maintain them notwithstanding an order made against him under section 488, Criminal Procedure Code, the Courts have no authority to refuse to him the custody of the children under section 25 of the Guardians and Wards Act. A more exhaustive decision of the subject was delivered by Kaikaus, J. in *Muhammad Bakhsh* v. *Mst. Ghulam Fatima* PLD 1953 Lah. 73. In construing the clause 'consistently with the law to which the minor is subject' the learned Judge laid down that 'all rules of Muhammadan Law relating to the guardianship and custody of the minor are merely application of the principle of benefit of the minor to diverse circumstances. Welfare of the minor remains the dominant consideration and the rules only try to give effect to what is minor's welfare from the Muslim point of view'. These observations are confined to the construction of section 17 of the Guardians and Wards Act, but the same considerations were applied to section 25, which does not contain the provision 'consistently with the law to which the minor is subject', on the following reasoning:—

> It may be objected that if every rule of Muhammadan Law is subordinate to the interests of the child, how do the rules affect a case under section 25 at all. The answer is simple. We will regard the rules as raising a presumption till exceptional circumstances are proved. The above question from Tyabji's Muhammadan Law is substantially to the same effect. If I were dealing with an application under section 17, I would have to apply Muhammadan Law because of the words 'consistently with the law to which the minor is subject' in that section. But the Act recognizes the father as natural guardian and the only application he can

file is under section 25. If I do not apply Muhammadan Law in this case it would create an anomaly in that if a relative other than the father applies under section 17 he can have all the rights which personal law gives him, whereas the father, because he has to apply under section 25, would not get the benefit.

With utmost respect to the learned Judge, I may venture to say that a father can, in no circumstances, be placed at a disadvantage in comparison to any other relative of the minor, who may apply under section 17 of the Guardians and Wards Act for appointment as a guardian. A father is a natural guardian of his minor children and, as observed by the learned Judge at page 81 of the report even when the minor children are in the custody of the mother, the legal control of the children vests in the father. This cannot be said of any other relative who is appointed as a guardian of the minor. In determining the question whether the custody of a minor shall be given to such a relative under sections 17 and 25 of the Guardians and Wards Act, the Court will be primarily guided by the welfare of the minor and if, on the facts of a given case, a father does not succeed as against the mother in obtaining the custody of the children, no Court would give their custody to a relative, other than the father, who applies under section 17 of the Guardians and Wards Act.

8. The more important question which falls for determination in the case is, 'What is the law to which the minor is subject?' Mr. A. R. Sheikh (as he then was), learned counsel, brought to my notice various Text Books on Muslim Law in which there is a divergence of opinion as to the age of a minor son and daughter at which the mother loses the right of their custody. In view of this conflict, one of the questions referred to the Full Bench was 'In case of conflicting views expressed in text books on Muslim Law, such as Hedaya, Fatawai-i-Alamgiri, Radd-ul-Mukhtar, Muhammadan Law by Sayyed Amir Ali, etc., how are the Courts to determine which view is correct?' The answer given by the Full Bench is that where there is no Quranic or Traditional Text or an Ijma' on a point of law, and if there be a difference of views between A'imma and Faqihs, a Court may form its own opinion on a point of law. In support of this view reliance was placed on the following questions and answer in Al-Risala by Imam-Al-Shafei'.

He asked: 'I have found the scholars in former and present times, in disagreement on certain (legal) matters. Is it permissible for them to do so?' (Shafei') replied: 'Disagreement is of two kinds; one of them is prohibited, but I would not say the same regarding the other.' He asked: 'What is prohibited disagreement?' (Shafei'): 'On all matters concerning which God provided clear textual evidence, His book or (a Sunna) uttered by the Prophet's tongue, disagreement among those to whom these (texts) are known is unlawful. As to matters that are liable to different interpretation or derived from analogy, so that he who interprets or applies analogy arrives at a decision different from that arrived at by another, I do not hold that (disagreement) of this kind constitutes such strictness as that arising from textual (evidence).'

On this view, it would be permissible for Courts to differ from the Rule of Hizanat stated in the Text Books on Muslim Law for there is no Quranic or Traditional Text on the point. Courts which have taken the place of Qazis can, therefore, come to their own conclusions by process of Ijtihad which, according to Imam-Al-Shafei', is included in the doctrine of Qiyas. It has been mentioned earlier that the rule propounded in different Text Books on the subject of Hizanat is not uniform. It would, therefore, be permissible to depart from the rule stated therein if, on the facts of a given case, its application is against the welfare of the minor. I am fortified in this view by the instance in which a Qazi finding hardship in the application of a rule of law to which the parties belonged sent the case to the Qazi of another School of Law which took a liberal view of the matter.

9. Turning to the merits of the present case, it is not difficult to pronounce where the welfare of the minors lie. It has been found that the mother does not suffer from any mental ailment and by now has for the last 9 years brought up the two children without any apparent shortcoming. Both of them attend school and no complaint was made by Sheikh Latif Ahmad Munawwar about their physical well-being. It has, therefore, to be seen whether it would be in the welfare of the minors to give them in the custody of the father. It is an admitted fact that uptil now Sheikh Latif Ahmad Munawwar has not contributed a single penny towards their maintenance. In fact, he has not even seen them once since 1953. In the circumstances, if the custody of Khalid Latif and Robeena Khatoon is given to Sheikh Latif Ahmad Munawwar, they shall find themselves, more or less, choked in the custody of a stranger, who has had such a long drawn and bitter ligation with their mother. In the circumstances, it is likely that if they are removed from the affection of their mother, their emotional and mental growth may be retarded.

The plea raised in the written statement that the petition under section 25 of the Guardians and Wards Act by Sheikh Latif Ahmad Munawwar was a counterblast to the civil suit and the complaint under section 488, Criminal Procedure Code, instituted by *Mst.* Zohra Begum against him rather than motivated by a sudden outburst of affection for the welfare of the minors [?].

10. In the result, it is found that it is in the welfare of Khalid Latif and Robeena Khatoon, minors, to remain in the custody of their mother, *Mst.* Zohra Begum. F. A. O. No. 88 of 1962 by Sheikh Latif Ahmad Munawwar, accordingly, stands dismissed and F.A.O. No. 65 of 1962 by Mst. Zohra Begum allowed; but, in the circumstances of the case, there will be no order as to costs in both the appeals.

Appeal accepted.

44

Muhammad Haneef v. Abdul Samad

JUDGMENT

FAQIR MUHAMMAD KHOKHAR, J. The petitioner Late Muhammad Haneef (now represented by his legal heirs) instituted, on 26-7-1980, a suit for declaration in that by virtue of sale Mutation No. 63 attested on 12-6-1967, he was owner of agricultural land measuring 72 kanals situated in Chak No. 52/4-R Tehsil Haroon Abad District Bahawalnagar. He further prayed therein that the judgment and decree, dated 27-7-1973, passed by the Senior Civil Judge Bahawalnagar, followed by Mutation No. 197, dated 19-3-1979, registered sale-deeds, dated 28-6-1979 and 12-3-1980 by Mst. Ghulam Fatima, the respondent No. 7, in favour of respondents Nos. 1 to 5 coupled with Mutations Nos. 202 to 205 attested on 15-11-1997 and Mutation No. 209 attested on 2-4-1980, be declared illegal, ex parte, collusive, void and inoperative qua his rights. By way of consequential relief, the possession of the suit-land was sought for. It was averred in the plaint that Mst. Ghulam Fatima, the respondent No. 7 was the original owner of the suit-land, who alienated the same by way of exchange in favour of her mother Mst. Rabia, the respondent No. 6, through Mutation No. 62, dated 30-5-1967. Mst. Rabia, the respondent No. 6, purportedly sold out the suit-land in favour of plaintiff/petitioner through Mutation No. 63 attested on 26-7-1967. Then the respondent No. 7 obtained ex parte decree on 27-4-1973, from the Senior Civil Judge, Bahawalnagar, whereby the exchance Mutation No. 62, dated 30-5-1967 was set aside. Subsequently, Mutation No. 63 was also cancelled by the Assistant Commissioner/Collector Haroon Abad, vide order, dated 14-1-1974, on account of violation of provisions of Land Reforms Regulations, 1959 (M. L. R No. 64 of 1959). The petitioner agitated the matter before the Member (Revenue), Board of Revenue, Punjab, Camp at Bahawalpur, who vide order, dated 11-3-1980, held that there was no violation of M.L.R. No. 64 of 1959 as Mst. Rabia, had acquired some other land by way of inheritance after the sale of the suit-land.

2. On the other hand, respondents Nos. 1 to 5 also filed a civil suit for declaration of their title over the suit-land on the basis of registered sale deeds, dated 28-6-1979 and 12-3-1980, followed by Mutations Nos. 202 to 205 and 209. They also called in question the validity of order dated 11-3-1980 passed by the Member (Revenue) Board of Revenue in favour of the petitioner.

3. Both the suits were consolidated. The respondent No. 7 Mst. Ghulam Fatima in her written statement to the suit of the petitioner took the position in that she was a minor girl of tender age at the time of attestation of exchange Mutation No. 62, dated 30-5-1967 and that her mother Mst. Rabia, the respondent No. 62, having not been appointed guardian of her property, by any Court, was not competent to alienate the suit-land by way of exchange or otherwise. The Senior Civil Judge, Bahawalnagar framed as many as 28 issues and subsequently added issues Nos. 6-A, 6-B and 6-C on the divergent pleadings of the parties. The trial Court, vide judgment and decree, dated 11-2-1989, dismissed

the suit of the petitioner and decreed the one filed by the respondents Nos. 1 to 5. However, the appeal of the petitioner was allowed and his suit was decreed by the District judge, Bahawalnagar, vide judgment dated 20-4-1989. Therefore, the respondents Nos. 1 to 5 preferred Civil Revision No. 187-D of 1989, which was accepted by a learned Single Judge of the Lahore High Court, Bahawalpur Bench, vide impugned judgment, dated 5-7-2001 and the suit of the petitioner was dismissed.

4. The learned counsel for the legal heirs of late Muhammad Haneef petitioner vehemently argued that Mst. Rabia, the respondent No. 6 being de facto guardian had herself got alienated the suit-land of her daughter Mst. Ghulam Fatima, the respondent No. 7, in her favour by way of exchange which the respondent No. 6 further sold to the petitioner on receipt of the consideration. Therefore, the respondent No. 7 could not be allowed to take a somersault on the plea of minority particularly in order to repudiate the sale of the suit-land to the petitioner. The principle of approbation and reprobation was attracted against the respondents Nos. 6 and 7. It was further argued that the invalidity of transaction of exchange would not ipso facto nullify the transaction of sale of the land duly made by its owner the respondent No. 6. Since the suit-land had already been sold to the petitioner by virtue of sale Mutation No. 63, therefore, the same could not be sold out by the respondent No. 7 to the respondents Nos. 1 to 5. The Member (Revenue), Board of Revenue, by order, dated 11-3-1980, had also upheld the sale Mutation No. 63 in favour of the petitioner. Therefore, the same could not be ignored by the Civil Courts. It was lastly contended that Mst. Rabia was the ostensible owner of the suit-land. Therefore, the transaction of sale of the suit-land by her to the petitioner could not be set aside on the ground that she was not authorized to sell the suit-land. The sale was protected by section 41 of the Transfer of Property Act, 1882.

5. On the other hand, the learned counsel for the respondents supported the impugned judgment of the High Court as well as that of the trial Court and prayed for dismissal of this petition.

6. We have heard the learned counsel for the parties and have also perused the available record with their able assistance. The bare perusal of exchange Mutation No. 62, dated 30-5-1967 passed by the Assistant Collector would make it manifestly clear that Mst. Ghulam Fatima, the respondent No. 7, was a minor at that time and that her mother

Mst. Rabia, the respondent No. 6, got transferred in her favour the suit-land of her minor daughter, by way of exchange. There is nothing on record to show that Mst. Rabia was ever appointed by any competent Court to be the guardian of the property of her minor daughter Mst. Ghulam Fatima. The respondent No. 6, albeit mother of respondent No. 7, was not the natural guardian to deal with property of her minor daughter, the respondent No. 7, under the Mohammadan law. At the most, she was the de facto guardian of the property of her daughter. Therefore, the exchange Mutation No. 62 showing exchange of suit-land between the mother and her minor daughter was illegal.

7. In the Principles of Muhammadan Law by D. F. Mulla, (Pakistan Edition) (1995), it is stated in section 359 that the following persons are entitled in the order mentioned below to be the guardians of the property of a minor:- (1) the father; (2) the executor appointed by the father's will; (3) the father's father; (4) the executor appointed by the will of the father's father. In section 360, it is provided that in default of the legal guardians appointed in section 359, the duty of appointing a guardian for the protection and preservation of the minor's property falls on the Judge as representing the State. As regards a de facto guardian, it is laid down in section 361 a person may neither be a legal guardian (section 359) nor a guardian appointed by the Court (section 360) but may have voluntarily placed himself in charge of the person and property of a mi-nor. Such a person is called de facto guardian. A de facto guardian is merely a custodian of the person and property of the minor. Section 364 leaves no doubt that a de facto guardian (section 361) has no power to transfer any right or interest in the immovable property of the minor.

8. The legal position of alienation of immovable property of a minor by his/her mother, brother, uncle and other close relatives as de facto guardians of the minors, has been examined by superior courts in a number of cases.

In the case of Ahmed Khan and others v. Rasool Bakhsh and others (PLD 1975 SC 311), a sale-deed was executed by a widow mother alien-ating property of her minor son purporting to be his de facto guardian in order to pay off certain outstanding debts of her deceased husband. It was held that such a sale was not merely voidable but void under the Muslim Law and that a de facto guardian of a minor had no power to transfer any immovable property of the minor. In Haji Abdullah Khan and others v. Nisar Muhammad Khan and others (PLD 1965 SC 690), this

Court took the view that it was only a guardian which could enter into a contract on behalf of a minor. Under Mohammadan Law, the guardians of the property of a minor were the father and grand-father or their executors or persons appointed as guardins by their will. Since the uncle of the minor was nowhere found in the list of guardians, therefore, he was not competent to enter into an agreement on behalf of the minor for alienation of property. In the case of Imambandi and others v. Haji Mutsaddi and others (AIR 1918 P. C. 11 = 45 Indian Appeals 73 = 1918 47 Indian Cases 513), the following observations were made by the late Right Hon'ble Syed Amir Ali:—

> Under the Mahomedan Law the mother is entitled only to the custody of the person of her minor child up to a certain age according to the sex of the child. But she is not the natural guardian; the father alone, or, if he be dead, his executor (under the Sunni Law), is the legal guardian. If the father dies without appointing an executor (Wasi) and his father is alive the guardianship of his minor children devolves on their grandfather. Should he also be dead, and have left an executor, it vests in him. In default of these de jure guardians the duty of appointing as guardian for the protection and preservation of the infant's property devolves on the Judge as the representative of the sovereign. When the mother is the father's executrix or is appointed by the Judge as guardian of the minor she has all the powers of a de jure guardian.

In Muhammad Ejaz Hussain and another v. Muhammad Iftikhar Hussain and others (AIR 1932 PC 76), it was held that the mother as a de facto guardian could not enter into reference to make award binding upon the share of minors nor could she enter into family arrangement on their behalf. It was further held that the subsequent appointment of the mother as a guardian would not validate the arbitration agreement. To the same effect are the cases of Mst. Abdara v. Salim Khan and others (PLD 1992 Peshawar 98), Mst. Subhan Bibi and another v. Mst. Musarrat Jabeen and others (PLD 1969 Karachi 563), Musali Khan v. Nazir Ahmed and others (PLD 1952 Peshawar 1), Ziarat Gul v. Mian Khan (PLD 1950 Peshawar 69), Zinda and others v. Mst. Roshna and another (AIR 1928 Lahore 250) and Rang Ilahi and another v. Mahboob Ilahi (AIR 1926 Lahore 170).

9. A somewhat similar view has been taken by the Indian Supreme Court and High Courts in Methiyan Siddqu v. Muhammad Kanju (AIR 1996 SC 1003), Naeem Iqbal v. Noreen Saleem (AIR 2009 SC 757),

Mahboob Sahab v. Ismail (AIR 1995 SC 1205), Mt. Anto v. Mt. Reoti Kuar and others (AIR 1936 Allahabad 337), Muhammad Moizuddin Mia and others v. Nalini Bala Devi (AIR 1937 Calcutta 284), Bhikaji Ramchandra Shimpi v. Ajagarally Sarafally Bohori and others (AIR 1946 Bombay 57), Sk. Md. Zafir v. Sk. Amiruddin and others (AIR 1963 Patna 108) and Ali Muhammad v. Rammviwas and another (AIR 1967 Rajasthan 258).

10. We, therefore, hold that the exchange mutation of the suit-land of the respondent No. 7, by respondent No. 6 in her own favour, acting in her capacity as a de facto guardian being mother of the respondent No. 7 was invalid. Therefore, the petitioner being transferee of the suit-land would not acquire or claim any title of the suit-land. It seems to us that the petitioner late Muhammad Hanif belonged to the same village where the suit-land was situated. He could not be said to be ignorant of the factual and legal position of the exchange Mutation No. 62 which itself clearly showed that the respondent No. 7 was a minor girl and respondent No. 6 to be her de facto guardian. The petitioner purchased the suit-land from respondent No. 6 within a few days thereafter through Mutation No. 63.

11. In the circumstances, the petitioner could not be said to have taken any reasonable care or having acted in good faith to find out whether or not the respondent No. 6 had the power to make the transfer of the suit-land on the strength of exchange Mutation No. 62, dated 30-5-1967. In our view, the petitioner was not entitled to take the protection of section 41 of the Transfer of Property Act. The impugned judgment of the High Court is plainly correct to which no exception can be taken.

12. For the foregoing reasons, we do not find any merit in this petition which is dismissed and leave to appeal is refused accordingly.

Petition dismissed.

45

Sardar Muhammad v. Nasima Bibi

JUDGMENT

MUHAMMAD AFZAL CHEEMA, J.
This petition under Article 98 of the Constitution seeks quashment of two orders, Annexures 'A' and 'C'. The first order dated 23rd May 1962, was passed by the Chairman, Union Committee No. 2, Gujrat, whereby he allowed respondent No. 1 and her daughter a maintenance allowance at the rate of Rs. 70 per mensem, and directed the petitioner to pay to the respondent Rs. 718 in lump sum as arrears of maintenance from 15th July 1961, *i.e.*, the date of the enforcement of the Family Laws Ordinance, to 23rd May 1962, the date of the disposal of the petition. The petitioner was further directed that he should continue to make payment in future at the stipulated rate of Rs. 70 per mensem. The second impugned order dated 12th November 1963, was passed by the Collector Gujrat, dismissing the petitioner's revision as time-barred.

2. The facts giving rise to this Writ Petition may be summarized as follows:

The petitioner Sh. Sardar Muhammad who is a Head Constable in the police department was married to respondent No. 1 on 24th May 1957. The spouses lived happily for about a year and a quarter and a daughter was born to them. According to the respondent's allegations, the petitioner brought her to Gujrat, left her with her parents and never bothered himself about her again. On 7th February 1962, respondent

No. 1 applied to the Chairman Union Committee No. 2, Gujrat under section 9 of the Family Laws Ordinance, in which she claimed dower money to the tune of Rs. 4,000, monthly allowance at the rate of Rs. 80 per mensem in addition to the jewellery, clothes, furniture, etc., which was given as dowry at the time of her marriage. It appears that the Chairman issued three notices to the petitioner under registered cover at his home address in Union Committee No. 3, in Jalalpur Jattan, district Gujrat, followed by two notices sent to him through the Chairman of that Committee. According to the report of the Chairman, Union Committee, Jalalpur Jattan, one notice was affixed on the door of the petitioner's residential house. Finally, a notice was also published in the daily 'Kohistan' in its issue dated the 30th of March 1962. In spite of all this, the petitioner failed to respond and as such an Arbitration Council was constituted without a representative of the petitioner against whom *ex parte* proceedings were taken. As regards the respondent's claim for the dowry and jewellery she was directed to approach a competent Court, but her prayer for maintenance was allowed as stated earlier. This order was unsuccessfully challenged in revision by the petitioner before the Collector on 2nd October 1963, who dismissed his petition on 12th November 1963, as time-barred.

3. The learned counsel for the petitioner has raised the following contentions before us:

(1) That the allegations against the petitioner were those of total neglect and refusal to maintain and as such, section 9 of the Family Laws Ordinance which deals with only cases of inadequate maintenance could not be invoked.

(2) That the first impugned order was illegal inasmuch as the proceedings were taken against the petitioner *ex parte* by an Arbitration Council which was not properly constituted, besides the order appears to have been passed by the Chairman in his personal capacity.

(3) That the date of the application before the Chairman was 7th February 1962, whereas the arrears have been granted from 15th July 1961, which was illegal inasmuch as no decree could be passed for past maintenance under Muhammadan law. Reliance was placed on I L R 6 Cal. 631, Baillie 447 and Hedaya 142.

(4) Lastly, that the impugned order clearly stated that the allowance of Rs. 70 per mensem had been granted both for the petitoner's wife

as well as his minor daughter whereas no provision existed in the Family Laws Ordinance for grant of allowance to a child.

4. In order to appreciate the first contention raised by the learned counsel, the two relevant provisions, *i.e.*, the one under section 488 of the Code of Criminal Procedure, and the other in section 9 of the Family Laws Ordinance will have to be considered in juxtaposition, and are reproduced below:

Section 488 of the Criminal Procedure Code:

488.(1) If any person having sufficient means neglects or refuses to maintain his wife or his legitimate or illegitimate child unable to maintain itself, the District Magistrate, a Sub-Divisional Magistrate or a Magistrate of the first class may, upon proof of such neglect or refusal, order such person to make a monthly allowance for the maintenance of his wife or such child, at such monthly rate, not exceeding four hundred rupees in the whole, as such Magistrate thinks fit, and to pay the same to such person as the Magistrate from time to time directs.

(2) Such allowance shall be payable from the date of order, or if so ordered from the date of the application for maintenance.

Section 9 of the Muslim Family Laws Ordinance, 1961:

9. *Maintenance.*—(1) If any husband fails to maintain his wife adequately, or where there are more wives than one, fails to maintain them equitably, the wife, or all or any of the wives, may in addition to seeking any other legal remedy available apply to the Chairman who shall constitute an Arbitration Council to determine the matter, and the Arbitration Council may issue a certificate specifying the amount which shall be paid as maintenance by the husband.

(2) A husband or wife may, in the prescribed manner, within the prescribed period, and on payment of the prescribed fee, prefer an application for revision of the certificate, in the case of West Pakistan, to the Collector, and in the case of East Pakistan to the Sub-Divisional Officer concerned and his decision shall be final and shall not be called in question in any Court.

(3) Any amount payable under subsection (1) or (2), if not paid in due time, shall be recoverable as arrears of land revenue.

The expression used in section 488, Cr. P. Code is 'neglects or refuses to maintain his wife', whereas sections 9 of the Ordinance says: 'fails to maintain his wife adequately'. The two expressions are differently worded and might seemingly have different connotations, but on a close examination the difference between the two is reduced to nothingness. Considering language used in section 488, if a person agrees or offers to give to his wife an inadequate allowance say Rs. 20, per mensem as against a reasonable amount of Rs. 100, per mensem, his agreement to pay the inadequate sum would certainly amount to a refusal to maintain, as maintenance would mean an adequate, proper and reasonable maintenance, and a person offering an inadequate allowance cannot on that pretext escape or avoid the invocation of section 488, Cr. P. Code. Similarly, although the expression used in section 9 of the Muslim Family Laws Ordinance mentions only the failure on the part of the husband to maintain his wife adequately, a case of total absence of maintenance or refusal to maintain cannot be excluded from the purview of this section as a case of total absence of maintenance does not become identical with one of adequate maintenance. A case of refusal to maintain at all would be a still worse form of inadequate maintenance. In fact, the word 'adequately' has been employed only to emphasise that the maintenance should be proper and reasonable, and that an inadequate maintenance may be considered no maintenance at all. It is a well settled principle of interpretation of statutes that the interpretation should be beneficial and one which should advance the object of legislation and not the one which should lead to its frustration. Keeping in view the background of the Muslim Family Laws Ordinance which was enacted on the recommendations of the Commission on Marriage and Family Laws, giving rise to country-wide controversy, we are in no manner of doubt that the underlying object in making this provision was to furnish a simpler, cheaper and more expedient remedy to neglected wives than the one which was already available to them under section 488 of the Code of Criminal Procedure. It certainly does not appear to have been the intention of the law-giver to classify cases of maintenance into two different categories, *i.e.* those of a total absence of maintenance and those of inadequate maintenance. We have thus no hesitation in saying that a case of inadequate maintenance also includes a case of total absence of maintenance and the new remedy now made available to a neglected wife under the Muslim Family Laws Ordinance is not alternative in nature, so as to be invoked by inadequately maintained wives only, but has been made available in addition to a similar remedy already provided in section 488, Cr. P. Code. The two remedies in our view are available to all cases of lack of maintenance whether adequate or inadequate, and we see no reason to hold that both relate to different kinds and categories of such cases.

Coming now to the second contention, regarding the *ex parte* proceedings and improper constitution of the Arbitration Council, the argument is patently devoid of force as the impugned order clearly shows that every effort was made to serve the petitioner whose substituted service appears to have been properly effected. In his absence there was no question of the nomination of his representatives on the Arbitration Council, and under sub-rule 5(3) of the relevant Rules, proceedings before the Arbitration Council cannot be vitiated on account of the failure of any person to nominate his representative. No doubt, in the impugned order first person has been used by the Chairman giving the impression as if it were an order passed by him in an individual capacity and not by the Arbitration Council as such, but this seems to us to be merely due to inadvertence. The coutention has no force.

5. In the next contention, it is argued by the learned counsel that under the Muhammadan Law, a wife is not entitled to a decree for past maintenance, unless the claim is based on a specific agreement, and as such, the Arbitration Council was not competent to grant allowance to respondent No. I from 15th July 1961, *i. e.*, the date of the enforcement of the Family Laws Ordinance. The point to be determined by us is whether an Arbitration Council can issue certificate in respect of arrears of maintenance, or to put it more precisely from what date could an allowance be allowed to a neglected wife; from the date when the cause of action arises or the date when she makes the application before the Arbitration Council or the date on which the order is made in her favour. Placing reliance on *Abdool Futteh Moulvie* v. *Zabunnessa Khatun* I L R 6 Cal. 631, it was argued by the learned counsel for the petitioner that maintenance could only be paid to respondent No. I from the date of the decree and not even from the date of making application, *i.e.*, 7th February 1962. In this D. B. authority, reliance has been placed on the following observation in Baillie's Digest at page 443:

> When a woman sues her husband for maintenance for a time antecedent to any order of the Judge or mutual agreement of the parties, the Judge is not to decree maintenance for the past.

Reference has also been made to the Hedaya. We have carefully considered this question and it would be advantageous to reproduce the following passage from Baillie which lends further support to this view:

When maintenance has been decreed against a husband at so much the month, or the parties have come to a mutual agreement for so much each month, and several months are allowed to pass without his giving her anything, and she in the meantime raises her maintenance on credit, or disburses it out of her own property, and then either the husband or the wife happens to die, the whole of what has been so raised or disbursed drops, or can no longer be recovered. And in like manner, if he should repudiate her, any arrears of maintenance that may have accumulated after the decree of the Judge are irrecoverable.

6. A similar view has been expressed at page 142 of *Hamilton's* Translation of Hedaya:

Arrears of maintenance not due unless the maintenance have been decreed by the Kazee or the rate of it previously determined on between the parties.—If a length of time should elapse during which the wife has not received any maintenance from her husband, she is not entitled to demand any for that time, except when the Kazee had before determined and decreed it to her, or where she had entered into a composition with the husband respecting it, in either of which cases she is to be decreed her maintenance for the time past, because maintenance is an obligation in the manner of a gratuity, as by a gratuity is understood a thing due without a return, and maintenance is of this description, it not being held (according to our doctors) to be as a return for the matrimonial propriety; and the obligation of it is not valid but through a decree of the Kazee, like a gift, which does not convey a right to possession but through seisin, which establishes possession; but a composition is of equal effect with a decree of the Kazee, in the present case, as the husband by such composition, makes himself responsible, and his power over his own person is superior to that of the Magistrate. This reasoning does not apply to the case of dower, as that is considered to be a return for the use of the wife's person.

7. The proposition cannot be questioned that it is incumbent on a Muslim husband to maintain his wife, subject of course to her loyalty and readiness to perform marital obligations. The following passage from Ameer Ali's Muhammadan Law may be reproduced with advantage in which reliance has been placed on Fatawa-i-Alamgiri and Radd-ul-Muhtar:

If the husband be a minor and the wife an adult, and the incapacity to complete or consummate the contract be solely on his part, she is entitled to maintenance. If the minor has no property, the obligation of maintaining the wife devolves on his father with a right of recovery against him when he is in a position to repay the amount expended on his behalf. When both husband and wife are minors and cohabitation is impossible, there is no liability, for maintenance.

It makes no difference in the husband's liability to maintain the wife, whether he be in health or suffering from illness, whether he be a prisoner of war or undergoing punishment, 'justly or unjustly' for some crime, whether he be absent from home on pleasure or business, or gone on a pilgrimage, and whether he be rich [or] poor. In fact, as long as the status of marriage subsists and the wife is subject to the marital power, she is entitled to maintenance from him. Nor does she lose her right by becoming afflicted with any disease after marriage.

But when she becomes ill before she has taken up her abode in the conjugal domicile there is no obligation on the husband to provide for her maintenance.

8. A woman is also entitled to her maintenance though refusing herself to her husband on the ground that he had not paid her dower. Mulla in his Principles of Muhammadan Law at page 238, 1961 Edn. has observed as follows:

> *Husband's duty to maintain his wife.*
>
> The husband is bound to maintain his wife (unless she is too young for matrimonial intercourse) so long as she is faithful to him and obeys his reasonable orders. But he is not bound to maintain a wife who refuses herself to him, or is otherwise disobedient, unless the refusal or disobedience is justified by non-payment of proper dower, or she leaves the husband's house on account of his cruelty.

Thus, it is abundantly clear that the husband's obligation to maintain his wife commences with the performance of marriage subject to certain conditions. But the authorities cited earlier and relied upon by the learned counsel for the petitioner seem to lay down in unmistakeable terms that in the absence of an agreement between the spouses or a decree by the Kazee, a wife is not entitled to a decree for past maintenance. The reasoning seems to be that if the wife has somehow managed to get along without maintenance and has not cared to approach the Kazee, a decree for past maintenance may be justifiably refused to her. In other words, the argument is that a person who does not care to promptly seek a legal remedy or has somehow managed to do without it may be afforded a relief only when he seeks it and not for an earlier period of time. This position seems to be rather inconsistent with the view expressed in the above cited authorities that normally obligation to maintain a wife starts from the time of marriage.

9. It appears necessary to appreciate the difference between dower for which the word 'ajar' (singular) or 'ajur' (plural) has been used in the Qur'an and maintenance or 'nafaqa'. Marriage in Islam being in the nature of a contract, dower is the consideration agreed between the parties which the husband has to pay to the wife either promptly or subsequently in accordance with the terms of the agreement. On the contrary, maintenance is an obligation which is one of the essential incidents of marriage, liable to suspension or forfeiture under certain circumstance. The two incidents, therefore, proceed on entirely different bases. So far as the payment of dower is concerned once it is stipulated, its payment becomes obligatory on the husband and even if the wife is divorced by the husband before she is touched, he is bound to pay half of the dower money as would be clear from the following verse No. 236 of Sura Albaqra.... It could, of course, be quite different if the wife voluntarily foregoes the dower.

10. As against this, the obligation of the husband to maintain his wife has been derived from an earlier verse No. 232 of the Sura Albaqra which enjoins upon the father of a suckling child to feed and cloth [sic] his wife according to usage.... This finds further support from the famous tradition of the Holy Prophet (peace be upon Him):...The argument in favour of forfeiture of arrears of maintenance for the past seems to have been based on the assumption that maintenance is an obligation in the manner of a gratuity... *i.e.*, an *ex gracia* [sic] grant which is paid by way of sympathy and charity which cannot be claimed as of right. This is clearly laid down in Hamilton's Translation of Hedaya of which the relevant portion has been reproduced earlier in this judgement. In all humility and with the utmost respect we find it difficult to endorse this view as the consensus of opinion as shown from the authorities cited earlier seems to be that the maintenance of a wife is the bounden duty of a husband, irrespective of his minority, illness or imprisonment or the richness of the wife, so much so that the obligation devolves on the father of a minor husband with a right of recovery against him when he is in a position to repay the amount as held by Amir Ali on the authority of 'Fatawa-i-Alamgiri' and Radd-ul-Mukhtar, alluded to earlier. It is thus difficult to say that it is in the nature of an *ex gracia* [sic] payment which cannot be claimed for a past period of time.

11. The question of the forfeiture or suspension of maintenance with the passage of time has been discussed by Ibne Qayyum under a separate heading, at pages 149-50 of the Fourth Volume of his famous work *Zaadul Maad*, 2nd Edition, published in Egypt. It is mentioned therein that it was a disputed question. Imam Abu Hanifa the founder of the Hanafi School of thought was definitely is favour of the forfeiture of arrears of maintenance, while on the contrary, the three other Jurists, namely, Imam Shaafi, Imam Ahmad Hambal and Imam Malik, unanimously held the view that the arrears of maintenance being a just charge could be realized from the husband. It would be advantageous to reproduce the original version in Arabic in this regard....

(People have differed on three versions on the question of forfeiture of maintenance of wives and relatives: whether it stands forfeited or not in both cases or whether maintenance of relations alone forfeits and not that of wives. One view is that it forfeits in both cases with the passage of time and this is the view of Abu Hanifa, and one of the authorities is from Ahmad. The second view is that it does not stand forfeited in either case, if the relative is a child. This is the Shaafi view. The third view is that it is the maintenance of the relative and not of the wife that forfeits. This is the generally accepted view and was held by Shaafi, Ahmad and Malik).

12. The main argument which formed the basis of the Hanafi view is that Hinda, the wife of Abu Sufian, approached the Holy Prophet complaining about her inadequate maintenance by Abu Sufian, when the Prophet allowed her husband so much as was sufficient to maintain her.... From the absence of any reference to past maintenance, it is argued from this that the same stood forfeited. This argument is met by the other school of thought by a counter argument that since Hinda never claimed arrears of maintenance, as such, there was no occasion for the Holy Prophet to allow her a relief which was never prayed for. Another incident on which both sides seem to have relied in support of their respective views is that Caliph Umar wrote to his army officers in distant countries that the Muslim soldiers who were away from their wives should be ordered either to pay maintenance to their wives or divorce them. It was further directed that in the event of divorce they should also remit arrears of past maintenance. It is not disputed that no exception was taken to this directive of Caliph Umar. The argument of the Hanifites is that the payment of arrears was ordered only in case

of divorce and not otherwise. On the contrary it is argued by the other schools of thought that this direction of Caliph Umar amounts to a clear dictum in favour of the validity of past maintenance and only in the event of divorce was it insisted that it should be sent along with the divorce, and as such, it does not necessarily mean that it stands forfeited if the wife is not divorced. Further support is lent to the latter view from the fact that the competency of the Kazee to grant maintenance for the past has also been admitted by the Hanafi school of thought as is clear from the following Heading of the excerpt from Hamilton's Hedaya quoted earlier which reads: '*Arrears of maintenance not due unless have been decreed by the Kazee or....*' Thus the competency of the Courts of today which have stamped into the shoes of the Kazees for the purposes of adjudication of these matters flows as a necessary corollary therefrom. The mere fact that a neglected wife has been hesitant in promptly coming to the Court or has been pursuing alternative remedies out of Court cannot in all fairness be so construed as to deprive her of the right of maintenance from the day when the cause of action accrued to her. The Courts have thus the jurisdiction to grant such maintenance subject of course to considerations of limitation and the relevant circumstances of each case, and we hold accordingly.

13. Even if a different view may be taken from this, and the period intervening between the time of the accrual of the cause of action and of filing the suit is excluded there can be no difference of opinion on the grant of maintenance to a neglected wife from the date she files an application in Court. This position is not inconsistent with the one taken by the Division Bench authority I L R 6 Cal. 631 based on Baillie's Hedaya, and the apparent inconsistency if any is capable of being easily reconciled. In the earlier days when Kazees used to adjudicate upon the rights of the litigants and performed the same functions which the Courts are now called upon to perform today, a complainant could get expeditious relief without loss of time, and it was inconceivable that a petition could linger on for months and years, as it often happened in civil litigation of this kind in this country particularly before the promulgation of the Muslim Family Laws Ordinance. Thus in those days there was no intervening period between the date of the filing of the suit and the date of passing of the decree, and the gap if any would be negligibly small. That promptitude is certainly very difficult, if not impossible to achieve in the complicated legal system and complex

social set up of a much more sophisticated society of today where the Courts have found it difficult to cope with the ever-increasing volume of multifarious litigation.

14. In the instant case, maintenance was allowed to respondent No. I from 15th July 1961, *i.e.*, the date of the promulgation of the Muslim Family Laws Ordinance. It was argued by the learned counsel for the petitioner that by that time, even the relevant rules relating to the constitution of the Arbitration Council and procedure to be followed by it had not yet been framed, which came into existence only on the 20th of July 1961, and as such, the order could not be maintained. Having held in favour of the competency of the Court to grant arrears of maintenance we see no force in this contention, as once the respondent is found entitled to maintenance and it is established that the cause of action accrued to her before the promulgation of the Muslim Family Laws Ordinance, we see nothing wrong with the impugned order granting her arrears with effect from the date of the promulgation irrespective of the fact that the rules were framed sometimes later. In these circumstances, the right would accrue to the respondent from the 15th of July 1961, *i.e.*, the date of the promulgation of the Ordinance, as retrospectivity of the rules of procedure could be inferred from that date. The relevant date in fact, is the date of enforcement and not the date on which the Rules were framed, if it had been the intention of the Legislature to make the Ordinance operative with effect from the date of framing of Rules it would have clearly said so. In the absence of such a proviso, the retrospectivity of the Rules from the date of enforcement of the Ordinance can be safely presumed.

15. The next point, which is the last contention raised by the learned counsel for the petitioner, has obviously lot of force in it, and we are straightway inclined to concede that position. Muslim Family Laws Ordinance contains no provisions for the maintenance of children unlike the one contained in section 488, Cr. P. C. Section 9 in the relevant section which only deals with the maintenance of neglected wives. This does not appear to us to be an omission on the part of the law-giver, as the remedy provided in section 9 is made available in addition to the one already in existence under section 488 of the Cr. P. C. Since the respondent invoked section 9 of the Muslim Family Laws Ordinance, she had obviously no right to any maintenance allowance for her minor daughter. As the stipulated allowance at the rate of Rs. 70 per mensem

was fixed by the Arbitration council for both the respondent as well as her daughter, it cannot be sustained under the law, and as such a patent illegality cannot be allowed to be perpetuated merely because the order was challenged in revision beyond limitation.

16. For the foregoing reasons, we accept the petition, quash the impugned orders and remand the case to the Arbitration Council concerned for deciding afresh according to law the allowance which should be paid to the Respondent's wife. The parties are left to bear their own costs.

SECTION IV

BANGLADESH

Makbul Ali v. *Manwara Begum*

JUDGMENT

ANWARUL HOQUE CHOWDHURY, J. This Rule arises out of an application under section 561A of the Code of Criminal Procedure for quashment of the proceeding in C. R. Case No. 156 of 1985 pending in the Court of the Upazilla Magistrate, Chhatak, District Sunamganj, in so far as it relates to petitioner No. 2 Manwara Begum, the alleged second wife.

2. Facts are that Manwara Begum, the first wife as complainant filed a petition of complaint in the Court of Upazilla Magistrate, Chhatak, District Sunamganj alleging that she is the married wife of Makbul Ali. The marriage was solemnized on 16-4-74 and out of that wedlock a son, now aged about 10 years and a daughter now aged about 7 years were born. Her husband Makbul Ali is a wage earner in London and comes home occasionally. He came home in the month of October, 1984 and the complainant Manwara Begum, the first wife was sent to her father's house for a visit during the last part of October, 1984. On 8-12-84 her husband in violation of the provision of section 6 of the Muslim Family Laws Ordinance took a second wife namely another Manwara Begum, who has been made accused No. 2.

3. Cognizance was taken by the learned Upazilla Magistrate who issued warrant of arrest against Makbul Ali and Manwara Begum under section 6(5) of the said Ordinance and also issued search warrant for recovery of his International Passport. Makbul Ali and Manwara Begum

surrendered before the learned Upazilla Magistrate on 26-6-85 and prayed for bail. Manwara Begum was granted bail but the petitioner No. 1 Makbul Ali remained in hajjat. Subsequently he is also released on bail.

4. It is the case of the husband, petitioner No. I before this Court that in October, 1984 he divorced the complainant, his wife, by a letter written to her. Similar letters were also written to the local Chairman and also to the father of the petitioner No. I to this effect. The petitioner husband has annexed those letters in this petition and also submitted the certified copies of the certificates of the local Chairman.

5. It is stated by the petitioner husband after arrival from London he was advised to divorce the first wife again by Talak which he did and stated that there existed no marital tie with the complainant opposite party, the first wife, at the time when the petitioner No. I married the petitioner No. 2. As such there was no violation of the provision of section 6 of the Muslim Family Laws Ordinance.

6. No one appeared for the petitioner. We have heard the learned Deputy Attorney General for the State who submitted that the proceeding may be quashed in respect of petitioner No. 2 the alleged second wife because she can not be said to have violated the Muslim Family Laws Ordinance. She having no criminal liability the proceeding against her be quashed being an abuse of the process of the court.

7. In the instant case it appears that this Court was pleased to issue a Rule to show cause why the proceeding in C. R. Case No. 156 of 1985 pending in the Court of Upazilla Magistrate Chhatak, District Sunamganj in so far as it relates to the petitioner No. 2 Manwara Begum be not quashed. Hence in this Rule we are concerned only with petitioner No. 2 Manwara Begum.

8. We have examined the provisions of Muslim Family Laws Ordinance. It appears that the Muslim Family Laws Ordinance of 1961 was promulgated to give effect to certain recommendation[s] of the Commission on Marriage and Family Laws. The said Ordinance as it stood originally included a non-obstante clause as spelt out in section 3 of the said Ordinance which provided that the provision of the said Ordinance shall have effect notwithstanding any law, custom or usage. But the said clause was omitted by Act 52 of 1974 for obvious reasons as in Muslim Personal Law polygamy is not totally prohibited.

9. The provisions of Muslim Family Laws Ordinance also did not prohibit polygamy altogether but allowed it under certain conditions.

A man can thus take second wife, in spite of the fact that he has other wife or wives living provided that he took previous permission from the Arbitration Council in writing in which application he should state the reasons for doing so and also should mention whether he has obtained the consent of his existing wife or wives in this regard.

10. The Arbitration Council shall after hearing the petitioner and the representative of his existing wife or wives decide and in deciding whether it is just and proper to allow the application the Council shall have regard to such circumstances such as sterility, physical infirmity, physical unfitness for the conjugal relation, wilful avoidance of a decree for restitution of conjugal rights, infirmity, physical unfitness for the conjugal rights, or insanity on the part of an existing wife as provided under Rule 14 of the Muslim Family Laws Rules. It also provided that the said application for permission be signed by the applicant who wishes to contract another marriage with a woman during the continuance of an existing marriage and shall be accompanied by a fee. Obtaining prior permission before contracting another marriage by a man during continuance of his existing marriage or marriages is thus made obligatory under the Ordinance and it is followed by a punishment for violation of the same.

11. Sub-section (5) of section 6 of the Ordinance provided that:—

Any man who contracts another marriage without permission of the Arbitration Council shall (a) pay immediately the entire amount of dower whether prompt or deferred due to existing wife or wives, which amount, if not so paid, shall be recoverable as arrears of land Revenue, (b) on conviction upon complaint be punishable with simple imprisonment which may extend to one year, or with fine which may extend to Tk. 10,000/- or with both.

12. Under sub-section (5) of section 6 of the Ordinance criminal liability will thus be incurred by the husband being the 'man' referred to in that sub-section and not by the woman whom he marries. The restrictions are put upon man who wishes to contract another marriage with a woman during the continuance of the existing marriage, and nowhere the said Ordinance casts any such duty upon the woman who is married by a man already married either to apply for permission to marry or to suffer any imprisonment for the fault of his [*sic*] husband's taking her as a wife during the continuance of her husband's existing marriage or marriages without permission nor she was obliged to undergo the punishment as an abettor.

13. Penal Statutes need be strictly construed. While interpreting penal provisions in an attempt to find out the person or persons who would come within the mischief of the same no violence need ever be made to the language of the statute either by extending the plain meaning of the specific expression used or by extending the operation of the same by way of an analogy drawn from other laws on somewhat similar field or by taking recourse to the provision of the General Clauses Act but rather care need be taken to see that no one is dragged into it who is not within the express language of the statute.

14. In order to determine as to whether other persons are also within the mischief and thus within the intention of the legislature to be so punished, the language of the statute must authorize the Court to say so. If the legislator [*sic*] remained silent as to others it must be taken to have remained silent consciously.

15. In the instant case the complaint was filed by the previous wife namely, Manwara Begum, daughter of Aftabuddin, both against her husband Mokbul Ali and the second wife, another Manwara Begum under section 6(5) of the Muslim Family Laws Ordinance and prayed that proceedings be drawn against both. On this the learned Magistrate initiated a proceeding against both the husband and the second wife.

16. The proceeding against the second wife, drawn under section 6(5) of the Ordinance is thus, unwarranted. The Court initiated the proceeding against the second wife by taking a wrong view of the law. It thus need be quashed.

In the result, this Rule is made absolute. The instant proceeding pending in the Court below under section 6(5) of the Muslim Family Law Ordinance in so far as it relates to petitioner No. 2 is hereby set aside after being quashed. She is to be released from her bail bonds immediately.

ABDUL BARI SARKER, J. I agree.

50

Hosna Jahan v. Md Shahjahan

JUDGMENT

MUSTAFA KAMAL, J. This petition for leave to appeal by the defendant-petitioner is from the judgment and order dated 2-4-98 passed by a learned Single Bench of the High Court Divison in Civil Order No. 1423 of 1998 dismissing a revisional application summarily.

2. Respondent No. 1 as plaintiff instituted Family Suit No. 27 of 1996 in the Court of the learned Senior Assistant Judge, Chauddagram, Comilla for restitution of conjugal rights impleading his wife i.e. the petitioner, her parents, brother and brother-in-law as defendants contending that after a prolonged love affair between him and the petitioner the plaintiff married the petitioner through a registered Kabinnama on 28-8-95 at a dower of Taka 1 lakh and thereafter started living together as man and wife. The petitioner's parents did not take kindly to the marriage and apprehending an untoward incident the plaintiff had sworn two affidavits, one before a Notary Public on 30-8-95 and other before a Magistrate, 1st Class, Brahmanbaria on 4-10-95 acknowledging the factum of Kabinnama dated 28-8-95. The parents of the plaintiff informed him that they had decided to accept the marriage and also decided to hold a wedding reception at their house and accordingly, defendant No. 5, the brother-in-law of the petitioner, came and took the petitioner to her father's house on 1-11-95. Thereafter defendant Nos 2-5 confined the petitioner and pressured her to disown the marriage and even physically punished her. The plaintiff sent a relation to bring back the petitioner to his house but his relation was roughly treated and was told that the petitioner would never again return to the plaintiff's

house. The plaintiff sent a notice through registered post on 6-12-95 asking his father-in-law, defendant No. 2, to send the petitioner to his house but on receipt of the notice on 12-12-95 defendant No. 2 filed GR Case No. 165 of 1995 with the Chauddagram Police Station alleging false and frivolous accusations against the plaintiff. The plaintiff was thus constrained to file the family suit for restitution of conjugal rights.

3. All the defendants including the petitioner as defendant No. 1 filed a joint written statement denying the assertions and allegations contained in the plaint. They denied the love affair, the marriage and living together as man and wife. They denied the Kabinnama and termed it as collusive and forged. The affidavits are also collusive and forged. The plaintiff is unemployed and lives an immoral and anti-social life whereas the petitioner is a student of Degree College. On 25-9-95 while the petitioner was returning home from College by a rickshaw the plaintiff in the company of his associates gagged her with a scarf and took her to a house near by. She was shifted from place to place. Under intimidation and coercion she was made to sign affidavit and kabinnama. On 26-9-95 the petitioner's father defendant No. 2 made a GD Entry at Chuddagram PS and lodged an FIR on 28-9-95 which gave rise to Nari-O-Shishu Nirjatan Case No. 8 of 1996. The plaintiff having obtained bail from the High Court Division on 26-9-96 filed the false family suit as a counter-blast to wriggle out of the criminal case. The family suit was filed on 30-9-96.

4. After the close of evidence as many as four dates were fixed for hearing arguments but the defendants on this plea or that took adjournment after adjournment. Then the defendant-petitioner filed an application on 8-1-98 for stay of all further proceedings of the family suit till the disposal of the pending Nari-O-Shishu Nirjatan Case. The trial Court rejected the application by order dated 8-1-98. Then the petitioner filed an application on 3-2-98 under section 6 (8) of the Family Court Ordinance, 1985 for rejection of the plaint alleging infringement of the provisions of sections 6 (5) and 6 (7) of the said Ordinance and alleging also that the suit is hit by Article 28 (2) of the Constitution of Bangladesh and prayed for rejection of the plaint.

5. By judgement and order dated 3-2-98 the Family Court rejected the petitioner's application for rejection of the plaint. Thereafter the petitioner preferred Civil Order No. 1423 of 1998 under section 115 (1) CPC in the High Court Division which as already noticed was summarily rejected by a learned Single Judge.

6. Syed Mahmud Hossain, learned Advocate appearing with the leave of the Court for the petitioner, repeated the submissions which were unsuccessfully made before the High Court Division. He has relied on the case of *Nelly Zaman vs Giasuddin Khan, 34 DLR 22*, where it was held that a direction for restitution of conjugal rights is opposed to the principles laid down in Articles 27 and 31 of the Constitution.

7. The High Court Division found that marriage is a contract under Muslim Law. In section 5B of the Family Court Ordinance, restitution of conjugal rights has been specifically mentioned as a subject matter for trial and disposal by a Family Court. This Ordinance came into force on 30-3-85 and the aforesaid case reported in *34 DLR 221* was decided in 1982. The subsequent conscious policy of the legislature will prevail over the earlier decided case, held the learned Single Judge.

8. The better view is that under the High Court Rules a Single Judge has no jurisdiction to decide any question affecting the interpretation of any provision of the Constitution. He has to refer the matter to the learned Chief Justice for deciding a constitutional matter by an appropriate Division or Special Bench, in which the referring Judge may also be a party.

9. The case reported in *34 DLR 221* has therefore been passed without jurisdiction and is not a validly-given decision at all.

10. Syed Mahmud Hossain further relied upon the case of *Sharmin Hossain alias Rupa vs Mizanur Rahman alias Tuhin, 2 BLC 509* in which a learned Single Judge of the High Court Division went a step further and held that the law of restitution of conjugal rights is void while disposing of a Rule arising out of an application under section 24 CPC

11. The High Court Division held that this decision has to give way to section 5B of the Family Court Ordinance simply because a Single Judge exercising jurisdiction under section 115(1) CPC was not invested with the jurisdiction to strike down a piece of legislation which is the absolute and exclusive jurisdiction of a properly constituted court exercising jurisdiction under Article 102 of the Constitution. The reasonings given by the High Court Division appear to us to be proper and sound and we do not find any reason to differ from it. The case reported in *2 BLC 509* has also been decided without jurisdiction and is not a validly given decision at all. Syed Mahmud Hossain did not urge any other point.

The petition is dismissed.

51

Hosne Ara Begum v. Alhaj Md Rezaul Karim

JUDGMENT

KAZI EBADUL HOQUE, J. These two Rules arise from analogous judgment and decrees dated 20-2-1990 passed in Family Court Appeal Nos. 42 and 43 of 1989 by the Additional District Judge, Chittagong setting aside analogous judgment and decrees dated 30-4-1989 passed in Family Court Case No. 1 of 1988 filed by the wife petitioner and Family Court Case No. 1 of 1989 filed by the husband, opposite party No. 1 and remanding both the cases to the Family Court for trial.

2. The petitioner admittedly was married to the opposite party No. 1 on 10.4.82 on the basis of the registered Nika-nama Ext. 1 and in the said Nika-nama dower was Tk. 1,00,001.00 out of which Tk. 40,000.00 was shown as satisfied on account of value of gold ornaments given to the wife. Tk. 50,001.00 was shown as prompt dower and Tk. 10,000.00 was shown as deferred dower and Tk. 1000.00 per month was shown as maintenance of the wife per month.

3. The wife petitioner filed Family Court Case No. 1 of 1988 against her husband opposite party No. 1, her father-in-law, opposite party No. 2 and sister of her husband opposite party No. 3 claiming recovery of dower of Tk. 60,001.00, maintenance of Tk. 14,000.00 for 14 months for being compelled to reside in the house of her father and maintenance of Tk. 14,000.00 each for the two older children and Tk. 3,000.00 for the third child born on 11-7-87 while she had been residing at her father's

residence and also Tk. 80,000.00 as value of the gold ornaments misappropriated by the defendant opposite parties, Tk. 10,000.00 as expenses borne during delivery of the third child, Tk. 15,000.00 as expenses of clothings [*sic*] for her and her children and Tk. 10,000.00 as medical expenses for her and her children while residing at her father's residence.

4. The Family Court after hearing Family Court Suit No. 1 of 1988 filed by the petitioner analogously with Family Court suit No. 1 of 1989 filed by the husband opposite opposite party No. 1 for restitution of conjugal rights decreed the suit filed by the wife petitioner in part allowing claim for prompt dower of Tk. 50,001.00, maintenance of two older children of Tk. 19,600.00 and third child Tk. 3,000.00 and her own maintenance of Tk. 14,000.00 and dismissed the suit filed by the husband opposite party No. 1 for restitution of conjugal rights and also dismissing other claims made by the wife on the ground that Family Court has no jurisdiction to allow the same.

5. The opposite party No. 1 filed Family Court Appeal Nos. 42 and 43 of 1989 against the same and by the impugned analogous judgment both the appeals were allowed and both the suits were remanded to the trial Court for hearing afresh.

6. The only question raised in these two Rules is whether the Court of appeal below was justified in setting aside the judgment and decrees of the Family Court and in remanding the two suits to the Family Court for retrial.

The Family Court on consideration of the pleading and evidence on record came to the conclusions that the plaintiff petitioner was compelled to do domestic work in the house of her husband and she was not even allowed to go to her father's house and as a result a salish was to be held to bring her to her father's house and the plaintiff was subjected to physical and mental toture; that the plaintiff was under apprehension that she might be killed if she returned to her husband's house; that father and sister's husband of the plaintiff are very prosperous businessman and it was not believable that they were responsible for breaking conjugal life of the plaintiff; that there was no proof that the defendant No. 1 ever went to bring his wife and children from her father's house; that there are sufficient grounds on the part of the plaintiff's residing in the house of her father and as such she and her children are entitled to get maintenance from the defendant No. 1; that the defendant No. 1 failed to prove that he repaid the prompt dower of Tk. 50,000.00 by presenting new ornaments after marriage; that admittedly the plaintiff has been residing in her father's house from 5-11-86 with one son and one daughter and another son was born on 11-7-87 at her father's residence; that the plaintiff is entitled to get maintenance at the rate of Tk. 1,000.00 per month for herself and for her two older children at the rate of Tk. 700.00 per month each as maintenance from 5-11-86 and for her third child at the rate of Tk. 500.00 per month as maintenance from 11-7-87 and that the plaintiff was not entitled to recover other claims as the same were beyond the jurisdiction of the Family Court.

7. The Court of appeal below without considering the pleadings in their proper perspective and without discussing and considering the evidences on record and without setting aside specifically the findings of facts arrived at by the trial Court jumped to the conclusion that the plaintiff is not entitled to maintenance by residing in the house of her father on the ground of physical and mental torure and for being compelled to do domestic works avoiding conjugal right of the husband and that she is not also entitled to recover prompt dower as she never demanded the same from her husband; that if the husband pays the prompt dower then there will remain no cause of action for her suit; that by the impugned decrees Family Court gave the plaintiff right to reside in her father's house permanently though the petitioner did not pray for dissolution of her marriage in the face of the suit for restitution of conjugal rights filed by the husband opposite party; that the Family Court could have considered the question of restitution of conjugal right subject to payment of prompt dower and also whether prompt dower at all or any portion thereof was paid; that for physical and mental torture by the husband there is provision for punishment under the provisions of Cruelty to Women (Deterrent-Punishment) Ordinance, 1983.

8. The Court of appeal below it appears was guided by the archaic concept of absolute dominion of the husband over the wife and children when the wife and children were treated as chattels under the Roman law and could be sold by the husband to pay his debt to the creditor and they even could be killed by him. Such absolute right of the husband is known as *patrea* [*sic*] *protestas* under the Roman law. But the learned Court of appeal below forgot that even under the Muslim Law several rights have been recognized to the wife and she can refuse to subject to the conjugal domain of the husband if the husband treats her with

cruelty when it is of such a character as to render it unsafe for the wife to return to her husband and her prompt dower is not paid on demand. Cruelty has been defined by section 2(viii) of the Dissolution of Muslim Marriages Act, 1939. Under the said provision, amongst others, physical assault and making the life of the wife miserable by cruelty of conduct even if such conduct does not amount to physical ill-treatment are cruelty. The trial Court found on consideration of evidence on record that both the families are in business and petitioner's father and sister's husband are prosperous businessmen. As such in the well-to-do family of the parties compelling the wife to do domestic work is also physical and mental torture. The petitioner was subjected to physical and mental torture and she was under apprehension that she might be killed if she returned to her husband's house. Such finding of fact was made by the Family Court on consideration of evidence.

9. Court of appeal below also failed to consider that physical and mental torture to the wife is not only an offence punishable with imprisonment and fine under the said Ordinance but is also a valid ground to refuse restitution of conjugal right to the husband and to allow maintenance to her in terms of the Nika-nama as she was compelled to leave her husband's house on account of his cruelty (See the case of *Amir Md. vs. Mst Bushra* reported in AIR 1956 Raj. 102).

10. The learned Court of appeal below failed to notice that in the reply dated 15-6-87 sent by lawyer of the wife (Ext. 2 Ka) to the lawyer's notice dated 2-5-87 sent by the Advocate of the husband prompt dower as well as maintenance were demanded from the husband and that the petitioner is entitled to maintenance at the rate of Tk. 1,000.00 per month under the terms of the nika-nama dated 10-4-1982 executed by the husband opposite party No. 1 in favour to the wife petitioner and marked as Ext. 1 in the suit. Moreover, filing of the suit by the wife for prompt dower is sufficient demand for the same. The husband without paying the same contested the claim on the plea of satisfaction of the same by presentation of fresh gold ornaments which he failed to establish by evidence. So the Court of appeal below was wholly wrong to set aside the decree for recovery of prompt dower and maintenance and to send back the suit on remand to the Family Court to consider whether prompt dower was paid wholly or in part and whether the husband is prepared to pay prompt dower and whether restitution of conjugal rights could be allowed if not reasons therefor.

11. Apart from the fact that the judgment of the court of appeal below cannot be sustained for not specifically setting aside the findings of the trial Court on considering the evidence on record the Court of appeal below failed to notice that the scheme of the Family Court was quick disposal of a case between the husband and the wife and for that purpose under section 20 of the Family Court Ordinance, 1985 provisions of the Evidence Act and the Code of Civil Procedure (except sections 10 and 11 thereof) have been excluded. Under the provisions of section 17 of the Ordinance the court of appeal below can only decide the appeal and sub-section (6) of section 17 shows that on receipt of the order passed by the District Judge in appeal the Family Court shall modify or amend the judgment, decree or order accordingly and this clearly shows that no power to send the case on remand to the Family Court has been given to the Court of appeal below.

12. Mr. Mozammel Hossain, the learned Advocate for the opposite parties referred to the case of *AKM Ruhul Amin vs. District Judge, Bhola,* reported in 38 DLR (AD) 172 in support of his contention that the court of appeal below has the powers of a civil court under the provisions of the Code of Civil Procedure and as such can send the case on remand after setting aside the judgment of the Family Court. We have noticed in that decision that under rules 47 and 48 of Union Parishad (Election) Rules, 1983 the Election Tribunal shall try the case in accordance with the procedure for trial of suits under the Code of Civil Procedure and the Tribunal shall have all the powers of the Civil Court. But no such corresponding provisions in the Family Courts Ordinance or rules made thereunder. So the *ratio decidendi* of the said decision is not applicable in this case and the decision is clearly distinguishable.

13. In the result the Rules are made absolute and the impugned judgments and decrees of the court of appeal below are set aside and the judgment and decree of the Family Court in Family Court Case No. 1 of 1988 is restored with the modification that the same is decreed only against the husband defendant No. 1 with cost and dismissed against the other defendants and judgment and decree of dismissal of Family Court case No. 1 of 1989 is also restored with costs.

FAZLE HUSSAIN MOHAMMAD HABIBUR RAHMAN, J. I agree....

52

Gul Newaz Khan v. Maherunnesa Begum

JUDGMENT

This second appeal at the instance of the defendant is from the decision of the subordinate Judge, Second Court, Comilla in Title Appeal No. 350 of 1959, affirming that of the Munsif, 3rd Court Comilla in Title Suit No. 25 of 1959.

2. The defendant married the plaintiff, respondent according to Muslim law on 4-11-55, on a dower of Rs. 5,000. He executed a *kabinnama* by which he delegated to the plaintiff the right to repudiate the marriage on the happening of any of the contingencies mentioned therein, including non-payment of prompt dower on her demand and non-maintenance. After the marriage, the plaintiff stayed in her father's house where the defendant used to go at times. But since 31-3-56, the defendant did not take care of the plaintiff and give her any maintenance. Nor did he give her prompt dower though demanded; rather the defendant treated her with cruelty and neglect. Thereupon the plaintiff, in the exercise of the right delegated to her in the *kabinnama* (*talak-i-tafweez*) repudiated the marriage on 30-6-58, and got a *talaknama* registered in token thereof.

3. The defendenat contested the suit. He denied the plaintiff's allegation about non-payment of prompt dower and maintenance and the alleged cruelty and neglect on his part. According to him, the plaintiff did not ever make any demand for prompt dower and maintenance from him. But he, of his own accord, paid her Rs. 3,200 towards prompt

dower and maintenance on different dates. Accordingly, the defendant contended that the right to exercise *talak-i-tafweez* did not really accrue to her and as such, the marriage was not dissolved according to law. His further contention was that the suit was an outcome of a grudge of the plaintiff's brother against him.

4. The trial Court held, amongst others, that the defendant did not pay the plaintiff the prompt dower in spite of her demand for it and that he did not give her maintenance either. In view of this finding, the trial Court, having regard to the plaintiff's delegated power to repudiate the marriage, conferred by the *kabinnama* Exh. 1 and the actual repudiation of the marriage on 30-6-58, by her in the exercise of that power as per *talaknama* Exh. 2, decreed the suit declaring that the marriage between the parties was legally dissolved by the due exercise of *talak-i-tafweez* by the plaintiff.

5. The defendant appealed against the judgment and decree of the trial Court. The lower appellate Court agreed with the trial Court that the defendant failed to pay the plaintiff's prompt dower in spite of her demand, but took a different view with regard to maintenance on the ground that she had been voluntarily living in her father's house from the time of her marriage when she was studying in a local school. However, the lower appellate Court held that non-payment of the prompt dower in spite of the plaintiff's demand was a valid ground for repudiating the marriage in exercise of the power delegated to her in the *kabinnama*. Accordingly, the lower appellate Court upheld the judgment and decree of the trial Court. The defendant has appealed to this Court against the decision of the lower appellate Court.

6. Mr. Md. Fazlul Karim, learned advocate for the appellant, has pressed only one point in this appeal, namely. Ground No. 1 in the memorandum of appeal which runs thus: 'For that the Court of appeal below erred grievously in law in holding that non-payment of prompt dower simpliciter, specially after consummation of marriage, can be a valid reason for dissolution of a Muslim marriage.'

7. The *kabinnama*, Exh. 1, is admitted. In clause (5) of the *kabinnama*, the defendant delegated to the plaintiff the power to repudiate the marriage in the event of happening of any of the contingencies mentioned therein. Non-payment of prompt dower on demand and non-maintenance are two of the several contingencies mentioned in the said clause. After careful and elaborate analysis of the evidence on record, both the

Courts below came to a concurrent finding that the plaintiff did, in fact, make a demand of prompt dower and that the dower so demanded was not paid by the defendant. Thus, one of the contingencies mentioned in clause (5) of the *kabinnama*, according to the concurrent finding on the Courts below, stood satisfied in this case. The learned advocate for the appellant, however, contends that once the marriage is consummated, the mere non-payment of promt dower cannot, under the Muslim law, be a valid ground for repudiating the marriage by the wife in the exercise of her deligated power. I have been unable to lay my hands on the opinion of the Muslim jurists on this point. Two reported decisions relating to this point, have, however, been cited in this case on behalf of the plaintiff respondent. In the case of *Hamidulla v. Faizunnissa* ILR 8 Cal. 327, it was held that non-payment of prompt dower on demand is a valid condition for the exercise of the delegated power of divorce by the wife. This decision was followed by this Court in the case of *Abdul Sukur v. Sm. Machuma Khatun* 7 DLR 451. In the latter case, it was held that the wife can validly exercise the delegated power on the failure of the husband to pay the prompt dower on demand. Dower is the essential condition of Muslim marriage. Judicial opinions appear to be unanimous that a wife may live separately from the husband in case of non-payment of prompt dower on demand and claim maintenance from the husband while living separately from him. To provide for maintenance of the wife by the husband is enjoined by the Muslim Law, but to pay prompt dower on demand is all the more enjoined by that Law, the same being an essential condition of a contract of Muslim marriage. Under the Dissolution of Muslim Marriages Act, wilful non-payment of maintenance by the husband for two years gives a right to the wife to seek a dissolution of the marriage. When non-maintenance of the wife is a valid ground for the dissolution of a Muslim marriage, there is no reason why the marriage cannot be lawfully repudiated by the wife in the exercise of the delegated power in case of non-payment of prompt dower on demand. The exercise of such power by the wife of the husband's failure to pay the prompt dower on demand does not appear to be against the public policy or the principles of Muslim Law. Thus the point raised in this appeal has no merit. As regards actual repudiation of the marriage by the plaintiff in the exercise of her delegated power, the evidence of the plaintiff and the *talaknama* Exh. 2 are sufficient to establish it.

8. The appeal, therefore, fails and is dismissed. But, having regard to the point of law raised in this case, I do not saddle the appellant with any costs.

53

Hasina Ahmed v. *Syed Abul Fazal*

JUDGMENT

This second appeal at the instance of a plaintiff-wife is directed against a judgment of the lower appellate Court affirming a judgment of the Trial Court dismissing the plaintiff's suit for dissolution of her marriage with the defendant.

2. The present appellant was admittedly married with the respondent in November, 1963 and after about 9 years the plaintiff instituted a suit for dissolution of her marriage with the defendant in May, 1972 on various ground including both physical and mental ill-treatment with the wife, failure to maintain the wife, sale of wife's property and ornaments, false allegations against wife's moral character and husband's immoral conduct and association with bad women etc. All these grounds were specifically alleged by the wife and denied by the husband concerned and on that account evidences were led with by the wife and husband. In support of the plaintiff five witnesses including the plaintiff herself appeared and deposed in this suit. On consideration of the evidence on record both the Courts below came to a finding that no ground was established which could entitle the plaintiff-wife to a divorce against her husband. As against the aforesaid concurrent judgment in

the negative the wife has preferred this second appeal which is presently under disposal.

3. Of all the grounds specifically raised by the plaintiff-wife there is one ground over which there is no dispute and is admitted by both the plaintiff-wife and the defendant-husband. The wife in order to obtain divorce against her husband alleged, as one of the grounds, that her husband used to suspect her as having illicit connection with one of her cousins Borhanuddin and this suspicion had caused a mental agony on the part of the wife which had compelled her to institute this suit for the dissolution of her marriage with the defendant. The allegation about the husband's suspicion, about her involvements with her cousin Borhanuddin was not only pleaded in the plaint but was also stated by the wife in her deposition as P. W. I. The defendant husband not only did not dispute this allegation of the plaintiff but admitted the same position by alleging and reiterating the same allegation against his wife in his written statement and also in his deposition before the Court as defendant No. 1. Thus the undisputed and admitted position in fact is that the husband is alleging that his wife has illicit connection with her cousin Borhanuddin who was responsible for the institution of the present suit. On the face of it the wife's allegation against her husband, about the husband's allegation against his wife that she has an illicit connection with her cousin Borhanuddin has been fully established not only by admission in the pleadings but also in the deposition of the witnesses concerned.

4. In the aforesaid facts and circumstances of the case where the husband has been found to have made consistent allegation about his wife's involvement with her cousin and the same allegation being repeated by the husband to his wife concerned definitely is a 'cruelty' within the meaning of sub-clause (a) of Clause VIII of section 2 of the Dissolution of Muslim Marriages Act No. VIII of 1939. It provides that a woman married under Muslim law shall be entitled to obtain a decree for the dissolution of her marriage if the husband treats her with 'cruelty' that is to say makes her life miserable by 'cruelty' of conduct even if such conduct does not amount to physical ill-treatment. In this connection it may be mentioned that under the Muslim Personal Law in the Principle of 'Lian' or Imprecation, the wife is entitled to sue for a divorce on the ground that her husband has falsely charged her with adultery. Having considered the aforesaid facts and circumstances of the case it appears

that both the Courts below never attempted to adjudicate the present case on the basis of the admitted position in fact with regard to the husband's allegation and charge against his wife about her complicity and illicit connection with her cousin. That allegation was made by the husband against his wife consistently for a long time is borne out by the husband's statement in the written statement and the deposition. That this allegation by itself constitutes 'cruelty' within the meaning of sub-clause (a) of clause VIII of Section 2 of the Dissolution of Muslim Marriages Act is not at all in dispute. In this connection reference may be made to a Division Bench decision of the erstwhile High Court reported in P.L.D. 1963, Dacca 947, wherein their Lordships held that the imputation by the husband as to the fidelity of a wife will always give the wife a right to have a decree for divorce and that the allegation by the husband as to the chastity of a woman cuts to the heart and this itself gives a bonafide cause for obtaining a divorce at the instance of the wife against her husband.

5. In the present case it further appears that the wife while instituting the suit for dissolution of her marriage with the defendant explicitly expressed her willingness to part with her dower money amounting to Tk. 14,000/ in consideration of a divorce with her husband. It is quite clear from the plaint case and the deposition of P. W. I. that the wife is willing to surrender her claims against the husband in consideration of her release from marriage bond itself. The appellant has specifically filed an affidavit before this Court to that effect. It is a well-known principle in Muslim Personal Law that apart from the unilateral right of 'Talak' at the instance of the husband the wife can claim divorce by consent or agreement with her husband which is known as 'Khula' in Muslim Personal Law. This is of course as against a consideration and that consideration includes the wife's surrender of the dower money and other claims against her husband. This divorce by way of 'Khula' if not obtained with the consent and agreement between the parties, can, by analogy, be obtained from a Court of law before whom the case of dissolution of marriage is pending. In this connection refer-ence may be made to a Full Bench decision of the Supreme Court of Pakistan reported in P. L. D. 1967 (S.C.) 97 wherein there Lordships have elaborately discussed the Muslim Personal Law on divorce with reference to a 'Khula'. The question that fell for consideration in that case was whether a wife is entitled as of right to claim 'Khula' despite

the unwillingness of the husband to release her from the matrimonial tie. Their Lordships of the Supreme Court concurred in their opinion that under Muslim Law the wife is entitled to 'Khula' as of right, if she satisfies the Court that there was no possibility of their living together consistently with their conjugal duties and obligations and further if she satisfies the conscience of the Court that it will otherwise mean forcing her into a hateful union. This judgment of the Supreme Court is a classic and monumental example where the principle of Muslim Law on divorce by consent by way of 'Khula' has by analogy been made a rule of the court, so that an unwilling wife is not forced to live with her husband against her expressed will. In the present case the plaintiff-wife has all through alleged and claimed that she cannot live with her husband and on that account prayed for a divorce. For the reason stated hereinbefore, in support of which the aforesaid judicial decisions have been referred to, it is quite clear that the plaintiff has successfully established her right to obtain a divorce as against the defendant. The judgments of the Courts below did not at all consider the present case with due consideration as to the actual reasons upon which the plaintiff's suit for dissolution of the marriage with the defendant was based and for that reason erred in law for the grounds stated hereinbefore.

6. Before concluding it must be observed that the Courts while adjudicating on family dispute and administering personal law shall take into account not only the factual and the legal position and questions involved in a particular case but also consider the social dynamics when concept of law is changing in a changing society. Previously decades before where a wife's claim for a divorce could be resisted for well-established reasons it cannot be resisted for the salf-same reason because of the very basic fact that with the changing society women are coming of their own and their independence of mind and will must be respected while considering the legal and contractual obligation in marriage between man and woman as such. The decision reported in P. L. D. 1967 (S.C.) 97 has merely tried to extend the principle of 'Ijtehad' in bringing about the change in the concept of the Muslim Personal Law with regard to their application in a changing society. It would be beneficial to society as such if the Court concerned takes the same attitude to interpret the Muslim Law as has been done in the aforesaid decision of the Supreme Court of Pakistan.

7. In the aforesaid fact and circumstances of the case and for the reasons stated hereinbefore the judgments of the Courts below are set aside. The plaintiff's suit for her dissolution of marriage with the defendant is decreed. The plaintiff's marriage with the defendant is hereby dissolved. This appeal is accordingly allowed with costs.

The respondent's prayer for leave to appeal under Clause 15 of the Letters Patent is refused.

55

Amena Khatun v. *Sherajuddin Sardar*

JUDGMENT

This appeal arises out of a suit for dissolution of marriage. Plaintiff's case is that she was a minor when her parents died leaving behind herself and a younger brother as his [*sic*] heirs. Defendant who is her cousin, used to look after the properties left by her parents. She is said to be a good-looking woman and it appears that she inherited one-third share of 70 bighas of land together with a house left by her father. Considering the social status of the parties of the suit, plaintiff's inheritance was by no means inconsiderable. Allured by her properties and her physical beauty, defendant married her when she was about 16 years of age, according to Kabinnama, and much younger, according to her. Defendant is much older than her and is not at all good-looking. It is her case that in accordance with the terms of Kabinnama, defendant undertook to stay in her house (viz., the house of plaintiff's father) and to look after her properties. It is a kind of undertaking, which, in this country, for want of better expression, is known as 'domesticated son-in-law'. Such an arrangement is stated to be the primary object of what appears to be an unequal match. Defendant also undertook to maintain her and to give her a sum of Rs. 12 per month for her maintenance in case he lived in some other house, which is not plaintiff's residence. The marriage took place in the year 1353 B.S. corresponding to February, 1947. Defendant was already married at the time when the aforesaid marriage with plaintiff took place. She has alleged that in Jaistha, 1360 B.S. that is near about 1953, defendant left her house and has ever since then been living separately with his first wife. He has several children by the latter and none by her. She has also alleged that defendant has neither given her any maintenance nor has he ever lived with her subsequent to Jaistha, 1360 B.S. She has made allegations of beating and ill-treatment against the defendant. On the aforesaid grounds she has asked for dissolution of the marriage.

2. The defence is a traverse of plaintiff's case although the marriage with plaintiff is admitted. It is contended by defendant that one Quader Baksh has enticed away plaintiff and has induced her to bring this suit. It further transpires that plaintiff (defendant) instituted a criminal case against the aforesaid Quader Baksh for enticing away his wife, namely, plaintiff. The other averments in the pleadings filed by parties need not be repeated here.

3. The points for decision in this suit have been properly enumerated by the Trial Court as follows: '1. Negligence and failure to maintain her for 2 years. 2. Failure to perform marital obligations for more than 3 (three) year[s]. 3. Cruelty. 4. Unequal treatment to her and her co-wife. 5. Violations of the conditions of the marriage contract. 6. Non-payment of the dower.'

4. On a consideration of the evidence led by the parties learned Munsif, who tried the suit, decreed the same and directed that the marriage between plaintiff and defendant be dissolved subject to payment of a sum of Rs. 200/- by plaintiff to defendant. It was also directed that plaintiff be debarred from realizing her dower or any part thereof from defendant.

5. Against the judgment and decree passed by learned Munsif, defendant preferred an appeal which was heard and disposed of by the District Judge of Rajshahi. Learned District Judge allowed the appeal

and dismissed the suit reversing the judgment and decree passed by the Trial Court. Hence this appeal.

6. At the hearing of this appeal I was taken through the judgments pronounced by the Courts below. The Trial Court, in a somewhat lengthy judgment, has fully dealt with the material points in this case and has recorded finding which, if allowed to stand, would furnish good reasons for passing the decree that was obtained by plaintiff in that Court. But, the judgment pronounced by the Appellate Court below can hardly be described as a proper judgment. The learned District Judge has hardly assessed the evidence in an appropriate manner. Furthermore, he has not adverted to some vital points which have been discussed and decided by the Trial Court. The learned District Judge did not discuss a number of material issues which arise in this suit. In answer to plaintiff's case that the husband has violated the terms of the Kabinnama by living separately from her, he has, without giving a decision on the point, merely observed that the husband lives in a separate home appertaining to the same homestead. He then proceeded to observe: 'So, prima facie, it appears that the plaintiff has started her [*sic*] with a malafide intention and attempted to mislead the Court.' The learned District Judge seems to have been misled by his own misconception of plaintiff's case. It is evident from what I have observed that the judgment and decree passed by him must be set aside on the ground, among various other grounds, that he has not properly applied his mind to the facts and circumstances of this case.

7. That being the position, the course which is open to me is to either send back the case to him for re-hearing the appeal or, in the alternative, to decide the suit in this Court, having regard to the facts and circumstances of this case.

8. Learned Advocate for appellant has urged that this is a case where I should exercise the jurisdictions vested in this Court, to decide the suit on the evidence already on record, if such evidence can lead to a decision. I think that this submission of learned Advocate for the appellant is consonant to reason and justice. The points in issue are simple and more than sufficient evidence has been led by parties. The suit can be properly and effectively decided by me and I propose to do so.

9. This case, inter alia, attracts the provisions of the Dissolution of Muslim Marriages Act, 1939. The relevant provisions of section 2 of the said Act may be quoted thus:

2. A woman married under Muslim Law shall be entitled to obtain a decree for the dissolution of her marriage on any one or more of the following grounds namely ... (ii) that the husband has neglected or has failed to provide for her maintenance for a period of two years: ... (iv) that the husband has failed to perform, without reasonable cause, his marital obligations for a period of three years; ... (viii) that the husband treats her with cruelty, that is to say,—

(a) habitually assaults her or makes her life miserable by cruelty of conduct even if such conduct does not amount to physical ill-treatment, or ... (f) if he has more wives than one, does not treat her equitably in accordance with the injunctions of the Quoran: (ix) on any other ground which is recognized as valid for the dissolution of marriages under Muslim Law.

10. From the evidence which has been led by the parties it must be accepted that the marriage between plaintiff and defendant took place on the aforesaid date and, in the circumstance alleged by plaintiff. The aforesaid Kabinnama appears to be genuine. The Trial Court accepted the same as genuine and I have no hesitation to do so. No attempt has been made by defendant to show that the Kabinnama is not genuine. As a matter of fact, reliance has been placed on the aforesaid Kabinnama by both parties appearing before me in support of their respective cases. In accordance with the terms of the Kabinnama defendant had undertaken to live in the house of plaintiff as 'Ghar Jamai'. This fact strengthens my belief in the case made out by plaintiff that defendant entered into a marriage of convenience with her at a time when he was already married to another woman. Plaintiff's positive evidence is that her husband left her to live separately in Jaistaha, 1360 B.S., i.e. about seven years after the said marriage. She is corroborated by the rest of the witnesses examined on her behalf. Defendant has not been able to controvert this but has said that the place where he lives with his first wife is a part of the same homestead. This seems to be the gravamen of the contention of the defendant, a contention which has impressed the Appellate Court below. The question is that even if a husband lives separately with another wife in the same homestead but in a separate home he has violated the undertaking given by him in the Kabinnama, namely, to live in the household of plaintiff's father (i. e., the household of plaintiff). The suit was instituted in the year 1960 when defendant had already been living continuously away from his wife in a separate household with another wife for over a period of seven years. This is

a fact which stares one in the face. It is also clear from the evidence, which has been led by parties that defendant has failed to pay the plaintiff a sum of Rs. 12 per month for this period, namely, approximately between 1953 and 1960, when the suit was instituted. I have no hesitation in accepting this evidence.

11. Pausing here for a moment, it must be found that defendant has failed to provide for plaintiff's maintenance for a period of more than two years, in fact, for a period of about 15 years up till today. I had asked learned advocate for respondent, namely, plaintiff's husband, whether defendant has up till today paid her a single pice by way of her maintenance. The answer was that the husband was entitled to refuse such maintenance having regard to the fact that defendant had reasons to suspect a questionable liaison between her and another person. The appellate Court below seems to have taken the view that the husband was absolved of the duty to maintain her because the wife was a woman of means. I do not think that legally such a proposition is tenable. The competence of the wife does not absolve the husband of a duty to maintain her. Having considered the evidence led by the parties I am led to the conclusion that, on an assessment of the evidence and circumstances in this case, it must be held that defendant had failed to maintain his wife for more than two years contrary to the specific stipulation in the Kabinnama.

12. It would next be seen that there is no escape from inference that relationship between the husband and wife has been, unfortunately, very unhappy for about 15 years at the time when I heard the appeal. Without apportioning blame to any party it is evident that the husband has failed to perform his marital obligations for more than three years. Defendant's contention is that he has good reasons to suspect his wife's fidelity, but it is not his case that he has performed his marital obligations ever since 1960 when the suit was filed.

13. It is also clear that defendant was unable to offer equal treatment to plaintiff in relation to the other wife of defendant. The case that has been made out by defendant amounts to saying that plaintiff can only blame herself for such inequality of treatment.

14. On behalf of the plaintiff evidence has been led that husband used to beat her from time to time. Having regard to the facts and circumstances of this case, there is hardly any good reason to disbelieve the corroborative evidence which has been led on behalf of the plaintiff to

the extent that, at least, occasionally the husband has exercised violence upon her.

15. From what has been stated above, it is clear that for about 15 years up till today the relationship between plaintiff and defendant has been anything but happy. For long 15 years there has not been even the semblance of a marital relationship between the parties. The marriage between the parties was shipwrecked at an early stage and since then there has been a perpetual state of hostility and antagonism between the parties. From the allegations, which have been made by parties, it appears that hardly any feeling of love and affection existed between the parties. It is evident from what has been discussed above that it is almost impossible to weigh the evidence of the parties in the balance. The truth probably lies somewhere in the middle. It appears that, on the whole, the scale turns a little in favour of the plaintiff.

16. In this background, I may revert to the finding arrived at by me to the effect that the husband has failed to maintain her for more than two years in violation of the marriage contract, namely the Kabinnama. In these circumstances, it must be held that plaintiff has succeeded in establishing her right to claim a dissolution of marriage in accordance with the terms of section 2 of the Dissolution of Muslim Marriages Act, 1939.

17. The husband has been living with another wife for about 20 years. The plaintiff has hardly known a married life. No marital relationship exists for a long time. There cannot be any equality of treatment between the co-wives in the face of the strained relationship.

18. There are various other considerations upon which the aforesaid marriage can be dissolved. For instance, the relationship between the parties as made out by them, brings it within the ratio of the decision of a Full Bench of the West Pakistan High Court in the case of *Mst. Balquis Fatima vs. Najm-ul-Ikram Qureshi* 1959 11 DLR 93 (W. P.). The aforesaid decision has overruled the case of *Mst Umar Bibi vs. Muhammad Din* A I R 1943 Lahore 51, and that of *Mst Saeeda Khanam vs. Muhammad Samir* 1952 4 D L R Lahore 134 (Full Bench). I do not think it necessary for me to express any final opinion on the points mooted and decided in the case of *Mst. Balqis Fatima vs. Najm-ul-Ikram Qureshi* D L R 93 (W. P.).

19. I would prefer to base my decision on the ground that defendant has failed to provide for plaintiff's maintenance for a period of two years in breach of the terms of the Kabinnama. The plain fact is that

on a total assessment of the relationship between the parties it would amount to cruelty to the plaintiff to continue the marital tie. Another important factor in this case is that if the marital tie is not dissolved it would be impossible for the wife to live within the limits of the shariat. Islam does not ignore the propensities of human nature.

20. I also hold that in the situation with which one is confronted in this case the order that could be given is one that has been passed by the learned Munsif. The order strikes a via media and a division of the blame between the parties. The question is: can the Dissolution of Muslim Marriages Act, 1939 be applied to the facts of this case. I have found that it does apply.

In the result, I allow the appeal and set aside the judgment and decree passed by the Appellate Court below and affirm those passed by the Trial Court without any order as to costs of this case.

56

Abdul Aziz v. *Rezia Khatoon*

JUDGMENT

This Rule was obtained by Moulvi Abdul Aziz, opposite-party in an application under section 488 Cr. P. C. filed on 17.9.66 by one Musammat Rezia Khatoon. Her case in short was that Moulvi Abdul Aziz who had sufficient means, being a Nayeb Marriage Registrar, married her some 6 or 7 years before the application, and that in January 1966 she was driven out by Moulvi Abdul Aziz who took a second wife. She, therefore, claimed maintenance at the rate of Rs. 60/- per mensem.

2. The petitioner, Moulvi Abdul Aziz, did not dispute the marriage. He did not also dispute that he was the Nayeb Marriage Registrar of Sutrapur in Dacca city and that as such he was in a position to pay maintenance, as claimed by Rezia Khatoon. Briefly stated, his plea was that Rezia Khatoon was a disobedient and impertinent woman of loose morals, and that on 18.1.66 as the situation became absolutely intolerable he divorced her. His further case was that on 19.1.66 he duly served notice of the divorce on the Chairman in terms of sub-section (1) of section 7 of Muslim Family Laws Ordinance, 1961 (hereinafter called the Ordinance) and supplied a copy thereof to Rezia Khatoon. It was contended on his behalf before the learned Magistrate that the divorce being of the earlier date the application under section 488 Cr. P. C., which was filed on 17.9.66, was not maintainable.

3. Rezia Khatoon, the applicant, examined herself and two other witnesses. Moulvi Abdul Aziz did not examine any witness other than himself. He produced two documents that were marked as Exts. A and B.

4. Ext. B is a petition of complaint in Bengali filed by Rezia Khatoon in a different case. It was contended on behalf of Moulvi abdul Aziz before the learned Magistrate that the contents of Ext. B would show that in it Rezia Khatoon clearly admitted that she was divorced by him. This contention was not accepted. I have myself perused that document. The word used there is 'parityag' which can only mean desertion, and not divorce, as construed also by the learned additional Sessions Judge who declined to refer the case to this Court under section 438 Cr. P. C. The other document, namely, Ext. A, which is dated 23.2.67, purports to be a certificate under the hand of the Chairman acknowledging receipt of a notice of divorce. The learned Magistrate observed that the contents of this document were not proved by examining the maker thereof, nor the alleged original notice was called for. The learned Magistrate also observed that though, Moulvi Abdul Aziz's case was that Ext. A was granted by the Chairman against a notice of divorce alleged to have been served on the Chairman on 19.1.67, Ext. A bears the date 23.2.67. He could not, therefore, place any reliance on this document; nor could he, in the absence of any corroboration accept Moulvi Abdul Aziz's case that a copy of such a notice was supplied to Rezia Khatoon who denied having received any such notice. There being no other evidence on record in support of Moulvi Abdul Aziz's claim that he had divorced Rezia Khatoon, the learned Magistrate could not also arrive at any firm

conclusion on this issue upon the bare statement of Moulvi Abdul Aziz. The learned Magistrate was, however, of the opinion that even if the story of divorce were true it was not legally effective, since it was not proved that an Arbitration Council was constituted in terms of sub-section (4) of section 7 of the Ordinance and further that it took necessary steps for reconciliation of the parties. Accordingly, the learned Magistrate rejected Moulvi Abdul Aziz's contention that Rezia Khatoon was not entitled to maintenance. He allowed the application under section 488 Cr. P. C. and directed Moulvi Abdul Aziz to pay maintenance to Rezia Khatoon at the rate of Rs. 60/- per mensem with effect from 17.9.66, the date of the application.

5. The learned advocate appearing in support of the Rule, which is at the instance of Moulvi Abdul Aziz, contended before me that Ext. A, the certificate granted by the Chairman, conclusively proved that notice of the divorce was served on the Chairman on 19.1.66. The learned advocate contended further that the bare statement of Moulvi Abdul Aziz that he divorced Rezia Khatoon was sufficient proof of divorce, if not on 18.1.66 at least on the date that he made the statement on oath before the learned Magistrate. He also contended that the learned Magistrate's view that a divorce would not be legally effective unless an Arbitration Council constituted in terms of sub-section (4) of section 7 of the Ordinance made an attempt at reconciliation was erroneous.

6. On behalf of Rezia Khatoon it was contended that Ext. A which is a mere certificate issued by the Chairman furnished no proof of service of notice on the Chairman. Her learned Advocate contended further that in the absence of proof of the actual words used in pronouncing the alleged *talaq*, the learned Magistrate was right in refusing to act upon Moulvi Abdul Aziz's bare statement in court that he divorced Rezia Khatoon. He also contended that unless an Arbitration Council was constituted and such a council failed to bring about a reconciliation between the parties, a divorce could not be legally effective in view of the provisions of section 7 of the Ordinance.

7. Mr. Razzaq Rahman who appeared at my request took me through the text of the Ordinance, including section 7 thereof which consists of six sub-sections. It is sub-sections (1) and (3), he contended, that are relevant for the disposal of this Rule, and not sub-section (4) which weighed so much with the learned Magistrate. For a proper

appreciation of Razzaq Rahman's submissions it is necessary to refer to the contents of sub-sections (1), (3) and (4) of section 7. These three sub-sections are reproduced below:-

> 7. *Talaq.* (1) Any man who wishes to divorce his wife shall, as soon as may be after the pronouncement of *talaq* in any form whatsoever, give the Chairman notice in writing of his having done so, and shall supply a copy thereof to the wife....
>
> (3) Save as provided in subsection (5), a *talaq* unless revoked earlier, expressly or otherwise, shall not be effective until the expiration of ninety days from the day on which notice under sub-section (1) is delivered to the Chairman.
>
> (4) Within thirty days of the receipt of notice under subsection (1), the Chairman shall constitute an Arbitration Council for the purpose of bringing about a reconciliation between the parties, and the Arbitration Council shall take all steps necessary to bring about such reconciliation.

8. Sub-section (5) of which reference has been made in sub-section (3) is not relevant for the purpose of this Rule. Sub-section (5) fixes the period on the expiry of which *talaq* would be effective, if the wife be pregnant at the time *talaq* is pronounced. It was not the case of Rezia Khatoon that she was pregnant at the time of the alleged divorce. Mr. Razzaq Rahman pointed out that sub-section (4) of section 7, which makes it obligatory on the Chairman to constitute an Arbitration Council and directs that Council to take all steps necessary to bring about reconciliation between the parties, does not say what would be the consequence if the Chairman does not appoint an Arbitration Council or if such a Council, duly constituted, fails to take such steps as it is required to take. On the other hand, Mr. Razzaq Rahman further pointed out, sub-section (3) lays down in clearest terms that the *talaq* shall not be effective until the expiration of the period mentioned in it from the day on which notice under sub-section (1) is delivered to the Chairman. In the present case, which does not involve the question of pregnancy, Mr. Razzaq Rahman submitted, the alleged divorce could be effective only on the expiry of ninety days from the day it could be proved that such a notice as required be sub-section (1) was delivered to the Chairman. I am thankful to Mr. Razzaq Rahman for the lucid exposition of the legislative intent expressed in section 7 as to the date on which a *talaq*, otherwise valid, can be legally effective. I am in complete agreement with Mr. Razzaq Rahman that it is sub-section (3) of section

7 which determines the date on which a *talaq* becomes effective in law, and that the parties have little to do with sub-section (4) for a violation of the provisions of which it is not they but the Chairman or the Arbitration Council, if it has come into existence, will be responsible. If the Chairman fails in his duty or the Arbitration Council in its, the *talaq*, if otherwise valid, cannot but be effective in law on the expiry of the period mentioned in sub-section (3).

9. The contention of the learned Advocate for the petitioner Moulvi Abdul Aziz that the learned Magistrate was in error in holding that in the absence of proof of an Arbitration Council having been constituted under sub-section (4) of section 7 of the Ordinance, the alleged divorce was not legally effective, cannot but, therefore, be accepted. But I have noticed above how the learned Magistrate came to be of the view that service of notice under subsection (1) of section 7 was not established in the evidence. It is true that the petitioner stated on oath before the learned Magistrate that such a notice was served on the Chairman. But the learned Magistrate could not rely on this statement in the absence of any corroboration, and in view of this original notice from the office of the Chairman who was not examined nor any one from that office having been examined to prove delivery of any such notice in the office of the Chairman. It is true that a certificate under the hand of the Chairman, Ext. A, purports to be an acknowledgment of receipt of such a notice is on record. But this certificate can hardly have any evidentiary value. The adversary could not test the correctness of the statement appearing therein, since the maker thereof did not subject himself to cross examination. The relevant Register was not produced, nor the original notice that was alleged to have been delivered in the office of the Chairman. In the circumstances, there can be no reason to hold that the learned Magistrate was wrong in not acting upon Ext. A. I agree with the learned Magistrate that the petitioner Moulvi Abdul Aziz failed to prove compliance with the provision of subsection (1) of section 7 of the Ordinance, with the consequence that the alleged *talaq*, if it was pronounced by him, was not effective in law, so that in the eye of law the marriage between him and Rezia Khatoon subsists. She is, therefore, entitled to maintenance. Whether petitioner Moulvi Abdul Aziz's statement on oath before the learned Magistrate alleging divorce constituted a valid pronouncement of *talaq* need not be considered in this case, as that can be of no avail to the petitioner who has to serve a

notice on the Chairman in terms of subsection (3) of section 7 in order to make such a *talaq* effective.

10. For the foregoing reason I find no merit in this Rule which is discharged.

58

Md Abu Baker Siddique v. *S.M.A. Bakar*

JUDGMENT

FAZLE MUNIM, C.J. This appeal arises from F. M. A. No. 184 of 1984 decided by a Single Judge of the High Court Division, Dhaka (Mr. Justice Sultan Hossain Khan) on 29th May 1985.

2. Appellant filed an application under section 25 of the Guardians and Wards Act, (Act VIII of 1890) in the court of District Judge, Dhaka for custody of his minor son named Suja. The boy then about 8 years old, was born on 22nd May 1976. He married respondent No. 3 who is an M. B. B. S. Doctor on 10th June 1973. On 16th July 1977 respondent No. 3 on getting a job left for Saudi Arabia leaving the boy with the appellant. In July, 1978 she came back home and after two months again left for Saudi Arabia. This time she took the boy with her. Appellant also went to Saudi Arabia and lived with respondent No. 3 but came back in April 1981 leaving the boy with respondent No. 3. In a suit for dissolution of marriage filed at the instance of respondent No. 3, her marriage with the appellant was dissolved in June 1982. In May 1984 respondent No. 3 returned with her son to Bangladesh and went back

to Saudi Arabia keeping the boy with her relations, namely, respondent No. 1 and her sister respondent No. 4. (Note: No. 4 in lines 2, 7 and 15 of para 7 and in line 3 of para 15 should be read as No. 3 (i.e. mother).)

3. At this stage appellant filed an application under section 25 of the Guardians and Wards Act for the custody of the boy. Respondent No. 1 and his wife respondent No. 2 filed a written objection denying allegations made in the aforesaid application. It was stated that the boy has been suffering from severe ailment called Hirshtring. Steps were taken to take the boy to U.K. where he might require operation. Welfare of the boy would be best served if he was allowed to live with his mother's relation. Besides examining the appellant and respondent Nos. 1 and 4 the boy was also asked several questions by the Court. On hearing the case and on consideration of the evidence the learned District Judge dismissed the application. Appellant preferred the above mentioned appeal in the High Court Division which was, however, dismissed.

4. Being aggrieved, appellant moved this Court and obtained special leave to appeal on the following terms:

> Mr. Fazlul Karim, learned Advocate for the petitioner, contends that the petitioner is a Superintending Engineer and he has sufficient means to look after his minor son and that he is also in a position to arrange his son's medical treatment wherever it is available, and as such, rejection of his application for custody of his son is clearly arbitrary. Mr. Karim contends that the welfare of the petitioner's son cannot be expected at the hand of the divorced wife who may re-marry at any time. The question raised merits consideration. Leave prayed for is granted.

5. Mr. Fazlul Karim, Counsel for the appellant, submitted that since the boy is over 7 years of age, appellant, his father, was entitled to his custody. Besides, appellant who is a Superintending Engineer had sufficient means to provide for the boy's medical treatment and, therefore, the refusal to order the custody of the son to the appellant was arbitrary.

6. Appellant's Counsel mentioned that since respondent No. 3 may take to a second husband there is clear possibility of the boy being neglected by her. Moreover the very fact that she left the boy with her relations amounted to cruelty. Also, the mother, being divorced, would teach him disrespect for appellant.

7. Mr. Md. Nurul Huq, Advocate-on-Record, who appeared for the respondents submitted that respondent No. 4 has been taking utmost

care in looking after the boy and providing him all necessary treatment in Bangladesh and abroad. On the advice of the doctors she took the boy to U.K. where he has already undergone operation. Doctors in U.K. expressed the opinion that the boy may need another operation. Appellant never looked after the boy nor spent money over his treatment. She was even beaten up by the appellant in presence of the boy. On the other hand, respondent No. 4 spent a huge amount of money in taking the boy to U.K. and in bearing his entire medical and other expenses there. Further, the boy being stricken with a critical disease as mentioned above is very much dependent on his mother who alone can give him tender affection and take proper care, both medically and otherwise. It was never true that the boy was ever maltreated by her brother or brother's wife, respondent Nos. 1 and 2, or that they were creating hatred in the mind for the appellant. Also, the boy, being quite intelligent, expressed his preference to live with his mother and her relations when asked by the learned District Judge. This being an intelligent preference has been regarded, and quite rightly, by the court. It is only for the sake of love and affection for the boy that respondent No. 4 gave up her highly remunerative job in Saudi Arabia and came back to Bangladesh to live with her boy and take all necessary care, both medical and otherwise. So, the allegations of cruelty, irresponsibility and neglect made against her are false and malicious.

In this background the only question for determination is whether appellant or respondent No. 1, is entitled to the custody of the person of the minor boy.

8. Mr. Fazlul Karim, appellant's Counsel referred to the principles of Muslim Law regarding the custody of the person of minor children, male and female, and asserted that having regard to these principles which have been enunciated with a view to securing the welfare of minor children, it would have been just and proper if appellant father was given the custody of the boy. Principles as stated in Mullah's Principles of Mohammadan Law are:

> 352. Right of mother to custody of infant children. The mother is entitled to the custody (hizanat) of her male child until he has completed the age of seven years and of her female child until she has attained puberty. The right continues though she is divorced by the father of the child, unless she marries a second husband in which case the custody belongs to the father.

357. Right of father and paternal male relation to custody of boy over seven and of girl who has attained puberty. The father is entitled to the custody of a boy over seven years of age and of an unmarried girl who has attained puberty. Failing the father, the custody belongs to the paternal relations in the order given in sec. 355 above, and subject to the proviso to that section.

If there be none of these it is for the Court to appoint a guardian of the person of the minor.

9. Quite emphatically, the learned Counsel asserted that these principles cannot be departed from, but conceding, however, that the custody of a boy above 7 years of age can be taken away from the father only upon the ground of welfare of the boy. In support of his contention that the rule of Islamic law should be regarded and, in so regarding it, the custody of the boy should be given to the father who is entitled to it under Muslim Law, appellant's Counsel referred to the following cases, namely, *Muhammad Bashir Vs. Mst. Ghulam Fatima, PLD 1953 Lah. 73, Zainab Bibi Vs. Feroze-ud-Din, PLD 1954 Lah. 704, Ali Akbar Vs. Mst. Kaniz Maryam, (1956) 8 DLR Lah. 43, Mst. Sultana Begum Vs. Muhammad Shofi,(1965) 17 DLR Kar. 119, Mst. Munawar Jan Vs. Master Muhammad Afsar Khan, PLD 1962 Lah. 142 and Rahimullah Chowdhury Vs. Mrs. Sayeda Helali Begum,(1968) 20 DLR 1 SC.*

10. These decisions, while recognizing the principle of Islamic Law as to who is entitled to the custody of a minor son with reference to his or her age and sex simultaneously took into consideration the welfare of the minor child in determining the question. Courts in all these cases seem reluctant to give automatic effect to the rule of hizanat enunciated by Islamic jurists. If circumstances existed which justified the deprivation of a party of the custody of his child to whose custody he was entitled under Muslim Law, courts did not hesitate to do so. It may be argued, as the appellant's Counsel did, that the welfare of the child would be best served if his custody is given to a person who is entitled to such custody. Nevertheless, court's power to determine the entitlement of a party to the hizanat is not limited to mere observance of age rule so as to exclude the consideration of the interest of the child which would, however, depend on the facts and circumstances of a given case.

11. Rules of hizanat as formulated in Islamic law find place in Hedaya. There, the following tradition of the Holy Prophet (upon whom be peace) is quoted:

A woman once applied to the Prophet, saying O Prophet of God: that is my son the fruit of my womb, cherished in my bosom and suckled at my breast, and his father is desirous of taking him away from me into his own care, to which the Prophet replied, thou hast a right in the child prior to that of the husband so long as thou do'st not marry with a stranger (Chapter XIV— 'on Hizanat').

In the *Hedaya* there is also mention of the reason as to why the mother should have the hizanat of an infant child. Thus, it is stated that: 'a mother is naturally not only more tender, but also better qualified to cherish a child during infancy, so that committing the care to her is of advantage to the child'.

12. Muslim jurists appear to have considered the reasons for different age limits for boys and girls with respect to their hizanat. In *Hedaya*, it is stated:

The right of hizanat with respect to a male child appertains to the mother, until he becomes independent of it himself, that is to say, he becomes capable of shifting, eating, drinking and performing other natural functions without assistance after which the charge devolves upon the father, or next paternal relation. The hizanat with respect to a boy, ceases at the end of seven years, as in general a child at that age is capable of performing all the necessary offices himself, without assistance. But the right of hizanat with respect to a girl, appertains to a mother, grandmother, and so forth, until the first appearance of the menstrual discharge, that is to say, until she attains the age of puberty, because a girl has occasion to learn such manners and accomplishments as are proper to women, to the teaching of which the family relations are most competent, but after that period the charge of her properly belongs to the father, because a girl, after maturity, requires some person to superintend her conduct and to this the father is most completely qualified.

13. As against his submissions, Mr. Md. Nurul Huq. Advocate-on-Record for the respondents, contended that the main consideration in determining who is entitled to the custody of the person of the minor child, in other words, when there is contest regarding his guardianship is his welfare. Facts of this case show that the boy is suffering from a serious ailment, namely, 'Hirshtring', whose proper treatment required him to be taken to U.K. where he underwent operation in the hands of expert surgeons involving considerable expenses which were entirely borne by the mother, the need for a second operation which may, according to doctor's opinion, also have to be done there and the urgent

necessity for his constant care which only the mother could give, specially when she is herself a doctor, the determination of custody should be decided in favour of the mother.

14. Referring to the principle of guardianship or entitlement to the custody of a minor male child under Islamic Law, the learned Advocate cited a few cases on this point, namely, *Mst. Zohra Begum Vs. Sh. Latif Ahmed Munawar*, (1965) 17 DLR (WP) 134; PLD 1965 Lah 695, *Mst Rashida Begum Vs. Shahab Din*, PLD 1960 Lah 1142, *Mst Tahmida Begum Vs. Habib Ahmed*, PLD 1968 Lah 1112 and *Jamshed Sultan Taimoori Vs. Mst. Anisa Begum*, PLD 1980 Kar 299. He submitted that in all these cases, the concept of the welfare of the minor would appear to be the deciding factor.

15. In these cases as well as those cited by the appellant's Counsel the concept of the welfare of the minor child, whether below or above the age limit, seems to have been of paramount importance. In appointing the mother, respondent No. 4, the guardian in the instant case, the Court has been satisfied that the welfare of the boy requires that the order should be made in her favour.

16. It appears that the mother who has been away to Saudi Arabia in connection with a job in a hospital came back to Bangladesh on 17th May 1985, presumably to live here permanently. The learned Single Judge of the High Court Division, after considering all the facts and circumstances of the case and hearing the arguments of the parties' Counsels, concluded as follows:

> In view of the changed circumstances that the mother has come to Bangladesh and the minor is with the mother should the father be refused custody in preference to the mother. The mother being a doctor, she is better suited to look after the minor than the father in view of the peculiar illness of the minor and therefore the present position regarding custody of the minor should not be disturbed.

17. As regards reference to the binding nature of Islamic Law regarding custody of a minor child which was repeatedly emphasised by the learned Counsel for the appellant, it will be admitted on all hands that there is absolutely no reason to differ from this position as long as the particular rule of law to be applied is found either in the Quran or Sunnah, nor is there any reason to differ from a clear interpretation of any rule of the Quran or formulation of principle based on Quranic text represented by the dominant opinion of a particular school of law, such as Hanafi, one of the four major schools of law governing

Sunnis in Bangladesh. Needless to mention that so far as personal laws of Muslims are concerned when legal dispute arises between Muslims, rules enunciated in the Hanafi school of law are applied.

18. Other reasons also led to the departure from the rule regarding the guardianship of minor children. Rules of hizanat or custody are seen to differ from school to school, namely, Hanafi, Shafei, Maliki and Hanbali. This shows that there was no consensus among the jurists of these schools on the question of guardianship of minor children leaving scope for difference of opinion, there being no definite rule in the Quran or Sunnah on the matter.

19. It appears that superior Courts in the Indian Sub-continent considered it permissible for Courts to depart, from such rule, that is to say, when there is no uniformity among the jurists of these schools of law and facts and circumstances of the particular case justified such departure.

20. During British rule in India also this was the position. Courts used to take guidance regarding these rules from the standard translations of two very distinguished classical compilations on Sunni Law, namely, the Hedaya and the Fatawa Alamgiri. Thus the Judicual Committee of the Privy Council recognised the value and importance of these two books. It was observed:

> The Hedayah and the Fatawai-Alamgiri are recognized as standard authorities in India on the Hanafi branch of the Sunni Law.... The English versions of the Hedayah and of the Fatawai-Alamgiri [by Hamilton and Neil Baillie respectively] are valuable works on Mohammedan Law.
> (*vide, Imambandi vs. Haji Mutsaddi*, AIR 1918 PC 11)

21. It is true that, according to Hanafi school, father is entitled to the hizanat or custody of the son over 7 years of age. Indisputably, this rule is the recognition of the prima facie claim of the father to the custody of the son who has reached 7 years of age, but this rule which is found neither in the Quran nor Sunnah would not seem to have any claim to immutability so that it cannot be departed from, even if circumstance justified such departure. For example, on proof of the unfitness of the father to the custody of a male child over 7 years of age, courts are seen to exercise the discretion against his entitlement according to the Hanafi rule.

22. Mr. Nurul Huq, Respondents' Advocate, in supporting this view referred to the case of *Zohra Begum Vs. Latif Ahmed Munawar*, (1965) 17 *DLR (WP)* 134; *PLD* 1965 *Lah 695*. Here, the Court observed as follows:

...It would be permissible for Courts to differ from the Rule of Hizanat stated in the Text Books on Muslim Law for there is no Quranic or Traditional Text on the point. Courts which have taken the place of Qazis can, therefore, come to their own conclusions by process of Ijtihad which, according to Imam-al-Shafei' is included in the doctrine of Qiyas. It has been mentioned earlier that the rule propounded in different text books on the subject of Hizanat is not uniform. It would, therefore, be permissible to depart from the rule stated therein, if on the facts of a given case, its application is against the welfare of the minor. I am fortified in this view by the instance in which a Qazi finding hardship in the application of a rule of law to which the parties belonged sent the case to the Qazi of another school of law which took a liberal view of the matter.

23. In cases involving the question of guardianship their decisions are seen to be influenced by the concept of welfare of the minor child concerned. In this connection it may be mentioned that under the provisions of Guardians and Wards Act, the Court to whom an application is made under that Act is to be satisfied that the welfare of the minor required the appointment of a particular person as his guardian, but the court is to make the appointment consistently with the law to which the minor is subject. Indeed, the principle of Islamic Law (in the instant case, the rule of hizanat or guardianship of a minor child as stated in the Hanafi school) has to be regarded, but deviation therefrom would seem permissible as the paramount consideration should be the child's welfare. We think in the present case the learned Single Judge, while considering the welfare of the boy, has rightly determined the question which need not be disturbed. Facts as mentioned above clearly point out that the welfare of the boy requires that his custody should be given to the mother or that she should be appointed as his guardian.

For the reasons stated above, the appeal is dismissed. There will, however, be no order as to costs.

Jamila Khatun v. *Rustom Ali*

JUDGMENT

MUSTAFA KAMAL, J: Appellant Jamila Khatun is the wife of respondent Rustom Ali. On 6.1.86 she filed Family Court Case No. 1 of 1986 in the Family Court and Upzila Munsif, Fulbaria against the respondent praying for balance dower money of Taka 250.00 and maintenance at the rate of Taka 500.00 per month for 11 years 1½ months which comes to Taka 66,750.00, in total Taka 67,000.00 and for a decree of dissolution of marriage. By judgment and decree dated 31.5.86, the trial Court decreed the suit for Taka 30,287.50 representing maintenance for 11 years 1½ months for her child @ Taka 75.00 per month amounting to Taka 10,012,50, maintenance for herself for the same period @ Taka 125.00 per month amounting to Taka 20,025.00 and balance of dower money amounting to Taka 250.00 and also decreed dissolution of marriage. On appeal by the respondent, OC Appeal No. 243 of 1986, the 2nd Court of Subordinate Judge, Mymensingh, by judgment and decree dated 25.5.87 dismissed the same and affirmed the judgment and decree of the trial Court. In the revision taken by the respondent, Civil Revision No. 1078 of 1987, a learned Single Judge of the High Court Division by judgment and order dated 19.6.90 set aside the judgment and decree of the lower appellate Court insofar as the decree for past maintenance is concerned, keeping undisturbed all the other reliefs granted to the appellant. The High Court Division allowed maintenance to the appellant with effect from the date of filing of the case, i.e., 6.1.86 till the expiry of 3 months from the date of decree of the trial Court (31.5.86) and also granted maintenance to the child from 6.1.86 till the decree of the Court below.

2. Leave was granted from the said judgment and order of the High Court Division to consider the appellant's submission that the right to maintenance is guided by the personal law of the appellant and her son and that the High Court Division wrongly held that the appellant was not entitled to past maintenance in the absence of a written document.

3. The suit was filed by the appellant as plaintiff on the allegations, inter alia, that the appellant and the respondent were married on 3.8.72, the dower being fixed at Taka 500.00. On the same date the respondent transferred 11 acres of land to the appellant by a saf kabala. The couple lived together happily as man and wife and when the appellant was in the family way the respondent sent her to her paternal home. There she gave birth to a male child. Two months after the birth of the child the respondent took back his wife to his house and gradually started assaulting and torturing her physically and mentally. On the 5th Magh, 1381 BS corresponding to 18.1.75, the respondent after mercilessly beating the appellant drove her and her son out from the conjugal home retaining all her ornaments and wearing apparels. The appellant has since been living at her parental home and the respondent has not given her or her son any maintenance since then. A year later she approached the village madbars for a salish which failed. Thereafter the dispute was successively referred, twice each, to a Village Peace Committee and to the Chairman of the Union Parishad, but for four years the dispute remained unresolved. The respondent never gave her possession of 11 acres of land and although he is a man of substance he is denying the appellant and her son of their due maintenance, but he has paid her half of the dower. Hence the suit.

4. The respondent in his written statement admitted that he was married to the appellant on 3.8.72 and also admitted the dower amount. He admitted that the appellant was not given possession of 11 acres of land even though a saf kabala was registered in her favour. When the appellant gave birth of a male child only 7 months and 15 days of the marriage a suspicion arose in his mind that the child was not his. The appellant is a woman of easy virtue and the respondent divorced her on the 3rd Falgoon, 1379 BS and a talaqnama along with maintenance for 3 months and the dower money was duly sent to the appellant's paternal home. The salish was denied altogether.

5. Both the trial Court and the lower appellate Court concurrently held that the male child was born in wedlock, that the respondent never divorced the appellant, that the suit was not barred by limitation, that it was maintainable and that the appellant was entitled to the decree prayed for with modification in the amount of maintenance claimed.

6. Relying upon section 278 of Mulla's Principles of Mohammadan Law (18th Edition) and the case of *Abdul Futtee Moulvie vs. Zabunesa Khatun, (1881) ILR 6 (Cal) 631*, a learned Single Judge of the High Court Division held that a wife is not entitled to past maintenance in the absence of a prior written agreement. She can be allowed maintenance from the date of institution of the suit till three months after the decree of dissolution of marriage i.e. during the period of iddat. Relying further on the case of *Mst Ghulam Fatima vs. Sheikh Muhammad Bashir, PLD 1985 (WP) (Lahore) 596*, the learned Single Judge further held that past maintenance of a child is also not available to a Muslim wife in this country.

7. Mrs. Rabeya Bhuiyan, learned Counsel for the appellant, submits that the traditional Hanafi Law on past maintenance to a wife has been stated in Baillie's Digest at page 223 as follows: 'When a woman sues her husband for maintenance for a time antecedent to any order of the Judge or mutual agreement of the parties, the Judge is not to decree maintenance for the past.'

And further

> When maintenance has been decreed against a husband at so much a month, or the parties have come to a mutual agreement for so much each month, and several months are allowed to pass without his giving her anything, and she in the meantime raises her maintenance on credit, or disburses it out of her own property, and then either the husband or the wife happens to die, the whole of what has been so raised or disbursed drops or can no longer be recovered. And in like manner, if he should repudiate her, any arrears of maintenance that may have accumulated after the decree of the Judge are irrecoverable.

8. Further, Mulla's Principles of Mohammadan Law (18th Edition), section 278 reads as under:

> 278. Order for maintenance—If the husband neglects or refuses to maintain his wife without any lawful cause, the wife may sue him for maintenance, but she is not entitled to a decree for past maintenance,

unless the claim is based on a specific agreement. Or, she may apply for an order of maintenance under the provisions of the Code of Criminal Procedure, section 488, in which case the Court may order the husband to make a monthly allowance for her maintenance not exceeding five hundred rupees.

9. Mrs. Rabeya Bhuiyan further submits that at page 142 of Hamilton's translation of Hedaya it has no doubt been stated as follows:

Arrears of maintenance not due unless the maintenance has been decreed by the Kazee or the rate of it previously determined on between the parties—If a length of time should elapse during which the wife has not received any maintenance from her husband, she is not entitled to demand any for that time, except when the Kazee had before determined and decreed it to her, or where she had entered into a composition with the husband respecting it, in either of which cases she is to be decreed her maintenance for the time past, because maintenance is an obligation in the manner of a gratuity, as by a gratuity is understood a thing due without a return, and maintenance is of this description, it not being held (according to our doctors) to be as a return for the matrimonial propriety; and the obligation of it is not valid but through a decree of the Kazee, like a gift, which does not convey a right to possession but through seisin, which establishes possession; but a composition is of equal effect with a decree of the Kazee, in the present case, as the husband, by such composition, makes himself responsible, and his power over his own person is superior to that of the Magistrate. This reasoning does not apply to the case of dower, as that is considered to be a return for the use of the wife's person.

10. Mrs. Rabeya Bhuiyan does not dispute that these are the traditional views of Hanafi Law on past maintenance to wife but she contends that these views have been considered in detail with reference to the Holy Qur'an, Hadith of the Holy Prophet and Ibne Qayyum's famous work Zaadul Maad published in Egypt and after a thorough discussion of the law and literature on the subject a Division Bench of the Lahore High Court held in the case of *Sardar Muhammad vs. Mst. Nasima Bibi and ors, 19 DLR (WP) 50=PLD 1966 (Lahore) 703* (which we shall henceforth refer to as Sardar Muhammad's' case) as follows:

14 The argument in favour of forfeiture of arrears of maintenance for the past seems to have been based on the assumption that 'maintenance is an obligation in the manner of a gratuity' ... i.e. an *ex gracia* grant

which is paid by way of sympathy and charity which cannot be claimed as of right. This is clearly laid down in *Hamilton's Translation of Hedaya* of which the relevant portion has been reproduced earlier in this judgment. In all humility and with the utmost respect we find it difficult to endorse this view as the consensus of opinion as shown from the authorities cited earlier seems to be that the maintenance of a wife is the bounden duty of a husband, irrespective of his minority, illness or imprisonment or the richness of the wife, so much so that the obligation devolves on the father of a minor husband with a right of recovery against him when he is in a position to repay the amount as held by Amir Ali on the authority of 'Fatawa-i-Alamgiri and Radd-ul-Muhtar, alluded to earlier. It is thus difficult to say that it is in the nature of an *ex gracia* payment which cannot be claimed for a past' period of time....

16. The main argument which formed the basis of the Hanafi view is that Hinda, the wife of Abu Sufian, approached the Holy Prophet complaining about her inadequate maintenance by Abu Sufian, when the Prophet allowed her husband so much as was sufficient to maintain her.... From the absence of any reference to past maintenance, it is argued from this that the same stood forfeited. This argument is met by the other school of thought by a counter argument that since Hinda never claimed arrears of maintenance, as such, there was no occasion for the Holy Prophet to allow her a relief which was never prayed for. Another incident on which both sides seem to have relied in support of their respective views is that Caliph Umar wrote to his army officers in distant countries that the Muslim soldiers who were away from their wives should be ordered either to pay maintenance to their wives or divorce them. It was further directed that in the event of divorce they should also remit arrears of past maintenance. It is not disputed that no exception was taken to this directive of Caliph Umar. The argument of the Hanifites is that the payment of arrears was ordered only in case of divorce and not otherwise. On the contrary, it is argued by the other schools of thought that this direction of Caliph Umar amounts to a clear dictum in favour of the validity of past maintenance and only in the event of divorce was it insisted that it should be sent along with the divorce and, as such, it does not necessarily mean that it stands forfeited if the wife is not divorced. Further support is lent to the latter view from the fact that the competency of the Kazee to grant maintenance for the past has also been admitted by the Hanafi school of thought as is clear from the following heading of the excerpt from *Hamilton's Hedaya* quoted earlier which reads:

'Arrears of maintenance not due unless the maintenance have been decreed by the Kazee or...'.

Thus the competency of the Courts of today which have stamped into the shoes of the Kazees for the purposes of adjudication of these matters flows as a necessary corollary therefrom. The mere fact that a neglected wife has been hesitant in promptly coming to the Court or has been pursuing alternative remedies out of Court cannot, in all fairness, be so construed as to deprive her of the right of maintenance from the day when the cause of action accrued to her. The Courts have thus the jurisdiction to grant such maintenance subject of course to considerations of limitation and the relevant circumstances of each case, and we hold accordingly.

11. Mrs. Rabeya Bhuiyan submits that the above decision of the Lahore High Court, given on the 5th May, 1964, is holding the field for the last 32 years and the said decision escaped the notice of the learned Judge of the High Court Division. She also submits that the Lahore decision has not only been followed by a Division Bench of the High Court Division in the case of *Sirajul Islam vs. Halena Begum and ors., 48 DLR (HCD) 48*, but has consistently been affirmed first by the Pakistan Supreme Court in the case of *Muhammad Newaz vs. Mst. Khurshid Begum, PLD 1972 (SC) 302, at pp 304 305* in which a comparison was made between the provisions of section 9 of the Muslim Family Laws Ordinance, 1961, hereinafter referred to as the Ordinance of 1961, and those of section 488 of the Code of Criminal Procedure and the Supreme Court of Pakistan, in support of granting past maintenance to the wife, gave an additional reasoning which is as follows:

> The Legislature must have been conscious of the phraseology of section 488, CrPC. In spite of that it did not place any restriction on the powers of the Arbitration Council to award maintenance. In our opinion, under this provision of law, the Arbitration Council is competent to award maintenance for the past subject, of course, to the question of limitation. In the present case, the High Court has considered the question of limitation and has come to the conclusion that Article 120 of the Limitation Act applies to the facts of the present case and the claim of the respondent was not barred by limitation. In this view of the matter, we are satisfied that the High Court has rightly held that the Arbitration Council was competent to award past maintenance.

12. Sardar Muhammad's case has next been affirmed by the Pakistan Supreme Court in the case of *Ghulam Nabi vs. Muhammad Asghar, PLD 1991 (SC) 443*. She therefore submits that the High Court Division has

failed to take into account the latest Sunni Law on past maintenance prevalent in the sub-continent.

13. Having heard Mrs. Bhuiyan on this question and having considered the frank submission of Mr. Gour Gopal Shaha, learned Advocate for the respondent that he cannot lay his hands on any decision contrary to Sardar Muhammad's case, we find that the word 'maintenance' is 'nafkah' in Arabic. Syed Ameer Ali says in his Muhammadan Law, Volume 11 (5th Edition) at page 404 as follows:

> In the language of the Arabs,' in other words, literally, 'nafkah means what a man spends over his family.': In the language of the law, it signifies food, clothing and lodgment. This has been mentioned by Imam Mohammed.... The nafkah of a person becomes incumbent upon another from three causes; (a) from being a wife; (b) from being a relation; (c) from being a slave or servant.

Syed Ameer Ali says further at the same page—

> The husband is legally bound to maintain his wife and her domestic servants whether she and her servants belong to the Moslem Faith or not. 'It is incumbent on the man to maintain his wife,' says the Fatawai Kazi Khan, 'whether she be Moslemah or non-Moslemah (lit. zimmia), poor or rich, whether there has been copula or not; whether grown-up (adult) or young, so that intercourse with her is possible.

14. We also find in Syed Ameer Ali's above edition of Muhammadan Law the background of the Holy Prophet's award of maintenance to Hinda. That was in the context of fixing a proper amount of maintenance. The learned author says at pp. 404 405:

> Karkhi has said that in fixing the amount of maintenance regard is to be paid to the condition of the husband and not to the position of the wife, and this is the Zahir-ur-Rawayet (most approved doctrine) and also the doctrine of Imam Shafiei. But Kassaf has said, and so it is stated in the Hedaya, that when the condition of the husband and the wife are not equal, in other words, when one is rich and the other poor, a proper mean should be adopted between the two; and on this is the Fatwa. And the Hedaya supports its view by the hadis in the Sahih-ul-Bokhari from Ayesha that on one occasion Hinda, daughter of 'Otba, came and complained to the Prophet that her husband Abu Sufian was a miser, and did not support her and child properly. The Prophet said, take what is necessary, but be moderate. (Radd-ul-Muhtar, Vol. 11, p. 1063)

15. Further, in *Kazhikoti Khadir Pallivetil Mahamed Haji vs. Moideen Veettil Kalimabi, 41 ILR (Madras) 211*, Mr. Justice Abdur Rahim and Mr. Justice Srinivasa Ayyangar in a case of recovery of arrears of maintenance for about a year and a half in respect of a couple both belonging to Shafi School of Muhammadan Law observed that in Minhajet Talabin of Nanawi, a high authority on the Shafi Law and recently translated by Messrs. Van Lean Beg and Howard, it was stated (at page 385 of the translation):

> During his stay in Egypt, Shafi adopted the doctrine that a wife's maintenance is obligatory only if she puts herself at her husband's disposition and not in virtue of the contract of marriage...; consequently, a husband owes his wife no maintenance so long as she refuses to come to him; but owes it from the moment he hears she is willing to put herself at his disposition.

Then further on it was laid down,

> When a husband during his marriage becomes so insolvent that he can no longer give the minimum maintenance prescribed, but his wife in spite of this continues to live with him the maintenance become a debt due to her from him and exigible at any moment.

16. The learned Judges made it clear that the position of Shafi School that the maintenance is a debt on her husband even if it was not decreed by the Kazee is nevertheless a Sunni law. The decision in *Abdul Futtee Moulvie vs. Zabunesa Khatun, (1881) ILR 6 (Cal.) 631*, the learned Judges opined, 'is according in the Hanafi School of law which is followed by the Mohammadans of Bengal generally'.

17. Although the view taken in Sardar Muhammad's case does not literally embrace the exposition of Hanafi Law in *Baillie's Digest* and in Hamilton's translation of Hedaya, and advances closer to the Shafi School of thought, we find that the advance by way of ijtihad has been made in the right direction, with strong reason so far undisputed and of course within the bounds of Sunni Law. We therefore find no reason why the enunciation of law on past maintenance made in 1964 by the Lahore High Court and governing the field for 32 years without being reversed by either this Court or Pakistan Supreme Court, on the contrary being re-affirmed twice by the Pakistan Supreme Court, should be overlooked or discarded without demolishing the reason given therefor. We hold therefore that the High Court Division was wrong in denying past

maintenance to the appellant on the ground of a lack of prior agreement and further hold that past maintenance is available to the appellant.

18. Mr. Gour Gopal Shaha only contends that past maintenance can be given only from the date of coming into force of the Family Courts Ordinance, 1985, hereinafter referred to as the Ordinance of 1985, i.e., from 15.6.86, as was given in Sardar Muhammad's case from the 15th July, 1961, i.e., the date of enforcement of the Ordinance of 1961. Mr. Shaha's last fallback position is that Article 120 of the Limitation Act will apply in this case and the appellant can only recover past maintenance for a period upto 6 years before the institution of the suit and he relies upon the case of *Muhammad Nawaz vs. Mst Khurshid Begum, PLD 1972 (SC) 302* for this proposition.

19. Mrs. Rabeya Bhuiyan however submits that the Ordinance of 1985 is not a legislation on substantive Muslim Law but is merely a procedural law governing the forum and procedure for resolution of some specified family disputes. The parties to the dispute come to the Family Court with all their accrued rights under the Mohammadan Law and the Ordinance of 1985 only provides the forum for adjudication of the accrued rights. The question of limitation, according to the Hedaya, quoted earlier, was not relevant at all upon filing of cases before the Kazee and similarly, there was no law of limitation under the Ordinance of 1961 in filing petitions/applications under section 6 (polygamy), section 7 (talaq) or section 9 (maintenance). The parties obtained remedies from when the cause of action accrued and not from when the petition was filed before the Arbitration Council. Also in guardianship and custody cases, there was no period of limitation in filing cases, although appeals and revisions were governed by statutory periods of limitation. Section 5 of the Ordinance of 1985, she says, confers jurisdiction on the Family Courts to dispose of any suit on matters relating to or arising out of (a) dissolution of marriage, (b) restitution of conjugal rights, (c) dower, (d) maintenance and (e) guardianship and custody of children. If any concept of limitation is imported into such suits then inevitable complications, hardships and harassments will ensue in the resolution of all the above matters, which was not the intention of the legislature. She further draws our attention to section 3 of the Ordinance of 1985 which is as follows: '3. Ordinance to override other laws—The provisions of this Ordinance shall have effect notwithstanding anything contained in any other law for the time being in force.'

She submits that section 3 has debarred the application of the law of limitation to suits filed in the Family Courts.

20. We will take up Mr. Shaha's first submission with regard to grant of past maintenance from the date of enforcement of the Ordinance of 1985 upon the analogy of relief given in Sardar Muhammad's case, in which the cause of action for past maintenance accrued to the wife before the coming into force of the Ordinance of 1961 but she filed her application before the Arbitration Council on 7.2.62. The Arbitration Council granted her past maintenance from the 15th July, 1961, the date of enforcement of the Ordinance of 1961, but the wife did not prefer any revisional application therefrom to the Collector, Gujrat. It is the husband who filed a revision which was dismissed as time-barred. The husband then challenged the Arbitration Council's order and the revisional order by way of a writ petition before the Lahore High Court, when it was argued on behalf of the husband-petitioner that past maintenance could not be granted to the wife respondent from the date of coming into force of the Ordinance of 1961, because the relevant rules relating to the constitution of the Arbitration Council came into existence on the 20th July, 1961. It was argued that the Arbitration Council's order could not be maintained. It was in the context of the said argument that the Lahore High Court held in Sardar Muhammad's case that the relevant date is the date of enforcement of the Ordinance and not the date on which the Rules were framed.

21. The argument which Mrs. Bhuiyan has now advanced in support of her submission that the Ordinance of 1985 is only a procedural law and that the law of limitation does not apply at all to such kinds of law were neither mooted nor decided in Sardar Muhammad's case. This case is no authority for the proposition, advanced by Mr. Shaha, that as a general principle relief, if any, can be granted to a plaintiff in a suit under the Ordinance of 1985 only from the date of enforcement of the said Ordinance, i.e. from 15.6.85 and not beyond that date. Nor do we otherwise find any legal basis to hold so.

22. With regard to the second contention of Mr. Shaha, namely, the applicability of Article 120 of the First Schedule to the Limitation Act, it should be borne in mind that sections 5 and 6 of the Ordinance of 1985 make it quite clear that what has to be filed before a Family Court is a 'suit' and not an 'application' as was the case with the Ordinance of 1961. In the case of an 'application' to an Arbitration Council (which was

not a Court) under the Ordinance of 1961, even the residuary Article 181 of the First Schedule did not apply, as applications under Article 181 are restricted to applications under the Code of Civil Procedure (see *Tamizul Huq vs. Shamsul Huq 43 DLR (AD) 34*.) But in respect of 'suits' section 3 of the Limitation Act will apply or section 29 (2) of the said Act will apply, if the suit is filed under a special or local law, unless the Limitation Act has been expressly excluded from the purview of such suits. Section 3 of the Ordinance of 1985 only means that if there are provisions in the Ordinance which are different from or are in conflict with the provisions of any other law then the provisions of the said Ordinance will prevail over the provisions of any other laws. If, for example, any special period of limitation is prescribed in the Ordinance of 1985 then that will govern the field, and not the Limitation Act, 1908. Section 3 does not debar the application of Limitation Act to suits filed under the Ordinance of 1985, as contended by Mrs. Bhuiyan. Section 20 of the Ordinance of 1985 is also instructive on this point:

> 20. Application and non-application of certain laws—(1) Save as otherwise expressly provided by or under this Ordinance, the provisions of the Evidence Act, 1872 (1 of 1872), and of the Code except sections 10 and 11 shall not apply to proceedings before the Family Courts. (2) The Oaths Act, 1873 (X of 1873) shall apply to all proceedings before the Family Courts.

23. It may be noticed that the legislature has taken care to mention certain specific laws which shall not apply to proceedings before the Family Courts and in enumerating such laws the Limitation Act, 1908 has not been mentioned. Applying the well-known maxim of interpretation of statutes *Expressio unius est exclusio alterius* (the express mention of one thing implies the exclusion of another), it can be safely held that the express mention of the Evidence Act and the Code of Civil Procedure necessarily implies the exclusion of Limitation Act from the purview of non-applicability to suits under the Ordinance of 1985. Moreover, in section 7 a time-limit has been prescribed for appearance of the defendant as also for submission of a written statement which will prevail over the time-limit, if contrary, provided by the Code of Civil Procedure. Under sub-section (6) of section 9 a defendant may apply to the Court for setting aside a decree passed *ex parte* against him within 30 days of the passing of the decree and sub-section (7) of section 9 provides that the provisions of section 5 of the Limitation Act,

1908 shall apply to an application under sub-section (6). These provisions clearly indicate that the Ordinance of 1985 is a special law. Under section 29 (2) of the Limitation Act section 3 thereof shall apply and sections 4, 9 to 18 and 22 are applicable unless excluded and other sections are not applicable unless included.

24. From a reading of the entire Ordinance of 1985 we find substance in the contention of Mrs. Bhuiyan that the provisions thereof are intended to provide for the establishment of Family Courts and for matters connected therewith and are not intended to make provisions for modification or amendment of Mohammadan Law or any other substantive law. The Ordinance is indeed procedural in nature, as was held in the case relied upon by Mrs. Bhuiyan, namely, the case of *Adnan Afzal vs. Sher Afzal, PLD 1969 (SC) 187*, a case in relation to the West Pakistan Family Courts Act, 1964. This Ordinance of 1985, therefore, does not in any way diminish or curtail the rights already possessed by a litigant with regard to the matters mentioned in section 5.

25. But diminution or curtailment of rights already possessed by a litigant with regard to the matters mentioned in section 5 is not the same thing as the loss of those rights or a part of those rights owing to the operation of the law of repose, i.e. the law of limitation. The existence of an accrued right may be accepted or acknowledged expressly or impliedly by a procedural law, but if the law of limitation is attracted, that right may be diminished or curtailed or even extinguished altogether. The fact that the Ordinance of 1985 speaks of 'suit', 'plaint', 'written statement', 'decree', etc. clearly attracts the Limitation Act under section 29 (2) thereof.

26. The Limitation Act does not specifically provide for any particular period of limitation in filing suits by a Muslim for arrears of maintenance although Articles 128 and 129 of the First Schedule provide a period of 12 years each by a Hindu for arrears of maintenance and for a declaration of his right to maintenance respectively and the time from which period begins to run is when the arrears are payable and when the right is denied respectively. No such corresponding provisions exist in respect of suits filed by a Muslim for a corresponding relief. In our opinion, residuary Article 120 of the First Schedule, providing for a period of limitation of 6 years from the time when the right to sue accrues in respect of a suit for which no period of limitation is provided elsewhere in the First Schedule will be applicable to a suit for maintenance under Ordinance of 1985.

27. We find indirect support for our view in Sardar Muhammad's case, in which it was held as follows:

> The Courts have thus the jurisdiction to grant such maintenance subject of course to considerations of limitation and the relevant circumstances of each case, and we hold accordingly.

28. We find further indirect support for our view in the case of *Muhammad Nawaz vs. Mst. Khurshid Begum, PLD 1972 (SC) 362*, in which the Supreme Court of Pakistan found that the High Court of West Pakistan, Lahore, from whose decision the appeal was taken by leave, considered the question of limitation and found that Article 120 of the Limitation Act was applicable and that the wife's claim was not barred by limitation. No exception was taken to the consideration of Article 120 by the High Court, although it was a case under section 9 of the Ordinance of 1961.

29. We do not foresee, as apprehended by Mrs. Bhuiyan, that by applying the law of limitation to the Ordinance of 1985 serious difficulties, hardships or harassments are likely to occur which will frustrate the purpose of the Ordinance. In the case of dissolution of marriage, restitution of conjugal rights and guardianship and custody of children we do not foresee any problem because the right to sue in such cases is of a continuous nature and the plaintiff's right to sue is always likely to accrue within the period mentioned in Article 120 of the First Schedule. In respect of dower, under Articles 103 and 104 of the First Schedule a period of 3 years has been prescribed in each case as the period of limitation in filing a suit by a Mohammadan for exigible dower (mu'ajjal) and for deferred dower (mu'wajjal) and the time from which period begins to run in each case is different. We find that in the present case the appellant is well within the said Articles, whichever is applicable, in claiming the remaining dower money of Taka 250.00 and is also well within Article 120 in seeking dissolution of marriage with the respondent, but in respect of past maintenance, the appellant is not entitled to the same more than 6 years back from 6.1.86, the date of filing of the suit.

30. That disposes of the question of limitation in a suit for past maintenance.

31. Mr. Gour Gopal Shaha, however, has supported the judgment of the High Court Division on the further ground that the Courts below

wrongly allowed maintenance, including past maintenance to the child, first, because, all the disputes under section 5 of the Ordinance of 1985 are between husband and wife. Section 23 of the Ordinance of 1985 provides that nothing in this Ordinance shall be deemed to affect any of the provisions of the Ordinance of 1961 or the Rules made there-under and section 9 of the Ordinance of 1961 enables only the wife to claim maintenance for herself and not for the child, a proposition supported in even Sardar Muhammad's case, and as such, her claim of maintenance for the child was not entertainable under the Ordinance of 1985. Secondly, past maintenance is not available to a child under Mohammadan Law and thirdly, in the prayer portion of the plaint the plaintiff did not specifically pray for past maintenance of the child, but prayed for her own past maintenance only.

32. We do not see any force in the argument of Mr. Shaha that section 5 of the Ordinance of 1985 deals exclusively with disputes between husband and wife or that section 23 of the said Ordinance read with section 9 of the Ordinance of 1961 precludes a wife from claiming maintenance for her child in a suit before a Family Court. Section 5 of the Ordinance of 1985 mentioned 'Maintenance' as a general subject for adjudication by the Family Court. Section 5 does not specifically say that a suit for maintenance can only be filed by the wife for herself. On the contrary, we find that the operation of section 9 of the Ordinance of 1961 has been widely extended by the provisions of section 5 of the Ordinance of 1985 by using the general expression *'Maintenance'*. In Hamilton's translation of Hedaya it has been stated in the Introductory Address by the composer of the Persian Version at page liii.

> The place and title of Chapter XV (Of Nafkah, or Maintenance) would only lead us to conclude, that it treats in particular of the alimony payable to a divorced wife during the term of probation. This, however, is by no means the case; for it is made to comprehend those rights of every person which come under the denomination of Maintenance,—not of the wife alone, but also of parents, children, poor or disabled relatives and slaves.

33. Under section 5 of the Ordinance of 1985 therefore it is not only the wife who can file a suit in a Family Court for her own maintenance but also for the maintenance of her child. Children in easy circumstances under Mohammadan Law are bound to maintain their poor parents, although the latter may be able to earn something for themselves. These

poor parents may also file a suit in a Family Court for maintenance from their opulent children. Similarly, poor or disabled relatives, even servants of the wife can maintain a suit for maintenance under the Ordinance of 1985 under circumstances enjoined by Mohammadan Law. But whether the parents, relatives and servants can claim past maintenance is not the subject matter of this case and we do not express ourselves on this question. Similarly, the claim for dower can not only be made by the wife but also by her heirs under certain circumstances. In guardianship and custody cases, besides the parents, grandparents, uncles and other relations may be plaintiffs in appropriate cases. Hence it is not correct to say that all the six subjects mentioned in section 5 relate to suits exclusively between husband and wife.

34. With regard to the second argument of Mr. Shaha, Mrs. Rabeya Bhuiyan quoted from *Hamilton's* translation of Hedaya, Volume 1, page 146 which is as follows:

A father must provide for maintenance of his infant children—The maintenance of infant children rests upon their father; and no person can be his associate or partner in furnishing it (in the same manner as no person is admitted to be associated with a husband in providing for the maintenance of his wife).

35. She also quotes from Volume II of Syed Ameer Ali's Muhammadan Law, 5th Edition, page 427, as follows:

The Musulman Civil Law imposes on parents the duty of maintaining their children and of educating them properly. This obligation rests naturally upon the father.... In all cases concerning the maintenance of infant children consideration is chiefly to be paid to the interest of the children. So long as the father is able to maintain them, it is incumbent on him to do so, and debt incurred on their behalf by any person are recoverable from him.

36. Mrs. Rabeya Bhuiyan also relies upon the previously cited case in PLD 1991 (SC) 543 in which it was held that the Supreme Court while permitting the grant of past maintenance did not make any exception with regard to the children as distinguished from past maintenance to a wife. It held:

Otherwise too it looks unfair that while the wife gets past maintenance the children should, as contended by the learned Counsel, be deprived of this benefit. Cases are not lacking where, while granting maintenance to the wife, Courts have taken into account her needs, vis-à-vis, any minor child which she might be supporting in the same household.

37. The wife, therefore, can claim past maintenance for the child if she has been supporting the child in the same household without any contribution from the father whose duty it is to maintain the child. But if she does not claim separate maintenance for the child, the Court will consider her overall needs, keeping in view the fact that she has been supporting a child in the same household. In either case, the claim is subject to Article 120 of the First Schedule.

38. We however find considerable force in the third argument of Mr. Shaha that the plaintiff did not specifically pray for the child's maintenance in the prayer portion of the plaint. In paragraph 6 of the plaint she gave a break-up of her claims against the respondent but here too she did not specify any separate amount claimed for the child's maintenance. The trial Court gave a break-up of the amount due to the child and the appellant by specifying separate amounts, and in decreeing the suit also so specified. Mr. Shaha submits that such division was uncalled for in the absence of a specific prayer in the plaint by the appellant.

39. We do not find however that this is a case where we should overlook the overall needs of the appellant. Admittedly, she has been supporting the child in the same household where she lives. Taking the overall needs of the appellant into consideration we do not think that the amount given to her by way of past maintenance for herself including that of her son is excessive or extravagant. Rather we find that while she claimed maintenance at the rate of Taka 500.00 per month the trial Court granted her maintenance at the rate of Taka 225.00 per month, including maintenance for the child at the rate of Taka 75.00 per month. We allow the same amount to the appellant as a consolidated sum, but she will be entitled to past maintenance at the rate of Taka 225.00 per month for only 6 years prior to the filing of the suit on 6.1.86, all other reliefs granted by the trial Court remaining unchanged.

In the result, the appeal is allowed in part. No costs. The trial Court's decree is to be amended accordingly.

A Comparative Survey of Muslim Personal Law in South Asian Countries

After two hundred years of British rule, India and Pakistan became sovereign states in 1947, and Bangladesh seceded from Pakistan in 1971. In Part I of the book we have given the gist of sixty-one cases—colonial India: thirteen, India: seventeen, Pakistan: sixteen, and Bangladesh: fifteen—under three heads: issues of law involved in each case, case summary and court decisions, and short comments. In Part II we have reproduced the text of thirty-five cases—colonial India: eight, and India, Pakistan, and Bangladesh: nine each. The selection of cases is representative of the judicial trends in the four jurisdictions, and due weight has been given to each of them. India is a secular republic, Pakistan an Islamic republic, and Bangladesh a people's republic with Islam as the state religion. Keeping these aspects in mind, in the concluding chapter, an assessment is made of the differences in judicial trends between pre-independence and post-independence decisions as well as the similarities and dissimilarities between judicial rulings delivered in the post-independence period by the three separate judicial regimes of India, Pakistan, and Bangladesh. In view of the fact that the three countries have inherited the same legal history and tradition, legal institutions and laws, including Muslim personal law, of pre-1947 India, another issue discussed here is whether they can share their post-independence experiences.

Colonial India

The Muslim rulers of India applied Muslim personal law only to Muslims and allowed the other religious communities to be governed by their own religion-based laws and usages. The British inherited and followed this enlightened policy. Regulation II of 1772 provided that 'in all suits regarding inheritance, marriage and caste and other religious usages and institutions, the laws of the Koran with respect to Mahomedans and those of the Shaster with respect to gentoos [Hindus] should be invariably adhered to'. Muslim personal law comprised all questions relating to family relations, namely marriage, dower, divorce, maintenance, guardianship of children, succession and inheritance, religious usages and institutions, and dispositions of property by gift, will and waqf.

Codification of Muslim law

The colonial rulers did not make any attempt to reform or codify these personal laws, because any such attempt was bound to hurt the religious susceptibilities of the people. They agreed to introduce legal reform only when the religious community itself desired it. It was on the basis of consensus amongst the Muslim community that the two principal legislations of the colonial period, the Muslim Personal Law (Shariat) Application Act, 1937 and the DMMA were enacted. The first restored the application of sharia law to all Muslims of India and did away with customary laws contrary to it. The second gave all Muslim wives, irrespective of sect and school of law, the right to judicial divorce on any of the following grounds: (i) disappearance of husband for four years or more; (ii) his failure to provide maintenance for two years or more; (iii) imprisonment for seven years or more; (iv) failure to perform marital obligations for three years or more; (v) impotence since marriage; (vi) insanity for two years, or leprosy, or virulent venereal disease; (vii) wife's exercise of 'option of puberty'; (viii) husband's cruelty; and (ix) any other grounds recognized by Muslim law. The DMMA has been hailed as one of the most progressive enactments passed by colonial legislature.

Special features of Muslim law in South Asia

Certain special features of Muslim law as administered by the colonial courts of South Asia have turned it into an independent and discrete legal system, substantially different in many cases from its original formulations by classical jurists. In the first place, contrary to the Islamic tradition of a single court and single qadi, Muslim law has been administered in South Asia through a hierarchy of secular courts with an elaborate system of appeal from the lower courts to the higher courts, the highest court of appeal being the Judicial Committee of the Privy Council which exercised considerable influence on the development of Muslim law in South Asia. In many countries sharia law is applied only by sharia courts. Second, the judges in the higher courts, which alone were competent to give authoritative rulings on points of law, were mostly British but with no specialized training in Muslim law. The British judges were ignorant of the laws, customs, usages, and institutions of the country, and unfamiliar with the Arabic language, Arabic texts of law, technical Arabic expressions, and legal phraseology. As a result they encountered great difficulty in ascertaining the terms of law on the issues before them. One interesting example of the ignorance of the British judges about Muslim law was their inability to recognize any distinction between the Sunnis and the Shias until 1842. Ameer Ali, J., an eminent Indian jurist of Muslim law, says that owing to their ignorance of the law and its language, the judges were reluctant to give effect to the rules of Muslim law and invoked English law, and sometimes even Hindu law, 'either to cut down or to explain away the meaning of the Mahommedan Law' (1985 [1912]: 1). Third, the courts of South Asia apply the Muslim law as a case-law system like all other civil and criminal laws, but it is foreign to the Islamic legal system. A South Asian judge cannot decide a case in opposition to the decisions of the high courts, the Supreme Court, or the Privy Council. Disputes arise everyday in the law courts on the interpretation of Muslim law texts and the best way of reconciling them. But when an authoritative judgment has been pronounced by a superior court, it becomes a binding precedent. The principle of precedent has been criticized on the grounds that: (i) by according binding authority to past judicial reasoning it constrained future decision-making in the name of consistency and (ii) 'the decision rapidly acquired a broad authority that displaced the jurisprudence of Islamic text'(Khare, *Perspectives on Islamic Law*, 75).

Rules of interpretation of Muslim law

The common law doctrine of *stare decisis* or precedent is somewhat similar to the traditional Islamic doctrine of taqlid which claims that the principles and rules of law as settled by recognized scholars of the classical period are sacrosanct and immutable and must be obeyed by subsequent generations of Muslims. By applying the two doctrines in the two celebrated cases, *Aga Mahomed* v. *Koolsom Bee Bee* (Case 1) and *Baker Ali Khan* v. *Anjuman Ara* (Case 2), the Judicial Committee of the Privy Council laid down the following rules of interpretation of Muslim law. Where the interpretation of a text of the Qur'an is at issue, it is the duty of the courts to see how it has been interpreted by classical jurists of recognized merit and authority and follow their authoritative exposition of the law. They should not, as a rule, put their own construction on any Qur'anic text in opposition to the express rulings of classical jurists. Thus, where a Qur'anic verse was interpreted in a particular way both in the *Hedaya* and *Imamia*, it is not open to a judge to construct it in a different way. Neither the ancient texts nor the precepts of the Prophet of Islam should be taken literally so as to deduce from them new rules of law. New rules are not to be introduced because they seem to present-day lawyers to follow logically from the authoritative classical texts when the classical jurists themselves have not drawn those conclusions.

Misinterpretation of rules of law

Blind obedience to the rules of interpretation and misunderstanding or misinterpretation of the provisions of substantive law sometimes led to sad legal and social consequences. According to *Fatawa Alamgiri*, where a man has divorced his wife by triple talaq and has continued to live with her without her marrying a stranger and then getting a divorce from him, the marriage is fasid or irregular and not batil or void, and the children are legitimate. But in *Saiyid Rashid Ahmad* v. *Anisa Khatun* (Case 8), the Privy Council held that such a marriage was void and the children were illegitimate and could not inherit their father's estate. The error of the Privy Council caused the gravest injustice to the wife and children in the instant case and has continued to cause unspeakable misery to countless men and women ever since. Again, according to *Fatawa Alamgiri*, the marriage of a man to two sisters simultaneously or one after the other in the lifetime of the first is irregular and not void and the children are legitimate. But in *Azizunnisa* v. *Karimunnisa*, it was held: 'The marriage with the sister of a wife who is legally married is void. The children of such marriage are illegitimate and cannot inherit' (Saksena 1963:37). Syed Ameer Ali held that the decision was wholly wrong and ought to be set right either by judicial declarations or by legislative enactment (1985 [1928]: 342). In *Ahmad Kasim Molla* v. *Khatun Bibi* (Case 9), the issue was whether the wife had been validly divorced. Her lawyer argued that a Muslim husband could not divorce his wife without a just cause. Costello, J., held that 'any Mahomedan may divorce his wife at his mere whim and caprice'(*Ahmad Kasim Molla* v. *Khatun Bibi*; Case 9, p. 29). Post-independence Indian decisions will show that this is not so. In a maintenance suit filed by the wife in *Abdool Futteh Moulvie* v. *Zabunnessa Khatun*, the Calcutta High Court held that where a husband neglects or refuses to maintain his wife without any lawful cause, the wife is entitled to maintenance only from the date of the court decree; she cannot claim arrears of maintenance from the day the cause of action arises. The decision is manifestly unjust. Again, in *Abdul Kadir* v. *Salima* (Case 5), a Full Bench of the Allahabad High Court decided that after consummation of the marriage a wife is not entitled to refuse herself to her husband on the ground of non-payment of prompt dower. As we would see later, the Pakistani courts held that both the suits were wrongly decided. Muslim law does not recognize the doctrine of *legitimatis per subsequens matrimonium*. But, in *Sibt Mohammad* v. *Mohammad Hamid*, the court declared legitimate a Muslim child, born within six months of the marriage of his parents. Similarly, in *Hamira Bibi* v. *Zubaida Bibi*, the Privy Council allowed to a widow six percent interest per annum on the dower debt due to her. Asaf Fyzee, a renowned lawyer and scholar of Muslim law, maintains that Islamic law does not countenance payment of interest in view of the clear text of law contained in the Qur'anic verse 2:275 (66 *Bom.L.R.*, 122). The most notorious misinterpretation of sharia law occurred with regard to the law of waqf or charitable endowments. A waqf exclusively for the benefit of the settlor's family without any provision for charity is valid in Muslim law. But in *Abul Fata* v. *Russomoy Dhur Chowdhury*, the Privy Council held that such a waqf was invalid. Wrong decisions like this led Muhammad Ali Jinnah to say: 'The Privy Council have on several occasions absolutely murdered Hindus and slaughtered Mohammedan law' (Rashid, *Islamic CLQ* 3: 161). The decision went against the fundamental notions of sharia law, and so great was the uproar that the legislature had to intervene and pass the Mussalman Wakf Validating Act, 1913 validating family waqf retrospectively.

Justice, equity, and good conscience

Cases where the law was misunderstood or misinterpreted by the colonial courts have been discussed above. However, there are also areas where the British administration of justice proved to be a blessing. One such example is the introduction of the principle of English common law and equity in the domain of sharia law. In cases where there was no specific rule of sharia law applicable, or the rule was uncertain, ambiguous, or too rigid or very much out of tune with the requirements of a changing society, the judges decided them according to the dictates of 'justice, equity and good conscience'. In traditional law a gift is only valid when possession has actually been delivered to the donee. This rule may turn out to be harsh or inequitable; to give relief to the donee in such cases, the courts developed the doctrine of constructive delivery. Unpaid dower of a widow is an unsecured debt due to her from her deceased husband's estate. But, by a rule known as the 'widow's lien', the widow is given a privileged position and allowed to retain possession of her husband's estate, when such possession has been lawfully acquired, until her dower debt is satisfied. The law governing the legal transaction of pardanashin women is perhaps the best illustration of the most beneficial impact of the application of English principles of equity. The courts felt that a pardanashin woman, being completely secluded from normal community life, needed their special protection, and developed the rule that for the validity of any transaction, for example, a gift made by her, contrary to the general rule of presumption, it is the donee who will have to satisfy the court that she understood the nature and effects of the transaction and that she acted freely and, where necessary, on independent legal advice. The leading case of *Farid-un-Nisa* v. *Mukhtar Ahmad*, gives an exhaustive statement of the law on the subject. English common law infiltrated into the rule governing the administration of a deceased's estate. According to Hanafi law, the deceased fictitiously survives and remains owner of the estate until his debts have been paid. In *Jafri Begum* v. *Anis Muhamad*, it was held that the deceased's estate devolved on his heirs, as in English law, in accordance with their share in the inheritance at the moment of death and any heir could pass a valid title to his share of inheritance before the debts have been paid.

Agreement to regulate marital relations

Validity of an agreement designed to regulate marital relations between the spouses is another field where, after some initial hesitation, the colonial courts came down in favour of agreements, which were: (i) reasonable; (ii) not contrary to public policy and Islamic norms; and (iii) pro-wife. In *Bai Fatima* v. *Alimahomed Aiyeb*, an agreement provided for the first wife to live separately and claim maintenance from the husband if he took a second wife and that led to family dissension. The court held that the agreement provided for and encouraged future separation between the spouses and was, therefore, void as being against public policy. In sharp contrast to *Bai Fatima*, in *Mansur* v. *Azizul* (Case 7), another court held that if a Muslim married a second time, found that his first wife could not pull on well with the second wife and, for preserving family peace, agreed to give her maintenance even if she lived apart from him, that agreement was not against public policy. The Lahore High Court saw nothing monstrous or mad or unreasonable in a similar postnuptial agreement in *Sadiqa Begum* v. *Ata Ullah*. A decade earlier, an antenuptial agreement had gone still further. It provided that in case of dissension between the couple the husband and his father would be bound to pay the woman a monthly allowance of Rs. 15 *for life*. When the husband divorced her, she filed a suit claiming the monthly allowance. The Allahabad High Court held that the agreement did not offend against the provision of Section 23 of the Indian Contract Act, 1872 or encourage and facilitate separation between the spouses, and the wife was entitled to receive the allowance as provided in the contract (*Muhammad Muin-ud-din* v. *Jamal Fatima*).

An assessment

Abdul Rahim, the renowned author of *Muhammadan Jurisprudence* (1911), maintains that necessity and the wants of social life are the two all-important guiding principles recognized by Islamic jurisprudence. In applying Muslim law, the court is entitled to take into account the circumstances of real life and the changing habits and modes of life. Analysing the rulings of the colonial courts, he was of the view that in Muslim personal laws governing domestic relations and succession, the colonial courts had allowed themselves a much narrower margin of freedom in applying the rules laid down in the medieval texts to the changed circumstances of modern life than in matters relating to disposition of property by gift, waqf, and will (1911: 44–5). Our survey of the court decisions supports his findings. The principle of equity was a welcome tool to soften the rigours of some sharia rules and adapt them to modern notions of social justice. But the fields where the principle could be applied were very narrow indeed, and by and large sharia law and society remained stagnant during the colonial period. In the following pages we will see how far the courts of India, Pakistan, and Bangladesh have responded to the challenges of changing social values and attitudes.

India

India is a secular constitutional democracy, as opposed to Pakistan, an Islamic republic, and Article 44 of the Indian Constitution stipulates that 'The state shall endeavour to secure for the citizens a uniform civil code throughout the territory of India'. It would have been expected that in secular India judicial interpretation of Muslim law would take the path of activism and liberalism, and in Islamic Pakistan, passivity and conservatism. In fact, in the first thirty years after independence, the reverse was the case. During these years while the Indian courts held that they were bound by the doctrine of *stare decisis* to follow the rules of interpretation of Muslim law, as laid down by the Privy Council in *Aga Mahomed* and *Baker Ali Khan* (Cases 1 and 2), the Pakistani courts refused to abide by these decisions and exercised their right of independent interpretation of the rules of sharia law as laid down in the Qur'an and Hadith. The result of the two different approaches is quite interesting. Muslim law remained more or less rigid and conservative in India in those years but became flexible and progressive in Pakistan; and laws in Pakistan and Bangladesh diverged in a number of cases from those in India. The case law discussed below will show that during the period under review the judicial trend in India was more or less the same as in the colonial epoch. In *Imdad Ali* v. *Ahmad Ali*, the High Court restated the rule of interpretation of Muslim law as follows: Where authoritative classical jurists had interpreted a rule of law in a particular way, it is not open to a judge to refer back to the original authorities and reach a different conclusion; he must follow the interpretation given by the great jurists. In *Amad Giri* v. *Begha*, the husband pronounced talaq on his wife in the bid'at form. The lower court referred to a number of Qur'anic verses, Hadith, and other texts and concluded that the talaq was absolutely invalid and the marriage subsisted. The High Court, using the picturesque language of Batchelor, J. in *Sarabai* v. *Rabiabai* held that talaq-i-bid'at, though bad in theology, is good in law and had put an end to the marital relations. The court further said that talaq-i-bid'at is the most prevalent form of talaq in India and judicial interpretation is not the appropriate method of changing this law. In *Mohd Ismail* v. *Abdul Rashid*, a case concerning Hanafi law of pre-emption, a Full Bench of the Allahabad High Court held:

> Where a rule of Mohamedan Law is well settled in the view of the ancient expositors of the Mohammedan Law, it is not open to us to disregard or to reject it on the ground that to us it appears to be illogical or unsound, provided, of course, it is not contrary to equity, justice and good conscience… (p. 4).

One glaring instance of incorrectly decided cases due to misunderstanding of the rules of sharia law is *Tufail* v. *Jamila*. In a case of li'an or mutual imprecation, the wife is entitled to sue for dissolution of her marriage on the ground that her husband has falsely charged her with committing adultery. But the court decided that if the husband retracts the charge, she cannot insist on divorce. The decision is a clear violation of the letter and spirit of the law of li'an and a prominent scholar has considered this outrageous (Mahmood 1997:42). In *Haji Mokshed Mondel* v. *Del Rousan Bibi*, the court equated dower with consideration in a contract of marriage. As early as 1911 Abdul Rahim authoritatively defined dower as 'an obligation imposed by the law on the husband as a mark of respect for the wife' and refuted the idea that it was consideration (1911: 334). Enforcement of dower law also has given rise to conflicting case law in India and Pakistan. In *Rabia Khatoon* v. *Mukhtar Ahmad* (Case 16) the question before the court was whether a wife could refuse herself to her husband after consummation of the marriage on the ground of failure by the husband to pay prompt dower. Imam Abu Hanifa maintains that the wife is entitled to refuse herself to her husband at any time during the marriage until payment of dower but his two disciples, Imam Abu Yusuf and Imam Muhammad, hold that once the marriage has been consummated, the wife loses the right. *Abdul Kadir* adopted the view of the two disciples and now the Allahabad High Court followed *Abdul Kadir*. In a well-argued critique B.P. Bhatnagar (1966: 416) questions the rule and submits that it should be reconsidered 'to make the law more realistic and to bring it in accord with the Islamic concerns of social justice'. This is precisely what a Pakistan High Court had done eleven years earlier in *Rahim Jan v. Muhammad* (Case 34).

There were also a number of progressive decisions in this period. For example, in *Saifuddin Sekh v. Soneka Bibi* (Case 18), an antenuptial agreement provided that if the husband brought either of his two other wives, who were not living with him at the time of the third marriage, to stay with him without the third wife's consent, she would be entitled to exercise the delegated power of divorce. The court held that a contract that served to ensure peace and domestic happiness should not be treated as opposed to public policy and invalid. In *Itwari v. Asghari* (Case 17), the question was whether taking a second wife would constitute cruelty to the first wife and was a valid ground for her to live separately from her husband and claim maintenance. The husband contended that the Qur'an granted him the right to take four wives and if the first wife was allowed to live separately merely because he had taken a second wife, that would be virtual denial of his polygamy right. Referring to the Qur'anic verse 4:3, the court stated that 'the right to four wives appears to have been qualified by "a better not" advice, and husbands were enjoined to restrict themselves to one wife if they could not be impartial between several wives' (*Itwari v. Ashgari*, p. 686). In considering the question of cruelty in a particular case, the court cannot ignore the prevailing social conditions and changes in people's habits and modes of living. The court decided that under the prevailing conditions the very act of taking a second wife, in the absence of a weighty and convincing explanation, raises a presumption of cruelty to the first wife. On the facts of the case, the court further held that it would be inequitable to compel the first wife to live with her husband. The decision has been warmly supported and also vehemently opposed. Irrespective of controversy over the decision, *Itwari* is the forerunner of judicial activism in the sphere of Muslim law in India.

Our analysis of the state of Muslim personal law in India in the first thirty years after independence has shown that the courts refrained from giving their own interpretations to Muslim law and with a few exceptions followed the decisions of the colonial courts. It is interesting to note that in the 1970s, while, due to the introduction of the Islamization of laws programme by the military regime, Pakistani courts became more circumspect in activist interpretations of Muslim law, Indian courts abandoned their dependence on colonial precedents and took an activist and liberal stance. 'Judicial activism' signifies a dynamic court's perception of its duties in a changing and developing society. Where the judges are literalist and conservative, beneficial and progressive legislation may be whittled away by narrow interpretation of law and social advancement thwarted. But where they are activist, liberal, and forward-looking, they can act as engines of social change and progress. A.S. Anand, C.J., describes the concept as follows: "'judicial activism" to my mind, thus involves the role of a judge, in a given system, as an instrument for developing the law to make it useful and relevant in an ever changing society' (Bhatia 1990: 11). He holds that courts have a vital role in providing social justice to people and fulfilling their hopes and aspirations as enshrined in the Constitution. P.N. Bhagwati, C.J., categorically asserts that justice devoid of social justice is meaningless (Bhatia 1990:156). In the following pages we will mainly discuss those areas where judicial activism has been most pronounced.

Registration of marriage

Registration is not an essential or formal requirement of a Muslim marriage and unlike Pakistan and Bangladesh, Indian statutory law does not provide for compulsory registration of Muslim marriage and divorce. Statutory provisions are, however, available in West Bengal, Bihar, Assam, and Odisha for optional registration of Muslim marriages. *M. Jainoon* v. *M. Ammanulla Khan* is an interesting example of compulsory registration of Muslim marriages under a customary practice prevailing in one area of Tamil Nadu. Here the court held that, once it is established that the Muslim community of any area has developed a custom to have their marriages registered, it assumes the character of a customary right and its violation is actionable.

Marriage expenses

In *Noor Mohammad* v. *Mohammad Jiauddin* (Case 14), the minor bride's father refused to pay for the services of a nautch girl, hired by the bridal party and an angry bridegroom and his father returned home, leaving the bride in her father's house. The question before the court was whether the father of the bride was bound to pay the marriage expenses incurred by the bridegroom and his father. The court held that the contract of marriage conferred on the bride rights of residence and maintenance in her husband's house. The bridegroom was duty bound to take her to his house immediately after marriage and the bride or her father was under no obligation to pay the marriage expenses incurred by him or his father. In Indian society, the court further held, 'abandoning the wife at the marital hall' is regarded as derogatory to women's dignity and by doing so the bridegroom and his father had challenged the 'dignity of the women', in violation of their fundamental duty contemplated under Article 51A of the Constitution. Incidents such as the one outlined above are very common and the activist role of the court in these situations is laudable.

Restitution of conjugal rights

In a husband's suit for restitution of conjugal rights against a wife, the Bombay High Court decided, in *Shakila Banu* v. *Ghulam Mustafa*, that the wife's evidence about her husband's cruelty does not require corroboration. The rule of corroboration is generally one of prudence and practice to be applied reasonably having regard to all the circumstances of a case. If, for example, the wife were beaten inside the husband's house it would not be possible for her to produce witnesses. In *Shahina Parveen* v. *Mohd Shakeel* the court was of the opinion that instituting criminal cases against the wife and her relations, and then vigorously pursuing them constituted cruelty, entitling the wife to live separately. One legal scholar has argued that the concept of restitution of conjugal rights is foreign to Islamic ideology and has been engrafted in it by colonial courts. In *Saroj Rani* v. *Sudarshan Kumar Chadha*, the Supreme Court has held that under Hindu law, it is a right inherent in the very institution of marriage.

Remarriage

In *Khadissa* v. *Muhammed* (Case 15), the issue was the validity of remarriage of a couple without an intervening marriage of the wife with a third person and the status of children of such a marriage. Contrary to the Privy Council decision in *Saiyid Rashid Ahmad*, the Kerala High Court has held that such a marriage is only irregular, not void; the children born of such marriages are legitimate, and entitled to claim maintenance and inherit their father's estate. The decision is a welcome departure from the unjust and harsh rule laid down in *Saiyid Rashid Ahmad*. The latest case on the subject is *Masroor Ahmed v. State*, where Ahmed, J. maintained that 'harsh abruptness of triple talaq has brought about extreme misery to divorced women and even men' and that its abolition would not be contrary to any basic tenets of Islam. He held that a triple talaq should be regarded as one revocable talaq. The decision is in full accord with the law prevailing in most Muslim countries including the two neigbours, Pakistan and Bangladesh.

Talaq law

The branch of law where the courts' activist role has made a major impact is traditional talaq law. *Sarabai* decided that a divorce without a just cause is valid in Muslim law, and *Ahmad Kasim Molla* held that any Muslim may divorce his wife at his 'mere whim and caprice'. This was the position until the 1980s when the Gauhati High Court, in two successive decisions, *Jiauddin Ahmed v. Anwara Begum* and *Rukia Khatun v. Abdul Khaliq Laskar* rejected the old decisions and decided that: (i) talaq must be for 'a reasonable cause'; (ii) be preceded by 'attempts at reconciliation' by the nominees of the spouses; and (iii) it 'may be effected' only if the said attempts fail. These two decisions were hailed by Professor Tahir Mahmood as 'a very brilliant and refreshing analysis of the true Islamic law of divorce as laid down in the Holy Qur'an and the Sunnah' (1982b: 222). In *Zeenat Fatema Rashid v. Md Iqbal Anwar* (Case 19) the same High Court agreed with the two decisions and further held that talaq must be proved—the husband's verbal or written statement that he has already divorced his wife is not enough. A Full Bench of the Bombay High Court held in *Dagdu Chotu Pathan v. Rahimbi Dagdu Pathan* (Case 20) that the view taken by the Gauhati High Court in the above cases is more in tune with the ethos of Muslim personal law. The husband's plea in his written statement that he had given talaq at an earlier date shall not amount to dissolution of marriage from the date on which such a statement was made unless such a talaq is duly proved and it is further proved that it was given by following the conditions precedent to a valid talaq, that is, 'the reasons for divorce, appointment of arbiters, the arbiters resorting to conciliation proceedings so as to bring about reconciliation between the parties and the failure of such proceedings' (*Dagdu Pathan* v. *Rahimbi Pathan*, Case 20, p. 631).

In *Shamim Ara* v. *State of U.P.* (Case 21), the wife applied for maintenance under Section 125 of the CrPC, 1973. In his written statement submitted in December 1990 the husband claimed that he had divorced her in July 1987 and, therefore, she was not entitled to any maintenance. The court agreed with the rules of talaq laid down in *Jiauddin Ahmed* and *Rukia Khatun* and held that there was no proof of talaq having taken place on 7 July 1987. A mere plea in the written statement of a divorce having been pronounced sometime in the past cannot by itself be treated as effecting talaq on the date of filing of the statement in court or delivery of a copy to the wife. The court expressly overruled those cases, including *Chand Bi* v. *Bandesha*, where a mere plea of previous divorce in the written statement, though unsubstantiated, was accepted as proof of talaq, terminating the marriage from the date of filing the statement in court. In *Iqbal Bano* v. *State of U.P.*, the facts were similar. The Supreme Court reaffirmed the rule laid down in *Shamim Ara* and held that the husband's plea of divorce was not sustainable, and the wife was entitled to claim maintenance from him. In Pakistan and Bangladesh statutory provisions regulate the rules of talaq.

Talaq-i-bid'at

Pakistan and Bangladesh have abolished talaq-i-bid'at or triple talaq. The Indian courts declared it to be effective on the basis of the rule of binding precedent enunciated in *Aga Mahomed*. The recent judicial trend however indicates a liberal, pro-woman interpretation of talaq laws. In *Marium* v. *Shamsi Alam*, the Allahabad High Court held: 'A divorce pronounced thrice in one breath by a Muslim husband would have no effect in law, if it was given without deliberation and without any intention of effecting an irrevocable divorce; such divorce is a form of *talaq-i-ahsan*, and thus is revocable by husband before the *iddat* expires (Ephroz 2003:287).' Danial Latifi warmly supported the decision. However, the judgment of Tilhari, J., in *Rahmat Ullah* v. *State of U.P.* (1994) (12) Lucknow Civil Decisions, 463), invalidating triple talaq has led to intense controversy. The case concerned a land-ceiling dispute, where the husband and wife claimed that their marriage had been terminated by triple talaq twenty-five years ago. Thus, triple talaq was not an issue. But the court held that talaq-i-bid'at, that is, pronouncing divorce in an irrevocable manner, without allowing the period of waiting for reconciliation runs counter to the mandate of the Holy Qur'an. Besides, 'since the practice of triple talaq, denigrates women, it is violative of the Constitution' (Ahmad 2003:171).

Talaq-i-tafwid

Talaq-i-tafwid or delegated divorce is a powerful weapon in the hands of a Muslim wife to obtain her freedom from an undesirable marriage without court intervention. In *Mangila Bibi* v. *Noor Hossain* (Case 22), the court had to decide whether delegation of the power of divorce can be conditional or without any condition at all. The court found that the power to give divorce, which primarily belonged to the husband, may be delegated to his wife either absolutely or conditionally. It is not an inflexible rule of Muslim law that delegation of power to divorce cannot be absolute, but must be conditional. Earlier, in *Aklima Khatun* v. *Muhibur Rahman*, relying on the *Hedaya* and *Fatawa Alamgiri*, a Bangladesh court had given the same decision.

DMMA

In *A. Yousuf Rawther* v. *Sowramma* (Case 23) the Kerala High Court was required to interpret Section 2(ii) of the DMMA, which provides that a woman married under Muslim law shall be entitled to obtain a decree for dissolution of her marriage if 'the husband has neglected or has failed to provide for her maintenance for a period of two years'. The courts are sharply divided on the interpretation of the words 'neglected or failed' to provide maintenance. One view is that, for dissolution of marriage, the neglect or failure must be 'wilful'. Unless there was a duty on the part of the husband to maintain his wife, it cannot be alleged that the husband has failed to provide maintenance to her. The other view is that the husband's failure to maintain need not be wilful, mere failure without any fault on the part of the husband is sufficient for a decree. Krishna Iyer, J. held that a Muslim woman, under Section 2(ii) of the

DMMA, can sue for dissolution of her marriage on the ground that she has not as a fact been maintained, even if there was a good reason for it. In *Noor Bibi* v. *Pir Bux* (Case 38), which the judge cited approvingly, Tyabji, C.J., had held the same view. In *Mohammad* v. *Sainaba Umma*, the wife petitioned for divorce under Section 2(ix) of the DMMA on the ground of irretrievable breakdown of her marriage. The court held that the DMMA recognizes irretrievable breakdown of a marriage as a ground for dissolution of marriage. As cruelty and non-payment of maintenance by the husband, a habitual drunkard, and the wife's great hatred and aversion towards him were proved, the court dissolved the marriage. The court cited a Pakistan decision in support of its views. In a similar factual situation in *Amna Khatun* v. *Kashim Ansari*, while granting a decree for dissolution of marriage on the grounds of cruelty and irretrievable breakdown, the Jharkand High Court drew support for its decision from a Hadith where the Prophet allowed the marriage of Jamila with Sabit to be dissolved on ground of irretrievable breakdown. The court also quoted a judgment of Pakistan Supreme Court, reported in (1986) 1 Current Civil Cases 241, in support of its decision.

Children's custody and maintenance

Judicial activism of Indian, and also Pakistan and Bangladesh courts is most apparent in the application of children's custody and maintenance law. *Khurshid Gauhar* v. *Siddiqunnisa* (Case 24) contains an elaborate statement of law on the nature and extent of a mother's right to custody and reiterates the principle that the mother is best suited for rearing minor children. In *Irfan Ahmed Shaikh* v. *Mumtaz* (Case 25) the court held that the underlying principle of custody law is the welfare of the minor child and, contrary to the general rule, gave the custody of child to the mother notwithstanding her marriage with a man who was a 'stranger' to the child. The court cited a similar Pakistani decision, where the court had rejected the father's application for custody and allowed the mother to retain custody of the child. As in custody law, the courts have also guarded the maintenance rights of children and frowned upon attempts to deprive them of their rights. The Supreme Court held in *Noor Sabha Khatoon* v. *Mohd Qasim*: 'Thus, both under the personal law and the statutory law [Sec. 125 Cr PC] the obligation of a Muslim father, having sufficient means, to maintain his minor children, unable to maintain themselves… is absolute, notwithstanding the fact that the minor children are living with the divorced wife' (p. 240). The decision is a good example of the harmonization of modern secular law and personal law concerning children's maintenance (Pearl and Menski 1998: 437). In *Ibrahim Fathima* v. *Mohamed Saleem* the court had to decide whether a father's obligation to maintain his children was purely personal or attached to his property and could even be enforced against an alienee from the father. Relying on the old case of *Mahomed Jusab* v. *Haji Adam*, the defence contended that the obligation was a personal one; it could not be treated as a charge on the father's property. The Madras High Court held that it could not ignore the open dictates of a Hadith, reported in both *Bokhari* and *Muslim*, to the effect that a father's obligation to maintain his children attached to his property and ran with it. Dissenting from *Mahomed Jusab*, the court laid down the following rule: 'The children's right to maintenance in a Muslim household always attaches to the father's property in such a way and in such measure that it is not affected by any subsequent alienation by the father with notice of the charge or by alienation which is gratuitous' (p. 86). The decision is a creative restatement of the rules of classical law and conforms to the principle of justice, equity, and good conscience.

Maintenance of divorced women

Section 125 of the CrPC, 1973 provides that if any person, having sufficient means, refuses to maintain his wife, including a divorced wife, who is unable to maintain herself, the Magistrate may order him to make a reasonable monthly allowance for her maintenance. In *Mohd Ahmed Khan* v. *Shah Bano Begum* (Case 27) the husband resisted his divorced wife's claim for maintenance under Section 125, on the grounds that: (i) under Muslim personal law his liability to maintain her was limited to the iddat period and (ii) he had paid the amount of mahr or dower and maintenance for the iddat period to her. The Supreme Court held that Section 125 overrides personal law, if there is any conflict between the two. But, since Muslim personal law, which limits the husband's liability to provide for the maintenance of the divorced wife to the iddat period, does not contemplate or countenance the situation envisaged in Section 125, it could not be said that there was, in fact, such a conflict between statutory law and personal law. Quoting Qur'anic Verses 2:241–2, the

Court further held: 'These Aiyats [Verses] leave no doubt that the Quran imposes an obligation on the Muslim husband to make provision for or to provide maintenance to the divorced wife.'

The decision in *Shah Bano* led to controversy regarding a Muslim husband's obligation to pay maintenance to his divorced wife. To 'specify' the rights of a divorced wife, the MWA was passed. Under Section 3(1), a divorced woman is entitled to 'a reasonable and fair provision and maintenance to be made and paid to her within the *iddat* period by her former husband' and also 'an amount equal to the sum of *mahr* or dower' due to her and all the properties given to her as marriage gifts. The MWA purported to reverse the *Shah Bano* decision but the interpretation given to it by the Supreme Court in *Danial Latifi* v. *Union of India* (Case 29) gave statutory recognition to the decision. In this case the Court held as follows: a Muslim husband is liable to make reasonable and fair provision for the future of the divorced wife, which obviously includes her maintenance as well. Such a reasonable and fair provision extending beyond the iddat period must be made by the husband within the iddat period. The liability of a Muslim husband to his wife arising under Section 3(1)(a) of the MWA to pay maintenance is not confined to the iddat period. As the laws stand at present, in Pakistan and Bangladesh divorced Muslim women are entitled to claim maintenance from their husband for the iddat period only and not beyond it.

Pakistan

Sources and interpretation of Muslim law

All the three Constitutions of Pakistan (1956, 1962, and 1973) defined Pakistan as the Islamic Republic of Pakistan and the third one also declared Islam to be the state religion. All the Constitutions also provided that the Muslim citizens of Pakistan shall be enabled individually and collectively to order their lives in accordance with the injunctions of the Qur'an and Sunnah. No law shall be enacted which is repugnant to them, and all existing laws shall be brought in conformity with them. But in the first thirty years of Pakistan's chequered constitutional history no concrete steps were taken to implement the Islamic provisions. The superior courts themselves took an activist stance, exercised ijtihad, and asserted rights to interpret the Qur'an and Sunnah independently and differ from the doctrines of traditionally authoritative texts, not based on the Qur'an and Sunnah, and refused to follow the rules of interpretations of Muslim law laid down in *Aga Mahomed*. As early as 1959, while reinterpreting the Qur'anic verse 2:229 in *Balqis Fatima* v. *Najm-ul-Ikram Qureshi* (Case 36), the court categorically stated: 'On a question of interpretation we are not bound by the opinions of jurists. If we be clear as to what the meaning of a verse in the Qur'an is, it will be our duty to give effect to the interpretation irrespective of what has been stated by jurists' (p. 584). The leading case on the sources and interpretation of Muslim law is *Khurshid Jan* v. *Fazal Dad* (Case 31). Here the court stated that the known sources of law are the Qur'an, Sunnah, ijma (consensus of jurists), qiyas (analogical deduction), and ijtihad (independent judgement). A clear injunction in the Qur'an or Sunnah is binding. Ijma is also binding on all until changed or modified by another ijma. A court of law may differ with the qiyas of earlier jurists, but only on the basis of interpretation and extension of a rule of decision contained in the Qur'anic or Hadith text or ijma and not on the basis of what appears to be more agreeable to the judge. If there is no clear rule of decision in these sources, the court may resort to private reason in which case it will be undoubtedly guided by the rules of justice, equity, and good conscience. There can be no disagreements regarding rules contained in the Qur'an or Hadith or a subsisting ijma. In the case of qiyas, it is open to the courts to adopt any one of the conflicting views of earlier jurists. In sum, the court held, the courts must be given the right to interpret for themselves the Qur'an and Sunnah and to differ from the views of the earlier jurisconsults. Denial of such a right 'will not only be a negation of the true spirit of Islam, but also of the constitutional and legal obligation resting on all courts to interpret the law they are called upon to administer and apply in cases coming before them' (*Khurshid Jan* v. *Fazal Dad*, p. 612). The decision in effect denies the binding force of taqlid and re-establishes the right of ijtihad. It also endeavours to harmonize Islamic legal concept and those of justice, equity, and good conscience in English law (Liebesny 1975: 125). Applying the principles laid down in this case, the court held, contrary to the rules in authoritative texts, that the exercise of 'option of puberty' by a wife did not require a court decree for its validity. In the custody case of *Zohra Begum* v. *Latif Ahmad Munawwar* (Case 42), the court gave custody of the children to their mother, although under Hanafi law the father was entitled to it.

Dower

Non-payment of prompt dower on demand before consummation of marriage enables a wife to live separately from her husband and yet claim maintenance. In *Rahim Jan*, the court was required to decide whether the wife is entitled, even after consummation of the marriage, to refuse to live with her husband on the ground that her prompt dower has not been paid. Imam Abu Hanifa was of the opinion that the wife in entitled at any time to refuse to live with her husband until her prompt dower is paid; on the other hand his two disciples, Imam Abu Yusuf and Imam Muhammad, held that the wife's right of refusal is lost on consummation of marriage. In *Abdul Kadir*, the court accepted the opinion of the two disciples on the ground that according to the rule adopted by jurists, the opinion of the two disciples is to prevail, where they differed from Abu Hanifa. In *Rahim Jan*, the court cited a number of cases to show that there was no such rule as claimed in *Abdul Kadir*. On the contrary, the original authorities, called matan, accepted the opinion of Abu Hanifa without even mentioning the differences of opinion. The court held that even after consummation the wife retains the right to refuse performance of marital obligations till the prompt dower is paid. The decision restores to married women an important right denied to them since 1886. When this decision is considered vis-à-vis *Rabia Khatoon*, it will be obvious that Pakistani law gives a larger right to women in this area of law, as in some others, than Indian law.

Khula divorce

The first landmark decision based on judicial reinterpretation of Qur'anic verses is *Balqis Fatima*. The Qur'anic verse 2:229, which is the basis of the right of khula, permits termination of a marriage upon the wife passing consideration to the husband. The question in this case was whether the termination could be effected only by agreement between the spouses as held by the Hanafi jurists, or whether the wife can claim it even if the husband does not agree. Interpreting the verse the court decided that 'the wife is entitled to a dissolution of the marriage on restoration of what she received in consideration of marriage if the judge apprehends that the parties will not observe the limits of God' (p. 693), that is, a harmonious married life is not possible. The court dissented from the earlier case of *Sayeeda Khanam* v. *Muhammad Sami*, where incompatibility of temperament was proved but the court refused to accept it as a valid ground for dissolution of marriage. The significance of the judgment in *Balqis Fatima* has been explained thus: 'In one resounding stroke the court ... resolved in its own favor the great question as to who is competent to determine the precepts of Islam' (Hoebel 1965: 50). In *Khurshid Bibi* v. *Muhammad Amin* (Case 37) the Supreme Court endorsed *Balqis Fatima* and overruled *Sayeeda Khanam*. It refuted the view of the classical jurists that a Muslim must follow one school of law exclusively. To the husband's contention that his consent was absolutely necessary for khula under Hanafi law, the court replied: 'If the opinions of the Jurists conflict with the Qur'an and the Sunnah, they are not binding on courts and it is our duty, as true Muslims to obey the word of God and the Holy Prophet (*ati-ullah wa ati-ur-Rasool*).' (*Khurshid Bibi* v. *Muhammad Amin*, p. 140). The judgment has been hailed as 'social activism' (Pearl and Menski 1998: 322). Court decisions have also established the rule that a husband cannot claim compensation where the khula is due to his ill-treatment of the wife or behaviour which is detrimental to the continuation of marriage. A number of cases have also decided that non-payment of the stipulated compensation for khula does not invalidate the dissolution of marriage; it only creates a civil liability with regard to the benefits.

The legal consequence of the decisions in *Balqis Fatima* and *Khurshid Bibi* is that the courts of Pakistan and Bangladesh can now allow a wife judicial khula on the ground that the marriage has irretrievably broken down. The significance of the decisions lies in the facts that: (i) it establishes the right of the courts to independently interpret the original sources of Muslim law including Qur'anic texts and (ii) it grants to the wife for the first time a right of release from the marital tie which she did not have under Hanafi law. In India the law as enunciated in *Moonshee Buzul-ul-Raheem* v. *Luteefut-oon-Nissa* (Case 11), which requires husband's consent for a khula divorce, is followed.

MFLO

The MFLO, unquestionably the most progressive reform in the sphere of family law in Pakistan and Bangladesh, is primarily based on the recommendations of the Commission on Marriage and Family Laws, 1956.

It fixes the marriageable age for girls at sixteen and for boys at eighteen and provides for compulsory registration of marriages. It makes it obligatory for a man to obtain the permission of the Arbitration Council for contracting a polygamous marriage. For a talaq to be effective, it lays down certain procedural requirements including reconciliation efforts by the Arbitration Council. It also abolishes the arbitrary and instantaneous talaq-i-bid'at and allows the remarriage of a couple without an intervening marriage of the wife to a third person. Where the husband fails to maintain his wife adequately, it allows her to apply for maintenance to the Arbitration Council. Finally, it provides that the children of a predeceased son or daughter of the *propositus* will be entitled to inherit the property of the *propositus* to the extent of their parent's share in it.

Polygamy

Section 6 of the MFLO provides that no man, during the subsistence of an existing marriage, shall contract another marriage without the previous permission of the Arbitration Council. The Council may grant permission if the proposed marriage is necessary and just. Any man, who contracts another marriage without the Council's permission, will be liable to punishment with simple imprisonment or fine or both. The MFLO does not say what will be the legal effect of a marriage contracted in violation of Section 6. In *Syed Ali Nawaz Gardezi v. Muhammad Yusuf* (Case 39), which is the leading case on polygamy and divorce provisions of the MFLO, the Supreme Court held: 'The Ordinance of course only penalises the person in respect of a marriage, celebrated in contravention of the provisions of the Ordinance by making him liable to imprisonment, or fine or both but does not invalidate the marriage itself.' The decision has been followed in all subsequent cases.

Talaq

Section 7 of the MFLO provides that any man who wishes to divorce his wife shall immediately after pronouncement of talaq, give the Union Council Chairman notice of his having done so and send a copy of the notice to the wife. Any person who contravenes this provision shall be punishable with imprisonment or fine or both. A talaq, unless revoked earlier, shall not be effective until the expiration of ninety days from the date of the service of notice. During this period an Arbitration Council will try to bring about reconciliation between the parties. In this Section also the MFLO does not state what the effect of failure of the husband to notify the Chairman of the pronouncement of talaq would be. In *Syed Ali Nawaz Gardezi*, the Supreme Court held that where the husband did not give notice of talaq to the Chairman, he would be deemed to have revoked the talaq so that in the eyes of law the marriage between him and his wife subsisted. Similarly, in *Ghulam Nabi* v. *Farrukh Latif*, the Supreme Court held that failure to send a copy of the talaq to the wife would also make the talaq ineffective.

Custody of children

The Pakistani courts have consistently held that the paramount consideration in the matter of custody of minor children is the interest of the child and not the rights of parties. In *Zohra Begum*, absence of clear Qur'anic and Hadith texts and lack of unanimity and clarity regarding the rules of custody enabled the court to depart from the rules laid down by classical jurists and give custody of the children to the mother. In a study of reported case law on children's custody between 1947 and 1992, Casandra Balchin (1994: 186) has found that the number of cases where the mother was given preference by far outnumbered the cases where the minor's father or other relatives were awarded custody. According to the principles of traditional law, a mother's remarriage is a disqualification in granting custody of minor children to her, whereas that of the father is not: a detailed analysis of case law has shown that the courts have often disregarded this principle and acted on the paramount consideration of the welfare of the child in determining who is fit to be awarded custody (Balchin 1994: 166–9). Welfare considerations have also led the courts to overrule agreements conferring on the father custody of minor children, contrary to the general rule of custody. In *Hameed Mai* v. *Irshad Hussain*, the Supreme Court held: 'Issues of custody of minor in all cases cannot be effectively settled by private compromise: The Court's powers with regard to custody of minor are in the nature of parental jurisdiction. Therefore, the court must act in a way a wise parent would do'. The rule laid down in *Hameed Mai* was reaffirmed by the Supreme Court in *Razia Rahman* v. *Station House Officer*.

Maintenance of wives

According to Hanafi law a court decree awarding maintenance to a wife is enforceable only from the date of the decree. In *Abdool Futteh Moulvie*, citing the *Digest* and the *Hedaya*, the court held that maintenance is payable to the wife only from the date of the court decree and not from the date the cause of action accrued to the wife. In *Sardar Muhammad* v. *Nasima Bibi* (Case 45) the Lahore High Court dissented from this view. The court observed that the Hanafi rule is inconsistent with the sharia principle that a husband's obligation to maintain his wife commences with the performance of the marriage. Contrary to the Hanafi rule, the three other Sunni schools, namely, the Shafi'i, Hanbali, and Maliki, are unanimously of the view that arrears of maintenance, being a just charge, could be realized from the husband. The court held further: 'The mere fact that a neglected wife has been hesitant in promptly coming to the Court or has been pursuing alternative remedies out of Court cannot in all fairness be so construed as to deprive her of the right of maintenance from the day when the cause of action accrued to her.' In *Muhammad Nawaz* v. *Khurshid Begum*, the Supreme Court approved the decision. Regarding past maintenance of wives, India follows *Abdool Fatteh Moulvie*. Recent legislative enactment and judicial decisions have given maintenance rights to divorced women in India. In Pakistan, the Commission on Marriage and Family Laws, 1956 suggested that family courts should be vested with discretionary power to order a husband to pay maintenance to the destitute divorced wife for life or until her remarriage. The Women's Rights Committee, 1976 and the Pakistan Commission on the Status of Women, 1983 also made recommendations for granting maintenance rights to divorced wives. But neither the legislature nor the judiciary has taken notice of this serious socio-legal problem.

Appointment of women as judges and magistrates

One of the most controversial issues that the Federal Shariat Court had to decide in its early years is whether women can be appointed as judges and magistrates. In *Ansar Barney* v. *Federation of Pakistan*, the petitioner challenged women's appointment to these positions as violations of the injunctions of Islam. In what has been called a historic judgment, the

Court gave a clear ruling that the Qur'an and Sunnah do not prohibit, either expressly or impliedly, appointment of women as judges and magistrates. The court held that there is no law or custom or usage having the force of law for or against seclusion of women. The rule of Islamic jurisprudence is that what is not prohibited by the Qur'an or Sunnah is permitted. Differences on the issue are not new. While some schools of thought opposed appointment of women as heads of state or judges, others including Imam Abu Hanifa, Imam Malik, Imam Tabari, and Ibn Hazm supported it. There are also a number of historical instances of women acting as heads of state or qadi. The Prophet often consulted his wife Umme Salma on vital issues and acted on the evidence of women.

Women's property rights

Men often deprive their female relatives of their rightful shares in agricultural land by taking recourse to two devices: (i) brothers who tended the lands and were, thus, in possession of them, claimed title to them on the ground of adverse possession and (ii) mothers, sisters, and daughters, who are often dependent on their close male relatives, were coerced into relinquishing their shares in the inheritance. In *Ghulam Ali* v. *Ghulam Sarwar Naqvi*, the Supreme Court laid down the following principles for protection of their inheritance rights.

1. A brother cannot legally claim adverse possession against his sister.
2. The recognition and enforcement of inheritance law relating to female heirs by state agents including courts is a matter of 'public policy' in Islam.
3. The so-called 'relinquishment' by a female of her inheritance is opposed to public policy.
4. Alienation by way of sale or gift by a female heir in favour of a male heir would be subject to protection given by the law against undue influence.

In *Ami Chand* v. *Fajroo*, a man who had three daughters and no son allegedly executed a deed in favour of his male relatives. The donees failed to explain why the alleged donor had made a gift that deprived his own daughters of their share of inheritance. The Supreme Court struck down the gift deed.

Islamization of laws programme and after

In order to Islamize the legal system of Pakistan, in 1979 General Zia-ul-Huq promulgated the Constitution (Amendment) Order, 1979 whereby Shariat benches of the High Courts and a Shariat Appellate Bench of the Supreme Court were established. In 1986 the Shariat benches of the High Courts were replaced by a single Federal Shariat Court for the whole country. These courts were given jurisdiction to examine and decide whether any provision of law in Pakistan was repugnant to the injunctions of Islam. Muslim personal law was excluded from their jurisdiction. During this period liberal judges such as Aftab Hussain, C.J. were removed and judicial conservatives such as Tanzil-ur-Rahman were elevated to the bench. The Islamization programme significantly curtailed the independence of the judiciary and stalled the process of activist interpretation of law. In 1980, dealing with a petition challenging the legality of Section 4 of the MFLO, which gives orphaned grandchildren inheritance right to their grandparent's property, in *Farishta* v. *Federation of Pakistan*, the Shariat bench of Peshawar High Court held that the section was repugnant to the injunctions of Islam. On appeal, the Shariat bench of the Supreme Court set aside the judgment on the ground that Muslim personal law was outside its jurisdiction (*Federation of Pakistan* v. *Farishta*).

By far the most important and interesting case on the constitutionality and Islamization of the MFLO is *Mirza Qamar Raza* v. *Tahira Begum*. Professing to assume jurisdiction under Article 2A of the Constitution to judge the legality of Section 7 of the MFLO, the court held that providing for effectiveness of talaq on receipt of notice by the Union Council Chairman is against the injunctions of the Qur'an and Sunnah. Mere non-receipt of notice cannot render a talaq ineffective or void. Suspending the effects of talaq for ninety days from the date of receipt of notice is also against the injunctions of Islam. A talaq, if otherwise valid under the sharia law, takes effect immediately on pronouncement. The right to marry the same husband without an intervening marriage is also contrary to the injunctions of the Qur'an and Sunnah. In *Allah Dad* v. *Mukhtar Ahmad*, relying on *Mirza Qamar Raza*, it was held that even in the absence of notice under Section 7 of the MFLO, talaq becomes effective. However, in *Kaneez Fatima* v. *Wali Muhammad* (Case 40) the Supreme Court held that the jurisdiction of both the courts did not extend to the Constitution and family law and reiterated that the provisions of Section 7 must be complied with to effect a valid divorce. In the meantime *Mahmood Faisal* v. *Government of Pakistan* decided that Muslim personal law was not outside the scope of scrutiny of the Federal Shriat Court. In *Allah Rakha* v. *Federation of Pakistan*, the Federal Shariat Court took up the question of the validity of Sections 4, 5, 6, and 7 of the MFLO. The court found nothing wrong with Section 5 (compulsory registration of marriage) and Section 6 (restrictions on polygamy). It held that inclusion of orphaned grandchildren in the inheritance from the grandfather negates the scheme of inheritance envisaged in the Qur'an and therefore, Section 4 was repugnant to the injunctions of Islam. The court also held that Section 7(3) providing that talaq shall not be effective until the expiration of ninety days from the date of delivery of notice does not conform to Qur'anic requirements. The period of iddat prescribed by the Qur'an is different in different situations. But Section 7(3) has fixed ninety days iddat for all situations, which clearly violates Qur'anic injunctions. Similarly, Section 7(5), fixing ninety days' waiting period for pregnant women, is clearly violative of Islamic injunctions. The *Allah Rakha* judgment strikes at the very root and substance of the only significant post-colonial modernist legislation in Pakistani family law. The decision of the Shariat Appellate Bench of the Supreme Court in the appeal against *Allah Rakha* has been pending for the last fourteen years.

Bangladesh

Article 8 of the Constitution of Bangladesh proclaimed secularism as one of the fundamental principles of State policy. However, Article 149 provided that all existing laws shall continue to have effect but may be amended or repealed by law made under the Constitution. Thus, personal laws continue to be in force as existing laws. Second, one of the fundamental rights guaranteed to the citizens under Article 28(1) is that the state shall not discriminate against any citizen on the ground of religion. This provision not only ensures freedom of religion but also safeguards personal laws based on religion. The Constitution does not contain any provision for introduction of a uniform civil code for all citizens. In 1977 secularism as a fundamental principle was dropped from the Constitution and in 1988 the controversial Eighth Amendment declared that 'the state religion of the republic is Islam, but other religions may be practised in peace and harmony in the Republic'. These changes in the Constitution were not followed up by any measures to Islamize laws and institutions, as it happened in Pakistan. The principle of secularism was restored to the Constitution by the Fifteenth Amendment, 2011. Despite constitutional changes, the judiciary has been consistently moving away from religious norms and rules prescribed by classical jurists. In fact, Bangladesh has demonstrated remarkable judicial maturity in the field of Muslim personal law. Bangladeshi courts have not only accepted liberal interpretations and decisions of Pakistani courts given before and after 1971 but, as the cases analysed below will show, have also been responsive to new social needs and realities.

Registration of marriages

Section 5 of the MFLO, subsequently replaced by Section 3 of the Muslim Marriages and Divorces (Registration) Act, 1974, provides for compulsory registration of marriages. Non-compliance with the provision is punishable with imprisonment or fine or both. But the MFLO does not say anything about the legal effects of non-registration. In a clear and brief statement of law on the issue, which has been frequently quoted by the courts of Pakistan and Bangladesh, in *A.L.M. Abdulla* v. *Rokeya Khatoon* (Case 47) the High Court held that 'the solemnization of marriage if validly effected might not be affected for non-registration of the marriage. But non-registration of the marriage causes a doubt on the solemnization of the marriage itself'.

Dower

Dower is an essential condition of marriage and an important right of a wife. Dower-related matrimonial suits are frequent in Bangladesh. In *Saleha Khatun* v. *Saleh Ahmed*, the wife exercised delegated power of divorce for non-payment of prompt dower on demand by the husband and the latter challenged its validity. The court held the divorce to be valid and said: 'The exercise of such power by the wife on the husband's failure to pay the prompt dower does not appear to be against public policy or the principles of Muslim law' (*Saleha Khatun* v. *Saleh Ahmed*, p. 328).

Polygamy

Polygamy in Bangladesh is regulated by Section 6 of the MFLO. It provides that no man shall contract another marriage during the subsistence of an existing one without the previous permission of the Arbitration Council. For contracting a marriage without such permission, the husband shall be liable to punishment with imprisonment or fine or both. The vagueness of the provision raised a number of questions. What is, for example, the legal effect of a marriage contracted in violation of the provision? In *Syed Ali Nawaz Gardezi*, the court held that the Ordinance *only penalizes* the husband but *does not invalidate the marriage itself.* Second, is the existing wife's consent a prerequisite for contracting a second marriage? In *Abul Bashar v. Nurun Nabi*, it was held that the legislative intent of Section 6 was to restrict the practice of polygamy and permit it only in cases where it appeared to be reasonable to the Arbitration Council. Section 6 provided for punishment of husband for marrying without Arbitration Council's permission but it did not contemplate any punishment for marrying without the consent of the existing wife. Third, can the second wife be convicted for abetting an offence under Section 6(5)(b) of the MFLO? In *Makbul Ali v. Manwara Begum* (Case 49) the court held that criminal liability would be incurred only by the husband, being the 'man' referred to in that sub-section and not by the woman whom he marries. Pearl and Menski (1998: 270) welcome the decision and say: 'This is undoubtedly a correct interpretation of the Ordinance and it seems appropriate that such attempts to criminalise women who may be entirely innocent should be soundly rebuffed.'

The MFLO does not prohibit polygamous marriages; it merely imposes certain procedural restrictions on its unfettered exercise. But a Division Bench of the High Court has challenged the very concept of polygamy in *Jesmin Sultana v. Mohammad Elias*. In a wife's suit for dower and maintenance against her husband the court examined the question of whether Islam approves polygamy. The court was of the opinion that 'to be able to deal justly' between more than one wife, as ordained in the the Qur'anic verse 4:3, is a condition precedent to marry more than one wife. According to some commentators, the expression means only equality in maintenance and lodging. According to others, it implies equality in love and affection, and as such equality is impossible the verse virtually prohibits polygamous marriages. Accepting the latter view the court held that Section 6 of the MFLO which allows polygamy subject to the previous permission of the Arbitration Council is against the injunctions of Islam and legislation should be enacted prohibiting polygamy altogether. On appeal, the Appellate Division held that polygamy was neither an issue in the suit nor was relevant in the context of the pleadings of the parties and, therefore, the entire discussion on polygamy in Islam in the impugned judgment 'should be taken to be deleted' (*Mohammad Elias* v. *Jesmin Sultana*, 19 BLD (AD) (1999) 122).

Restitution of conjugal rights

Restitution of conjugal rights is a controversial issue. As with Hindu law in India, there are differences of views among Bangladeshi judges concerning the constitutional validity and legal propriety of this law (Serajuddin 2011: 198–203). According to some High Court decisions, it is a reciprocal right; it is neither discriminatory nor repugnant to the fundamental rights guaranteed by the Constitution. It helps to protect family values, preserve the sanctity of marriage as an institution, and prevents its break-up. According to others, it is inhuman and repressive, an engine for harassment of wives, a relic of a bygone age; more importantly, it is inconsistent with the fundamental rights of citizens. When the issue came up before the Appellate Division of the Supreme Court in *Hosna Jahan* v. *Md Shahjahan* (Case 50), the court refrained from giving any opinion on its constitutional validity. They preferred to base their decision on Section 5(b) of the Family Courts Ordinance, 1985 which specifically mentions restitution of conjugal rights as a subject matter for trial and disposal by a family court. They held that the conscious policy of the legislature would prevail over decided cases. The result of the decision is that like Hindu law in India, restitution of conjugal rights is valid law in Bangladesh.

Talaq

As in Pakistan, so in Bangladesh, a husband's exercise of talaq is no longer unilateral; it is governed by Section 7 of the MFLO, which provides that a man who intends to divorce his wife must, after pronouncement of *talaq*, give the Union Council Chairman notice in writing of his having done so. But it does not say what would be the effect of his failure to give notice. *Syed Ali Nawaz Gardezi* decided that giving notice to the Chairman is mandatory and non-compliance with it amounts to revocation of the talaq, so that in the eyes of law the marriage between the parties subsists. The liberal and activist interpretation of law given in this case is followed by the Bangladesh courts. In *Safiqul Islam* v. *State* the court said that the object of Section 7 of the MFLO is to prevent hasty dissolution of marriage by talaq pronounced by the husband unilaterally, without an attempt being made to bring about reconciliation between the parties. The MFLO gives the responsibility of reconciliation to a public authority. So, divorce is no longer a unilateral act of the Muslim husband. The latest decision on the subject, *Kazi Rashid Akhter Shahid* v. *Rokhshana Chowdhury*, categorically asserts that 'a talaq will not be effective even after the expiry of 90 days if any of the conditions of effectiveness of talaq, i.e., pronouncement as per Mohammadan law, service of notice on Chairman and a copy thereof to the wife is not complied with' (p.618). Section 7 of the MFLO has abolished the arbitrary and instantaneous talaq-i-bid'at and allowed remarriage of the couple after such a divorce without an intervening marriage with a third person. An investigation into the family court cases has shown that the procedural requirements of giving notice of talaq, constituting the Arbitration Council, and freezing the talaq for ninety days are curbing unilateral divorce by husbands and protecting the interest of wives (Monsoor 1990: 180–5). The conciliation procedure of the MFLO is also a Qur'anic requirement.

Talaq-i-tafwid

Talaq-i-tafwid or delegated divorce has been in vogue for a long time in both East Bengal, that is, present-day Bangladesh, and West Bengal. The exercise of delegated power of divorce may be conditional or unconditional. The most usual form of delegated divorce is the conditional one and two very common stipulations for its exercise are non-payment of maintenance and dower. In *Aklima Khatun* v. *Muhibur Rahman*, the husband pleaded that unconditional delegation of the right of divorce was illegal. Relying on the *Hedaya* and *Fatawa Alamgiri*, the court held that it was valid. Unlike unconditional divorce, conditional divorce requires court intervention and court interpretation of the reasonableness of stipulations. *Nelly Zaman* v. *Giasuddin Khan* is the best example of a conditional divorce. In this case the marriage contract provided that the wife could exercise the right of delegated divorce if the husband was unable to maintain her or there was mutual recrimination between the parties. The court held that there was sufficient recrimination between the spouses which led the wife to live separately and the husband to seek restitution of conjugal rights. Under the circumstances exercise of the right of divorce by the wife could not be said to be illegal. The MFLO has provided for an option for delegated divorce in the kabinnama and more and more women are taking advantage of this. A survey of the family court cases of Dhaka shows that women find it easier to dissolve undesirable marriages using this device (Monsoor 1990: 192–3).

Khula divorce

Judicial khula without husband's consent is a very important right of wives. In *Hasina Ahmed* v. *Syed Abul Fazal*, (Case 53) the court held that a wife could obtain divorce by way of khula from the court even if the husband did not agree and relied on *Khurshid Bibi* for its decision. The court further held that while adjudicating on family disputes the courts should take into account not only the factual and legal position but also the social dynamic. In *Sherin Alam Chowdhury* v. *Shamsul Alam Chowdhury* (Case 54), the wife prayed for a khula divorce alleging cruelty and ill-treatment by the husband and agreeing to surrender the dower money in consideration of khula. The court held that, for dissolution of marriage by khula, the question whether the husband treated his wife with cruelty was not of prime importance. The most important consideration was whether the parties could live together in peace and harmony. Following the Pakistan Supreme Court's decision in *Khurshid Bibi*, the court held that if the wife satisfied the court that there was no possibility of the couple living together consistently with their conjugal duties and obligations, the court would have the right to dissolve the marriage. In India the courts follow the traditional khula law which requires the consent of the husband.

Custody of children

Like India and Pakistan, hizana or custody law of minor children is gov-erned in Bangladesh by a combination of Muslim personal law and statute law, that is, the Guardians and Wards Act, 1890. Irrespective of what these laws provide, the courts have held that in custody cases, the paramount consideration is the welfare of the child and not the legal rights of the parties. In the leading Bangladeshi case, *Md Abu Baker Siddique* v. *S.M.A. Bakar* (Case 58), the court found that there are no Qur'anic or Hadith texts regarding custody of children. The custody rules are only juristic views and they differ from school to school. The court approved the rule laid down in *Zohra Begum* that it would be permissible for present-day courts to differ from the rules of hizana stated in textbooks like the *Hedaya*, the paramount consideration being the child's welfare. In *Romana Afrin* v. *Fakir Ahmed*, the court held that the opinions of jurists were their personal opinions based on social norms and conditions prevailing in their times and had no binding force. In *Ayesha Khanam* v. *Major Shabbir Ahmad*, the court emphatically asserted that the provisions of personal law of the parties, even those of statute law, are subject to the 'paramount need of the welfare of the child'. The court cited the case of *Surinder Kaur Sandhu* v. *Harbux Singh Sandhu*, where the Supreme Court of India had said: 'Section 6 of the Hindu Minority and Guardianship Act of 1956 constitutes the father as the natural guardian of a minor son. But that provision cannot supersede the paramount consideration as to what is conducive to the welfare of the minor' (*Ayesha Khanum*, p. 401). In *Abdul Jalil* v. *Sharon Laily Begum Jalil* (Case 59), the Appellate Division held that in custody proceeding 'it is not the right of the parties but the rights of the child which are at issue' (p. 59). The court found support for the mother's right to custody of the children in *Veena Kapoor* v. *Varinder Kumar Kapoor*. In the Bangladeshi case, the concept of custody is characterized as the 'entitlement' of the children to be with their mother. Is a mother bound by a voluntary agreement surrendering her right to custody of her minor children to their father? *Nargis Sultana* v. *Amirul Chowdhury* decided that in custody cases the welfare of the minor is the dominant consideration, not what the parents have agreed upon. An agreement between the parents cannot exclude the court's jurisdiction to decide what will serve the interest and welfare of the child.

Guardianship of minors

Imambandi v. *Haji Mutsaddi* (Case 13) laid down that the mother is entitled only to the custody of the person of her minor child, but she is not their natural guardian. The father alone or his executor is the legal guardian. If there is no father's executor, the grandfather or his executor is the legal guardian. In the absence of any legal guardian, it is the duty of the judge to appoint one. *Raihanuddin* v. *Azizun Nahar* is a unique and welcome decision relating to guardianship of a minor. Here, considering the facts and circumstances of the case, the court appointed the child's mother as its guardian in place of the grandfather. The decision is in consonance with the recommendation of the Commission on Marriage and Family Laws, 1956 that in the absence of the father it should be open to the court to appoint any person as guardian of the property of the minor including the mother.

Maintenance of wives

In Bangladesh, until recently there were two conflicting High Court decisions on the neglected wife's right to past maintenance. In *Rustom Ali* v. *Jamila Khatun*, relying on the old case of *Abdool Futteh Moulvie* the court held that the wife was not entitled to past maintenance; she could only be allowed maintenance from the date of the institution of the suit before the family court. In *Sirajul Islam* v. *Helana Begum* (Case 57), the High Court dissented from the above decision, and citing the statement of law laid down in the Pakistani case of *Sardar Muhammad* held that the wife was entitled to maintenance from the time when the husband started neglecting her without any reasonable cause. In *Jamila Khatun* v. *Rustom Ali* (Case 60) the Appellate Division of the Supreme Court reviewed the two conflicting decisions. Agreeing with the decision in *Sardar Muhammad*, the Court held that the wife is entitled to maintenance from the time the husband neglected or refused to maintain her. The classical law holds that following divorce maintenance is payable to the wife only for the iddat period. As this rule causes hardship to destitute divorced women, the Commission on Marriage and Family Laws suggested that courts should be vested with power to grant maintenance to an unjustly divorced wife for life or until remarriage. This was not done in Pakistan or Bangladesh. India has solved the problem by enacting the MWA. Recently, a valiant effort was made by a High Court division in *Md Hefzur Rahman* v. *Shamsun Nahar Begum*, to give them financial security by making their former husbands liable for their maintenance until their remarriage. In this suit, filed by the wife for her iddat maintenance, the court took up *suo motu* the legal query whether the divorced wife could have claimed maintenance beyond the iddat period. Accepting Abdullah Yusuf Ali's translation of Qur'anic verse 2:241 ['for divorced women maintenance (should be provided) on a reasonable (scale)'] as correct the court held: 'A person after divorcing his wife is bound to maintain her on a reasonable scale beyond the period of *iddat* for an indefinite period, that is to say, till she loses the status of a divorcee by remarrying another person' (*Hefzur Rahman* v. *Shamsun Nahar*, p. 57). But the Appellate Division of the Supreme Court overruled it in *Md Hefzur Rahman* v. *Shamsun Nahar Begum* (Case 61). It held that the word mataa in the verse has never been understood as maintenance. It is a 'consolatory offering' or parting gift to a divorced woman and being a gift it has never been judicially enforceable. But the court was also of opinion that statutory provisions, binding the husband to maintain an unjustly treated and destitute divorced wife, as has been done in several Muslim countries, would not be against Muslim personal law.

Pardanashin women

One class of people who need special protection of courts is pardanashin-women. In suits where they were parties special rule of onus was devised by the Privy Council to give them protection. In *Siddique Ahmed* v. *Gani Ahmed*, the Appellate Division reiterated the Privy Council rule that in case of any dispute regarding the validity of a transfer of property by a pardanashin lady, the onus is always on the donee or transferee to satisfy the court that she substantially understood the disposition and executed it with full understanding of what she was doing, and of the nature and effect of the transaction. Where the donee or transferee stands in a position of confidence or fiduciary relation with the lady he will have to prove that she had independent advice from disinterested advisers. In *Rokeya Khatun* v. *Alijan*, the Appellate Division decided that the person upon whom the property of the pardanashin lady would devolve by operation of law could challenge the legality of the disposition.

Concluding remarks

In this treatise we have made a comprehensive survey of the administration of Muslim law in South Asia, as represented in case law. The sources of this law and the agencies of their interpretation are the same

in India, Pakistan, and Bangladesh. However, in each country the prevailing political and social conditions have shaped its application and
development. Thus, some differences are inevitable. In India a Muslim
man is at liberty to marry up to the limit of four wives without the
intervention of any public authority. In Pakistan and Bangladesh he can
contract a second marriage only with the permission of the Arbitration
Council. In each country a wife is entitled to a judicial dissolution of
her marriage where the husband fails to treat the co-wives equally in
accordance with the Qur'anic injunction or where he breaks a condition
of the marriage contract that he will not take another wife during her
lifetime. In Pakistan and Bangladesh a wife can also seek dissolution
of her marriage if a husband takes an additional wife in contravention
of Section 6 of the MFLO. Talaq law is the most controversial area of
Muslim law. Section 7 of the MFLO, which applies to Pakistani and
Bangladeshi Muslims, abolishes the arbitrary and instantaneous talaq-
i-bid'at and allows a couple's remarriage without an intervening marriage of the wife. The MFLO also forces a cooling off period of ninety
days after pronouncement of a talaq so that attempts may be made
by the Arbitration Council to bring about reconciliation between the
spouses. Through activist judicial interpretation the Indian courts lave
also brought about changes in the colonial talaq law. A Muslim husband
can no longer divorce his wife at will. For a talaq to be valid, there must
be a reasonable cause for it, and it has to be preceded by attempts at reconciliation by nominees of the spouses. Two High Court decisions have
held that talaq-i-bid'at is revocable, and one has held that remarriage of
a couple without halala procedure is only irregular and not void. What
Pakistan and Bangladesh have aimed to achieve by enacting legislation,
India has attempted to achieve by judicial interpretation of the Qur'anic
and Hadith texts and subsidiary sources of law.

There is convergence of the rules of Muslim law of India, Pakistan,
and Bangladesh on children's custody and maintenance, restitution of
conjugal rights, talaq-i-tafwid, and interpretation of the provisions of
DMMA. Their courts have established the uniform rule that in matters
of custody and maintenance of children the paramount consideration
is the welfare of the minor children and not the rights of parties; if the
personal law and the welfare doctrine conflict on the issue, the welfare doctrine will have precedence. Though there were differences of
views among High Court judges regarding the constitutional validity

of the restitution of conjugal rights, the apex courts have declared that it is a valid law. Though the colonial courts were not comfortable with the concept of unconditional delegation of power of divorce (talaq-i-tafwid) by the husband to the wife, the courts of South Asia have held it to be valid. Again, all the three jurisdictions agree that husband's failure to provide for maintenance of his wife for two years or more entitles the wife to claim a decree for dissolution of her marriage under provisions of the DMMA, even if there was good reason for the failure.

Divergence is noticeable in the application of the laws of khula, maintenance, dower, 'option of puberty', and li'an. India follows the traditional Hanafi rule that husband's consent and the wife's surrender of dower and other benefits received by her are necessary for a khula divorce. Pakistani and Bangladeshi courts have established the rule that a wife is entitled to dissolution of her marriage, even without proving cruelty or any other specific misconduct of the husband, if she can satisfy the conscience of the court that she has developed an irremediable aversion to the husband. Where the fault of the husband is proved, she does not have to restore the dower money and other benefits received.

The old case of *Abdool Futteh Moulvie* decided that a court decree awarding maintenance to a Hanafi wife is enforceable only from the date of the decree. This is still the rule of law in India. Courts in Pakistan and Bangladesh have held that maintenance is due to her from the date on which the cause of action accrued. A major innovation in maintenance law in India is the rule that a husband is liable to make reasonable and fair provision for the future of the divorced wife, which includes her maintenance as well. Pakistani and Bangladeshi husbands are not liable to make any such provision. The divorced wife is entitled to maintenance only for the iddat period. India follows the rule laid down in *Abdul Kadir* that a wife, whose prompt dower has not been paid, has no right to refuse herself to her husband, if the marriage has earlier been consummated with her consent. But in Pakistan, even after consummation the wife retains the right to refuse performance of marital obligations till the prompt dower is paid. In Pakistan a wife, who exercises 'option of puberty' and repudiates her marriage, does not require a court decree for its validity. In India a court decree is essential. In cases of li'an or imprecation, a Pakistani wife is entitled to a decree for dissolution of her marriage on the ground that her husband has falsely charged her with committing adultery. But in India, if the husband retracts the charge the wife cannot insist on divorce.

India, Pakistan, and Bangladesh were one geographical and political entity until 1947. They have inherited the same legal history and tradition, legal institutions, and laws including personal laws. Therefore, there is no reason why they should not share their experiences after 1947. Danial Latifi, a renowned scholar and lawyer of Muslim law, has persuasively argued that the decisions of Pakistani courts on khula divorce are founded on the authority of an undisputed Hadith of the Prophet. They are in perfect harmony with classical law as well as the modern concept of family and should be adopted by Indian courts. Similarly there can be no objection for the Indian courts to accept the liberal Pakistani decisions on 'option of puberty' and li'an. Again, if the Pakistani and Bangladeshi Muslims can accept the Shafi'i rule regarding past maintenance of neglected wives, there is no reason why Indian Muslims cannot do the same. In *Shah Bano* and *Danial Latifi* the Supreme Court of India held that a divorced Muslim wife, who is unable to maintain herself, is entitled to claim maintenance from her husband. Maulana Ashraf Ali Thanvi, a great authority on sharia law, has held identical views. The Pakistan Commission on Marriage and Family Laws, 1956 has unequivocally recommended that family courts be vested with the power to grant maintenance to destitute divorced wives for life or until her remarriage. Though the Appellate Division of the Bangladesh Supreme Court did not agree with the interpretation given to the Qur'anic verse I2:241 in the above two cases, it has held that statutory provisions enjoining husbands to maintain their divorced destitute wives will not be against the law; on the contrary it will be in consonance with the idea of justice, tolerance, and compassion that the Qur'an enjoins upon all righteous Muslims. Thus, there is scope for reviewing the decision in *Hefzur Rahman* (Case 61) or enacting legislation such as the MWA in Bangladesh.

(The above survey draws on two earlier works of mine, *Shari'a Law and Society: Tradition and Change in South Asia* and *Muslim Family Law, Secular Courts and Muslim Women of South Asia: A Study in Judicial Activism,* and articles on the subject.)

Glossary

ahsan	most approved (form of divorce)
a'imma	juris-consult
aiyat	Qur'anic verse
a'kar	immovable property
barat	bridegroom's party
batil	void
bid'at	something disapproved or innovative
bigha	a unit of land measurement
din-al-fitrat	religion of nature
dyn-mohr	dower
faqih (pl. fuqaha)	a jurist, a legal scholar
fasid	irregular
faskh, fiskh-i-nikah	rescission, dissolution of marriage by the court
fatwa *(pl. fatawa)*	authoritative legal opinion, a juristic opinion or verdict
fiqh	the science of law or jurisprudence
fuzuli	a person busying himself in things not belonging to him or acting without authority
fuzuli beea	sale of another's property without his consent
guzara	maintenance
Hadith	sayings or traditions of the Prophet
hakam	arbitrator, judge
halala	to make something valid in law, legalizing remarriage between a man and his triply-divorced wife
Hanafi	followers of Imam Abu Hanifa
Hanbali	followers of Imam Ahmad bin Hanbal

hasan	approved (form of divorce)
hizana, hizanat	the care and custody of minor children
hudood (pl. of hadd)	punishment specified in the Qur'an
ibranamah	instrument by which wife waives her right to dower
iddat	wife's period of waiting after divorce or death of husband
ijma	consensus of the jurists, consensus of the community
ijma ul-ummat	consensus of opinion of the Muslim community
iqrarnama	deed of acknowledgement
isbatat	acts which create rights
isqatat	acts which extinguish rights
istidlal	juristic deduction or reasoning
ijtihad	independent judgment, systematic original thinking
istihsan	juristic preference, equity
istislah	setting aside, in public interest, a rule which causes general injury
kabinnama	marriage deed
kazi	a judge
khilafat	succession, vicegerency
khula	dissolution of marriage at wife's request
khulanama	deed of divorce by khula
khumar	a distilled preparation of dates, intoxicant
li'an	imprecation leading to divorce
madbar	village elder
mafqudulkhabar	absent without news, missing person
mahr	dower
majlis	conference, meeting
malik	owner
Maliki	followers of Imam Malik
mataa	provision, maintenance, gift, compensation paid to a woman by the husband, who has arbitrarily divorced her
matan	the text, 'ancient textbooks'

maulvi	a religious leader, an expert in sharia law who advised the British courts on legal points, a title of respect
mauquf	dependent
muaddat	affection
mu'ajjal	exigible (dower)
mubarat	dissolution of marriage by mutual consent
mufti	a legal scholar who pronounces a fatwa, a jurisconsult
mujtahid	a person who exercises independent judgment
mullah	a religious leader
mu'wajjal	deferred (dower)
nafkah	maintenance
nikah	marriage
nikahnama	marriage deed
panchayat	village council
parda	veil, seclusion
qadi	see *kazi*
qiyas	analogical deduction (as a source of Islamic law), juristic reasoning by analogy
raja	revocable
rehmat	blessing, grace
rukhsati	taking of bride to matrimonial home for cohabitation
saheeh	valid, authentic
salish	conciliation
Shafi'i	followers of Imam Shafi'i
Shia	followers of the Ithna Ashari, Ismaili and Zaydi schools of law, originally the followers of Hazrat Ali
sharia	the divine law
shubh	doubt
siqaq	breach or schism
sukoon	contentment, peace
Sunnah	the sayings and deeds of the Prophet and also the deeds of others tacitly approved by him, the model behaviour of the Prophet and the practices he endorsed and the precedents he set

Sunni	followers of the Hanafi, Shafi'i, Maliki, and Hanbali schools of jurisprudence
taka	Bangladesh currency
talaq	unilateral divorce of wife by husband
talaq al-hasan	approved form of divorce
talaq al-sunnah	divorce which conforms to the dictates of the Prophet
talaq-i-bain	irrevocable divorce
talaq-i-bid'at	disapproved form of divorce
talaq-i-tafwid	delegation of an authority or power to pronounce divorce, power given by the husband to the wife to divorce herself
talaqnama	divorce deed
taqlid	imitation, precedents, the principle of strict adherence to the law as expounded in the authoritative legal manuals
tola	unit of weight, equivalent to 11.664 grams
ulema (sing. alim)	Muslim theologians, learned persons
vokil (wakil)	attorney, agent
waqf	a charitable endowment
waqif	settlor of waqf
wasi	executor guardian
zid	obstinacy
zina	the offence of illicit sexual relations

Select Bibliography

Ahangar, M. Altaf Hussain, 'Classical Sources of Islamic Law: Judicial Responses in Pakistan', *Islamic and Comparative Law Review*, 12 (1992): 101–13.

Ahmad, Aqil, *Text Book of Mohammedan Law* (20th ed. by I.A. Khan, Allahabad, Central Law Agency, 2001).

Ahmad, Aziz, *Islamic Law in Theory and Practice* (Lahore, All Pakistan Legal Decisions, 1956).

Ahmad, Furqan, *Triple Talaq: An Analytical Study with Emphasis on Socio-Legal Aspects* (Regency Publications, New Delhi, 1994).

Ahmad, K.N., *Muslim Law of Divorce* (New Delhi, Kitab Bhavan, 1978).

Ali, Abdullah Yusuf, *The Meaning of the Glorious Qur'an: Text, Translation and Commentary* (Vols. I and II, Beirut, Dar Al-Kitab Al-Masri, Cairo and Dar Al-Kitab Allubnani, 1938).

Ali, Shaheen Sardar, 'Case book – Supreme Court on Khula', *Journal of Law and Society*, 4 (1985): 51.

——— and Rukhshanda Naz, 'Marriage, Dower and Divorce: Superior Courts and Case Law in Pakistan', in Farida Shaheed, Sohail Akbar Warraich, Cassandra Balchin, and Aisha Gazdar (eds), *Shaping Women's Lives* (Lahore, 1998), pp. 107–42.

Ali, Syed Ameer, *Mahommedan Law* (Vol. I, 4th ed., London, 1912; Vol. II, 5th ed., London, 1928; New Delhi reprint, 1985).

Ali, Zeenat Shaukat, *Marriage and Divorce in Islam: An Appraisal* (Bombay, Jaico Publishing House, 1987).

Anderson, J.N.D., *Islamic Law in the Modern World* (New York, New York University Press, 1959).

———, *Law Reform in the Muslim World* (London, Athlone Press, 1976).

Badawi, Gamal A., *Polygamy in Islamic Law* (Delhi reprint, 1996).

Baillie, Neil B.E., *A Digest of Moohummudan Law* (Part I, 2nd ed., London, Smith Elder and Co., 1875, Lahore reprint, Premier Book House, 1965; Part II, London, Smith Elder and Co., 1869).

Balchin, Cassandra (ed.), *A Handbook of Family Law in Pakistan* (2nd ed., Lahore, Shirkat Gah, 1994).

Bhatnagar, B.P., 'Marriage', *Annual Survey of Indian Law*, 1996, 411–16.

Bhatia, K.L. (ed.), *Judicial Activism and Social Change* (New Delhi, Deep and Deep Publications, 1990).

Bhuiyan, Rabia, *The Legal Rights of Muslim Women in Marriage and Divorce* (Dhaka, Women for Women, 1986).

———, 'Legal Status of Women in Bangladesh', in Q.K. Ahmed, M.A. Khan, Salma Khan, and J.A. Rahman (eds), *Situation of Women in Bangladesh* (Dhaka, Ministry of Social Welfare and Women's Affairs, 1985), 231–251.

Carroll, Lucy, 'Divorced Muslim Women and Maintenance', *Pakistan Legal Decisions Journal* 38 (1986): 1–6.

———, 'Mahr and Muslim Divorcee's Right to Maintenance', *Journal of the Indian Law Institute*, 27, no. 3 (1985): 487–95.

———, 'Talaq-i-Tafwid and Stipulations in a Muslim Marriage Contract: Important Means of Protecting the Position of the South Asian Muslim Wife', *Modern Asian Studies* 16,:2 (1982): 277–309.

Compendium of Islamic Laws: A Section-wise Compilation of the Rules of Sharia't Relating to Muslim Personal Law (2nd ed., New Delhi, All India Muslim Personal Law Board, 2001).

Coulson, N.J., *Conflicts and Tensions in Islamic Jurisprudence* (Chicago and London, University of Chicago press, 1969).

———, *A History of Islamic Law* (Edinburgh, Edinburgh University Press, 1964).

———, 'Reform of Family Law in Pakistan', *Studia Islamica* 7 (1957): 135–55.

———, *Succession in the Muslim Family* (Cambridge, Cambridge University Press, 1971).

Diwan, Paras, 'Claim of Maintenance under Criminal Procedure Code', *Journal of the Indian Law Institute*, 27:2 (1985): 292–317.

——— and Peeyushi Diwan, *Muslim Law in Modern India* (8th ed., Faridabad, Allahabad Law Agency, 2000).

Engineer, Asghar Ali, *The Shah Bano Controversy* (London, Sangam Books, 1987).

Ephroz, Khan Noor, *Women and Law: Muslim Personal Law Perspective* (Jaipur, New Delhi, Rawat Publications, 2003).

Esposito, John L., 'Women's Rights in Islam', *Islamic Studies* 14:2 (1975): 99–114.

Faruki, Kemal, *Islamic Jurisprudence* (Karachi, Pakistan Publishing House, 1962).

Fatima, Tanzeem, *Islamic Law and Judiciary* (New Delhi, Deep and Deep Publications, 2001).

Fyzee, Asaf A.A., *Cases in the Muhammadan Law of India and Pakistan* (Oxford, Clarendon Press, 1965).

———, *Cases in the Muhammadan Law of India and Pakistan* (2nd ed. by Tahir Mahmood, Delhi, Oxford University Press, 2005).

Fyzee, Asaf A.A., "The Impact of English Law on the Shariat in India", Bombay LR 66 (1964): 107–29.

———, 'The Muslim Wife's Right to Dissolving Her Marriage', *Bombay Law Review*, 38 (1936): 113–23.

———, *Outlines of Muhammadan Law* (4th ed., Delhi, Oxford University Press, 1974).

———, *Outlines of Muhammadan Law* (5th ed. by Tahir Mahmood, Delhi, Oxford University Press, 2009). Ganai, Nisar Ahmed, 'Judicial Contribution to Muslim Matrimonial Law in a Changing Society in India: Some Policy Perspectives', in K.L. Bhatia (ed.), *Judicial Activism and Social Change* (New Delhi, Deep and Deep Publications, 1990), pp. 406–27.

Gani, H.A., *Reform of Muslim Personal Law* (New Delhi, Deep and Deep Publications, 1988).

Haq, M. Fazlul, 'Islamic Personal Law and the Courts', *Kerala Law Times Journal* (1976): 43–4.

Hinchcliffe, Doreen, 'Divorce in Pakistan: Judicial Reform', *Journal of Islamic and Comparative Law*, 2 (1968): 13–25.

Hodkinson, Keith, *Muslim Family Law: A Sourcebook* (London, Croom Helm, 1984).

Hoebel, E. Adamson, 'Fundamental Cultural Postulates and Judicial Lawmaking in Pakistan', *American Anthropologist*, 67:6 (1965): 50.

Hoque, Ridwanul, *Judicial Activism in Bangladesh: A Golden Mean Approach* (Newcastle upon Tyne, 2011).

Hoque, Ridanwul and M.M.M. Khan, 'Judicial Activism and Islamic Family Law: A Socio-Legal Evaluation of Recent Trends in Bangladesh', *Islamic Law and Society*, 14: 2 (2007): 204–39.

Iyer, V.R. Krishna, *The Muslim Women (Protection of Rights on Divorce) Act* (Lucknow, Eastern Book Company, 1987).

———, 'Reform of the Muslim Personal Law', in Tahir Mahmood (ed.), *Islamic Law in Modern India* (Bombay, N.M. Tripathi, 1972), 17–33.

Jain, M.P., *Outlines of Indian Legal History* (Bombay, N, M. Tripathi, 1972).

Jain, P.C., 'Polygamy among Muslims', *All India Reporter Journal* (1969): 186–9.

Kamali, Muhammad Hashim, *Principles of Islamic Jurisprudence* (3rd ed., Cambridge, The Islamic Text Book Society, 2003).

Khan, Hamid, *Islamic Law of Inheritance: A Comparative Study with Focus on Recent Reforms in the Muslim Countries* (2nd ed., Lahore, Pakistan Law House, 1999).

Khare, R.S., *Perspectives on Islamic Law, Justice and Society* (Maryland, Rowman and Littlefield Publishers, 1999).

Latifi, Danial, 'Change and the Muslim Law', in Tahir Mahmood (ed.), *Islamic Law in Modern India* (Bombay, N.M. Tripathi, 1972), 99–113.

Latifi, Daniel. 'Outstanding Decision on Muslim Personal Law', *Islam and the Modern Age*, 3 (1972): 16.

———, 'The Triple Talaq and Fatwa by Ahl E Hadith Maulanas', *Annual Survey of Indian Law* 29 (1993): 174–80.

Lau, Martin, 'Country Surveys: Pakistan', *Yearbook of Islamic and Middle Eastern Law* 8 (2001–2): 312.

———, 'Country Surveys: Pakistan', *Yearbook of Islamic and Middle Eastern Law* 9 (2002–3): 372.

———, 'Country Surveys: Pakistan', *Yearbook of Islamic and Middle Eastern Law* 12 (2005–6): 443.

———, 'Opening Pandora's Box: The Impact of the SAIMA WAHEED Case on the Legal Status of Women in Pakistan', *Yearbook of Islamic and Middle Eastern Law* 3 (1996): 518–31.

Liebesny, Herbert J., *The Law of the Near and Middle East: Readings, Cases and Materials* (Albany, State University of New York Press, 1975).

Macnaughten, W.H., *Principles and Precedents of Moohummudan Law* (Calcutta, The Church Mission Press, 1825).

Mahmood, Sh. Shaukat, *Principles and Digest of Muslim Law* (3rd ed., Lahore, Legal Research Centre, 1976).

Tahir Mahmood, 'A Revolutionary Judgment on Divorce: Comments on a Recent Delhi High Court Decision', *Amity Law Watch* (Amity University, Uttar Pradesh) 12 (2007): 7.

———, 'An Unreported Judgment on the Islamic Law of Divorce', *Islamic and Comparative Law Quarterly* 2:1 (1982a): 38–53.

———, 'Another Unreported Indian Judgment on Muslim Divorce Law', *Islamic and Comparative Law Quarterly* 2:3 (1982b): 213–21.

———, *Islamic Law in Indian Courts since Independence: Fifty Years of Judicial Interpretation* (New Delhi, Institute of Objective Studies, Jamia Nagar, 1997).

———, (ed.), *Islamic Law in Modern India* (Bombay, N.M. Tripathi, 1972).

———, *The Muslim Law of India* (3rd ed., New Delhi, LexisNexis, 2002).

———, 'Personal Laws in Bangladesh – A Comparative Perspective', *Journal of the Indian Law Institute* 14:4 (1972): 583–9.

Mahmud, I., *Muslim Law of Succession and Administration* (Karachi, Pakistan law House, 1958).

Malik, Shahdeen, 'Saga of Divorced Women: Once again Shah Bano, Maintenance and the Scope of Marriage Contracts', *Dhaka Law Reports Journal* (1990) 34–40.

Malik, Vijay, *Muslim Law of Marriage, Divorce and Maintenance* (2nd ed., Lucknow, Eastern Book Company, 1988).

Mannan, M.A., *The Superior Courts of Pakistan* (Lahore, Zafar Law Associates, 1973).

Mansoori, Muhammad Tahir, *Family Law in Islam: Theory and Application* (Islamabad, Shariah Academy, International Islamic University, 2006).

Marghinani, Burhanuddin, *The Hedaya*, trans. by Charles Hamilton (2nd ed. by S.G. Grady, London, W.H Allen and Co., 1870; Lahore reprint, Premier Book House, 1963).

Mehdi, Rubya, *The Islamization of the Law in Pakistan* (Surrey, Curzon Press, 1994).

Menski, Werner F., 'Development in Muslim Law: The South Asian Context', *Supreme Court Cases Journal* 3 (2000): 9–18.

———, 'Maintenance for Divorced Muslim Wives', *Kerala Law Times Journal*, 1 (1994): 45–52.

———, *Modern Indian Family Law* (Richmond, Surrey, Curzon Press, 2001).

———, 'The Reform of Islamic Family Law and a Uniform Civil Code for India', in Chibli Mallat and Jane Connors (eds), *Islamic Family Law* (London, Graham & Trotman, 1990), 253–94.

Monsoor, Taslima, *From Patriarchy to Gender Equity: Family Law and Its Impact on Women in Bangladesh* (Dhaka, University Press Limited, 1999).

Mulla, D.F., *Principles of Mahomedan Law* (19th ed. by M. Hidayatullah and Arshad Hidayatullah, Bombay, N.M. Tripathi, 1990).

Munir, Muhammad, 'Stipulations in a Muslim Marriage Contract with Special Reference to Talaq-Al-Tafwid Provisions in Pakistan', *Yearbook of Islamic and Middle Eastern Law*, 12 (2005–6): 235.

Nasir, Jamal J., *The Islamic Law of Personal Status* (2nd ed., London, Graham and Trotman, 1990).

Nyazee, Imran Ahsan Khan, *Islamic Jurisprudence* (Islamabad, International Institute of Islamic Thought, 2000).

Patel, Rashida, *Islamisation of Laws in Pakistan?* (Karachi, Faiza Publishers, 1986).

———, *Women and Law in Pakistan* (Karachi, Faiza Publishers, 1979).

Pearl, David, 'Family Law in Pakistan', *Journal of Family Law*, 9 (1969): 165

Pearl David and Werner Menski, *Muslim Family Law* (London and Lahore, A.M. Shakoori, 1998).

Qadri, Anwar Ahmad, *Islamic Jurisprudence in the Modern World* (Lahore, Sh. Muhammad Ashraf, 1981).

Rahim, Abdul, *Muhammadan Jurisprudence* (Madras, 1911, Lahore reprint, Indus Publishers, 1968).

Rahman, A.F.M. Abdur, *Institutes of Mussalman Law: A Treatise on Personal Law According to the Hanafite School* (Calcutta, 1907, Lahore reprint, All Pakistan Legal Decisions, 1969).

Rahman, Fazlur, 'The Controversy over the Muslim Family Laws', in Donald E. Smith (ed.), *South Asian Politics and Religion* (Princeton, University Press, 1966), 414.

Rahman, Tanzil-ur-, *A Code of Muslim Personal Law* (Vol. I, Karachi, 1978; Vol. II, Karachi, Hamdard Academy and Islamic Publishers, 1980).

———, *Muslim Family Laws Ordinance – Islamic and Social Survey* (Karachi, Royal Book Company, 1997).

——— and Arshad Masood, 'Judicial Reform of Muslim Personal Law: The Thin Edge of the Wedge', *Aligarh Law Journal* (1978): 6)

Rashid, S Khalid, 'Impact of Colonialism on the Shari'a in India', *Islamic and Comparative Law Quarterly*, 3:3 (1983): 161–76.

Rashid, S. Khalid, *Muslim Law* (3rd ed., Lucknow, Eastern Book Company, 1996).

Saksena, K.P., *Muslim Law as Administered in India and Pakistan* (4th ed., Lucknow, Eastern Book Company, 1963).

Schatct, J., *An Introduction to Islamic Law* (Oxford, Clarendon Press, 1964).

———, *Origins of Muhammadan Jurisprudence* (Oxford, Clarendon Press, 1950).

Serajuddin, A.M., *Muslim Family Law, Secular Courts and Muslim Women of South Asia: A Study in Judicial Activism* (Karachi, Oxford University Press, 2011).

———, *Shari'a Law and Society: Tradition and Change in South Asia* (2nd ed., Karachi, Oxford University Press, 2001).

———, 'The Sharia Law, Society and South Asian Judiciary', *Islam and the Modern Age* 24 (1993): 87–106.

Shabbir, Mohammad, *Muslim Personal Law and Judiciary* (Allahabad, Law Book Company, 1988).

Shafqat, C.M., *The Muslim Marriage, Dower and Divorce* (Lahore, Law Publishing Company, 1979).

Sivaramayya, B., 'Legal Status of Muslim Women and Social Change', *Journal of Indian Law Institute*, 25 (1983): 2.

Tyabji, Faiz Badruddin, *Muslim Law* (4th ed., Bombay, N.M. Tripathi, 1968).

Usmani, Molvi Mohammad, 'Orphaned Grandchildren's Right to Inheritance in Islamic Law', *Islamic and Comparative Law Quarterly*, 3 (1983): 128–31.

Verma, B.R., *Muhammedan Law* (7th ed., Allahabad, Law House, 2000).

———, *Muslim Marriage, Dissolution and Maintenance* (2nd ed., Allahabad, Law Book Company, 1988).

Wani, M. Afzal, *The Islamic Law on Maintenance of Women, Children, Parents and Other Relatives: Classical Principles and Modern Legislations in India and Muslim Countries* (New Delhi, Noonamy Upright Study Home, 1995).

———, 'Quantum of *Mahr*: Classical Views and Judicial Response in India', *Cochin University Law Review*, 18 (1994): 203–26.

Wilson, R.K., *Anglo-Muhammadan Law* (6th ed., London, W. Thaker Company, 1930).

Zafer, M. R., 'Dissolution of Marriage', *Annual Survey of Indian Law* (1971): 450.

Index

About the Author

Alamgir Muhammad Serajuddin, a Ph.D in history from the University of London and Barrister-at-Law from Lincoln's Inn, London, is Professor Emeritus, Department of History (formerly Vice-Chancellor), University of Chittagong, Bangladesh.

Professor Serajuddin is the author *of Revenue Administration of the East India Company in Chittagong, 1761–1785* (1971), *Shari'a Law and Society: Tradition and Change in South Asia* (1999), and *Muslim Family Law, Secular Courts and Muslim Women of South Asia* (2011), as well as numerous articles on South Asian history and law in scholarly journals including, among others, *Journal of the Royal Asiatic Society*, London, and *Journal of the Economic and Social History of the Orient*, Leiden.